A History of British Magazine Design

A History of British Magazine Design

ANTHONY QUINN

V&A PUBLISHING

This book is dedicated to Linda, Kezia and Max – for putting up with all the boxes!

First published by V&A Publishing, 2016
Victoria and Albert Museum
South Kensington
London SW7 2RL
www.vandapublishing.com

Distributed in North America by Abrams, an imprint of ABRAMS

Hardback edition
ISBN 978 1 85177 786 0

Library of Congress Control Number 2013945524

10 9 8 7 6 5 4 3 2 1
2020 2019 2018 2017 2016

A catalogue record for this book is available from the British Library.

Front jacket: details from *London Life* (page 99), *Woman's Own* (page 121), *Time Out* (page 184), *City Limits* (page 176), *Woman* (page 152), *Punch* (page 205) and *John Bull* (page 85), *The Englishwoman's Domestic Magazine* (page 40).

Original design: Joe Ewart for Society
Copy-editor: Lesley Levene

New photography by the V&A Photographic Studio

Printed in China

New photography of periodicals held in the National Art Library or the collection of the author by the V&A Photographic Studio unless noted otherwise:

De Beer Collection, Special Collections, University of Otago, Dunedin: page 10; Reproduced by the kind permission of the Syndics of Cambridge University Library: pages 44; © The British Library Board: page 55, 61; Helen Thurlow / *Vogue* © The Condé Nast Publications Ltd: page 75; Eduardo Benito / *Vogue* © The Condé Nast Publications Ltd: page 86; Cecil Beaton / *Vogue* © The Condé Nast Publications Ltd: page 86; Edward Steichen / *Vogue* © The Condé Nast Publications Ltd: page 86; Horst P. Horst / *Vogue* © The Condé Nast Publications Ltd: page 112; Leigh Miller and Horst P. Horst / *Vogue* © The Condé Nast Publications Ltd: page 112; Courtesy of St Bride Library & Archive: page 94; Leigh Miller / *Vogue* © The Condé Nast Publications Ltd: page 113; Cecil Beaton / *Vogue* © The Condé Nast Publications Ltd: page 113; © The Economist Newspaper Limited, London 2015: pages 139, 202; David Bailey / *Vogue* © The Condé Nast Publications Ltd: page 151; Ronald Traeger / *Vogue* © The Condé Nast Publications Ltd: page 151; *The Sunday Times Magazine* / News Syndication: page 154; © Reed Business Information Ltd, England. All rights reserved. Distributed by Tribune Content Agency: page 161; *Vogue* © The Condé Nast Publications Ltd: pages 164–5; With thanks to likepunkneverhappened.blogspot.com: page 169; Patrick Demarchelier / *Vogue* © The Condé Nast Publications Ltd: page 190; Peter Lindbergh / *Vogue* © The Condé Nast Publications Ltd: page 190; Corinne Day / *Vogue* © The Condé Nast Publications Ltd: page 191; With kind permission of *The Spectator*: page 204; © Standpoint magazine: page 220.

We are grateful to all the publishers, institutions and individuals who have granted permission for the reproduction of their work in this book. Any omissions are entirely unintentional, and the details should be addressed to V&A Publishing.

V&A Publishing

Supporting the world's leading museum of art and design, the Victoria and Albert Museum, London

Contents

Foreword

If you have a passion or even just a love for magazines, you will find it hard to put down this beautiful book.

To discover that the V&A is such a treasure trove of magazine history must have been a eureka moment for the author: a collection of more than 80,000 magazines selected for their reflection of and influence on the fashion, design and attitudes of their day stored and catalogued within the Museum's archives.

Today, the press is blamed for a great deal, while also being praised for its role in defending democracy. Magazines are very much a part of that conversation. Indeed, the distinction between newspapers and magazines is narrowing all the time, both in design and in content, as new positions are carved out in the digital landscape. This alone would make this book timely.

Within these pages, I also find much that contributes to two enduring debates. The first is the question of whether the press is responsible for society's fashions and attitudes, or just a mirror for them.

The answer arguably is yes ... and yes. The one reflects the other and in so doing both are influenced. The good editor catches the public mood and sets up a resonance that echoes through society and so encourages sales. In almost two decades as chief executive of the Periodical Publishers Association, the magazine industry's trade association, I witnessed many examples where that catching of the mood brought great commercial success, which, of course, is a condition for a magazine's existence. Some titles have married commercial sense and creativity over many generations – *Vogue*, *Good Housekeeping* and *The Economist* are among those that come to mind here – while so many fade within a few years.

The other debate is whether magazines are themselves art. Without question, they can exhibit the most captivating and eye-catching design ideas. Indeed, the Victorian title *Graphic* so impressed Van Gogh that he wrote: 'For me, the English black-and-white artists are to art what Dickens is to literature.' While in this century, the self-portrait 'Me Me Me' by the photographer and *Dazed & Confused* founder Rankin is a memorable example of magazine art informing opinion.

Accustomed as we now are to digital manipulation of photographs, it is comforting, perhaps, to learn that photographs, like other illustrative forms, have been made to lie since their inception. The late and revered Bert Hardy's montage of Queen Elizabeth's arrival at the Paris Opéra for *Picture Post* in 1957 and the sequence showing the retouching Douglas Fairbanks's visit to Sun Printers are evidence of the power of such techniques even in the analogue age.

The author says that his aim in producing this book was to explore design over the past 170 years, and he has done this in a scholarly, exciting and captivating way. He has done much more than that, too, capturing some of the major technological and social changes that have influenced magazine readership, production and content.

The result is a celebration of a remarkable, diverse and enduring medium that reflects social history in an art form which this book records and celebrates so well.

IAN LOCKS
Master of The Worshipful Company of
Stationers and Newspaper Makers, 2014–15
PPA Chief Executive, 1989–2008

Preface

This book sets out to explore magazine design over the past 170 years. The starting point is the advent of two magazines, *Punch* and the *Illustrated London News*, that transformed the look of magazines fundamentally, and moved them away from the book.

In making this exploration, I have tried to identify turning points that changed design strategies. To do this requires establishing what the status quo was at any time: to know what has changed, one must know what went before. It is not a book solely for designers, and the trigger for change in the look of a magazine can be commercial or technological, or the influence of an art movement.

These pages can show how magazines look, but not how they feel in the hand – is the paper silky or rough? Is the cover glossy or just smooth? Nor can they put across the heft, or the distinctive smell of gravure printing or the linseed oil in the best art papers. In an era of digital competition, these are factors that are becoming increasingly important.

Core to the research has been the National Art Library at the Victoria and Albert Museum, with its archive of thousands of copies of some 8,000 titles from Britain and around the world. There are 557 active, paid periodical subscriptions, not including standing orders for yearbooks and irregular journals or donations and exchanges; each week, the library receives between 50 and 100 issues. Given such a potential volume of material, the focus has been on consumer magazines – those that you are likely to find in your local newsagent – though the research has ventured into the realm of trade and specialist magazines where relevant.

A magazine may look great and feel great, yet without attitude it won't get very far. Many magazines start off with a spark – 'I can do better than that'; 'Women's magazines are boring'; 'Why isn't there a magazine for people like me?' But they are reactive and no matter how good the people behind them, and no matter how brilliant the execution, such titles will ultimately fail unless they develop in a way that sets them on a positive path. The additional ingredient is attitude, a way of approaching the world. For *Dazed & Confused*, co-founder Jefferson Hack has identified the Fashion-Able cover (September 1998 issue) as 'the point where the magazine grew up'. 'With that issue we were on page two or three of the world's newspapers. We realized that you didn't have to be the best-selling magazine to have an influence on culture. That has been our philosophy ever since.' The Victorian illustrated weeklies exploited the latest technology and art techniques; the women's weeklies have sought to create a feeling of family and friendship among their readers; *Vogue* has spent more than a century honing its pursuit of quality; *Private Eye* has fought to remain a pain in the side of the rich and powerful; *Nova* found a unique way of exploring the issues of the day; and *The Economist* and *New Scientist* showed the way in presenting complex ideas.

Amid all this innovation, magazines are commercial entities that must earn their way to survive. Many titles that were lauded for their design – such as *Town*, *Nova* and *London Life* – were too expensive to endure and failed commercially. As one former fashion editor has said of *Nova*: 'We had no idea that you had to please the advertisers as well as the readers.' When publishers get things right – as Newnes, Harmsworth and Pearson did – magazines can be money-making machines that spawn some of the biggest media empires the world has seen. Yet, commercially driven decisions can starve magazines of the oxygen of creativity, an accusation frequently aimed at the 1960s merger of Britain's largest magazine publishers to create the giant IPC – since taken over by an American behemoth, Time Inc., and renamed after that company.

As magazines change hands, their company names – and even the magazine's very title – may change, and if these appear inconsistent within these pages it is probably because of such factors; so IPC becomes IPC Media and *Tit-Bits* becomes *Titbits*, for example. Furthermore, while the chapters are arranged chronologically, comparisons made within them may not be, so a copy of *London Opinion* from the First World War may find itself alongside a modern-day *Radio Times*, for reasons that, I hope, will be clear. The National Art Library has an excellent search engine that enables anyone to explore its 1 million holdings (catalogue.nal.vam.ac.uk), including the option to search only for periodicals. The V&A offers a similar facility (collections.vam.ac.uk) and a search on the museum number given in the text (for example, E.1428–2001) will take the enquirer to a page showing the object denoted by that number.

Magazines as a subject for study have been neglected in comparison with books and other media. The first book on magazine design, Ruari McLean's *Magazine Design*, was published back in 1969. Hopefully, this book will inspire many more to come.

ANTHONY QUINN

Introduction: How the magazine became a magazine

The history of magazine design over the past 170 years has been all about escaping the models set elsewhere, by books, academic journals and newspapers. Books and journals were originally aimed at an elite class with library shelves to fill, and in the early years magazines followed suit, designed by printers to be collated into volumes. The essence of design was the typography, focusing on text legibility and production requirements.

Many Georgian and early Victorian periodicals were reliant on the selling power of fiction, from writers such as Dickens, and had no illustrations, so these were made 'uniform' with the books that the same publishing companies produced. As authors might provide handwritten sheets that were, in turn, typeset by hand each week, straightforward typography was essential to speed the process. Publishers could then sell the same pages as magazines or bound as books, making it a successful commercial strategy: a publisher could get several bites of the cherry by selling a magazine weekly, monthly and half-yearly in numbers, parts and volumes. Furthermore, the volumes could be offered in bindings of varying quality to appeal to different readerships.

The desire for uniformity on readers' library shelves meant that many magazines kept the same page size and look for many years – in the case of *Blackwood's Magazine*, the *Cornhill Magazine* and *Punch* a century or more. Most of the leading magazine publishers were book publishers – *Punch* became the property of book printer Bradbury & Evans, which vied with Chapman & Hall to publish Dickens; Pearson's, Hodder & Stoughton and Longman all produced medium-format monthlies, most based on short stories and serial fiction, which from the 1880s faced competition from a new generation of periodical houses, led by George Newnes with the *Strand*.

What changed this approach, and liberated magazine design, was the growth of a mass-market readership as taxation fell, production became cheaper and the literate population grew. The upmarket *Illustrated London News* was selling 130,000 copies a week by 1851 – 10 times the daily sale of *The Times*, and more even than any of the popular Sunday papers. By the early 1890s, several weekly magazines were each selling half a million copies a week, and *Answers* reached the million mark ahead of the best-selling newspaper, *Lloyd's Weekly*. Magazines were a mass medium for a British population that more than doubled from 16 million in the first census in 1801 to almost 42 million a century later. For the most ambitious publishers, the Empire and the United States created an even larger market – another 10 million people combined in Canada, Australia and New Zealand, and 76 million in the US. The success of these magazines gave their founders the skills, techniques and financial resources to launch popular newspapers.

GENTLEMAN'S MAGAZINE (January 1731)

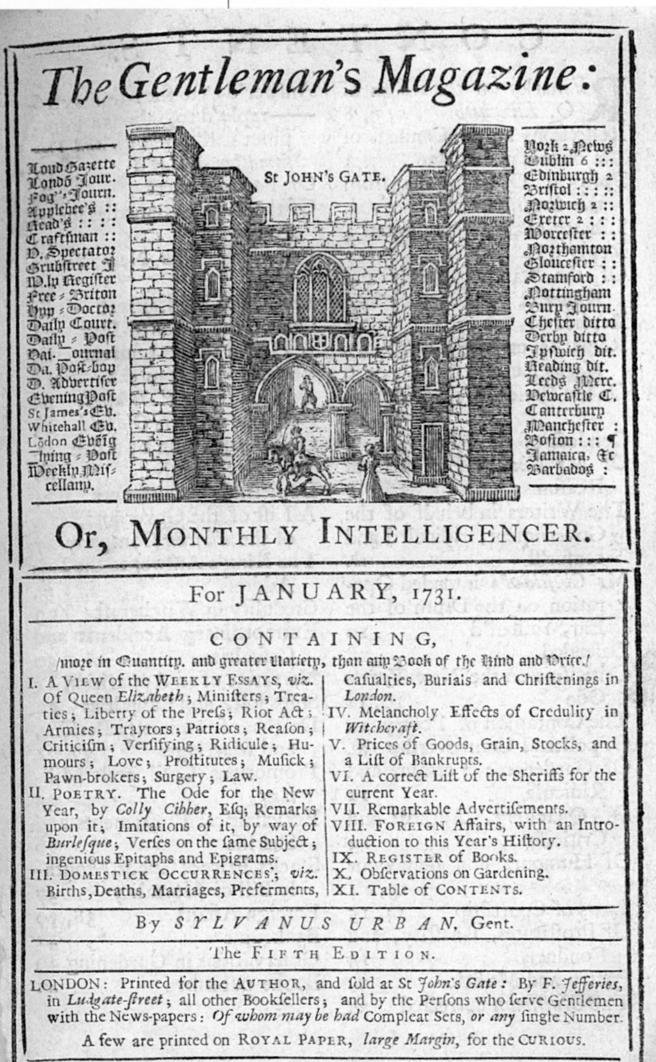

The Gentleman's Magazine:

Lond Gazette
Londō Jour.
Fog's Journ.
Applebee's
Read's
Craftsman
D. Spectator
Grubstreet J.
W.ly Register
Free Briton
Hyp Doctor
Daily Court.
Daily Post
Dai. Journal
Da. Post-boy
D. Advertiser
Evening Post
St James's Ev.
Whitehall Ev.
Lōdon Evēig
Flying Post
Weekly Miscellany.

St John's Gate.

York 2 News
Dublin 6
Edinburgh 2
Bristol
Norwich 2
Exeter 2
Worcester
Northamton
Gloucester
Stamford
Nottingham
Bury Journ.
Chester ditto
Derby ditto
Ipswich dit.
Reading dit.
Leeds Merc.
Newcastle C.
Canterbury
Manchester
Boston
Jamaica, &c
Barbados

Or, Monthly Intelligencer.

For January, 1731.

CONTAINING,

(more in Quantity, and greater Variety, than any Book of the Kind and Price.)

I. A View of the Weekly Essays, *viz.* Of Queen *Elizabeth*; Miniſters; Treaties; Liberty of the Preſs; Riot Act; Armies; Traytors; Patriots; Reaſon; Criticiſm; Verſifying; Ridicule; Humours; Love; Proſtitutes; Muſick; Pawn-brokers; Surgery; Law.
II. Poetry. The Ode for the New Year, by *Colly Cibber*, Eſq; Remarks upon it; Imitations of it, by way of *Burleſque*; Verſes on the ſame Subject; ingenious Epitaphs and Epigrams.
III. Domestick Occurrences; *viz.* Births, Deaths, Marriages, Preferments, Caſualties, Burials and Chriſtenings in *London*.
IV. Melancholy Effects of Credulity in *Witchcraft*.
V. Prices of Goods, Grain, Stocks, and a Liſt of Bankrupts.
VI. A correct Liſt of the Sheriffs for the current Year.
VII. Remarkable Advertiſements.
VIII. Foreign Affairs, with an Introduction to this Year's Hiſtory.
IX. Register of Books.
X. Obſervations on Gardening.
XI. Table of Contents.

By *Sylvanus Urban*, Gent.

The Fifth Edition.

London: Printed for the Author, and ſold at St *John's Gate*: By F. *Jefferies*, in *Ludgate-ſtreet*; all other Bookſellers; and by the Perſons who ſerve Gentlemen with the News-papers: *Of whom may be had* Compleat Sets, *or any* ſingle Number.

A few are printed on Royal Paper, *large Margin*, for the Curious.

The first periodical to call itself a magazine: the *Gentleman's Magazine* began as a 36-page weekly containing summaries of the contents of other newspapers and journals such as *Craftsman*, *Grubstreet* and *Daily Courant*. To these, it added lists of items such as commodity prices, births, domestic occurrences, laws of courtship, bankrupts, sheriffs and books published.

Sylvanus Urban
(203 × 124 mm, trimmed, 36 pages)

BLACKWOOD'S MAGAZINE (February 1960)

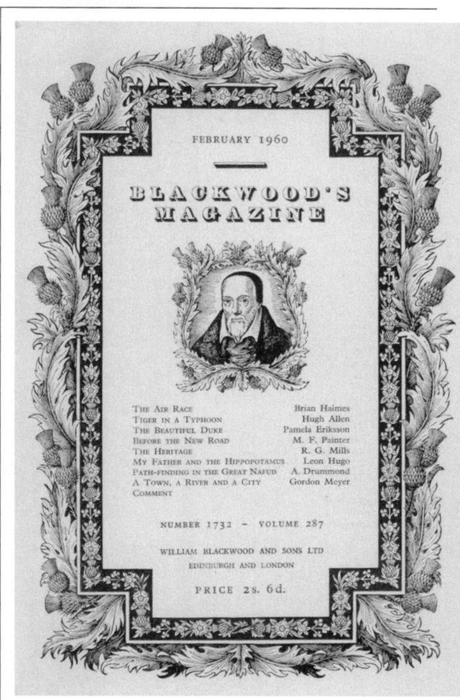

FEBRUARY 1960

BLACKWOOD'S MAGAZINE

The Air Race	Brian Haimes
Tiger in a Typhoon	Hugh Allen
The Beautiful Duke	Pamela Eriksson
Before the New Road	M. F. Painter
The Heritage	R. G. Mills
My Father and the Hippopotamus	Leon Hugo
Path-finding in the Great Nafud	A. Drummond
A Town, a River and a City	Gordon Meyer
Comment	

NUMBER 1732 – VOLUME 287

WILLIAM BLACKWOOD AND SONS LTD

EDINBURGH AND LONDON

PRICE 2s. 6d.

A bookish look that survived from 1817 into the 1960s: William Blackwood founded the monthly, with George Buchanan, a 16th-century Scottish historian, on the cover. Its reviewers caused controversy, but this was nothing compared to its rivalry with the *London Magazine*. The hostility was such that in 1821 *London's* editor John Scott challenged *Maga* (*Blackwood's* nickname) writer John Gibson Lockhart to a pistol duel. Lockhart's second, Jonathan Christie, faced Scott and mortally wounded him.

William Blackwood
(151 × 232 mm, book binding)

COUNTRY LIFE (8 January 1897)

COUNTRY LIFE ILLUSTRATED.

WITH WHICH IS INCORPORATED RACING ILLUSTRATED.
OFFICES. 20. TAVISTOCK ST LONDON. W.C.

VOL. I.—No. 1. *JANUARY 8th, 1897.* PRICE SIXPENCE.

HEDGES AND BUTLER,
ORIGINALLY ESTABLISHED A.D. 1667. WINE LISTS ON APPLICATION.
Wine Merchants to Her Majesty,
LONDON: 155, REGENT ST., W.

NO ALKALIES USED. "The Standard of highest purity."—*Lancet.*
CADBURY'S COCOA
Absolutely Pure, therefore Best.
As a sustaining, strength-giving Beverage, and a Nutritious Food, **CADBURY'S COCOA** fulfils every requirement.

Grand Hotel London
Unrivalled for its Situation, Comforts, and Cuisine.
The "Grand" Dinner, 6 to 8.30, Price 5/-
Proprietors: THE GORDON HOTELS, Limited.

OSMOND CYCLES
THE "OSMOND" LADYS' BICYCLE. REGISTERED DESIGN.
RECOMMENDED AS . . . THE MOST RIGID & EASY RUNNING LADY'S BICYCLE . . YET PRODUCED.
The OSMOND CYCLE Co., Ltd.,
"The Tower," BIRMINGHAM.

SHANNON DESKS.
THE LARGEST SELECTION IN GREAT BRITAIN.
Send for Illustrated Price List. ***Send for Illustrated Price List.***
SOME OF THE FINEST OFFICES AND LIBRARIES HAVE BEEN FITTED AND FURNISHED BY THE
SHANNON, LIMITED,
14 to 16, ROPEMAKER ST., LONDON, E.C.
F.W. SCHAFER, Managing Director.

WHIPS. BY APPOINTMENT TO THE QUEEN AND THE ROYAL FAMILY.
The New Raw Hide Riding Whip.
SWAINE & ADENEY,
185, PICCADILLY, LONDON.

THE FINEST OF SPIRITS IS
"Old Grans Special Toddy."
THE CREAM OF HIGHLAND WHISKIES (Registered) carefully blended under our own supervision. Guaranteed ten years old.
48s. per doz. 5% allowed for Cash.
CARRIAGE PAID ON 1 DOZEN AND UPWARDS.
CHARLES WRIGHT & SON, Wirksworth and London.
BONDED STORES: LEITH. Established 1795.

Country Life Illustrated was a relaunch of *Racing Illustrated* that broadened the title's appeal, turning it into an early lifestyle magazine. The word 'illustrated' was still important when marketing magazines, even 55 years after the advent of the *Illustrated London News*. *Country Life* used a format that would be adopted by society weeklies such as *Tatler and Bystander*: advertising on the cover, followed by a run of adverts, a frontispiece with a page portrait, an 'editorial well' and then advertising, once more, at the back of the issue. As befits the title, early issues focused on land-owning gentry – the Earl of Suffolk and Berkshire holding a book of the lunar month was in the launch issue – but the magazine became known for its 'girls in pearls', the daughters of such gentry, usually about to get married. The focus of the inside advertising pages in the first issue was rural property and today *Country Life* brands itself 'the home of premium property'.

Hudson & Kearns
(250 × 370 mm, stapled, 40 pages)

WOMAN AT HOME (Christmas 1903)

The *Illustrated London News* printed a colour cover to its Christmas supplement in 1855 and this became a tradition, as in Annie S. Swan's magazine with a Warwick Goble illustration. Swan, as editor, is named on the cover – a common practice at the time.

Hodder & Stoughton
(166 × 246 mm)

The broad audience for magazines encouraged experimentation in content, technology and design. Artists and engravers in the weeklies tried out new ways of portraying the explosions shown in illustrations of the Boer Wars, and new types of writing, such as science fiction, again encouraged a more imaginative approach, leading to different presentation techniques. The reproduction of photographs posed technical and design challenges – images were shown on the page as if in frames. This tradition lives on in many newspapers and magazines where house style dictates that photographs should be shown inside a box rule, unlike illustrations, which do not have a rule added.

Today, magazines normally have a colour cover printed on heavier paper than the main pages, with adverts everywhere but the cover and articles. There is a contents page somewhere near the front and a list of the staff (the masthead). Some have a square spine, which is seen as more upmarket and better for issues above about 200 pages. This may be achieved in several ways: perfect bound, where all the pages are glued in position; or stitched and then the cover is glued on; or side-stabbed with staples and then the cover is glued on. Stapled (saddle-stitched) binding is generally cheaper. Rarely, the pages of a magazine may simply be folded into each other and left loose, like a newspaper. The most common page size is slightly larger than A4, although an oversized A5 'travel' or 'handbag' format has also become popular in the past decade. But it was not always so. In fact, all sorts of questions come to mind: when is a magazine a magazine and not a newspaper (as *The Economist* describes itself)? Can you have an annual magazine? Why do we call some titles 'glossies' when they all seem to be glossy these days? Looking at things historically, it almost seems an accident that periodicals came to look the way they do. In fact, the magazine format has come about through many influences, from technology to cost and the intervention of individual editors and designers – along with practicalities of getting on to, and selling from, the newsagents' shelves.

By the mid-nineteenth century, British printers had cast aside heavy Gothic typefaces – which would stay in favour in countries such as Germany for the main body copy of many magazines and newspapers until the 1940s. In Britain, Gothic type would rarely be seen except for the mastheads of magazines and newspapers, such as the *Spectator* and *Daily Telegraph*. An aspect of evolving design that is soon clear when comparing modern-day and Victorian magazines is that, even though reading skills and printing techniques have greatly improved, type sizes have got larger. Conan Doyle's Sherlock Holmes pronounced himself an expert on typography and commented on it in *The Hound of the Baskervilles* (1902), telling Dr Mortimer:

> The detection of types is one of the most elementary branches of knowledge to the special expert in crime.

LONDON (January 1918)

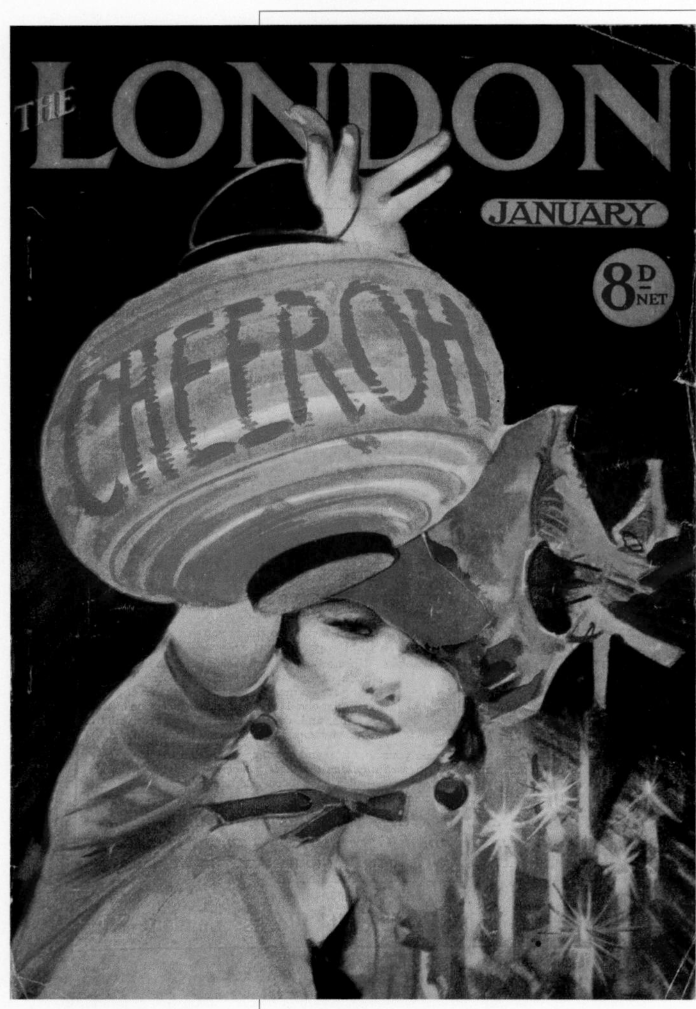

Harmsworth Popular Monthly was launched in 1898 as a rival to the *Strand* and changed its name to the *London* in 1908. Sales at the time were about 300,000 a month. The colour cover illustration is by William Barribal, who used his wife as the inspiration. As the century progressed, colour – and cover lines – became more common.

Amalgamated Press
(164 × 243 mm, side-stabbed, 136 pages)

A NEWS-STAND (1937–8)

Gravure dominated the 1930s news-stand: this promotional image from a Sun Engraving brochure shows only magazines that the Watford company printed (solely or partly) on its gravure presses. These presses were best at long runs, so among the 33 identifiable covers of issues published between 1937 and 1938 are some of the biggest-selling titles of the era, including *Picture Post*, *Weekly Illustrated*, *Picturegoer* and *Woman's Own*.

WORLD OF WONDER (17 November 1932)

World of Wonder was one of many money-spinning part-works for magazine publishers in the early 20th century. In essence, these were books published over a fixed period. In the 1980s, this part of the industry became the preserve of specialized companies focused on selling international rights as production costs soared due to 'collectable' items – such as videos, model cars or watches – with each issue. Note that the *World of Wonder* editor, Charles Ray, is credited on the cover. He worked on the *Children's Newspaper* for Arthur Mee, another prolific editor of encyclopedic works for children. Such cover credits were rarely seen after the war; publishing companies stressed their brand rather than the reputation of individuals.

Amalgamated
(216 × 278 mm, stapled, 32 pages)

He refers to the extra leading – space between lines of type – and the larger type size, in this case bourgeois, about 9 points (there being about 72 points to an inch). The Victorians would have referred to type sizes by a name – long primer, bourgeois or brevier, for example. The length of a line of type would be measured in ems. This is the width of a lower-case letter 'm', which, of course, varies for each size of type. The pica em, a 12-point em, is used as a standard measure. In the 1890s, text was generally dense on a page, in sizes as small as 7 point with a ½-point leading. Today, 12 point with 2-point leading would be more common, referred to as 12/14 for brevity.

The cover has become an essential marketing tool, screaming at potential buyers: 'Choose me!' But it was not so to wealthy Victorians, who subscribed to magazines or ordered them for delivery, while spurning the popular penny press. They saw the cover as protection for the contents, like a brown paper bag holding a pound of plums. It – and the adverts (with pages numbered in roman numerals on the front and back pages inside) – would be thrown away when the magazine pages 'proper' were bound together into a book once, twice, three or four times a year, along with an index and title pages. That's why the pages of each volume are numbered so, with editorial pagination in each issue continuing on from the previous one. The frequency of the volumes was dictated by practical considerations, such as the weight of the final book. For example, the first half-yearly volume of the *Sphere* weighs in at 8.5 kilos. The *Sphere* was a weekly with a jumbo page size (300 × 408 mm) and high-quality art paper. The habit of treating each issue of a magazine as part of a book died hard; *Punch* still expected to be bound in the Victorian manner into the 1980s. The computer magazine *Acorn User* – launched in 1982 – published an annual index and, like many titles then and now, sold binders to hold each year's issues. Although very few magazines today number their pages in a manner anticipating collection, many publishers still do not number their covers – *Vogue* publisher Condé Nast for one.

For some magazines, the wrapper was such a throwaway item that it was printed on a lesser-quality paper than the articles. *Tit-Bits*, which originally carried no advertising and is responsible for so much standard practice in both magazines and newspapers today, introduced a green cover after five years in 1886 to protect the magazine while it was being carried around by readers (who could claim insurance money if they were found with a copy in the case of a railway accident). The cover was made up of advertisements (to subsidize its production, said the publishers), and adverts stayed on the front until 1949; 'Tit-Bits green' survived as part of the cover design until 1967. When *Men Only* launched in 1935 in a pocket-sized format, the cover was not trimmed to the size of the article pages but left larger to better protect the issue. This suited the fact that so many people would be reading it while commuting. *Tit-Bits*

WEEKLY ILLUSTRATED ANNUAL (1936)

The man behind the camera is using a Leica. The German 35-mm format spurred photojournalism – and the growth of magazines such as *Weekly Illustrated* and *Picture Post*. This cover illustration also uses montage and spot colours to enliven the mono image. The annual was a 6d summary of the year in pictures collated from the weekly magazine.

Odhams Press
(258 × 345 mm, stapled, 64 pages)

TITBITS (13 September 1969)

Actress Susan George on the cover with a dramatically cropped photograph. It is a tabloid-style layout, but on a page only slightly larger than A4. *Titbits* has dropped its original green colour in favour of a warm red and has subtly changed its name.

IPC Magazines
(234 × 310 mm, stapled, 44 pages)

was relaunched regularly to keep up with the changing demands of its readers and to exploit the latest production technology while keeping costs low. There was a divide in formats in the 1930s, with the new photojournalism titles going for large page sizes – almost tabloid A3 – while *Men Only* made a pocket format popular again.

BOOK OR NEWSPAPER

Of course, dust jackets on hard-back books initially fulfilled the same protective function as magazine covers, but again have become an essential part of the reading experience – though the link between books and magazines has always been a little blurred, sometimes intentionally (in 1983 the designer David Hillman wrapped magazine *Information Management* with a blank cover inside a jacket). For some, treating a magazine as a book takes it upmarket and out of the realm of ephemera. Some publishers still refer to their magazines as 'books', Condé Nast again being an example. The company also still talks about an 'editorial well' – an unbroken sequence of editorial pages, with advertising before and after, that to this day defines the structure of *Vogue* and its other titles.

Issues of *Dazed & Confused*, *Intersection* and *AnOther Magazine* have been published with hardback covers. The tactic was also followed by men's monthly *Esquire*. In each of these cases, the aim was to stress the upmarket nature of the title. The terms 'bookazine' and 'mook' have both been used in recent decades for one-off publications that blur the divide between types of publication. But it's an approach that goes back to Aubrey Beardsley's *Yellow Book* at the Bodley Head in the 1890s and Ruari McLean's *Motif* at the Shenval Press in the 1960s.

In between the book and magazine were part-works, which, as serialized publications, go back centuries. Popular subjects included fiction and encyclopedias of general knowledge and etiquette. Bound sets could be marketed as books. Some of these were inspired by *Enquire within upon Everything*, an annual reference work published by Houlston and Sons of Paternoster Square for more than a century from 1856, which has been described by Tim Berners-Lee as an inspiration for the World Wide Web. Amalgamated Press – founded by Alfred Harmsworth in that same London square near St Paul's Cathedral – saw the potential of general-knowledge partwork publishing and set Charles Ray to produce *Everybody's Enquire Within*, an illustrated competitor in weekly instalments from 1937 to 1938. Almost 50 years later, the *Home Computer Course* in 24 issues for specialist part-work publisher Orbis was an important source of revenue for former *Oz* editor Felix Dennis. The market is now dominated by Italian group De Agostini and noted for television advertising in the new year.

At the 'other' end of the spectrum, magazines have blurred into newspapers. The illustrated titles of the Victorian era, from the

MEN ONLY (December 1935)

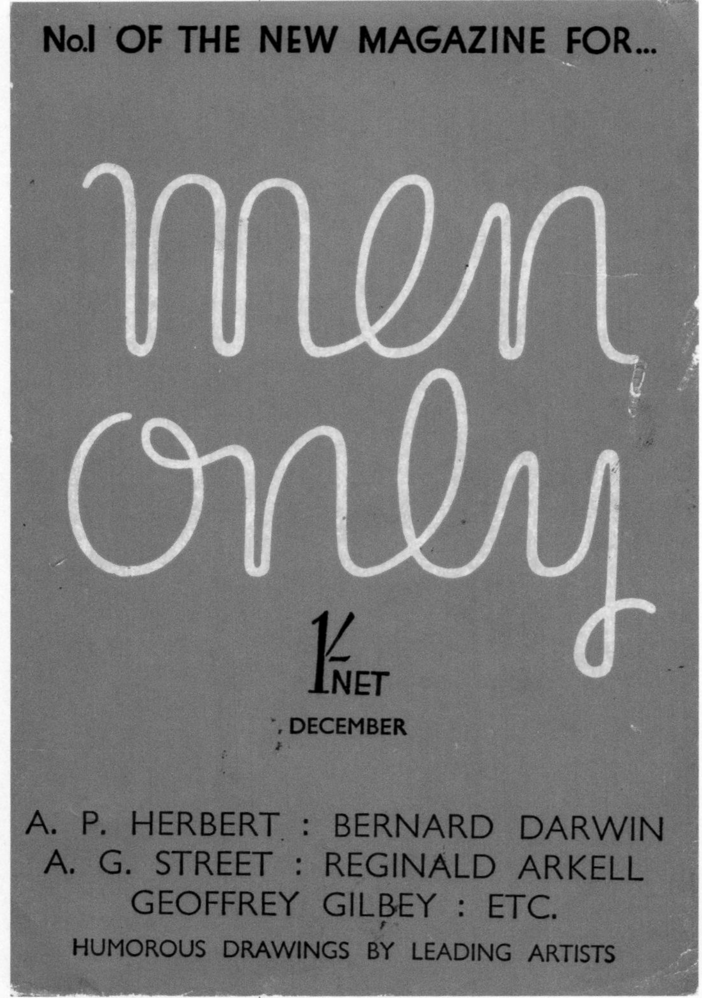

Early covers of this monthly about 'current male topics' consisted of the logo and cover lines. It was bound as a pocket book. In 1936, sketches of men were introduced and later full-cover caricatures by Edward Hynes until 1956. One reader commented: 'Your title led me to expect something more thrilling – by *Vie Parisienne* [a risqué French magazine dating back to 1863 that inspired *London Life*] out of *Esquire* [the US title that was only two years old] – and I find you too respectable for words.' It carried a colour pin-up from the start – 'Studio Peeps' – and later pin-ups from US *Esquire* artist Vargas.

C. Arthur Pearson
(124 × 182 mm, stitched book binding, 156 pages)

CARWEEK (13 October 1993)

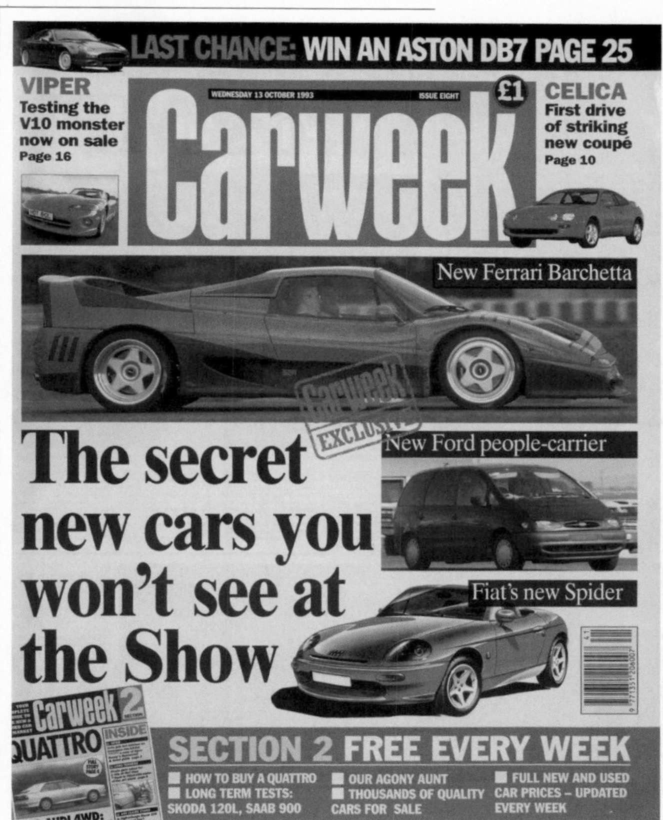

ROTATIONS (November/December 1996)

CARWEEK (24 August 1994)

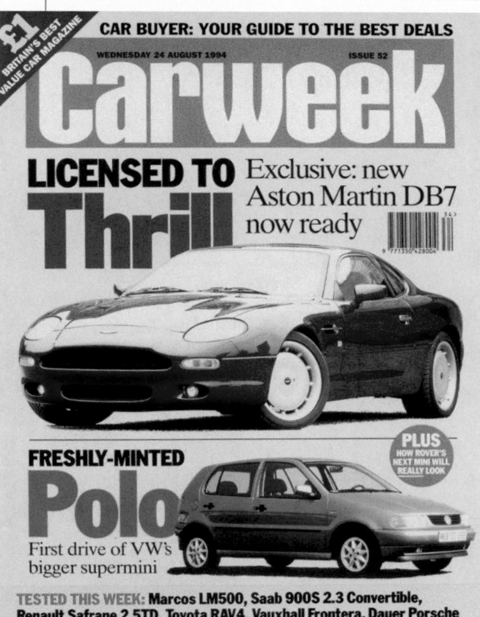

The Peterborough offices of Emap were used to producing magazines in a tabloid-newspaper format, but it did not suit the times: it did not fit on shop shelves alongside its competitors. Despite being relaunched in an A4 size, changing the editor and moving to offices in London, it folded.

Emap National Publications
(290 × 364 mm, stapled, 92 pages)

Emap National Publications
(230 × 298 mm, stapled, 92 pages)

Not a good format. This short-lived magazine came with a CD. It was mounted on card to stop it rolling off the shelves and was packaged in a plastic bag. A contents list was printed on the back of the card. Art direction, design and illustration were by Somewhere International. The articles were short because of the small pages and the overall effect was of a brochure or promotional item.

Rotations UK
(220 × 295 mm, stapled, 48 pages)

Illustrated London News onwards, might be seen as weekly papers. Several more were launched to serve the demand for images from the Boer Wars that newspapers could not meet because of the time and cost of processing images. The editorial strategy developed by George Newnes with *Tit-Bits* – editing down news and facts to their essence and presenting them as entertainment – influenced Alfred Harmsworth as he established both his rival, *Answers*, and the 'tabloid' news for the *Daily Mail* (1896), in a movement that would become known as 'new journalism'. The word 'tabloid' was derived from the invention of compressed (alkaloid) pills and related to the style of writing rather than the paper's format. Harmsworth's move from magazines into tabloids (the *Daily Mail* and then the *Daily Mirror* in 1903) was echoed by *Pearson's Weekly* publisher C. Arthur Pearson, who also went on to build a newspaper empire, starting with the *Daily Express* (1900). It was ironic, then, that in the long term the *Express*, once Britain's best-selling daily newspaper, was bought by Richard Desmond's Northern & Shell Group, magazine publisher, in 2000.

COLOUR AND PROCESS

The illustrated papers and mass-market weeklies were made possible by advances in printing, engraving and paper. Ever-faster presses – with the hand-operated machines that were little changed from the time of Johannes Gutenberg and Wynkyn de Worde being replaced by steam-powered rotary machines – enabled longer print runs; half-tones brought photography; and photogravure techniques improved image reproduction. Feeding a press from a continuous reel of paper – a web – again improved speeds over sheet-fed machines. Colour was initially applied from wooden blocks, one for each individual colour, or painted on by hand, but process colour printing, whereby the colours of an image are separated into primary colours – cyan (blue), magenta and yellow – by photomechanical means became steadily more widespread in the twentieth century. Although in theory cyan, magenta and yellow inks combine to make black, the result actually looks washed out, so a fourth colour, black – the 'key' colour – is also used.

The CMYK printing process is now the basis for most colour magazine (and book) work. In quality magazines, even seemingly black-and-white images are printed from four colours to achieve a greater depth and richness. Also, a fifth colour – for example, a metallic or fluorescent ink – might be used. The boom in photogravure, combined with 35-mm cameras, created the potential for photojournalism in the 1930s, along with far greater use of colour.

Speedier and cheaper reproduction of photographs spurred a switch from illustration to photography, particularly after the Second World War. The numerous star names of illustration largely disappeared, and photographers and their sitters arrived in their stead.

FORMATS

After the Second World War, *Tit-Bits* expanded to a tabloid size with pin-ups on the cover, a move that sparked a host of competitors, such as *Weekend* and *Reveille*, to follow. Then, in the 1960s, it shrank back to a magazine format. *Tit-Bits* has now long folded, but the debate over format has continued. When Emap (originally a local newspaper publisher, East Midlands Allied Press) launched *Carweek*, it adopted a colour tabloid-paper format, complete with motorsport pages reading in from the back. It envisaged the large images giving it an edge. However, the pubic preferred the glossy A4 format of the other weekly motoring magazines. An additional problem was that it was too big to fit on newsagents' shelves alongside its A4 competitors; instead, it was laid flat at the bottom of the shelves, where people were not expecting to find it. The company cut the size – twice – but it was too late and the title closed, losing £7 million.

It was a similar story for the 'inkies' – the tabloid-format weeklies such as *Melody Maker*, *New Musical Express*, *Sounds* and *Record Mirror* – so called because the ink came off on readers' hands. These all wilted in the face of competition from A4 music magazines such as *Smash Hits* and *Kerrang!*, which addressed themselves to smaller niches, there being fewer teenagers in the population and other young readers preferring style magazines. Several tried adopting an A4 colour format, but only *NME* survives today, with sales that are a fraction of its 1970s heyday. It maintains revenue by treating the title as a brand that can be applied to other products and 'channels' such as radio, the web and 'masthead television' programming.

COVER STRATEGIES

Even if the format is right, strategies for the cover vary enormously. In the late 1960s *Nova* was one of the most innovative magazines in its approach to the front image. David Hillman, one of its designers, credits Mark Boxer for the freedom he had:

> Boxer was probably the first [editor] ... whose design knowledge actually made the magazine. The *Sunday Times Magazine* had a high design content because he had an interest in words and pictures. He made it possible for others, such as myself later on at *Nova*, to be deputy editor as well as art editor. Art direction is something where to do the role properly, you have to be aware of both words and pictures.

Choices are influenced by design trends, whether it be Arts and Crafts, Swiss-driven modernism, photography against illustration, or a return to popularity of ornamentation. Many of these trends are created or built upon by magazines such as the Pre-Raphaelites' *Germ*, the *Studio*, the *Yellow Book*, *Blast*, *Design* or *Eye*.

The British magazine cover has evolved on a very competitive news-stand, where it must stand out from the competition, but at the

OBSERVER LIFE MAGAZINE (3 April 1994)

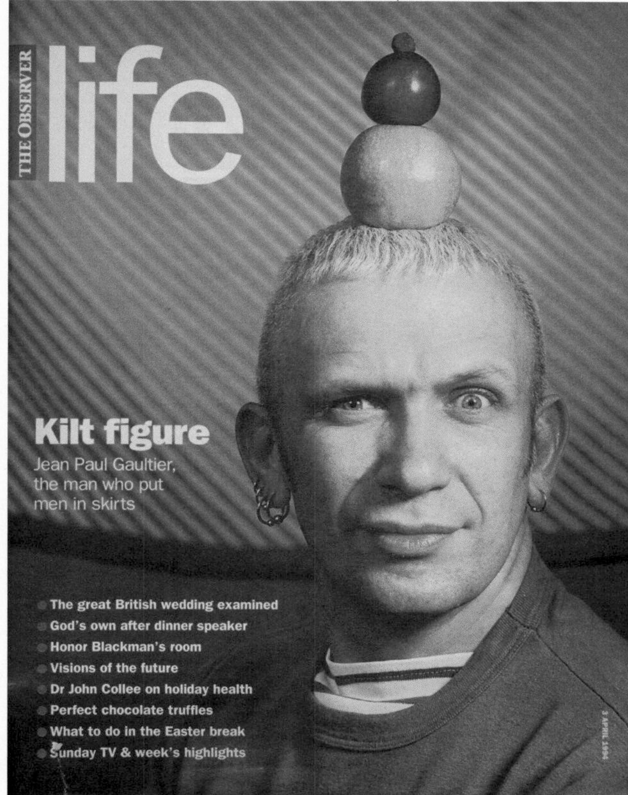

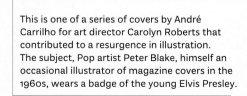

OBSERVER MAGAZINE (27 March 1994)

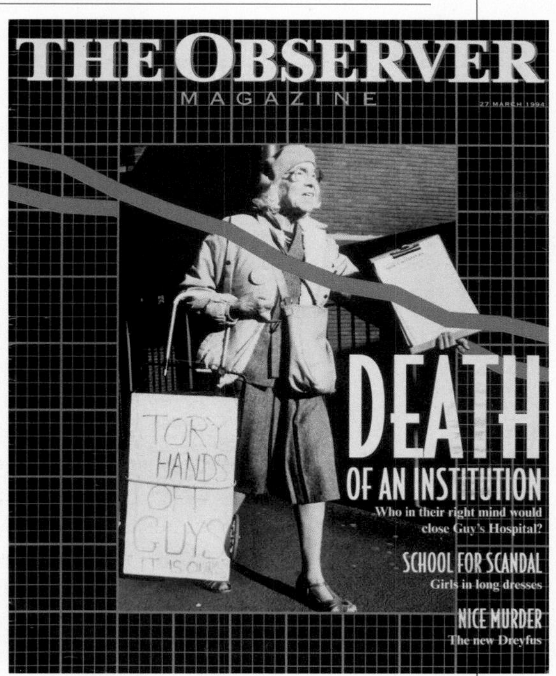

TALK OF THE TOWN (29 June 2003)

It is difficult to imagine a more downbeat cover than this. Compare it to another supplement with the same Sunday paper from the next week. The cover photograph was by Dario Mitidieri.

Observer supplement
(257 × 318 mm, stapled, 52 pages)

This cover seems designed to provide the maximum contrast with the previous week's. The subject, Jean Paul Gaultier, is one of those people who always seem to lead to an interesting image. Photo by Dan Burn-Forti.

Observer supplement
(287 × 373 mm, stapled, 56 pages)

This is one of a series of covers by André Carrilho for art director Carolyn Roberts that contributed to a resurgence in illustration. The subject, Pop artist Peter Blake, himself an occasional illustrator of magazine covers in the 1960s, wears a badge of the young Elvis Presley.

Independent on Sunday supplement
(210 × 296 mm, stapled, 48 pages)

same time fit in. In other words, it must not look out of kilter for its sector – too quirky an approach can hinder sales. Free Sunday supplements can take more risks. *Life*, a new magazine with the *Observer*, chose a different size and zany cover in what seemed to be an attempt to look as different as possible from the previous week's supplement. *Frank*, a woman's monthly from *Face* publisher Wagadon, was a name chosen to be deliberately 'both male and female' and 'upfront, candid and a little bizarre'. It was 'free' from horoscopes, letters and sex stories. But sales were disappointing and within a year the editor resigned, apparently over differences about long-term strategy, with Wagadon wanting *Frank* to be more mainstream. Fitting in is important: readers must know where to find a magazine. Glance into a large newsagent and you will see hundreds of titles grouped by topic and frequency – all the TV listings titles together and all looking similar. Any innovation will be quickly copied.

In the UK now most magazines are sold in newsagents – typically nine out of ten – whereas in the US that proportion is reversed in favour of subscriptions. Subsequently for British publishers a 'selling' cover is more important than a 'clever' design. In addition, British magazines tend to use heavier paper than their US counterparts (because postage weight is not such an issue) and page sizes are larger – giving more visual punch on the shelves.

For Victorian magazines, there was not such competition and covers tended to carry semi-display advertising, such as *Country Life*; an unchanging cover design (*Punch*, *Strand*); a design that provided a space for an engraving or a contributors or contents list (*Illustrated London News*, *Pall Mall*); or a unique cover for each issue (*Home Chat*, *Home Notes*). The most aggressive – *Home Chat* – approach was used in the most competitive sectors, and the Edwardian period saw most magazines adopt either an advertising cover or a unique cover for each issue. Even magazines that are regarded as having an unchanging design, such as *Punch* and *Strand*, introduced advertising, either in the margins around the main image (*Punch*) or by building ads into the image (*Strand*).

The name of the magazine as a logo – the title or masthead – is a branding device. Newnes used the *Strand* cover as a brand in the 1890s on the *Tit-Bits* almanac and its books, replacing the magazine's name hung from wires with the name of the publisher, George Newnes Limited. Titles for leading magazines tend to be designed by specialized typographers such as Reynolds Stone (*The Economist*), Dave Farey and Richard Dawson (*BBC Good Food*, *Maxim*, *Design Week*) and Matthew Carter (*Private Eye*). The need for visibility of the title dictates its position at the top of the cover and it has to be designed so that it can be recognized even if the cover is partly obscured by other magazines. This has led to the 'left third' rule – the vital area for the title and cover lines.

Within these constraints, editors and designers have coined rules of thumb for covers that will sell and also address the philosophy of a magazine. In the US, Dick Stolley, a founding editor of celebrity weekly *People*, came up with this mantra:

> Young is better than old.
> Pretty is better than ugly.
> Rich is better than poor.
> Movies are better than music.
> Music is better than television.
> Television is better than sports
> ... and anything is better than politics.

He later changed the last line to 'And nothing is better than the celebrity dead' after the 1980 murder of John Lennon. And to this day, the best-known photograph by Annie Leibovitz is arguably also the one that made her career – the image of a naked Lennon and Yoko Ono curled up together. It was taken the day the former Beatle was shot and it was used as the cover for *Rolling Stone* a month later. But Stolley had still left out the ultimate source of celebrity: royalty. The Lennon cover was *People*'s best-seller until the death of Princess Diana. Similarly, the Canadian-born editor of the modern *Vanity Fair*, Graydon Carter, has his own take on what sells his magazine: '[This] is a global magazine ... The only universal language is movies so you're stuck with it.' Such rules apply to a subset of magazines, but most editors and designers would do well to observe a maxim attributed to Haymarket art director Roland Schenk: that an editor should 'prostitute himself' for his covers.

Established publications with loyal readerships can run covers or editorials that reference previous issues, as in the *FT Magazine* mimicking its Tony Blair cover from 2003 two years later as a James Ferguson caricature (see page 25).

In less confident or more competitive times, magazines will seek to 'add value' using gimmicks. In the 1920s, rulers were printed up the side of back covers as a tool for readers. As commercial television began to eat into sales, *Picture Post* ran 3D photographs with red and blue lens glasses, and claimed the world's first colour 3D pin-up, of the glamour model Sabrina. Magazines from *Cabaret Girls* to *Wallpaper** have used the technology since. Cover gifts were popular in the First World War and appeared occasionally on many titles, but in the 1980s their use surged with cheap goods flooding in from China, such as flip-flops and paperbacks. Specialist titles have found flexidiscs, cassettes, CDs, videos and CD-ROMs essential at various times. Cover images have to be commissioned to sit around such items.

The past century has seen the control of design move from printers and typesetters to specialized art editors, directors and stylists.

RADIO TIMES (14 March 1998)

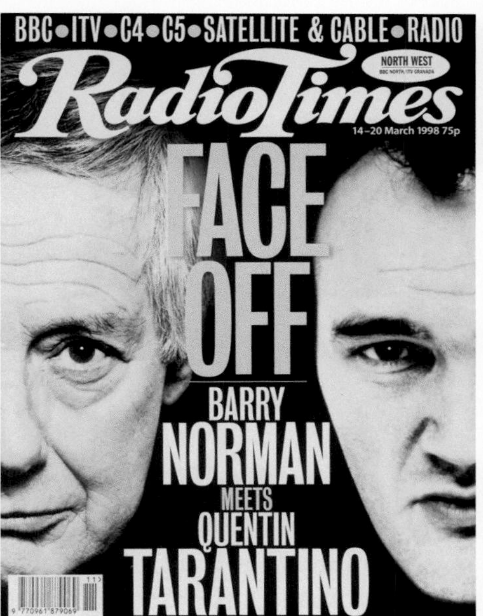

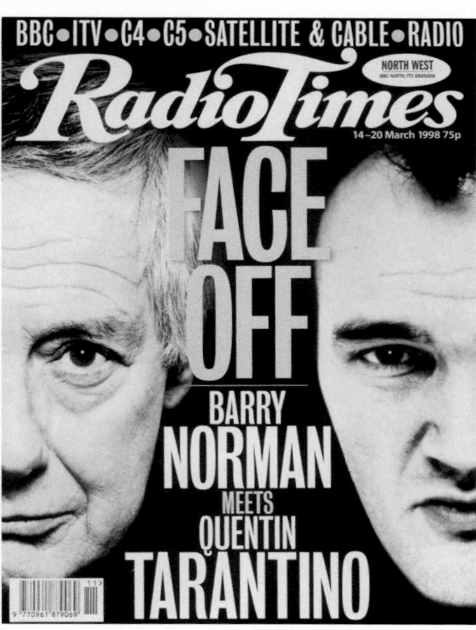

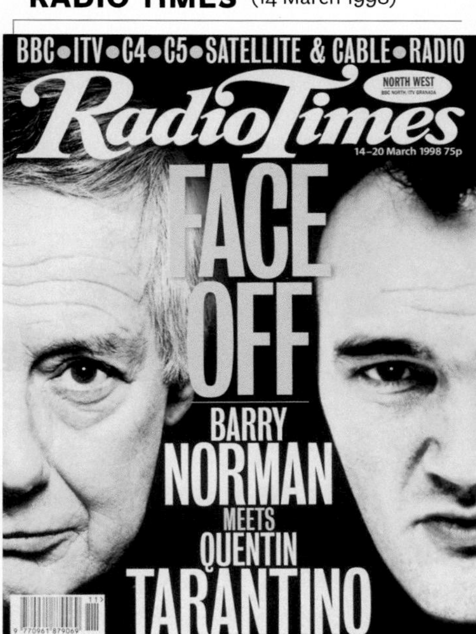

The cover promoting Barry Norman interviewing Quentin Tarantino looked particularly striking when several copies were placed side by side in newsagents. *Radio Times* also started to print issues with several different covers: for example, a cover for each of the four Teletubbies.

BBC
(226 × 296 mm, stapled)

YOUR GARDEN (May 1993)

The cover design and editorial strategy were a response to the success of BBC/Redwood's *Gardener's World*. Redwood also popularized cover gifts with *Gardener's World* and this IPC rival has responded with gardening gloves. Another challenge for the cover design!

IPC Magazines
(216 × 297 mm, stapled, 112 pages)

Much of this change has been driven by advertising art directors moving to magazines. Writers and photographers have also sought more influence. Yet all of this has to be done inside a commercial framework; even the most lauded designs – *Nova*, *Town* and *Queen* in the 1960s, for example – will fail if they cannot attract enough sales and advertising to pay the bills.

As for the 'best' cover, a public vote organized by the Periodical Publishers Association, the magazine industry trade body, resulted in a 2005 *Radio Times* being chosen. However, voting may well have been skewed by fans of Doctor Who and the Daleks (see opposite).

NEW ATTRACTIONS TO FIT IN

In 1912, Liverpool-born journalist Arthur Wynne devised a 'word cross' based on a childhood game for the *New York World*. The idea came back across the Atlantic, to *Pearson's Magazine* and *Queen* in 1922 and 1925 respectively. But it was not plain sailing for setters and compositors, as clue numbers 5A and 17A in *Queen* attest. The accompanying text read: 'The Crossword Puzzle has been given at the request of readers, and will be continued should a sufficient number of correspondents express their desire for one.' *The Sunday Express* followed the 'new-fangled puzzles' trend in 1924 and the *Daily Telegraph* in 1925.

British puzzles diverged from American crosswords by building on cryptic competitions and wordplay, such as *John Bull*'s Bullets and *Vanity Fair*'s 'double acrostics' and Doublets, the latter devised in 1880 by Oxford mathematics don Charles Lutwidge Dodgson, better known as Lewis Carroll. In a Doublet, the aim is to turn one word into another, one letter at a time, as in: 'monk, mock, cock, cork, core, come, Rome'. Edward Powys Mathers pioneered cryptic crosswords for the *Observer* as 'Torquemada' from 1926. A year later, a debate in the House of Commons heard that 13 million letters a year were being posted about such puzzles. In 1930, the *Listener*, *Country Life* and *The Times* adopted the approach. *The Economist* publishes a crossword in its Christmas number with instructions for US readers.

Victorian weeklies such as *Tit-Bits* pioneered all sorts of competitions and insurance schemes. In 1907, *London Opinion*'s limerick competitions were so popular that post offices ran out of the postal orders needed for entry and MPs debated declaring such competitions illegal lotteries. From the 1920s, the cheap weeklies were littered with prize crosswords and picture games, and by the 1950s were devoting anything up to a quarter of their issues to football pools, horse-racing and prize competitions. Today, there are puzzle magazines specializing in crosswords, or a more modern craze, such as Sudoku, the Japanese number squares popularized by *The Times* in 2004.

FLATPLANS AND THE RUN OF A MAGAZINE

Design Week once told an art department joke: 'How many art directors does it take to change a light bulb?' – 'Change? I'm not changing anything!' Where the demands of art editors, editors, advertising managers and production controllers come together each issue is with the flatplan. This diagram shows the spreads of a magazine as pairs of numbered rectangles. Each rectangle is marked as an advertising or editorial page. Simple really, but the editor has to develop a flow of articles that will draw readers through the magazine while satisfying production demands and giving the advertising sales people enough early spreads and 'CRHFMs' – colour, right-hand (pages) that face (editorial) matter. The sales department will be able to charge far more for these. But what happens if an advertiser wants three such pages consecutively in the first half of the book? Until the late 1990s, there was usually a limit on the number of colour pages in an issue and such pages fell in specific places, dictated by the interleaving of the colour and mono printed sections or sides. Conflicting demands for such colour sites could also lead to tension. Does the editor jiggle everything around, or reject advertising demands and risk losing a lucrative order? *GQ* editor Michael VerMeulen regretted allowing a 1993 split cover for an advertising request because he felt it had ruined the look of the magazine.

And editors have their own priorities. A stapled magazine will, for example, want to make the best use of the centre pages – a true spread where a photograph can run across the pages. Similarly, a decision has to be taken as to whether long fiction is left to run in the middle of a magazine or is turned to the back. Since the 1960s, most magazines have run editorial on the page facing the inside back cover to appeal to readers who open the book from the back, and also to increase the value of the 'IBC', as it is known, for advertising. The *Sunday Times Magazine*'s 'A Life in the Day' feature has run in that slot for 40 years. Crosswords and letters pages can create opportunities for advertising sites; indeed, some publications now seek sponsors for these 'landmark' positions.

'MAGAZINIZATION' AND OTHER MEDIA

The influence of magazines, and their design, can be seen throughout other media. They were the breeding ground for the tabloid strategy that revolutionized newspapers, and the pin-up page that was to reach its apogee in Rupert Murdoch's *Sun* in the 1970s was pioneered by *Tit-Bits*. *Telecrime*, one of the first televised drama series in 1938, was a spin-off from 'Photocrime', a feature in *Weekly Illustrated*. Similarly, broadcasters run 'magazine' programmes, and publishers now spin off radio stations and 'masthead television' programmes. And just as early radio and TV series were based on magazine formats, magazines ran serials based on soap operas, such the BBC's *Archers*, or told popular films as stories, with stills from the film. This 'magazinization' of the media continues.

RADIO TIMES (30 April 2005)

This was voted best magazine cover in a public poll organized by the PPA. Voters chose from 16 covers picked by a panel of editors. Of the 10,000 votes cast, more than a quarter voted Dalek. Rivals included the first issue of *Oz* (February 1967), *Nova* (September 1968), Patrick Demarchelier's *Vogue* cover of Princess Diana published after her death (October 1997), the first issue of the *Face* (May 1980), Vivienne Westwood as Margaret Thatcher for *Tatler* (April 1989), *Time Out*'s two-fingered salute to Winston Churchill on the 100th anniversary of his birth (29 November 1974) and *Loaded*'s graffiti cover of Kevin Keegan (April 1996).

BBC
(225 × 300 mm, stapled, 148 pages)

TIME OUT (13 July 2005)

The design chosen to mark the London bombings, which happened a week before the issue came out, was intended to show strength and resolution. The French satirical magazine *Charlie Hebdo* responded with similar fortitude on its website the day twelve people were murdered by terrorists at its offices: 'Je Suis Charlie' (7 January 2015).

Time Out Publications
(205 × 270 mm)

GUARDIAN WEEKEND (6 August 2011)

'The people vs The supermarkets' cover was by Bristol artist Banksy and entitled 'Tesco value petrol bomb'. The article was about protests around the country at Tesco and other big retailers opening more stores and threatening the trade of local shops. In the next few days, London suffered its worst bout of looting for decades and riots also broke out in other cities.

Guardian supplement
(244 × 290 mm, stapled, 80 pages)

THE BIG ISSUE (11 November 1996)

The magazine was set up by John Bird in 1991 to give homeless people an alternative to begging. This cover uses a duotone – a monochrome photograph scanned and printed in two colours, in this case black and blue. The technique can be used to give a sepia effect.

The Big Issue
(210 × 298 mm, stapled, 48 pages)

FRANK (October 1997)

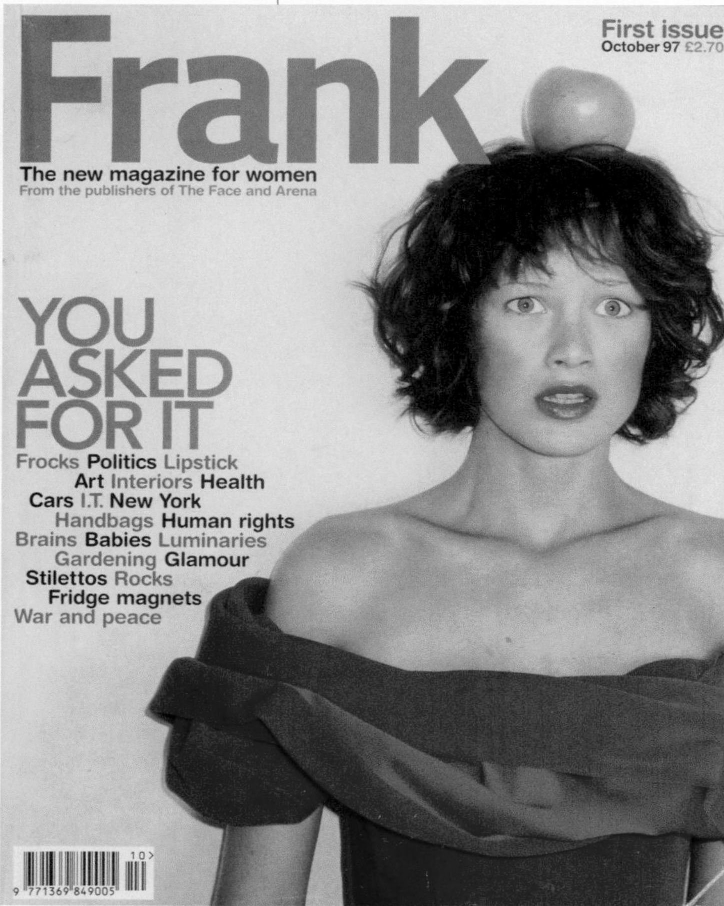

Editor Tina Gaudoin described a fraught time launching this title: 'This wasn't how it was meant to be ... we named *Frank* with 12 hours to go before the deadline ... the birth of *Frank* has been a total pain in the arse.' The art director was Jason Shulman. The magazine set out to be different from other women's monthlies, but was too quirky to gain sufficient sales.

Wagadon
(220 × 280 mm, perfect bound, 244 pages)

FINANCIAL TIMES MAGAZINE (26 April 2003)

Rankin (John Rankin Waddell) took this image of Tony Blair, then prime minister, for the launch issue of the *Financial Times Magazine* just weeks after US and British forces invaded Iraq. John Walsh wrote of the cover in the *Independent*: '"At 50, everyone has the face he deserves," wrote George Orwell in his 1949 notebook. But did Tony Blair, for all the ambiguities of his current position, really deserve the face he was given on the cover of last week's *Financial Times* magazine? Gaunt, deranged, apparently aghast at the cruelty of fate, he looked like a torture victim deprived of sleep for five days, then forced to wear a tight-fitting shirt and cruelly jaunty tie. The camera's "ring-flash" technique stamped two tiny Polo mints on his eyeballs. The receding hairline, the swooping lines on forehead and cheeks, a suggestion of liver spots about the cranium – it didn't seem a very celebratory portrait to mark the PM's 50th birthday. Then you noticed the cover line that accompanied the image: "The Believer". All was suddenly clear. This deeply troubled, terminally worried-looking man wasn't a victim after all, but something more spiritual – he was a martyr.'[1]

1 3 May 2003, p. 23.

Financial Times supplement
(210 × 296 mm, stapled, 48 pages)

FINANCIAL TIMES MAGAZINE (5 March 2005)

James Ferguson is a self-taught artist who illustrates the 'Lunch with the FT' interview, which at various times has been carried in either the Saturday paper or the *FT Magazine*. His caricatures are very much in the tradition of Ape in *Vanity Fair*, looking for a telling detail that will illuminate the interview. This painting takes the Rankin portrait and subtly exaggerates the features at a time when there was talk of Tony Blair being prosecuted for war crimes. Notice the disarranged tie and the prominent ears.

Ferguson points out that when he looked at the Rankin photograph, his reaction was that the 'ears had been pinned back or digitally altered', so he made them more prominent because Blair has 'sticky-out ears'; it is one of the features of his appearance for caricaturists. Rankin was surprised when he heard this comment and checked the negative. It turns out he had used a Mamiya RZ67 with a 50-mm lens – which acted as a wide-angle lens to slightly distort Blair's face, bringing the nose forward and, incidentally, diminishing the ears.

Financial Times supplement
(210 × 969 mm, stapled, 48 pages)

DAZED & CONFUSED (January 2004)

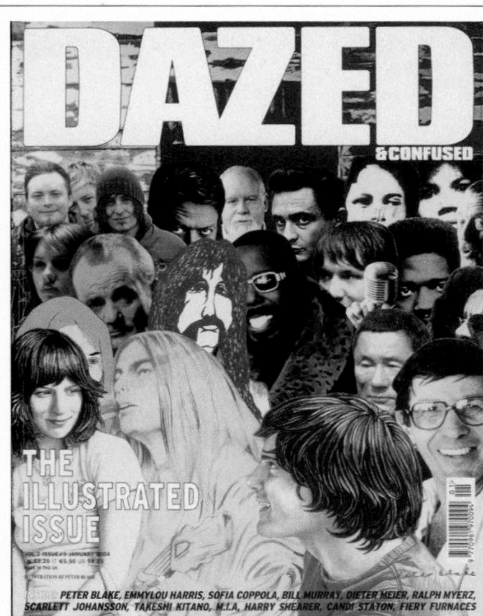

Pop artist Peter Blake peers out from the back of the crowd in his own cover illustration on an issue that celebrated the diversity and resurgence in the popularity of the art form.

Dazed & Confused Ltd
(210 × 275 mm)

Commercially, books, magazines and newspapers have long been intertwined. The *Daily Mail* carries an 'Answers to Correspondents' column with a logo that echoes the 1888 masthead of *Answers to Correspondents on Every Subject under the Sun* – the magazine that launched Lord Northcliffe as a newspaper baron and was the foundation for Daily Mail and General Trust, now a print, radio, television and digital conglomerate. When it was formed in the 1960s, the International Publishing Corporation (IPC) drew together Britain's three biggest magazine groups with the Daily Mirror group, printing plants and book publishing. It was the *Guardian* that led the launch of the first UK version of the US new media magazine *Wired*. Its owners, Guardian Media Group, also controlled *Auto Trader* and its many associated magazines until 2014.

In 2004, the broadsheet *Independent* responded to the need to cut costs and avoid competing for news with online sources and round-the-clock TV by becoming a tabloid 'viewspaper'. It was a term that had been used by editor Andrew Neil as he tried to transform the *European* newspaper into a magazine:'I want it to have the authority of *The Economist*, to be a viewspaper, with high-quality analysis.'[1] In design and content, newspapers are steering away from 'hard news' in favour of articles commissioned days or weeks in advance, with modular layouts and larger photographs. The layouts of some Saturday and Sunday papers, in particular, are simply magazine grids blown up to a bigger size.

The battle over whether to carry advertising or editorial on covers had been fought for centuries. Among consumer magazines, it appeared to have been won in favour of editorial in the 1950s, although *Tatler* reverted to a semi-display cover for a few years in the late 1960s. The battle seemed truly over when even *The Times* dropped advertising from its back page in 1981. However, the trend went into reverse from 1996 when the *Daily Mirror* turned blue: the issue had been bought for a day as a £1 million promotion by Pepsi to mark the drinks company changing the colour of its cans. The news was turned to 'blue-rinsed promotional puffery', said the *Guardian*. In a similar vein, Microsoft sponsored free copies of *The Times* for a year to promote Windows 95. A few years later, the *Spectator* allowed Mercedes to take every advertising page along with a wrap-around cover. With the launch of free daily papers such as *Metro* and free weekly magazines such as *Sport* and *Shortlist*, mainstream publications were pressed to allow aggressive advertising and wrap-around adverts. Many papers dropped editorial from their back pages in favour of a magazine-style full-page advert.

Since the 1990s, various 'multimedia' technologies have come and gone. CD-ROMs were seen as offering 'exciting' potential and IPC, Haymarket and Dennis experimented with magazines on discs. However, the idea fell flat and publishers turned to websites. These also failed as money-spinners but most keep ticking over with revenue from advertising, selling merchandise through web shopping portals or simply marketing for the magazines themselves. Later technologies led to 'virtual issues' or tempted readers to 'watch the cover move' using a mobile phone. The iPad and tablet craze led to another diversion, with a rush to turn out apps or sell digital subscriptions, often to little effect. *Wallpaper** and *Monocle* founder Tyler Brûlé reckons publishers have entered a blind alley:

> I'm very concerned for publishers who have chucked a hell of a lot of development money into making something that works on the iPad. Listen, guys: If your magazine isn't working at the moment in print or on the web, this isn't going to save you! ... I'd rather spend that $200,000 or $300,000 paying for more journalists.[2]

In fact, Brûlé has turned *Monocle* into an international brand, with an online radio station, a range of merchandise, shops in five cities around the world and a café in London. For him, publishers are not investing:

> In London and New York, magazines are charging more for a product that's inferior to what they were putting out 10 years ago! It's amazing! You're asking for more from your advertisers and readers, but your product is shit!

Instead, magazine publishers should return to a strategy that inspired *Punch*, *Picture Post*, *Prima* and many other British magazines over the years: look to publications overseas for ideas.

1 'The man who would be on the edge', Roy Greenslade. *Guardian* (2 June 1997)

2 'The amazing Mr Monocle', Dailyfrontrow.com (October 2010)

ENTER (March 2001)

Actress Amanda Holden was the cover subject for 'the magazine that moves'. In retrospect, CD-ROMs can be seen as an interim technology that would be overtaken by the web. Pornographic magazines were early users of digital video, both online and on CD-ROM.

Pure Communications
(220 × 300 mm, CD-ROM mounted on A4 card)

STYLIST (25 July 2012)

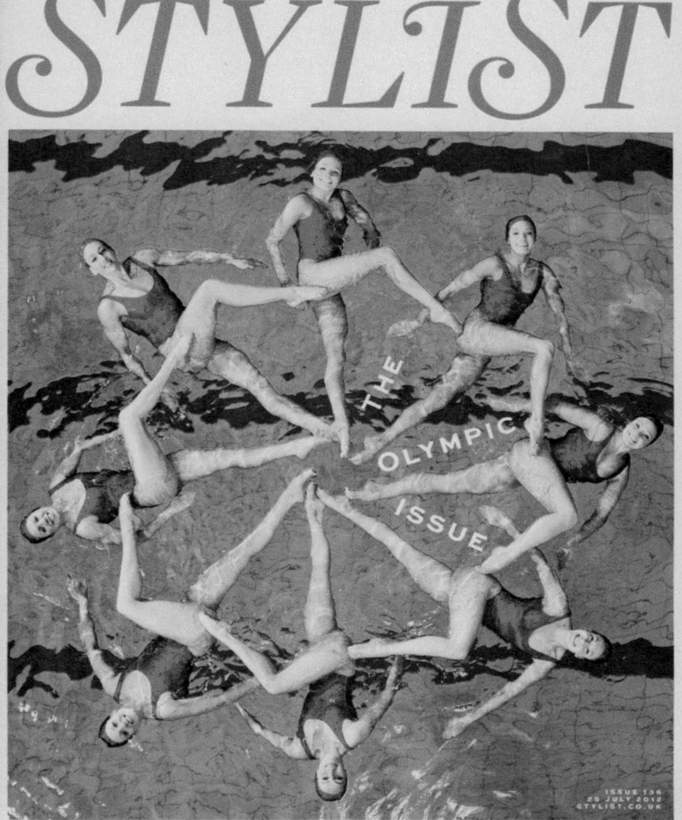

This was the 'first ever virtual issue' for the 'freemium' weekly. The Mark Harrison cover photo could be recognized by a tablet or smartphone using a Blippar app to be watched as a video. The digital artwork was by Happyfinish.com. The art director was Clare Ferguson.

Shortlist Media
(225 × 296 mm, stapled, 64 pages)

Punch and the illustrated magazine

Samuel Johnson listed the word 'magazine' in his dictionary of 1755: 'Of late this word has signified a miscellaneous pamphlet, from a periodical miscellany named the *Gentleman's Magazine*, by Edward Cave.' Johnson himself wrote for Cave and lived at 17 Gough Square, just off London's Fleet Street. The *Gentleman's Magazine* began as a 36-page weekly summarizing the contents of newspapers and journals such as the *Craftsman*, *Grubstreet* and *Daily Courant*. To these it added lists concerning business and current affairs (see page 10). The only illustration was an engraving as part of the masthead. Although it was very much for the aristocracy – it cost 6d an issue – it survived into the twentieth century and established a formula for popular content that would be taken up 150 years later (*Tit-Bits*) and again as the twenty-first century approached (the *Week*).

While the *Gentleman's Magazine* looked like a newspaper, other magazines, such as *Blackwood's*, published in Edinburgh from 1817, adopted a bookish, fiction-based approach. William Blackwood founded the monthly – nicknamed *Maga* – with a mix of literary and political articles and fiction. The cover on page 11 is from February 1960 and although the decorative border has changed, the face of George Buchanan, the sixteenth-century Scottish historian and early tutor to Mary, Queen of Scots, peered out from the first to the last issue. It was regarded as conservative – a virtue identified by its unchanging cover – and as valuing literary quality above commercialism. *Maga* was particularly well read in the colonies – the loss of which led to its ultimate decline: 'In tea plantations and hill stations, from the West Indies to India, across Africa and Burma, mildew and jungle have overtaken the bound volumes of *Punch* and *Blackwood's Magazine*, the cricket pitches and the billiard tables,' wrote Kenneth Allsop in the *Daily Mail* when Malta gained its independence (22 September 1964). It was bookish magazines such as *Maga* that gave many of the most prominent Georgian and Victorian authors their earliest showings, the most famous of all, Charles Dickens, first appearing in *Monthly Magazine* in 1833 with 'A Dinner at Poplar Walk'. *Oliver Twist* was published in *Bentley's Miscellany* in monthly instalments from February 1837 to April 1839 and Dickens would go on to 'conduct' (the contemporary phrase for an editor who had publishing control) his own magazines. Many book publishers produced periodicals devoted to fiction and were a big part of the magazine industry until the Second World War.

By 1840, railway networks were being established, paper made from mechanical wood pulp was far cheaper, the country had been at peace for 25 years, the penny post was coming in and there were more middle-class readers. The bookish magazine was established, but two other formats were about to liven up the industry, with a different focus at their core: humour and topical engravings.

Punch hit the news-stands in 1841 and became the most successful of the humorous weeklies. Its subtitle, 'the London Charivari', identifies its inspiration: the French magazine *Le Charivari*. Both brought together the Italian concept of *caricatura* – caricature – with satirical prints and journalism. The journalist and social researcher Henry Mayhew launched *Punch* with engraver Ebenezer Landells. Mayhew and Mark Lemon were joint editors. The magazine struggled to begin with and was taken over by Bradbury & Evans, book printers, in 1842. William Bradbury and Frederick Mullet Evans had set up their partnership in 1830 and after *Punch* brought them into regular contact with writers and illustrators, they were able to become a leading publisher of books and periodicals, with Dickens moving to them from Chapman & Hall in 1844. *Punch* also published almanacs and seasonal specials.

The *Illustrated London News* was the brainchild of Herbert Ingram, a printer, bookseller and newsagent in Nottingham. In 1840, one of the newspapers he sold published the portrait of a murderer. The level of demand inspired Ingram to bring out his weekly periodical of pictures with the help of Henry Vizetelly (who would found two rivals to the *ILN*, the *Pictorial Times* and the *Illustrated Times*, in 1843 and 1855 respectively). *Punch* ran a John Leech cartoon inspired by the popularity of the illustrated press, with an urchin telling a newsvendor: 'I vonts a nillustrated newspaper with a norrid murder and a likeness in it.' Engravings were used in other periodicals – the *Penny Magazine* with illustrations had been published by the Society for the Diffusion of Useful Knowledge since 1832, for example – but the *ILN* was bigger, better and dealt with newsworthy events. The first *ILN*, published in 1842, sold about 20,000 copies at a price of 6d. The Great Exhibition of 1851 boosted sales, and a string of wars, particularly the Crimean War of 1854–6, maintained the public's interest. The *ILN* sent six artists to the front and published engravings based on photographs from the pioneering war photographer Roger Fenton. In 1851, the weekly sale was 130,000, and circulation peaked in the 1860s at more than 300,000 copies a week. Issues were often reprinted for binding into volumes.

Magazines printed their illustrations from carved woodblocks, which were clamped into metal frames – formes – along with the handset type. The blocks were made as either a 'cut', where a knife is used to mark a softwood plank sawn parallel with the grain, or an engraving with the scoring done using special tools on a section of hardwood – usually boxwood – sawn across the grain. In both cases, wood is removed to leave a raised printing surface. The latter technique can produce a much sharper result, because the harder surface makes a finer line possible. Punch used the term the 'Big Cut' to describe its main political cartoon each week, which would have been on softwood for speed. Later titles such as *Once a Week*, *Good Words* and *Cornhill Magazine* raised the standard of engraving, and credited their artists. *Graphic* raised the game again from 1869, and was much admired by Vincent Van Gogh, who collected many of its illustrations, particularly from volumes published in the 1870s. He wrote in one letter to his brother Theo: 'For me, the English black-and-white artists are to art what Dickens is to literature.'[1]

For larger images, several woodblocks were glued or riveted together. This meant engravers could cooperate by taking a section of an image, either for speed or where one might specialize in, say, clouds, sea or people. Fine white lines across a print reveal where not enough care was taken joining the blocks.

In the middle of the nineteenth century engravers worked on an image drawn (reversed, of course, because of the direct printing process) by the artist on a white-coated block, but from the 1870s the image could be photographed on to a sensitized block, preserving the drawing. Photographic techniques were ultimately the nemesis of the engravers as photomechanical and half-tone processes were developed in the 1880s. *Punch*, for example, moved over to process blocks from 1892. Five years later, process techniques were dominant, as described by the editor of the *Process Year Book*:

> We have been told that high-class wood engraving is not dead yet, but we may well ask 'If it is not dead, where is it?' Certainly there is little to be seen in the illustrated papers and monthly magazines. Even in *The Graphic* – reputed as being the last stronghold of wood engraving – process forms a large part of block work.

The article cites the reproduction of wedding photographs in *Lady's Pictorial* as a great advantage of the technology. Furthermore, it describes artists as liking the photographic system, such as Sidney Paget expressing a 'great preference' for having his drawings reproduced by the process method in the *Strand*, as well as the late *Punch* cartoonist George du Maurier (who coined the phrase 'curate's egg'). In du Maurier's case, the switchover was triggered because his failing eyesight meant he could no longer achieve the level of detail needed for drawing on a wood block.[2]

The illustrated titles provided more employment for artists and the works of the Pre-Raphaelite Brotherhood are sprinkled through the pages of Victorian magazines such as *Once a Week*, *Cornhill Magazine*, *Graphic*, *Argosy* and *Good Words*. Their publicity skills were demonstrated when the Brotherhood launched their own magazine, *Germ*, in 1850, an idea that would be taken up by other art movements in later decades. *Germ* is an example of what academics would later call a 'little magazine', a non-commercial literary publication that aims to champion work by a few authors, or a particular style, or provide an overview of contemporary activities. At the other end of the scale was *The Economist*, another campaigning publication, launched in 1843 to fight the Corn Laws and promote free trade.

The *Cornhill Magazine* was founded by George Murray Smith in 1860 and named after the street at the heart of the City of London (a naming strategy seen later in the *Pall Mall Gazette* and the *Strand*). It was published until 1975. Smith set out to rival Dickens's *All the Year Round* and employed William Thackeray as editor. Like *Blackwood's*, the *Cornhill Magazine* used a consistent cover but differentiated itself with inside illustrations. An engraving of a John Everett Millais painting was in the first issue. An 1873 painting by Millais of his wife, Effie, the former wife of John Ruskin, shows her holding a copy of the *Cornhill Magazine*.

Stamp duty was removed from periodical publications in 1855, cutting prices and boosting sales. Stamped periodicals could be sent through the post for free. In addition, another market for magazines was forming, the middle-class woman who did much of her own housework. One of the first magazines to address this demographic was Samuel Beeton's *Englishwoman's Domestic Magazine*, which spun off *Beeton's Book of Household Management*. These magazines enabled fashions to be spread quickly, whether for bonnets and dresses, or the way homes should be decorated at Christmas. It was a virtuous circle: larger circulation paid for larger images and attracted more advertising, which paid for even more improvements and bigger issues.

New techniques enabled colour to be used more frequently and on larger runs, with woodblocks employed to add colour to engravings rather than doing the work by hand. The *Illustrated London News* used this technique for the cover of its 1855 Christmas supplement, establishing a tradition that was taken up by many weekly periodicals.

1 Quoted in Eric le Maré, 'The boxwood illustrators' in *Penrose's Annual: Process Year Book*, 1970 (vol. 63), pp.49–68

2 William Gamble, 'Process in magazine and book illustration' in *Penrose's Annual: Process Year Book*, 1897 (vol. 3.), pp. 3–16

PUNCH (17 July 1841)

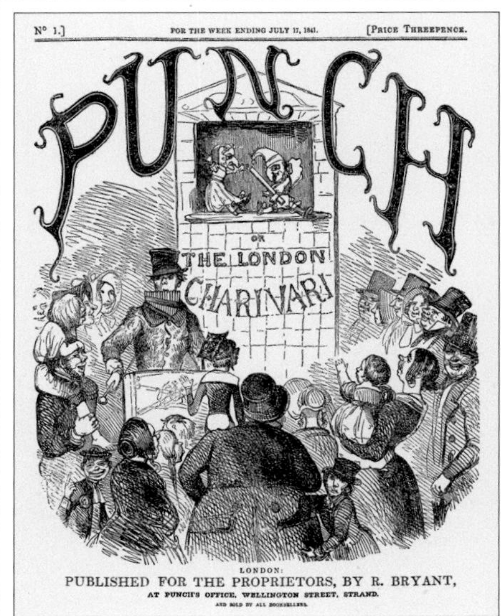
No 1.] FOR THE WEEK ENDING JULY 17, 1841. [PRICE THREEPENCE.

PUNCH OR THE LONDON CHARIVARI

LONDON:
PUBLISHED FOR THE PROPRIETORS, BY R. BRYANT,
AT PUNCH'S OFFICE, WELLINGTON STREET, STRAND.

Archibald Henning drew the first issue's cover. The design varied in the early years, with Richard Doyle creating what became the standard cover in 1849. Artists published in *Punch* in its first few decades included John Leech, Richard 'Dickie' Doyle, John Tenniel, Charles Keene, Harry Furniss, Linley Sambourne, Francis Carruthers Gould and Phil May. This group – the 'Brotherhood' – grew to incorporate Charles Dickens, who joined Bradbury & Evans after leaving Chapman & Hall in 1843. *Punch* authors and artists also contributed to another Bradbury & Evans literary magazine called *Once a Week* (1859–80), created in response to Dickens's departure from *Household Words*, as well as many books.

Initially published by the founders
(206 × 270 mm, 12 pages)

PUNCH (1843)

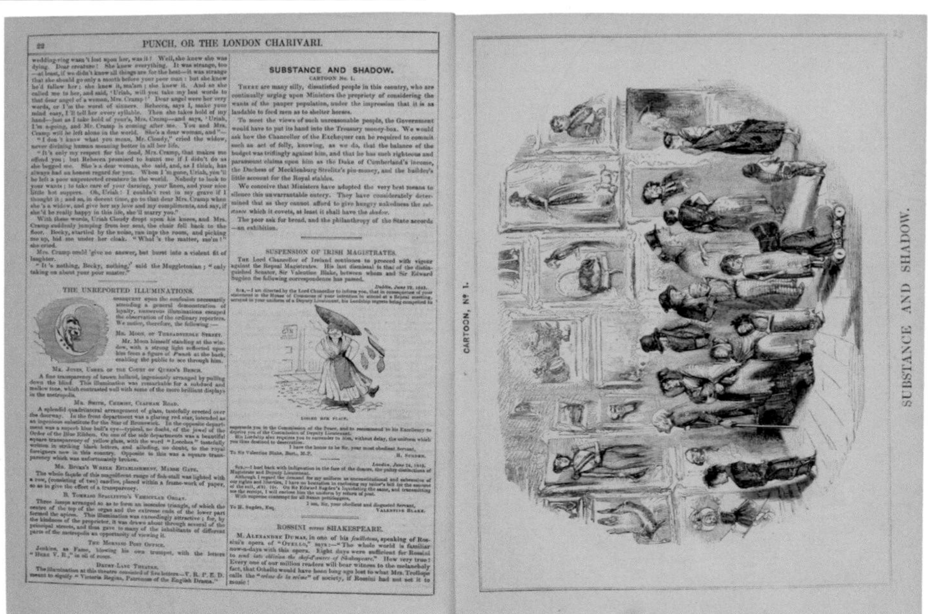
PUNCH, OR THE LONDON CHARIVARI.

SUBSTANCE AND SHADOW.

CARTOON, No 1.

SUBSTANCE AND SHADOW.

The right-hand page, 'Substance and Shadow', coins the use of the word 'cartoon' as a satirical drawing on a political topic. The cartoon became known as the 'Big Cut' among the staff. The commentary on the opposing page ends: 'The poor ask for bread and the philanthropy of the State accords – an exhibition.'

Bradbury & Evans
(206 × 270 mm)

PUNCH (1849)

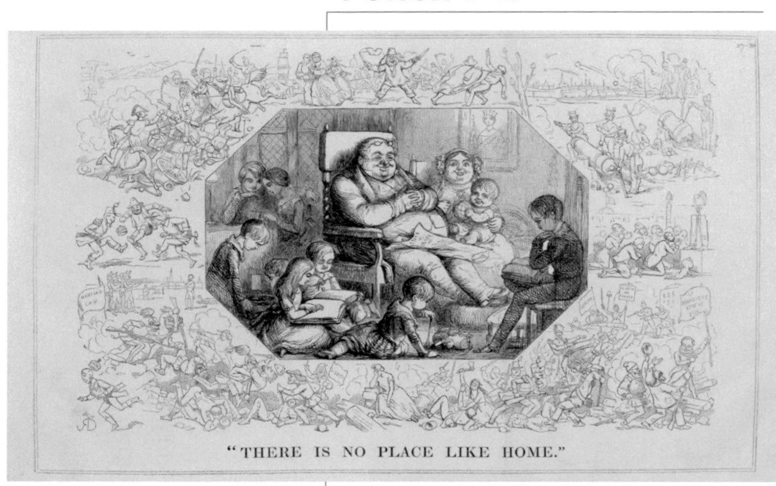
"THERE IS NO PLACE LIKE HOME."

A gatefold cartoon shows the domestic pleasures of home while all around is strife in the outside world – 'marital law', 'socialism', 'les droits des femmes', 'la propriété c'est le vol'. Note Doyle's 'dicky bird' signature in the bottom left corner.

Bradbury & Evans
(206 × 270 mm)

PUNCH (6 January 1849)

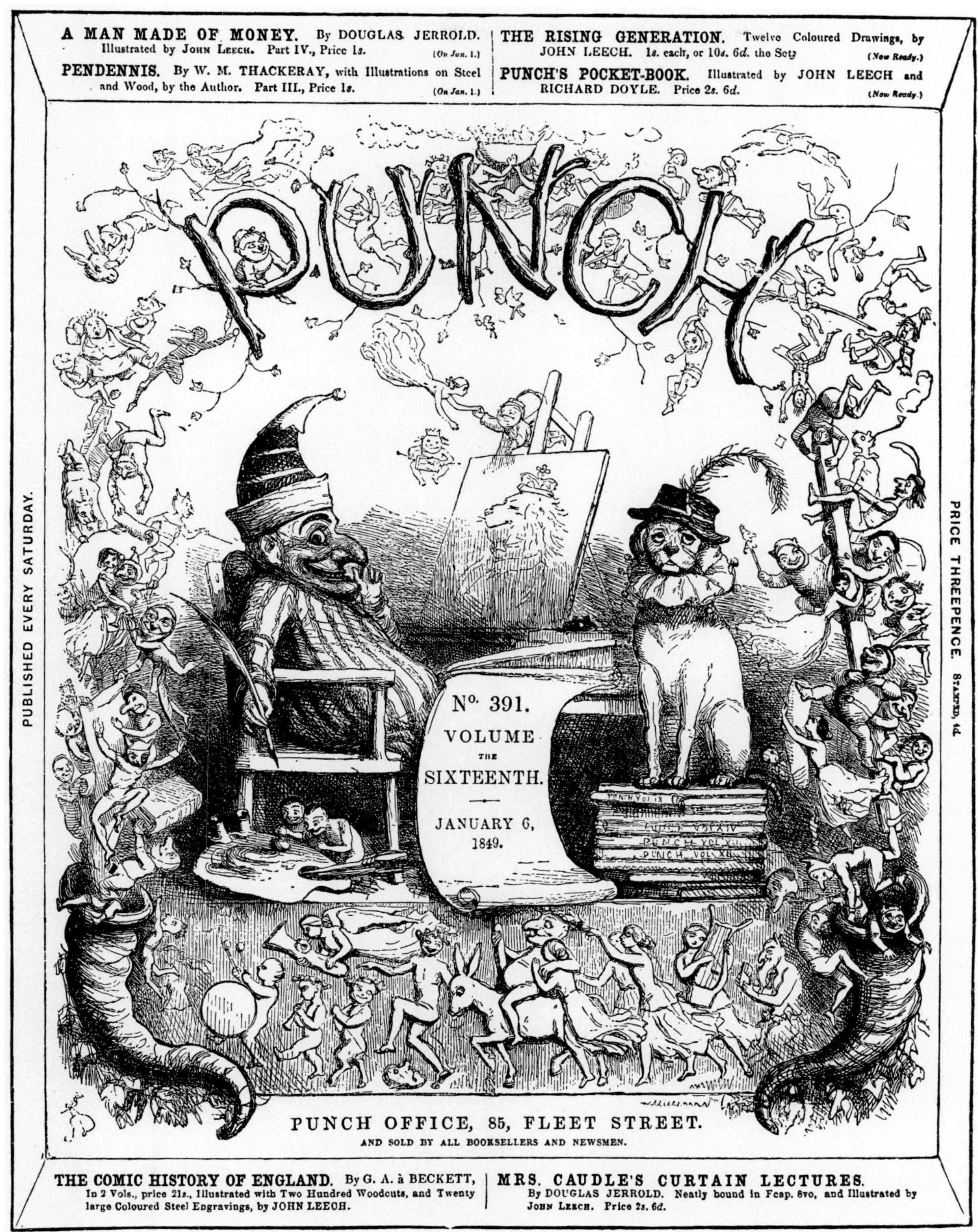
A MAN MADE OF MONEY. By DOUGLAS JERROLD. Illustrated by JOHN LEECH. Part IV., Price 1s. (On Jan. 1.)

PENDENNIS. By W. M. THACKERAY, with Illustrations on Steel and Wood, by the Author. Part III., Price 1s. (On Jan. 1.)

THE RISING GENERATION. Twelve Coloured Drawings, by JOHN LEECH. 1s. each, or 10s. 6d. the Set. (Now Ready.)

PUNCH'S POCKET-BOOK. Illustrated by JOHN LEECH and RICHARD DOYLE. Price 2s. 6d. (Now Ready.)

PUBLISHED EVERY SATURDAY.

PUNCH

No. 391.
VOLUME THE SIXTEENTH.
JANUARY 6, 1849.

PRICE THREEPENCE. STAMPED, 4d.

PUNCH OFFICE, 85, FLEET STREET.
AND SOLD BY ALL BOOKSELLERS AND NEWSMEN.

THE COMIC HISTORY OF ENGLAND. By G. A. à BECKETT, In 2 Vols., price 21s., Illustrated with Two Hundred Woodcuts, and Twenty large Coloured Steel Engravings, by JOHN LEECH.

MRS. CAUDLE'S CURTAIN LECTURES. By DOUGLAS JERROLD. Neatly bound in Fcap. 8vo, and Illustrated by JOHN LEECH. Price 2s. 6d.

Doyle changed the cover several times before *Punch* settled on this design for the next 107 years, with branches replacing the previous title in a fairground-style type. An earlier version had caused outrage by having Mr Punch lying on his back: 'his demonic grin and suggestive pose hinted at Mr Punch in the act of self-abusement'.[1] The title is made from old branches – 'old fashioned' in the sense that the ancient material imbues the title lettering, and hence the magazine itself, with a character and wisdom beyond its years. The procession at the base was modelled on Titian's *Bacchus and Ariadne*. Adverts on the frame above and below the illustration at first promoted the *Punch* almanacs and books illustrated by Leech and Doyle, and Thackeray's *Pendennis*. Later, branded goods moved into these slots. Doyle created several popular comic series for *Punch*, including 'Manners and Customs of Ye Englyshe', and the characters Brown, Jones and Robinson in 1850. The trio became household names, being used for the 'Hunnybuns at the Seaside' serial in the *Woman's Companion* later in the year and as names in 'The Struggles of Brown, Jones and Robinson' by Anthony Trollope in the *Cornhill Magazine* (1861–2). *Punch* ran a special comic tribute to Doyle in 1950 (2 February).

1 Richard Engen, *Richard Doyle*, The Artist and the Critic Series, vol. 2 (Stroud 1983), pp. 48–9

Bradbury & Evans
(206 × 270 mm)

ILLUSTRATED LONDON NEWS (23 March 1878)

THE ILLUSTRATED LONDON NEWS

Over the years, the *Illustrated London News* used more (and larger) engravings. The cover illustration of 'Darby and Joan' is by Kate Greenaway, whose first children's book, *Under the Window*, was published a year later and established her reputation as a children's illustrator. A medal in her name was established in 1955 and is awarded each year by the Chartered Institute of Library and Information Professionals for outstanding work in children's illustration. On 7 August 1964 *Private Eye* gave *Punch* the 'Kate Greenaway Award 1965' in a Ronald Searle cartoon, suggesting that the magazine had become too safe. In this issue of the *ILN*, 10 pages had no illustrations; there were five full-page and two half-page images, three smaller images (including the chess puzzle) and an inserted double-page illustration.

Illustrated London News Ltd
(280 × 398 mm, stapled, 24 pages)

ILLUSTRATED LONDON NEWS (14 May 1842)

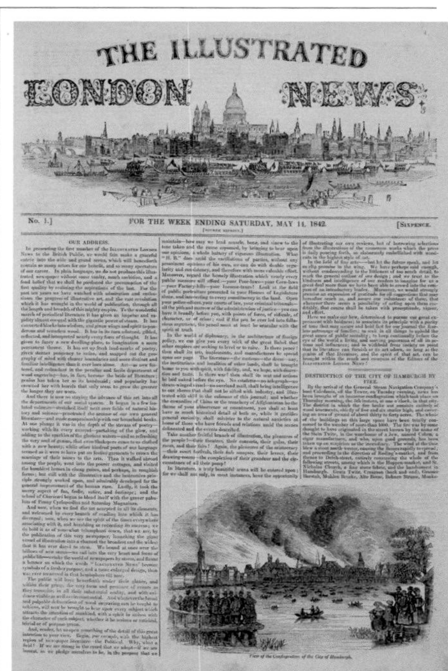
THE ILLUSTRATED LONDON NEWS

The first issue of the *Illustrated London News* carried 32 woodcuts. It was printed in 16-page sections arranged so that eight text-only pages fell on one side of the sheet and the pages with engravings on the other. The result was alternating spreads of engravings and pure text. The *ILN* later reduced its page size to approximately A4. It survived until 1982.

Illustrated London News Ltd
(280 × 390 mm, stapled, 16 pages)

ILLUSTRATED TIMES (5 December 1857)

Illustrated Times was one of many titles that mimicked the strategy of the *Illustrated London News*. Here a double-page spread shows the hull of Brunel's last and largest ship, *Leviathan* (later the *Great Eastern*), being built at Millwall, south London.

The engraving was made from a photograph by Robert Howlett (V&A: PH.255–1979). The issue announces a special number devoted to the launch of the 212-metre giant, with illustrations from photographs by Joseph Cundall and Howlett to include a full-length portrait of Brunel. An issue cost 2½d, or 3½d by post.

Illustrated Times Ltd
(260 × 374 mm, stapled, 16 pages)

GRAPHIC (4 December 1869)

THE GRAPHIC

GRAPHIC (25 December 1870)

THE EMPTY CHAIR, GAD'S HILL—NINTH OF JUNE 1870

The *Graphic* was founded by William Luson Thomas with a bias towards art and a campaigning attitude. Thomas aimed to use images to change public attitudes towards poverty and injustice. An artist, engraver and social reformer, he recruited other artists, such as Samuel Luke Fildes, Hubert von Herkomer, Frank Holl and John Everett Millais. Frederick Walker, the leader of the social realist movement, was an influence on this circle. The cover shows 'The Egyptian Girl' from a painting by Gustav Richter. The issue ran nine pages of engravings with three pages of advertising. One engraving had no print on the reverse so that it could be mounted and framed. An issue cost 6d, or 7d by post.

Illustrated Newspapers
(290 × 395 mm, stapled, 24 pages)

Charles Dickens died on 9 June 1870, inspiring Fildes to paint a memorial watercolour showing the writer's study, *The Empty Chair*, after his funeral. The *Graphic* ran several prints to mark the writer's death, including a woodcut after Fildes's painting (described as 'splendid' by Vincent Van Gogh) and a front page of Dickens's grave in Westminster Abbey (2 July 1870). John Everett Millais had brought Fildes to the attention of Dickens, who commissioned him to illustrate *The Mystery of Edwin Drood*. Fildes also produced caricatures for *Vanity Fair* under the *nom de crayon* 'ELF'.

In 1949, two decades after his death, Fildes's *The Doctor* (1891), inspired by the death of his eldest son, was used by the American Medical Association in a protest against proposals for a nationalized medical care system put forward by the Truman government. The image appeared on posters along with the slogan 'Keep politics out of this picture …', implying that more government involvement in medical care would damage the quality of treatment. The V&A is the principal repository of Fildes's drawings, many of which were probably for his published illustrative works.

Illustrated Newspapers
(290 × 395 mm, stapled, 24 pages)

GERM (January 1850)

Four issues of the literary monthly appeared under the editorship of Dante Gabriel Rossetti, starting in January, with poetry by Rossetti and his sister Christina, Thomas Woolner and James Collinson, together with essays on art and literature by associates of the Pre-Raphaelite Brotherhood.

Each issue came with a yellow cover and carried a page advert for Provident Life. However, it did not sell well and a planned fifth issue never appeared. This page includes two engravings on a single plate by William Holman Hunt to illustrate the poems 'My Beautiful Lady' and 'Of My Lady in Death' by Woolner.

Aylott & Jones
(145 × 224 mm, 52 pages)

GERM (March 1850)

This spread shows *Cordelia* by Ford Madox Brown. The etching shows a Shakespearean scene from *King Lear*, with Cordelia (right) being led away by the King of France, while she points back towards her older sisters Goneril and Regan (at left). In the centre background, Lear is heading outside with his crown in his hand and the Fool rests his head on the throne. There is a monogram in the lower left corner.

Each issue carried an etching. Others were *The Child Jesus* by James Collinson (February) and Walter Deverell's *Viola and Olivia* (April). William Morris followed other Pre-Raphaelites with his *Oxford and Cambridge Magazine* in 1856, which set out to promote art and poetry influenced by Arthurian romance and medieval design, but carried no illustrations.

Aylott & Jones
(145 × 224 mm, 52 pages)

HOUSEHOLD WORDS (1 April 1854)

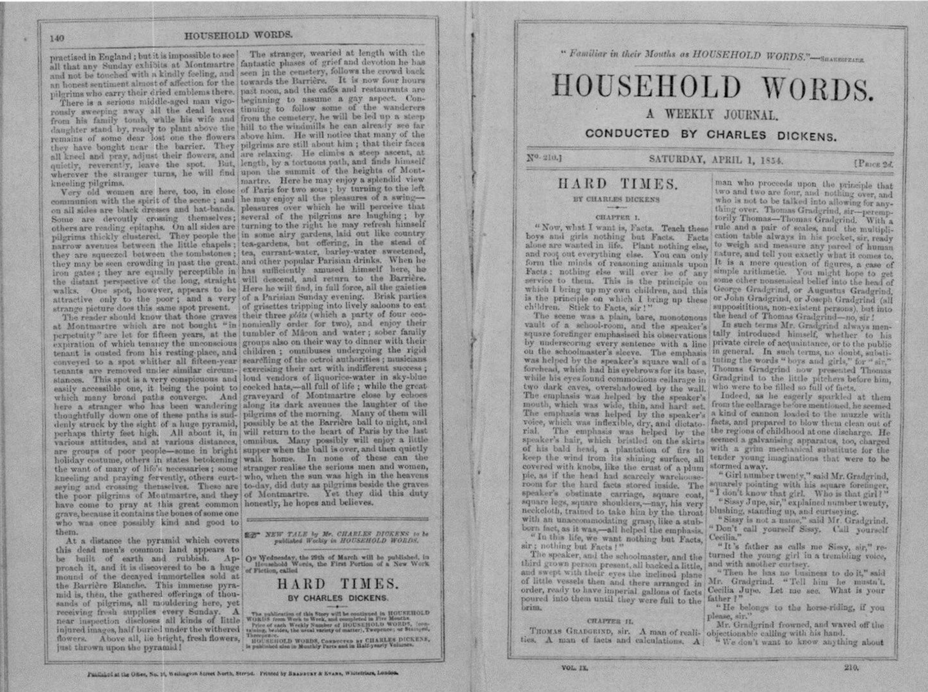

140 HOUSEHOLD WORDS.

practised in England; but it is impossible to see all that any Sunday exhibits at Montmartre and not be touched with a kindly feeling, and an honest sentiment almost of affection for the pilgrims who carry their dried emblems there.

There is a serious middle-aged man vigorously sweeping away all the dead leaves from his family tomb, while his wife and daughter stand by, ready to plant above the remains of some dear lost one the flowers they have bought near the barrier. They all kneel and pray, adjust their flowers, and quietly, reverently, leave the spot. But, wherever the stranger turns, he will find kneeling pilgrims.

Very old women are here, too, in close communion with the spirit of the scene; and on all sides are black dresses and hat-bands. Some are devoutly crossing themselves; others are reading epitaphs. On all sides are pilgrims thickly clustered. They people the narrow avenues between the little chapels; they are squeezed between the tombstones; they may be seen crowding in past the great iron gates; they are equally perceptible in the distant perspective of the long, straight walks. One spot, however, appears to be attractive only to the poor; and a very strange picture does this same spot present.

The reader should know that those graves at Montmartre which are not bought "in perpetuity" are let for fifteen years, at the expiration of which tenancy the unconscious tenant is ousted from his resting-place, and conveyed to a spot whither all fifteen-year tenants are removed under similar circumstances. This spot is a very conspicuous and easily accessible one, it being the point to which many broad paths converge. And here a stranger who has been wandering thoughtfully down one of these paths is suddenly struck by the sight of a huge pyramid, perhaps thirty feet high. All about it, in various attitudes, and at various distances, are groups of poor people—some in bright holiday costume, others in states betokening the want of many of life's necessaries; some kneeling and praying fervently, others curtseying and crossing themselves. These are the poor pilgrims of Montmartre, and they have come to pray at this great common grave, because it contains the bones of some one who was once possibly kind and good to them.

At a distance the pyramid which covers this dead men's common land appears to be built of earth and rubbish. Approach it, and it is discovered to be a huge mound of the decayed immortelles sold at the Barrière Blanche. This immense pyramid is, then, the gathered offerings of thousands of pilgrims, all mouldering here, yet receiving fresh supplies every Sunday. A near inspection discloses all kinds of little injured images, half buried under the withered flowers. Above all, lie bright, fresh flowers, just thrown upon the pyramid!

The stranger, wearied at length with the fantastic phases of grief and devotion he has seen in the cemetery, follows the crowd back towards the Barrière. It is now four hours past noon, and the cafés and restaurants are beginning to assume a gay aspect. Continuing to follow some of the wanderers from the cemetery, he will be led up a steep hill to the windmills he can already see far above him. He will notice that many of the pilgrims are still about him; that their faces are relaxing. He climbs a steep ascent, at length, by a tortuous path, and finds himself upon the summit of the heights of Montmartre. Here he may enjoy a splendid view of Paris for two sous; by turning to the left he may enjoy all the pleasures of a swing—pleasures over which he will perceive that several of the pilgrims are laughing; by turning to the right he may refresh himself in some airy gardens, laid out like country tea-gardens, but offering, in the stead of tea, currant-water, barley-water sweetened, and other popular Parisian drinks. When he has sufficiently amused himself here, he will descend, and return to the Barrière. Here he will find, in full force, all the gaieties of a Parisian Sunday evening. Brisk parties of grisettes tripping into lively saloons to eat their three *plâts* (which a party of four economically order for two), and enjoy their tumbler of Mâcon and water; sober family groups also on their way to dinner with their children; omnibuses undergoing the rigid searching of the octroi authorities; musicians exercising their art with indifferent success; loud vendors of liquorice-water in sky-blue cocked hats,—all full of life; while the great graveyard of Montmartre close by echoes along its dark avenues the laughter of the pilgrims of the morning. Many of them will possibly be at the Barrière ball to night, and will return to the heart of Paris by the last omnibus. Many possibly will enjoy a little supper when the ball is over, and then quietly walk home. In none of these can the stranger realise the serious men and women, who, when the sun was high in the heavens to-day, did duty as pilgrims beside the graves of Montmartre. Yet they did this duty honestly, he hopes and believes.

☞ *NEW TALE by Mr. CHARLES DICKENS to be published Weekly in HOUSEHOLD WORDS.*

On Wednesday, the 29th of March will be published, in Household Words, the First Portion of a New Work of Fiction, called

HARD TIMES.

BY CHARLES DICKENS.

The publication of this Story will be continued in HOUSEHOLD WORDS from Week to Week, and completed in Five Months.

Price of each Weekly Number of HOUSEHOLD WORDS, (containing, besides the usual variety of matter), Twopence; or Stamped, Threepence.

HOUSEHOLD WORDS, Conducted by CHARLES DICKENS, is published also in Monthly Parts and in Half-yearly Volumes.

Published at the Office, No. 16, Wellington Street North, Strand. Printed by Bradbury & Evans, Whitefriars, London.

"Familiar in their Mouths as HOUSEHOLD WORDS."—Shakespeare.

HOUSEHOLD WORDS.

A WEEKLY JOURNAL.

CONDUCTED BY CHARLES DICKENS.

No. 210.] SATURDAY, APRIL 1, 1854. [Price 2*d*.

HARD TIMES.

BY CHARLES DICKENS

CHAPTER I.

"Now, what I want is, Facts. Teach these boys and girls nothing but Facts. Facts alone are wanted in life. Plant nothing else, and root out everything else. You can only form the minds of reasoning animals upon Facts: nothing else will ever be of any service to them. This is the principle on which I bring up my own children, and this is the principle on which I bring up these children. Stick to Facts, sir!"

The scene was a plain, bare, monotonous vault of a school-room, and the speaker's square forefinger emphasised his observations by underscoring every sentence with a line on the schoolmaster's sleeve. The emphasis was helped by the speaker's square wall of a forehead, which had his eyebrows for its base, while his eyes found commodious cellarage in two dark caves, overshadowed by the wall. The emphasis was helped by the speaker's mouth, which was wide, thin, and hard set. The emphasis was helped by the speaker's voice, which was inflexible, dry, and dictatorial. The emphasis was helped by the speaker's hair, which bristled on the skirts of his bald head, a plantation of firs to keep the wind from its shining surface, all covered with knobs, like the crust of a plum pie, as if the head had scarcely warehouse-room for the hard facts stored inside. The speaker's obstinate carriage, square coat, square legs, square shoulders,—nay, his very neckcloth, trained to take him by the throat with an unaccommodating grasp, like a stubborn fact, as it was,—all helped the emphasis.

"In this life, we want nothing but Facts, sir; nothing but Facts!"

The speaker, and the schoolmaster, and the third grown person present, all backed a little, and swept with their eyes the inclined plane of little vessels then and there arranged in order, ready to have imperial gallons of facts poured into them until they were full to the brim.

CHAPTER II.

Thomas Gradgrind, sir. A man of realities. A man of facts and calculations. A man who proceeds upon the principle that two and two are four, and nothing over, and who is not to be talked into allowing for anything over. Thomas Gradgrind, sir—peremptorily Thomas—Thomas Gradgrind. With a rule and a pair of scales, and the multiplication table always in his pocket, sir, ready to weigh and measure any parcel of human nature, and tell you exactly what it comes to. It is a mere question of figures, a case of simple arithmetic. You might hope to get some other nonsensical belief into the head of George Gradgrind, or Augustus Gradgrind, or John Gradgrind, or Joseph Gradgrind (all supposititious, non-existent persons), but into the head of Thomas Gradgrind—no, sir!

In such terms Mr. Gradgrind always mentally introduced himself, whether to his private circle of acquaintance, or to the public in general. In such terms, no doubt, substituting the words "boys and girls," for "sir," Thomas Gradgrind now presented Thomas Gradgrind to the little pitchers before him, who were to be filled so full of facts.

Indeed, as he eagerly sparkled at them from the cellarage before mentioned, he seemed a kind of cannon loaded to the muzzle with facts, and prepared to blow them clean out of the regions of childhood at one discharge. He seemed a galvanising apparatus, too, charged with a grim mechanical substitute for the tender young imaginations that were to be stormed away.

"Girl number twenty," said Mr. Gradgrind, squarely pointing with his square forefinger, "I don't know that girl. Who is that girl?"

"Sissy Jupe, sir," explained number twenty, blushing, standing up, and curtseying.

"Sissy is not a name," said Mr. Gradgrind. "Don't call yourself Sissy. Call yourself Cecilia."

"It's father as calls me Sissy, sir," returned the young girl in a trembling voice, and with another curtsey.

"Then he has no business to do it," said Mr. Gradgrind. "Tell him he mustn't. Cecilia Jupe. Let me see. What is your father?"

"He belongs to the horse-riding, if you please, sir."

Mr. Gradgrind frowned, and waved off the objectionable calling with his hand.

"We don't want to know anything about

VOL. IX. 210.

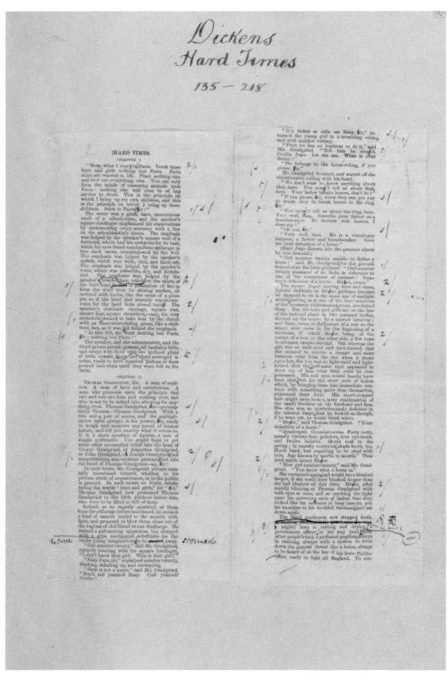

Household Words was published on Wednesdays by *Punch* owners Bradbury & Evans and 'conducted' by Charles Dickens. The name was taken from Shakespeare's *Henry V*: 'Familiar in their mouths as household words'. Only Dickens's byline was used, except for the authors of serialized novels. There were no illustrations or advertising and the target market was very broad: 'We hope to be the comrade and friend of many thousands of people, of both sexes, and of all ages and conditions.' An item in one edition hints at the magazine's attitude to advertising in its 'lost and found' columns: 'Found. Always. An immense flock of gulls to believe in preposterous advertisements.' Dickens published his *Hard Times* in parts in the magazine.

Bradbury & Evans
(235 × 150 mm, 24 pages)

Corresponding page from the *Hard Times* manuscript. Dickens wrote by hand using blue ink on blue sheets of handmade paper, which were folded and torn in half. Many of the sheets have corrections, some with cancelled text on one side.

Corresponding corrected galley proofs (upper right). Corrections were made by printer's proofreaders, who will also have incorporated the author's changes.

The manuscript, proof and printed magazine shown here are part of the Forster Collection, donated by John Forster, the critic and biographer of Dickens, to the V&A and held in the National Art Library. Forster inherited from Dickens the original manuscripts that the author still owned. A plaque at 76 Fleet Street marks the site of the former Bradbury & Evans offices, where the magazine was printed and published.

ONCE A WEEK (2 July 1859)

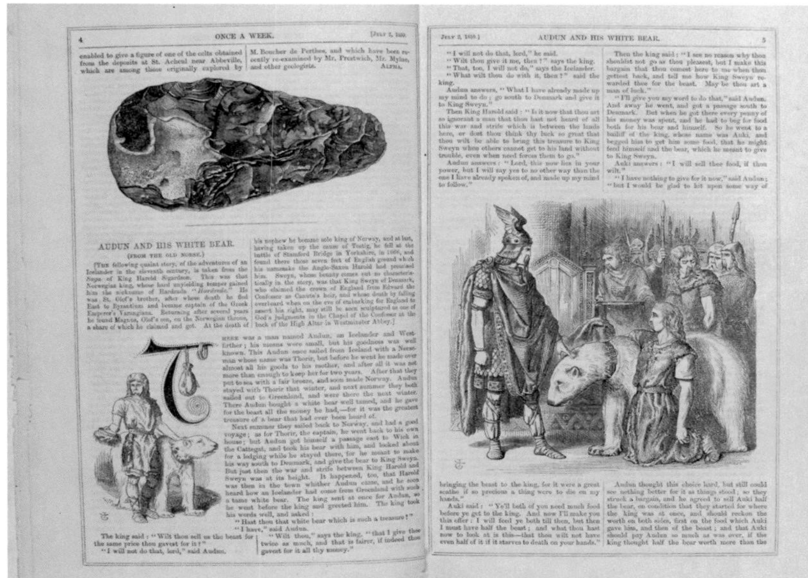
ONCE A WEEK.

AUDUN AND HIS WHITE BEAR.

This literary magazine was established by Bradbury & Evans when Dickens left to start *All the Year Round*. Its main visual difference from Dickens's title was the use of illustrations for its articles: in the example shown here about Norse and German legends, and biblical themes. This issue also included articles on cannibalism in Europe and the uses of English warships.

Bradbury & Evans
(165 × 242 mm, 40 pages)

CORNHILL MAGAZINE (January 1860)

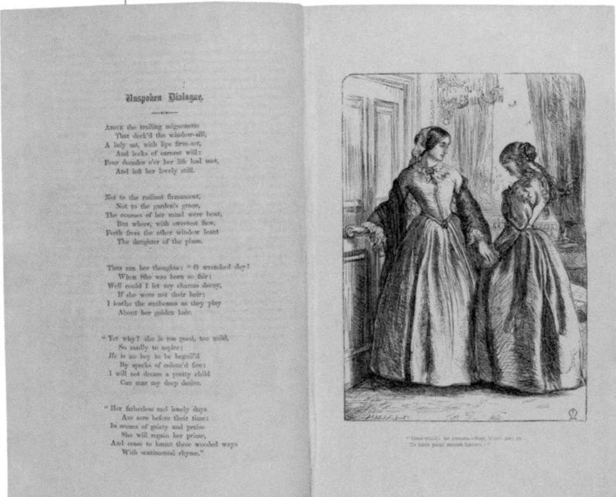

The first issue featured the opening instalment of *Framley Parsonage* by Anthony Trollope, with illustrations by John Everett Millais, and sold 120,000 copies. The seventh featured Elizabeth Barrett Browning's 'A Musical Instrument', with illustrations by Frederic Leighton. Serialization of novels by Thackeray and Trollope became a mainstay. The *Cornhill Magazine* also published *Leaves from the Journal of Our Life in the Highlands* by Queen Victoria in 1867 and its follow-up, in 1884, *More Leaves from the Journal of our Life in the Highlands*, which was compiled as a tribute to her gillie, the late John Brown.

Smith, Elder & Co.
(147 × 227 mm, book binding, 160 pages)

CORNHILL MAGAZINE (October 1876)

PRICE ONE SHILLING.

No. 202

OCTOBER

THE CORNHILL MAGAZINE

1876

LONDON:
SMITH, ELDER & CO., 15 WATERLOO PLACE

[*The right of publishing Translations of Articles in this Magazine is reserved.*]

Like *Blackwood's*, the *Cornhill Magazine* used the same cover design each time, but it carried illustrations by artists including George du Maurier, Edwin Landseer, Frederic Leighton and John Everett Millais alongside the fiction. There were 12 pages of illustrations in the first volume of six issues. The *Cornhill Magazine* was one of the many literary magazines that kept to a book format. The editorial pages were numbered sequentially (383–512 in this issue), with advertising pages bound in at the front and back. These pages were printed on a much inferior paper, because they were usually thrown away when the copies were bound.

Smith, Elder & Co.
(147 × 227 mm, perfect bound, 160 pages)

ENGLISHWOMAN'S DOMESTIC MAGAZINE (1852)

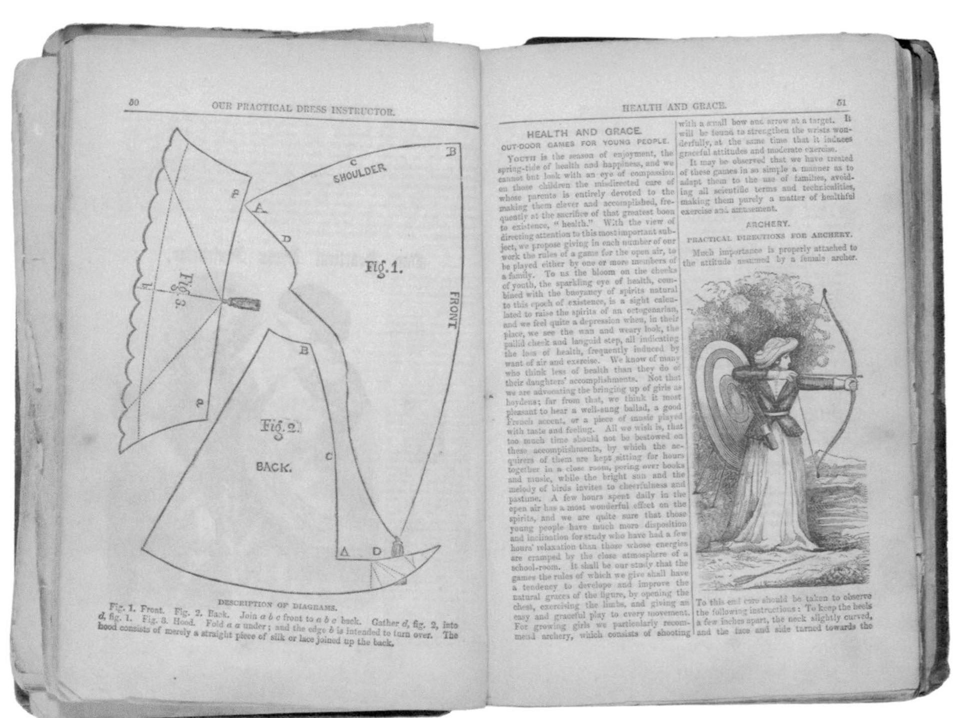

Samuel Orchart Beeton published an edition of *Uncle Tom's Cabin* by Harriet Beecher Stowe in 1852 and launched the *Englishwoman's Domestic Magazine* in the same year, with an excerpt from the book in the first issue. The annual bound volume has a front plate of the Duchess of Sutherland with her daughter based on an 1828 portrait by Sir Thomas Lawrence. Beneath the portrait is a scroll engraved 'From the ladies of England to their sisters in the United States. Sutherland'. The duchess had led the writing of a letter against slavery signed by half a million women that was given to Stowe in 1852. Ten years later during the American Civil War Stowe responded in the pages of the *Atlantic Monthly* to remind the British of which side they should support.

This spread shows a pattern for a summer cloak and hood. The right page shows a female archer – one of the sports thought suitable for a woman. The body text is set in 7 on 7½ point.

S.O. Beeton
(120 × 185 mm, bound volume, 376 pages)

ENGLISHWOMAN'S DOMESTIC MAGAZINE (May 1860)

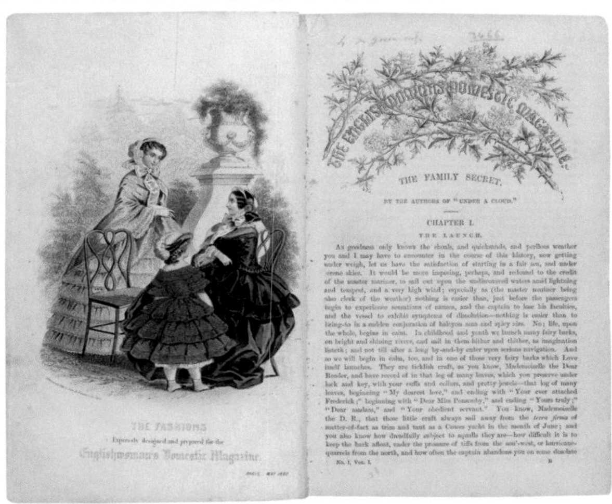

BILLS OF FARE FOR DINNERS IN MAY.

Soups.—Asparagus Soup, Soup à la Julienne, Potage Printanier or Spring Soup, Calf's Head Soup, Soup à la Reine.

Fish.—Carp, chub, crabs, crayfish, dory, herrings, lobsters, mackerel, red and grey mullet, prawns, salmon, shad, smelts, soles, trout, turbot.

Meat.—Beef, lamb, mutton, veal.

Poultry.—Chickens, ducklings, fowls, green geese, leverets, pullets, rabbits.

Vegetables.—Asparagus, beans, early cabbages, carrots, cauliflowers, cresses, cucumbers, lettuces, peas, early potatoes, salads, sea-kale —various herbs.

Fruit.—Apples, green apricots, cherries, currants for tarts, gooseberries, melons, pears, rhubarb, strawberries.

RECIPES.

Soup à la Julienne.

Ingredients.—½ pint of carrots, ½ pint of turnips, ¼ pint of onions, 2 or 3 leeks, ½ head of celery, 1 lettuce, a little sorrel and chervil, if liked, 2 oz. of butter, 2 quarts of stock.

Mode.—Cut the vegetables into strips of about 1¼ inch long, as shown in the engraving, and be particular they are all the same size, or some will be hard whilst the others will be done to a pulp. Cut the lettuce, sorrel, and chervil into larger pieces; fry the carrots in the butter, and pour the stock boiling to them. When this is done, add all the other vegetables, and herbs, and stew gently for at least an hour. Skim off all the fat, pour the soup over thin slices of bread, cut round about the size of a shilling, and serve.

Time.—1½ hour. *Average cost,* 1s. 3d. per quart. *Sufficient* for 8 persons.

Note.—In summer, green peas, asparagus-tops, French beans, &c., can be added. When the vegetables are very strong, instead of frying them in butter at first, they should be blanched, and afterwards simmered in the stock.

Potage Printanier, or Spring Soup.

Ingredients.—½ a pint of green peas, if in season, a little chervil, 2 shredded lettuces, 2 onions, a very small bunch of parsley, 2 oz. of butter, the yolks of 3 eggs, 1 pint of water, seasoning to taste, 2 quarts of stock.

Mode.—Put in a very clean stewpan the chervil, lettuces, onions, parsley, and butter, to 1 pint of water, and let them simmer till tender. Season with salt and pepper; when done, strain off the vegetables, and put two-thirds of the liquor they were boiled in to the stock. Beat up the yolks of the eggs with the other third, give it a toss over the fire, and at the moment of serving, add this, with the vegetables which you strained off, to the soup.

Time.—¾ of an hour. *Average cost,* 1s. per quart. *Sufficient* for 8 persons.

THE FLOWER GARDEN.

General Observations and Directions.—With the exception of June, this month is the driest in the year. The weather becomes gradually warmer, but, as an occurrence of severe frosts in the night is not unusual, it will be well to be provided against the injury which will be occasioned by these. In all gardens, by this time, all the walks ought to have been picked up, if necessary, all weeds removed, the lawns mowed, so as to give every chance for the flowers soon to display their beauties.

What Seeds to Sow.—Seeds of Brompton and Queen stocks, tiger flowers, mignonette, and annuals may be now sown to succeed those which were sown in April. The annuals should be sown in patches, and, as soon as they begin to show themselves, they should be gradually thinned, as this operation will greatly increase the strength of those which remain. Other seedlings also, which require it, should be pricked out and transplanted.

What Plants to Bed Out.—As fuchsias, geraniums, verbenas, and hydrangeas attain a much finer growth when placed in the open ground than when they are kept in the flower-pots, as do also all similar plants, it will be well to plant these out into the borders about the end of the month. Both verbenas and geraniums, being of a straggling growth, are not well adapted to mix with other flowers. When planted in small beds by themselves, circles, ovals, pine-shapes, &c., they will answer much better, and make a far more beautiful effect. Cupheas may now be planted, and little patches also of the dwarf blue lobelia, to which may be added the tall scarlet flower. Dahlias may also now be planted.

THE ORCHARD AND FRUIT TREES.

It will be very necessary to keep a sharp look-out for the insects which, now that the warm weather has invited them forth from their winter hiding-places, will very likely play "old gooseberry" with the fruit-trees.

THE KITCHEN GARDEN.

What Seeds to Sow and Vegetables to Plant.—A row of cauliflowers may be planted this month, in addition to those which have already been planted, and the ground should be well stirred amongst the latter. A further planting of potatoes may also be now made, and the ground earthed-up round the earlier ones, taking care, at the same time, to remove all weeds. Such rows of peas and beans which had not previously been hoed and staked, should now be attended to. Cabbages, lettuces, celery, and other crops of this kind, which require it, should now be pricked or planted out. Crops of vegetables to succeed those already in the ground may now be sown, and, if not already done, a full potato and scarlet-runner crop may be planted. Endive and broccoli should also be sown. Carrots, parsnips, and onions should also be thoroughly hoed, thinned out, and weeded, so that they may grow strongly and finely. At night and early in the morning, snails and slugs should be carefully removed from all young lettuces, cabbages, scarlet runners, and other vegetables.

THE FASHIONS.

We have just been inspecting the show-rooms of our first houses, and will describe two or three out-door garments for the beginning of the fine season. In the first place, for the country and sea-side, we saw a *demi-saison* made of a thin grey cloth, in the form of a jacket, with side-pieces. It had a narrow square collar bordered by a diminutive fancy trimming; buttons in front as far as the waist; close sleeves, with passementerie figuring a square opening. The back was quite straight, without a seam down the middle; pockets in front, with passementerie round the openings.

For a more dressy toilet, there was a mantilla forming a shawl, and trimmed with two deep flounces, the lower one draped at the sides by a bow of ribbon or gimp. The flounces terminate in a point in front, and the ground is decorated with two rows of gimp trimming.

As to dresses, they are all trimmed at the bottom only. One of the prettiest we have seen, intended for the spring season, had nine narrow flounces scarcely exceeding a nail in width. Just over the highest flounce, a row of buttons begins and runs up to the top. The body is plain and the waist short. The sleeves, wide, with an elbow, form a band just below the bend of the arm. A narrow frill is put on the revers. These sleeves are always accompanied by large puffed muslin under-sleeves.

Another dress has its flounces arranged in three groups; the bottom one consists of five, the next of three, and the third of two. The sleeves are puffed and slashed, with a ribbon bow in each of the slashes.

In ball dresses there is little novelty, for winter balls are almost over, and summer balls have not begun.

Dresses are worn so long behind that they form quite demi-trains, but in the front they are made only the ordinary length, just to touch the ground.

A new trimming for dresses we may here mention. It consists of rows of velvet squares round the skirt, each square touching at the corners. These squares are first cut in stiff muslin, and then covered with black velvet by turning over the edges and sewing on the under side. The squares are then slip-stitched on to the dress. Smaller squares form a trimming for the sleeves, which are made large and open. A small lace collar is worn with it, and puffed under-sleeves trimmed with lace.

Bonnets are worn rather large this season, slightly pointed in the front, raised at the top, projecting slightly over the face, and receding at the side. White crape bonnets are exceedingly fashionable. We may also mention a new trimming for bonnets: it consists of a straw chain, which may be looped on the bonnet in any way that taste and fancy may dictate. They are also trimmed with a bow at the top, without ends.

Plain crinoline bonnets are very suitable for the spring season, trimmed with black lace and some bright shade of ribbon—pink is very fashionable, also Eugénie blue and maize.

For head-dresses we have quite a change of style. The cachepeigne is no longer worn, but the trimming is placed high at the top of the head, and very little at the back. For the morning, ribbon is much used. A pretty head-dress is made of three rosettes of ribbon to the front, with a rosette of black lace between each; a piece of ribbon then passes down each side of the head, and finishes at the back with a knot and two short ends.

DESCRIPTION OF FASHION PLATE.

1. Walking Dress.—Bonnet of white crape, with a bunch of feathers at the side, and trimmed with white blonde. The front is wide at the bottom, and rather flat at the top, with a full white cap in the inside. On the right-hand side of the bonnet is a bunch of ostrich feathers, which should be so arranged as to fall a little over the front of the bonnet, and the tips fastened in the cap. On the left hand, inside, is a bunch of green and white daisies. The curtain is formed of one piece of crape, and is covered with a piece of blonde rather wider than the curtain, so that it just comes below all round. The strings are of plain white silk ribbon, with a very narrow fancy edge of the same colour.

Dress of white muslin, with a double shawl of the same material. The dress has seven flounces, each one trimmed with small ruchings of green. The edge of the shawl is trimmed to correspond.

2. Walking Dress.—White silk bonnet, bound with black velvet and trimmed with blonde and violet poppies. The front is bound with black velvet, covered with blonde. The curtain is made of black velvet, and trimmed with blonde to correspond, and should be made spreading. The crown is soft, and made of white silk. Three violet poppies are arranged on one side of the bonnet, rather forward, so that one of them comes into the cap. Full cap of white blonde, with white ribbon strings.

Dress with plain skirt in violet-coloured silk. Black silk mantle, falling over the shoulders, with two frills, the top one finished off by a puffing of black silk.

3. Dress for a little Girl of eight or nine years of age.—Straw hat, with turned-up edges, trimmed with green velvet. A feather is fastened in the front, and falls over to the back on the left side.

Dress of pink and white striped material, trimmed with strips of darker rose-coloured silk. The body is three-quarters high, and is trimmed with a berthe, which crosses in front. The sleeve forms a puff, with one frill; the waist is round, with a rose-coloured sash tied in front. The skirt is trimmed with three flounces. The width of the rose-coloured silk on the berthe and sleeves is an inch and a half; that on the bottom flounce, three inches; on the middle one, two inches and a half, and on the top one, two inches. The drawers are trimmed with muslin embroidery.

In 1860, Samuel Beeton relaunched the magazine with a new series beginning Volume I (it would have been Volume VII) in a larger format. It included coloured fashion engravings printed in Paris. Fiction was also important and elsewhere in the issue the 'book of the month' was George Eliot's *The Mill on the Floss*. The layout is very much like that of a book, but the 48 pages are enlivened with occasional small engravings. It was an illustrated journal combining practical information, instruction and amusement for middle-class women who ran a household. The wrappers contained a 'cheque' that could be sent in to claim readers' offers.

S.O. Beeton
(130 × 208 mm, stapled, 48 pages)

This spread includes recipes – collected by Samuel Beeton's wife, Isabella – and pieces about gardening and fashion. Note the illustration of vegetable strips. The recipes are laid out in what would become the standard form: ingredients, method and cooking time. Elsewhere in the issue was an article on 'spirit rappers, readers and writers. Or home-bug as it was exhibited in our town', involving a stool that moved around. The recipes were published as a supplement, which later became *Beeton's Book of Household Management*. The April 1861 issue of the magazine stated that the book 'will be 7s 6d or 8s, according to the number of parts to make a complete book. It is difficult to determine how many parts will conclude a book like this.' In fact, the 1,100-page work was published in monthly parts over two years and as a bound edition in December 1861. Though the book is commonly known as *Mrs Beeton's Cookbook*, Isabella is in fact identified as the book's editor and the foreword credits the 'many correspondents of the *Englishwoman's Domestic Magazine*, who have obligingly placed at my disposal their formulas for many original preparations'. *Beeton's Book of Needlework* was published in 1870 by Ward, Lock & Tyler, five years after Mrs Beeton's death at the age of just 28.

ENGLISHWOMAN'S DOMESTIC MAGAZINE (December 1870)

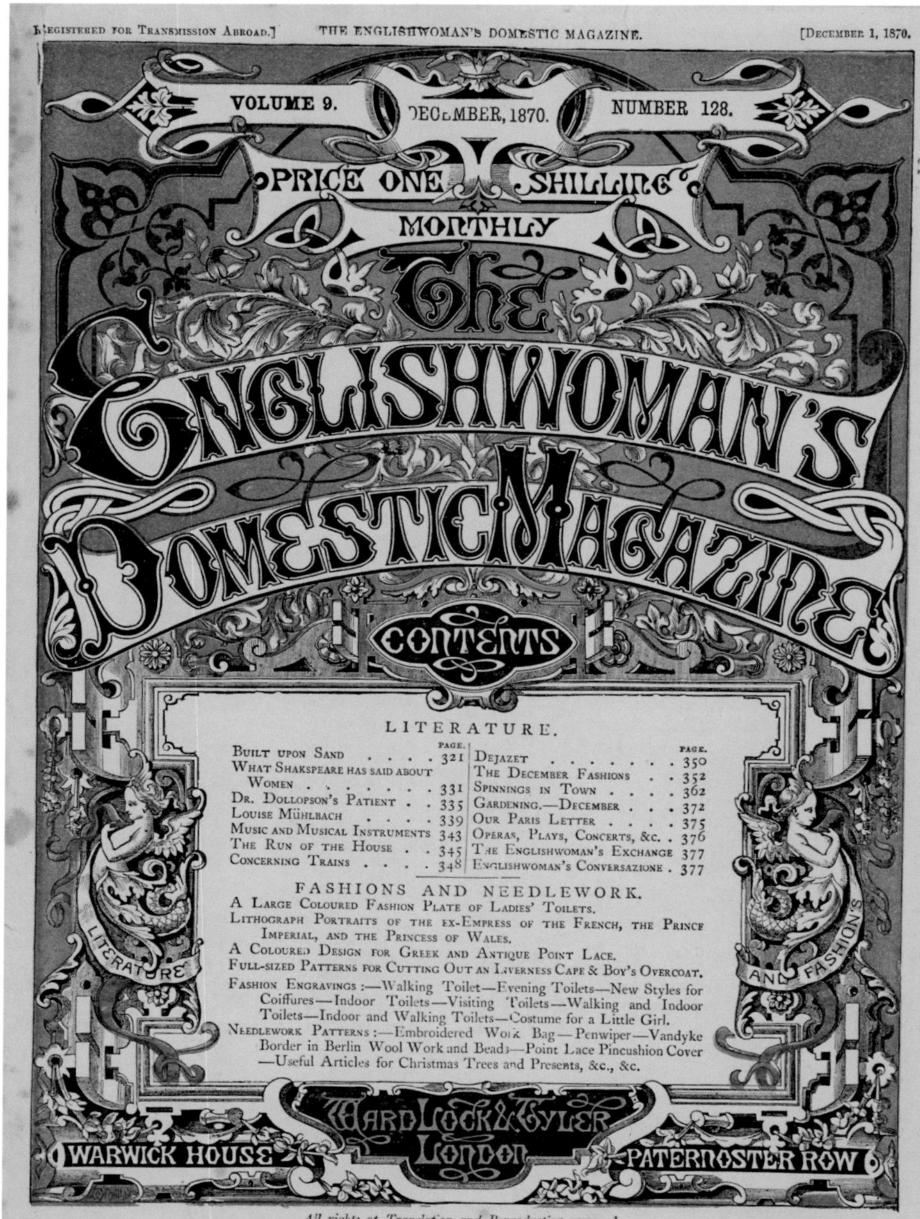
[Registered for Transmission Abroad.] THE ENGLISHWOMAN'S DOMESTIC MAGAZINE. [December 1, 1870.

VOLUME 9. DECEMBER, 1870. NUMBER 128.

PRICE ONE SHILLING MONTHLY

The Englishwoman's Domestic Magazine

CONTENTS

LITERATURE.

FASHIONS AND NEEDLEWORK.

A Large Coloured Fashion Plate of Ladies' Toilets.
Lithograph Portraits of the ex-Empress of the French, the Prince Imperial, and the Princess of Wales.
A Coloured Design for Greek and Antique Point Lace.
Full-sized Patterns for Cutting Out an Inverness Cape & Boy's Overcoat.
Fashion Engravings:—Walking Toilet—Evening Toilets—New Styles for Coiffures—Indoor Toilets—Visiting Toilets—Walking and Indoor Toilets—Indoor and Walking Toilets—Costume for a Little Girl.
Needlework Patterns:—Embroidered Work Bag—Penwiper—Vandyke Border in Berlin Wool Work and Beads—Point Lace Pincushion Cover—Useful Articles for Christmas Trees and Presents, &c., &c.

Literature and Fashions

Ward Lock & Tyler London
Warwick House Paternoster Row

All rights of Translation and Reproduction reserved.

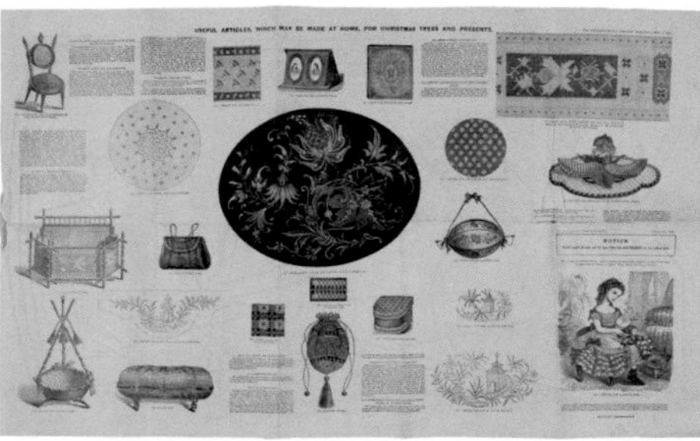

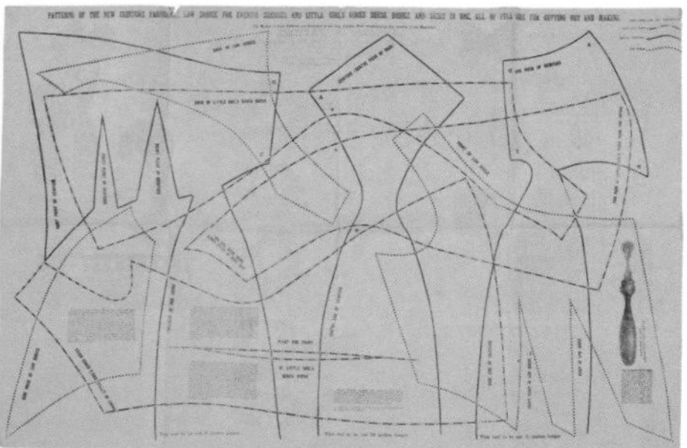

The magazine now has a new publisher, a larger format and is full of extras. There are 13 pages of engravings covering fashion, embroidery and gardening. In addition, there are several tipped-in sheets: lace patterns by Mrs Treadwin of Exeter on a large foldout blue sheet; a colour fashion plate; a monochrome fashion plate; a 10-page sheet of dress patterns with Christmas present ideas on the reverse side; an eight-page sheet with patterns and instructions for designs in tatting by Mrs Mee, the magazine's expert in the subject. Publishing paper patterns exploited the popularity of the latest domestic technology, sewing machines, which became widely available in the late 1850s and would have taken pride of place in many middle-class drawing rooms.[1] Such a craft-driven strategy can be seen again in Gruner & Jahr's successful upsetting of the British magazine market with the launch of *Prima* in 1986 (see page 179).

1 V&A: M.44:1–1991

Ward, Lock & Tyler (202 × 272 mm, stapled, 66 pages, including adverts printed on cheap paper)

LADIES' COMPANION (January 1852)

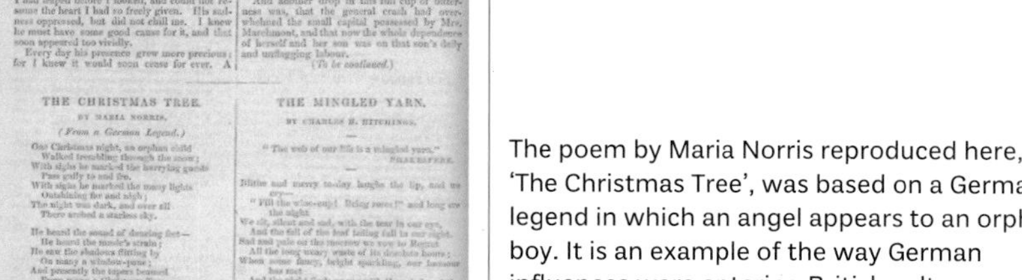

10 *The Christmas Tree.*

afford to marry. I had grown, not worldly hearted, but worldly wise among the inhabitants of Stillington Manor. I had heard so much of "good matches," and "the necessity of people waiting till they were rich before they married," the impossibility of being comfortably settled under three or four thousand a year, that I had begun to conceive how young men stifle the virtuous throbs of a pure first love, and addict themselves to clubs and "safe" flirtations.

When Effingham heard of my call at Mrs. Marchmont's his face clouded heavily. The next moment, with a forced laugh, he said—

"We must be civil to Ernest; his father was a great friend of ours."

So Ernest was invited to fish in the river, and to lunch and dine, and he came duly "as per notice," and his manner to me grew more expressive than ever, and his voice had softer and deeper tones; and yet he said no word of love. It was too late for me to think of prudence now. I had leaped before I looked, and could not resume the heart I had so freely given. His sadness oppressed, but did not chill me. I knew he must have some good cause for it, and that soon appeared too vividly.

Every day his presence grew more precious; for I knew it would soon cease for ever. A crueller shadow than even that of Death was falling over us—the shadow of helpless poverty. Strange rumours began to float around of my brother's conduct of the banking house. In a few months the storm broke, and we were all ruined.

I was in London when it was suddenly announced that the bank had stopped, that the liabilities were enormous, and that Mr. Effingham Stadlegh had hurried off to America!

It appeared that the affairs were embarrassed even before my father's death, and that Effingham, afraid and ashamed then to display the secrets of his management, had obtained a breathing time for arrangements, in hopes by vigorous speculation to set all to rights without exposure. His speculations, daring, rash, and far beyond his legitimate province as a banker, had unexpectedly failed, and he, conscience-stricken by his own folly, could not face the family he had wronged, and fled precipitately from the creditors.

And another drop in this full cup of bitterness was, that the general crash had overwhelmed the small capital possessed by Mrs. Marchmont, and that now the whole dependence of herself and her son was on that son's daily and unflagging labour.

(*To be continued.*)

THE CHRISTMAS TREE.

BY MARIA NORRIS.

(*From a German Legend.*)

One Christmas night, an orphan child
Walked trembling through the snow;
With sighs he marked the hurrying guests
Pass gaily to and fro.
With sighs he marked the many lights
Outshining far and nigh;
The night was dark, and over all
There arched a starless sky.

He heard the sound of dancing feet—
He heard the music's strain;
He saw the shadows flitting by
On many a window-pane;
And presently the tapers beamed
From many a Christmas Tree—
"I wish," the child in anguish cried,
"A bough were dressed for me!"

So passed he up and down the street
Till guests began to part:
Poor boy! Each kindly word they spoke
Breathed sorrow to his heart.
Each echo of their festal mirth
Called forth his tears like rain—
"I'll go," said he, "to yonder wood,
And pray to God again!"

He laid him down upon the snow—
The snow so soft and white—
And scarcely were his eyelids closed
When visions of delight,
Like sundawn beamed upon his soul—
"Dear child," an angel cries,
"Come quick with me, thy Christmas Tree
Is blooming in the skies!"

THE MINGLED YARN.

BY CHARLES H. HITCHINGS.

"The web of our life is a mingled yarn."
SHAKESPEARE.

Blithe and merry to-day laughs the lip, and we cry—
"Fill the wine-cup! Bring roses!" and long ere the night
We sit, silent and sad, with the tear in our eye,
And the fall of the leaf falling full in our sight.

[illegible]

For the smile and the tear are such neighbours, in sooth,
That the one from the other we cannot divide;
Like the wrinkle of age and the beauty of youth—
Like the sigh of the lone, and the blush of the bride.
Who shall look on the mirror upheld to the face
With the wisdom to say what its wearer may feel?

[illegible]

O'er the gems of the ocean the dark waters flow—
O'er the brightest of stars sweeps the thick veiling cloud;

[illegible]

The poem by Maria Norris reproduced here, 'The Christmas Tree', was based on a German legend in which an angel appears to an orphan boy. It is an example of the way German influences were entering British culture.

Samuel Beeton was not alone in bringing French colour engraving into mainstream women's magazines.

Bradbury & Evans (154 × 238 mm, stapled, 56 pages plus colour plate and wrappers)

LADIES' COMPANION (October 1852)

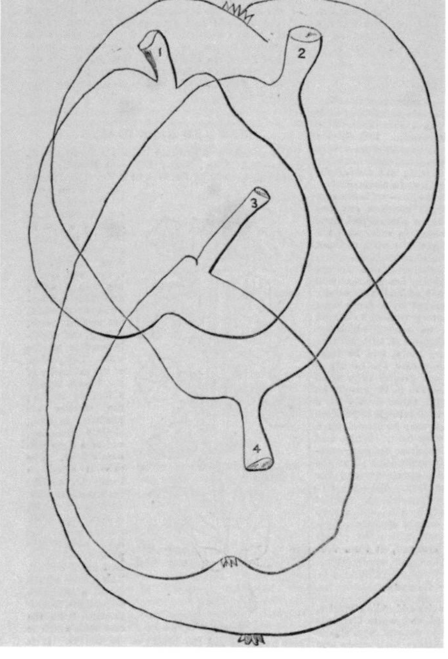

Engravings of royalty were popular in all the upmarket magazines. This is the Empress Josephine.

Pear-shaped: the diagram clearly demonstrates the differences in varieties of pears.

Bradbury & Evans (154 × 238 mm, stapled, 56 pages plus colour plate and wrappers)

QUEEN (12 January 1867)

The Queen
The Lady's Newspaper
& Court Chronicle.

SATURDAY, JANUARY 12, 1867.

[With Supplement and Traced Paper Pattern.—Price 6d.]

The cover was dominated by classified advertising for clothiers, materials and household goods. The office was at 346 The Strand, with printing by Horace Cox at that address. Samuel Beeton sought permission from Queen Victoria to launch the magazine in 1861. The subtitle *The Lady's Newspaper & Court Chronicle* was introduced when *Queen* took over that magazine. Windsor Castle is portrayed behind the lettering of the title. Such patronage was not unique: for example, *La Belle Assemblée*, which dated back to 1805 and published fashion plates, was relaunched under the patronage of the Duchess of Kent in 1835.

S.O. Beeton
(280 × 420 mm, 20 pages)

QUEEN & COURT CHRONICLE (16 March 1867)

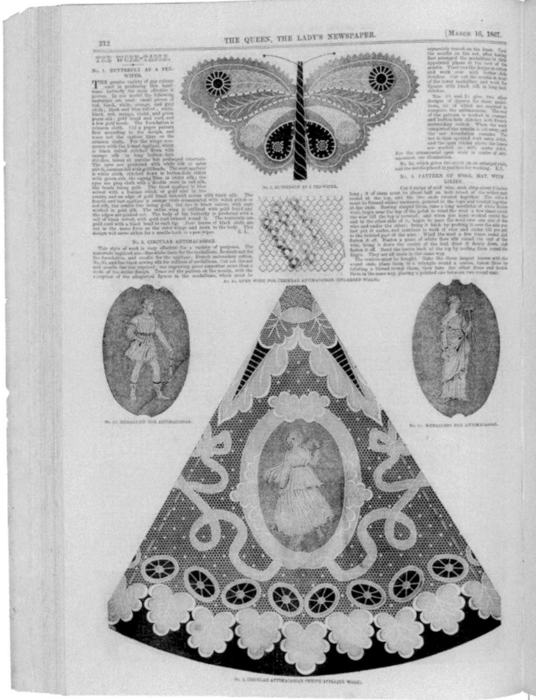
212 THE QUEEN, THE LADY'S NEWSPAPER. [March 16, 1867.

THE WORK-TABLE.

March 16, 1867.] THE QUEEN, THE LADY'S NEWSPAPER. 213

Spread of patterns for handicrafts. The 13 April issue gave subscribers a colour pattern design for a wooden box.

S.O. Beeton
(280 × 420 mm, 20 pages)

QUEEN (7 January 1899)

The QUEEN
THE LADY'S NEWSPAPER & COURT CHRONICLE
2715.—VOL. CV. SATURDAY, JANUARY 7, 1899. OFFICE: BREAM'S BUILDINGS, E.C. Registered.—Price 6d.

COSTUME DE PROMENADE.

4

A colour cover for the *Queen*. Colour plates were regularly used as supplements, but a colour cover was rare. The plate is credited to fashion illustrator Charles Drivon.

Fashion illustrations became a centrepiece for women's magazines, with this spread showing the latest fashions for a range of occasions.

S.O. Beeton
(280 × 420 mm, 42 pages)

ILLUSTRATED LONDON NEWS (22 December 1855)

Magazines were important in the dissemination of ideas that have become Christmas traditions for English-speaking peoples. The Christmas 1848 *Illustrated London News* showed a woodcut from a drawing by J.L. Williams of Victoria and Albert with their Christmas tree at Windsor Castle. This spread the Germanic tradition in Britain, and the image was copied and published in the US. This 1855 edition carried a supplement (pp. 729–36) with a colour cover produced using woodblocks, and three colour pages inside. As colour became more affordable it was used more frequently: for example, the 15 February 1879 issue carried a colour supplement to celebrate St Valentine's Day. The *ILN* also began to use better paper to reproduce paintings. The Christmas 1874 number ran colour on the main cover, with mistletoe and holly framing the cover in green, brown and red.

Illustrated London News Ltd (280 × 400 mm, 16 pages plus 8-page supplement)

BEETON'S CHRISTMAS ANNUAL (November 1887)

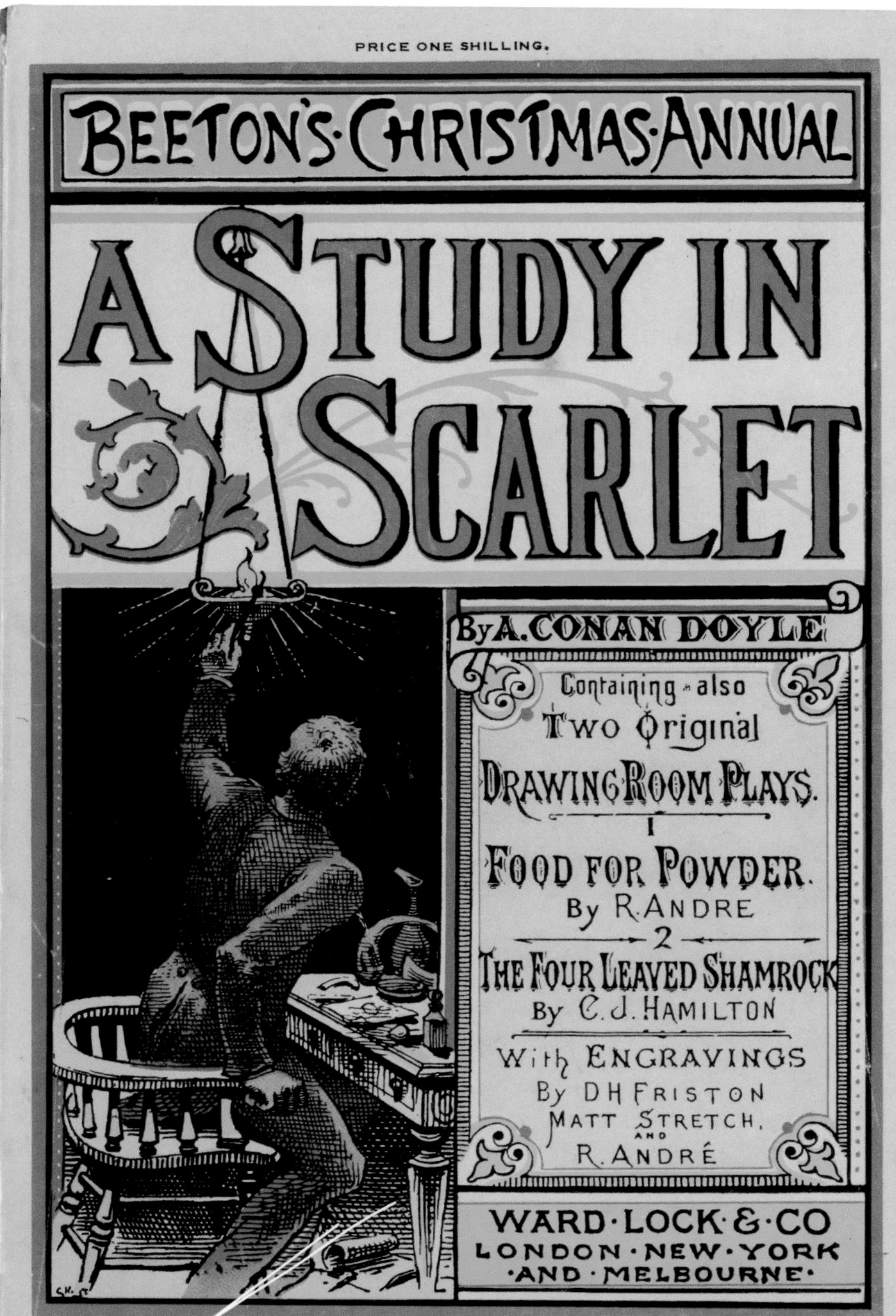

Sherlock Holmes made his first appearance in Conan Doyle's *A Study in Scarlet*. Each issue of *Beeton's Christmas Annual* carried a title that reflected that issue's contents. The 1887 edition had a colour pictorial wrapper (cover). It cost 1s and sold out before Christmas. The *Antique Trader Vintage Magazines Price Guide* describes this as 'the most expensive magazine in the world' because of its rarity and the popularity of Holmes. Conan Doyle had been to a Jesuit school in Feldkirch, Austria, where, in 1875, at the age of 16, he produced a 'scientific and monthly magazine' written and illustrated by hand. As an adult, he submitted short stories to magazines to supplement his earnings as a doctor.

Ward Lock & Co.
(140 × 215 mm)

QUEEN (7 January 1925)

Special Christmas issues – often doubling up for New Year – became a feature of many weekly magazines and are still common today. This Christmas number from the *Queen* was an extra issue, with many editorial pages and adverts printed in several colours. It cost 2s – twice as much as usual. Printing had moved south of the Thames to Hudson & Kearns, Hatfield Street, off Stamford Street, Southwark. The format was smaller and a second colour, after black, used. Rather than being gathered together in a front or back section, advertising was interspersed among the editorial pages, and given different folios in roman numerals.

Field Press
(260 × 338 mm, 52 pages)

RADIO TIMES (17 December 2011)

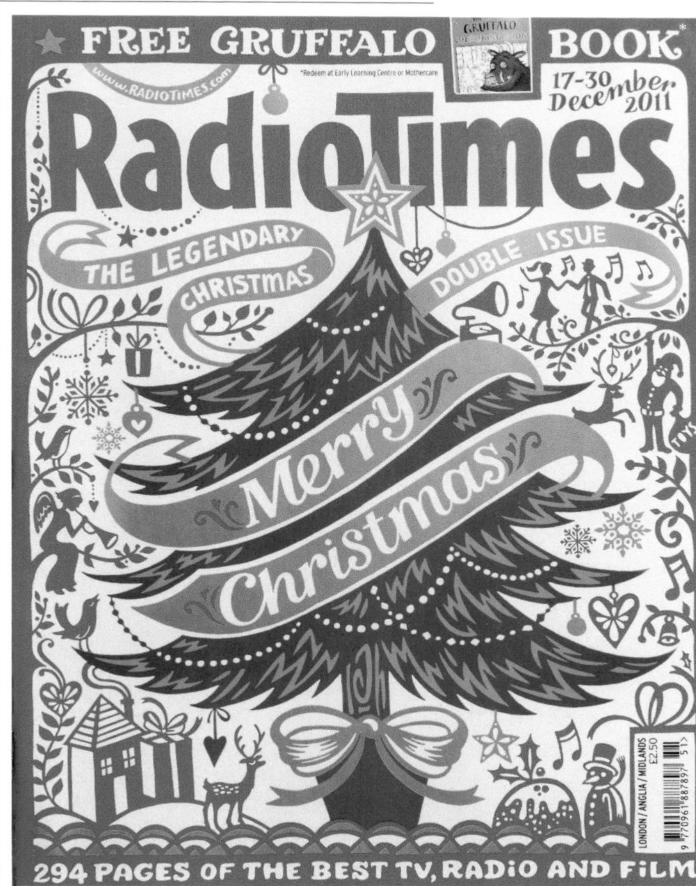

The cover illustration by Kate Forrester (with hand-drawn type) did not feature Father Christmas because the *Radio Times* has a tradition of dropping the jolly Santa when times are tough. Editor Ben Preston was quoted in the *Guardian* (2 December 2011): 'For many years Santa has been a cheery fixture ... but somehow that didn't feel right this year. Would Father Christmas be seen as a bloated, red-faced symbol of over-indulgence? At a time when so many people are hunkering down with friends and family and turning their backs on extravagant gift-giving, we wanted something different.' However, he added: 'If you look hard there's a little Santa hidden away.' There were two covesr: with a red tree and a green. Other Santa-less years were 1926, because of the General Strike; 1929, because of the stock market crash; 1976, because of Britain's bail-out by the International Monetary Fund; 1981, because of the recession; 1992, because of Black Wednesday, when the government was forced to withdraw sterling from the European Exchange Rate Mechanism; and 2000, when the dot-com bubble burst.

Exponent
(225 × 300 mm, stapled)

RADIO TIMES (17 December 1988)

The 1988 Christmas edition sold 11,220,666 copies – a record for a British magazine.

Exponent
(225 × 300 mm, stapled)

GAZETTE OF FASHION (1 February 1857)

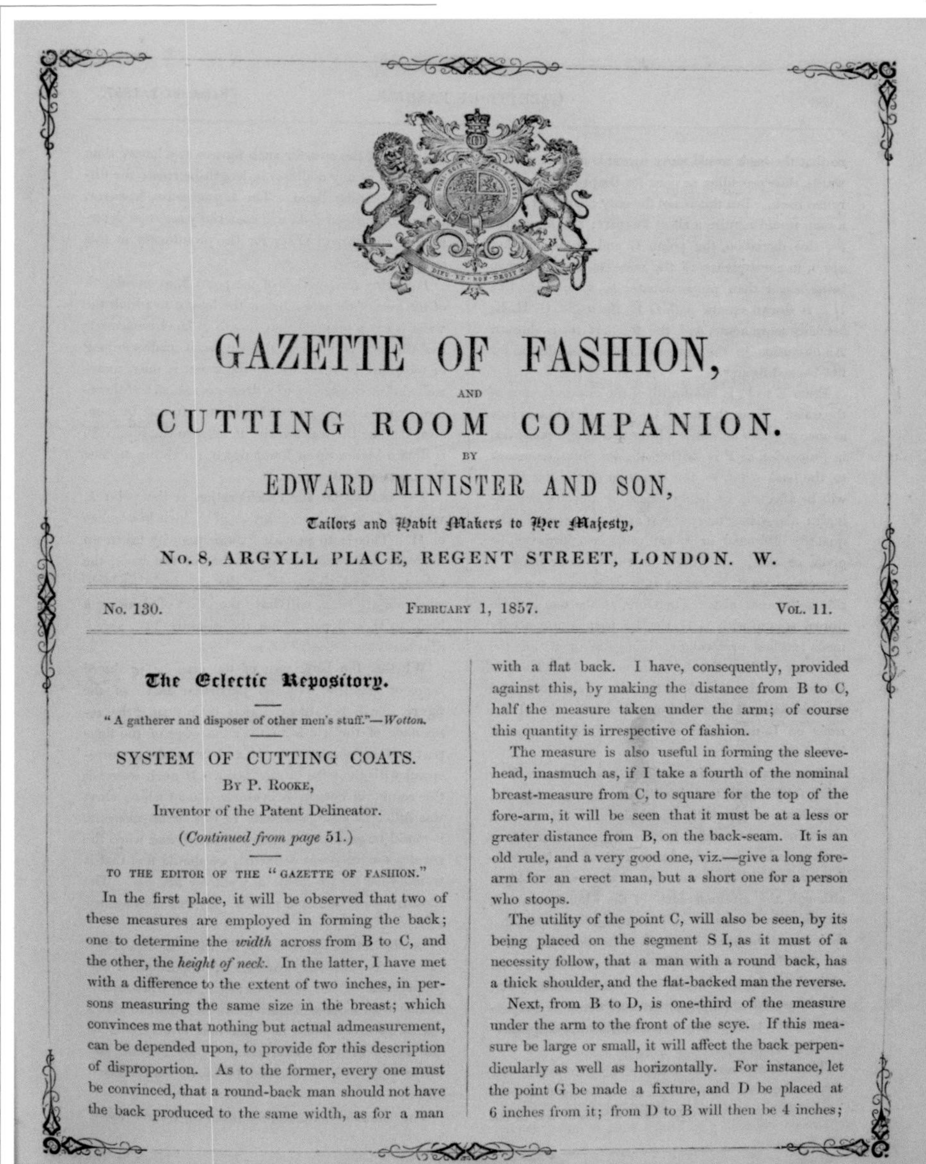

GAZETTE OF FASHION,

AND

CUTTING ROOM COMPANION.

BY

EDWARD MINISTER AND SON,

Tailors and Habit Makers to Her Majesty,

No. 8, ARGYLL PLACE, REGENT STREET, LONDON. W.

No. 130. FEBRUARY 1, 1857. VOL. 11.

The Eclectic Repository.

"A gatherer and disposer of other men's stuff."—*Wotton.*

SYSTEM OF CUTTING COATS.

BY P. ROOKE,

Inventor of the Patent Delineator.

(*Continued from page* 51.)

TO THE EDITOR OF THE "GAZETTE OF FASHION."

In the first place, it will be observed that two of these measures are employed in forming the back; one to determine the *width* across from B to C, and the other, the *height of neck*. In the latter, I have met with a difference to the extent of two inches, in persons measuring the same size in the breast; which convinces me that nothing but actual admeasurement, can be depended upon, to provide for this description of disproportion. As to the former, every one must be convinced, that a round-back man should not have the back produced to the same width, as for a man with a flat back. I have, consequently, provided against this, by making the distance from B to C, half the measure taken under the arm; of course this quantity is irrespective of fashion.

The measure is also useful in forming the sleeve-head, inasmuch as, if I take a fourth of the nominal breast-measure from C, to square for the top of the fore-arm, it will be seen that it must be at a less or greater distance from B, on the back-seam. It is an old rule, and a very good one, viz.—give a long fore-arm for an erect man, but a short one for a person who stoops.

The utility of the point C, will also be seen, by its being placed on the segment S I, as it must of a necessity follow, that a man with a round back, has a thick shoulder, and the flat-backed man the reverse.

Next, from B to D, is one-third of the measure under the arm to the front of the scye. If this measure be large or small, it will affect the back perpendicularly as well as horizontally. For instance, let the point G be made a fixture, and D be placed at 6 inches from it; from D to B will then be 4 inches;

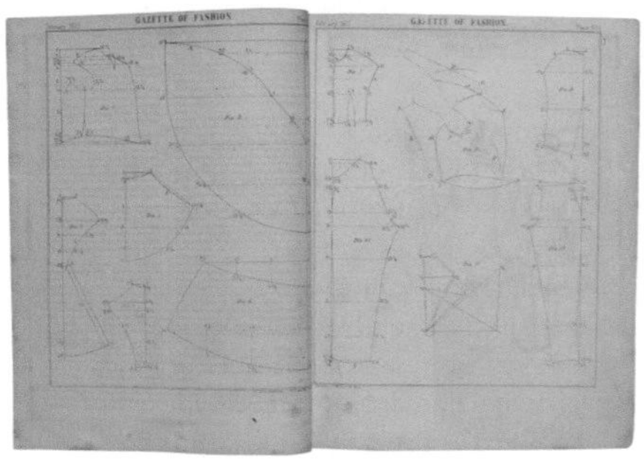

The *Gazette of Fashion* was published first by Edward Minister & Son, tailors and habit makers to Queen Victoria; then by Simpkin, Marshall & Co., a publisher based in Stationers' Court; and then by Kent & Co. of Paternoster Row – a move from ownership within the tailoring trade to a 'professional' publisher that would be repeated with *Man About Town* in the 1950s.

The first page to the right shows hand-coloured engravings depicting the latest in gentlemen's fashions. Such illustrations, along with the mono engraving and pages of patterns formed an important guide for other tailors. Whereas women's fashions were dictated by Paris, London's tailors and Savile Row in particular were the acme of men's fashion. The offices of *Gazette of Fashion* were across Regent Street from Savile Row.

Edward Minister & Son
(200 × 260 mm, 6 pages)

MILLION (3 June 1893)

REGISTERED AT THE G. P. O. AS A NEWSPAPER.

THE MILLION

EDITED = BY = GEO. NEWNES.

No. 63, Vol. 3.] FOR THE WEEK ENDING SATURDAY, JUNE 3, 1893. [Price One Penny.

People Who Are Talked About. No. 8—H.R.H. THE DUKE OF CAMBRIDGE.

Tit-Bits pioneer George Newnes followed the 1891 launch of the upmarket *Strand* (see page 55) by returning to his populist roots with the *Million*, the main innovation of which was to bring colour to the penny weekly market. This issue shows the Duke of Cambridge brought to vivid life with the use of red, yellow and blue inks over a line drawing signed 'EL'. The centre spread has the only other coloured illustrations, of a boat race, opposite a pencil sketch by Leslie Willson enlivened with flesh tones, which are also used for the stripes and dots on the dresses. Elsewhere in the issue is a full-page illustration, 'The Derby: Here They Come', by Louis Wain, who specialized in anthropomorphized cats; and a page by Alfred Chantrey Corbould illustrating a 'chat' with mountaineer Edward Whymper.

George Newnes Ltd
(214 × 290 mm, stapled, 24 pages)

VANITY FAIR (31 May 1894)

This 'skit' by Spy (Sir Leslie Ward) is of George Newnes, *Tit-Bits* and *Strand* founder, who by this time had been knighted and was an MP. Newnes's eponymous company lived on until it merged with IPC in the 1960s. From 1868 to 1914, *Vanity Fair* documented Victorian and Edwardian society, including the contemporary media barons, for people in the know. Its founder, Thomas Gibson Bowles, chose a better-quality paper than was used elsewhere at the time and, from issue 13 (30 January 1869), used full-page colour caricatures printed by chromolithography to record the personalities of the day. The images by Ape (Italian artist Carlo Pellegrini), Spy and their colleagues still grace the walls of homes, pubs, clubs, restaurants and hotels to this day. Bowles wrote the notes alongside the caricatures, which were humorous rather than malicious. Although done by various artists, the caricatures used a similar setting and pose for each of their subjects, and the regularity of the colours and size gives a *Vanity Fair* identity. In letters to the *Daily News*, Bowles referred to the illustrations as being in a tradition developed in Italy and France. 'There are grim faces made more grim, grotesque figures made more grotesque, and dull people made duller by the genius of our talented collaborator "Ape"; but there is nothing that has been treated with a set purpose to make it something that it was not already originally in a lesser degree.' The purpose of the caricature was to 'charge and exaggerate', as in the sense of the original Italian verb *caricare* and noun *caricatura*, using existing lines and tones.[1] Although the subject might look ridiculous, 'it is not to make fun of them, but rather to bring out the human qualities that so persistently elude the academician in a solemn portrait'.[2] Some caricatures were done at sittings or meetings; in others the artist 'stalked' the subject. Spy said: 'I abominate photos. I like to catch my man out, my favourite method being stalking my subject for a mile or two, and getting his peculiarities that way.' Harry Furniss described how 'I would rather have my man for a minute than all the photographs in the world', explaining that 'a caricature turns on the smallest point'. It was his view that 'Mr Gladstone will be known in the future by his caricatures, for I have never seen a good picture of him published'.[3] Pellegrini's influence would carry on down through Max Beerbohm, David Low and beyond.

1 Roy T. Matthews and Peter Mellini, *In Vanity Fair* (London 1982), p. 23
2 Randall Davies, in his introduction to Geoffrey Holme (ed.), *Caricatures of Today* (London 1928), p. 14
3 'How Caricaturists Catch Their Subjects', *Tit-Bits* (23 November 1889), p. 107

Vanity Fair
(278 × 390 mm)

VANITY FAIR (16 May 1895)

Alfred Harmsworth, later Lord Northcliffe, by Spy. Harmsworth had contributed to *Tit-Bits* and his *Answers to Correspondents* (see page 50) imitated that weekly. Its success gave him the resources to establish the Amalgamated/ Fleetway magazine group and found both the *Daily Mail* and the *Daily Mirror*.

Vanity Fair
(278 × 390 mm)

VANITY FAIR (17 November 1904)

Former *Tit-Bits* employee Cyril Arthur Pearson, who left Newnes to launch *Pearson's Weekly* and later the *Daily Express*, by Spy. Pearson's titles were taken over by Newnes after the former's death.

Vanity Fair
(278 × 390 mm)

VANITY FAIR (27 April 1889)

Carlo Pellegrini – known as Ape (Italian for 'bee') or Singe (French for 'ape') – portrayed in the year he did his last caricature, by AJM (Arthur Marks). Look at that claw of a left hand with its talons. And is that 'V' holding a cigar alluding to a victorious career, or a rather different sign of the times?

Vanity Fair
(278 × 390 mm, 22 pages)

The mass-market weekly

The 1870 Education Act laid down that all children had to go to school, again expanding the potential literate audience for magazines and creating a truly mass market. This audience was exploited by *Tit-Bits*, launched by George Newnes on 22 October 1881 in Manchester. It created a model for a cheap weekly by turning news and information taken from other publications into entertainment. It was much imitated – and itself can be seen as a populist version of the *Gentleman's Magazine* – but was able to see off most competitors through the inventiveness of its marketing schemes, which included competitions such as treasure hunts for gold sovereigns and a short-story prize of a villa in Dulwich. By 1890, *Tit-Bits* was selling 500,000 copies a week. In its footsteps came *Answers* (formerly *Answers to Correspondents on Every Subject under the Sun*) from Alfred Harmsworth and C. Arthur Pearson's *Pearson's Weekly* – both men had worked on *Tit-Bits*. All adopted a publishing model that was as cost-effective as possible.

Many magazines took their material from other titles and publishers made fortunes by releasing their own editions of books from overseas without paying any author royalties. Registration of a title at Stationers' Hall – a system that dated back to the sixteenth century – and common law gave some protection within Britain. The first international copyright laws came in the form of the Berne Convention in 1886.

In the same way that Newnes reduced the contents of the newspapers of the day to the best titbits, Harmsworth pioneered tabloid journalism – boiling down stories to their essence – to found the *Daily Mail* and the *Daily Mirror*. He later owned *The Times*, and was created Baron and then Viscount Northcliffe. Alongside this newspaper empire, his magazine company, Amalgamated, became the largest in Britain. This 'magazinization' of newspapers continued as Pearson launched the *Daily Express* in 1900.

As well as *Tit-Bits*, in 1890 Newnes founded *Review of Reviews*, a monthly digest of magazines and journals, with *Pall Mall Gazette* editor and pioneering investigative journalist William Thomas Stead. At the time, it was common for the daily papers to summarize and review the contents of magazines, in the way that they review books and films today. The digest model has now been revived, the most successful example being the *Week* (1995–), which, like *Review of Reviews*, is popular in the US (launched in 2001) as well as in Britain. Other recent examples include the weekly *Guardian* supplement the *Editor* in the late 1990s; *Cover*, a monthly digest of 'the best reading from the best publications in the world' (1997); and *Distill*, 'the best of the international fashion and style press' (2008). The free weekly *Shortlist* harks back to the *Gentleman's Magazine* and *Tit-Bits*.

When Harmsworth's *Home Chat* first appeared in 1895, 'Insistent, clamorous crowds besieged the publishing offices', according to a biography of Harmsworth. It cemented the cheap penny publishing model for women's weeklies.

For middle-class readers, Newnes offered the *Strand*, and there were also the *Harmsworth Popular Monthly* and *Pearson's Magazine* from the other two large publishers. These and their rivals, such as *Cassell's Magazine of Fiction* and Ward Lock's *Windsor*, adopted a similar format, with illustrations cut into the text and high-quality plates – increasingly in colour as the 1890s progressed. Fiction was essential to magazines, as exemplified by Conan Doyle's Sherlock Holmes, who appeared in the *Strand* for almost thirty years, gradually moving to complete short stories rather than serialized books. The *Strand* was forced into a smaller format during the Second World War before being swallowed up by *Men Only* in 1950. Such was the anger at the closure that *The Economist* wrote an editorial: 'A publishing house is a business enterprise whose projects must be financially sound, but it is also a trustee of the affections of the reading public, in Britain and overseas, and of that public's standards of taste. It is sad that George Newnes Ltd should have decided that of the three pocket monthly magazines which they publish, they should dispense with the *Strand* and concentrate on the publication of *London Opinion* and *Men Only*.'[1]

Photography began to make its mark in magazines in the mid-1880s. Although photographers such as Roger Fenton had documented the Crimean War of the 1850s and had their images reproduced as engravings, it was not until this time that the half-tone process enabled magazines to start using photographs more directly. The Boer Wars created a demand for a new genre, war photography, while illustrators experimented with ways of representing movement and explosions. Several illustrated newspapers were founded to cater for the demand, including the *Sphere*. Some of the engravers ousted by photographers turned to illustration themselves.

Illustrators were in great demand and magazines gave them the opportunity to test the popularity of their ideas: among them were Louis Wain with his anthropomorphized cats and Kate Greenaway with her overdressed children.

1 'The End of the Strand', *The Economist* (17 December 1950), p. 1342

TIT-BITS (11 April 1891)

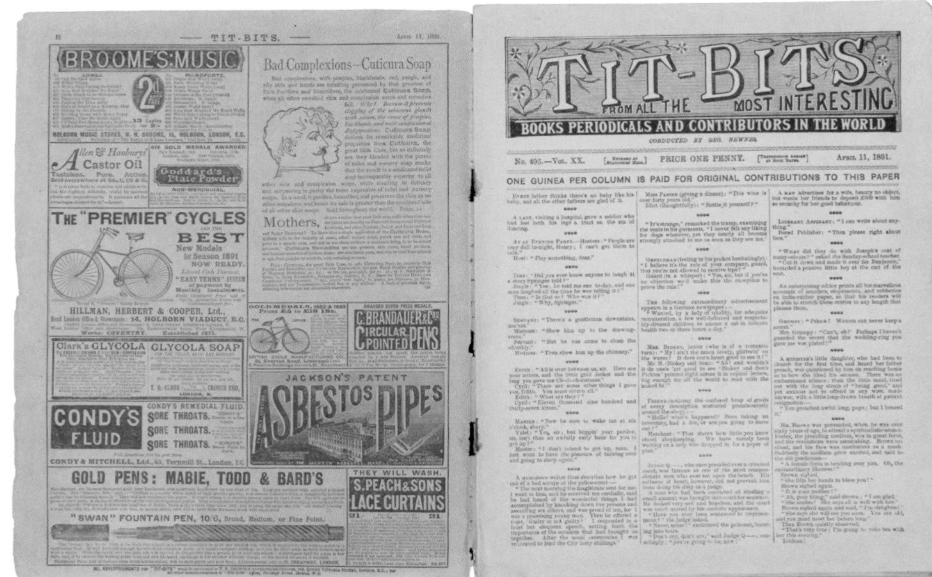

TIT-BITS.

BROOME'S MUSIC

Bad Complexions—Cuticura Soap

Allen & Hanburys Castor Oil

Goddard's Plate Powder

THE "PREMIER" CYCLES

BEST New Models for Season 1891 NOW READY.

HILLMAN, HERBERT & COOPER, Ltd., 14, HOLBORN VIADUCT, E.C.

Clark's GLYCOLA

GLYCOLA SOAP

CONDY'S FLUID

SORE THROATS. SORE THROATS. SORE THROATS.

C. BRANDAUER & Co CIRCULAR POINTED PENS

JACKSON'S PATENT ASBESTOS PIPES

GOLD PENS: MABIE, TODD & BARD'S

"SWAN" FOUNTAIN PEN

THEY WILL WASH S. PEACH & SONS LACE CURTAINS

TIT-BITS FROM ALL THE MOST INTERESTING BOOKS PERIODICALS AND CONTRIBUTORS IN THE WORLD

CONDUCTED BY GEO. NEWNES.

No. 495.—Vol. XX. PRICE ONE PENNY. April 11, 1891.

ONE GUINEA PER COLUMN IS PAID FOR ORIGINAL CONTRIBUTIONS TO THIS PAPER

TIT-BITS (11 April 1891)

A current copy of Tit-Bits is a Free Insurance Policy for £100 Railway Accident effected through the Ocean Accident & Guarantee Corporation, Ltd., Mansion House Buildings, London.

TIT-BITS FROM ALL THE MOST INTERESTING BOOKS PERIODICALS AND CONTRIBUTORS IN THE WORLD

CONDUCTED BY GEO. NEWNES.

No. 495.—Vol. XX. [Entered at Stationers' Hall.] PRICE ONE PENNY. [Transmission Abroad at Book Rates.] April 11, 1891.

THREE THOUSAND THREE HUNDRED POUNDS INSURANCE MONEY HAS BEEN PAID.

HIGHEST AWARDS EVERYWHERE.

London, Paris, Boston, Philadelphia, Santiago, Melbourne, Sydney, Adelaide, Edinburgh, &c.

Pears' soap

FOR TOILET AND NURSERY.

Specially prepared for the delicate skin of Ladies and Children, and others sensitive to the weather, Winter or Summer. Redness, Roughness, and Chapping prevented.

PROF. SIR ERASMUS WILSON, F.R.S.

Writes in the "Journal of Cutaneous Medicine,"

"The use of a good Soap is certainly calculated to preserve the skin in health, to maintain its complexion and tone, and prevent it falling into wrinkles. Pears is a name engraven on the memory of the oldest inhabitant; and

"PEARS' SOAP is an article of the nicest and most careful manufacture, and one of the most refreshing and agreeable balms for the skin."

YOU DIRTY BOY!

First launched in 1881 in Manchester, initally *Tit-Bits* carried no advertising. The green wrapper (numbered pages i–iv) was introduced with the explanation that it was to protect the magazine as it was carried on train journeys – and that advertising paid for it. The advertising was sold by a separate company, T.B. Browne, and gradually crept into the main part of the magazine.

George Newnes Ltd
(240 × 307 mm, stapled, 20 pages plus cover)

The editorial opened with the masthead – conducted by 'Geo. Newnes' – above the three-column layout used throughout the magazine. Items, in the form of questions and answers, are separated by a simple graphical device.

TIT-BITS (11 April 1891)

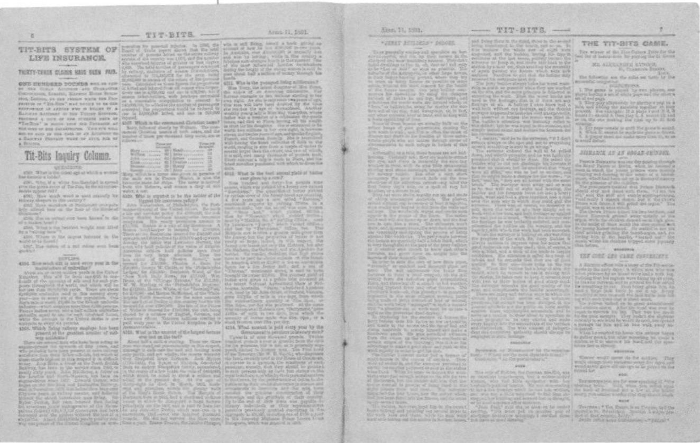

TIT-BITS.

TIT-BITS SYSTEM OF LIFE INSURANCE.

Tit-Bits Inquiry Column.

THE TIT-BITS GAME.

These pages demonstrate the extent of the design, with several decks of headline, the use of capitalization and extra leading on the text. The text was at about 8 point size (a 'point' being 1/72 of an inch). There were no illustrations, except in the advertising. As an example of self-publicity, one of the questions, numbered 4581, asks: 'Why, if a white handkerchief is spread over the green cover of *Tit-Bits*, do the advertisements appear red?' Another asks: 'What is news?' The answer most pleasing to the editor was: 'News is the truth concerning men, nations, and things. That is, truth concerning them that is helpful, or pleasant, or useful, or necessary for a reader to know.' Such ideas led to the development of the 'new journalism', which popularized newspapers.

THE WEEK (9 February 2008)

THE WEEK
THE BEST OF THE BRITISH AND FOREIGN MEDIA
Best British Articles
We're being conned about Heathrow 14
Talking Points
MPs on the make
Page 4
The hounding of Britney Spears 21
Best Foreign Articles
Fiddling while Kenya burns 16
Obituaries
The prankster we loved to hate 36
The Last Word
A boyhood behind barbed wire 44
9 February 2008 | Issue 651
£2.35
www.theweek.co.uk
ALL YOU NEED TO KNOW ABOUT EVERYTHING THAT MATTERS

In the footsteps of *Tit-Bits* and the *Gentleman's Magazine*, the *Week* summarizes the news of the previous seven days. The cover here by McBill (Howard McWilliam) draws on the con-man character Arthur Daley, played by George Cole, from the long-running ITV hit drama *Minder*. This, in turn, was a reprisal of his 'Flash Harry' from four *St Trinian's* films that were developed from the illustrations of Ronald Searle in *Lilliput*. The art director was Katrina Ffiske. A 'world at a glance' spread, plotting stories on a map of the world, is a device used in the 1930s by *Cavalcade* (see page 87) and *Wide World*.

Dennis Publishing
(210 × 298 mm, stapled, 48 pages)

JOHN BULL (4 January 1908)

JOHN BULL
Vol. IV No. 83. SATURDAY, JANUARY 4, 1908. ONE PENNY.
[Registered at the G.P.O. as a Newspaper.
For meaning of this number see page 5.
No 003667

The world is a bundle of hay;
Mankind are the asses who pull;
Each tugs it a different way,
And the greatest of all is John Bull
—BYRON.

Edited by
HORATIO BOTTOMLEY, M.P.

Contents

The World, The Flesh, and The Devil.
John Bull's Biscuits.
The Priest and the Girl.
What is Your Number?
The Newest Theology.
Our Public Trustee.
Among the Mummers.
Happy Old Year. By Jim Crow.
Among the Books.
John Bull's Post-cards.
The Cartoon.
John Bull in the City.
Bill Sikes' Romance.
The Hurly Burly.
Bull's Eyes. Letter Bag.
John Bull's Womenfolk.
Racing Notes, etc.

This vociferous penny weekly was edited by Horatio Bottomley, who helped launch the *Financial Times* in 1888 and was its first chairman. It became the best-selling magazine, boasting a (probably exaggerated) circulation of 1,350,000 in 1916. Although highly patriotic, it took an anti-establishment stance under mercurial editor Bottomley, who was twice an MP despite being hounded by accusations of corruption. Like *Daily Mirror* owner Robert Maxwell 60 years later, he tried using writs to silence journalists who campaigned against his fund-raising schemes, but he was ultimately imprisoned. The Bullets cryptic competitions from 1912 pre-dated crosswords and paid out £620,000 in prizes over 1,000 issues. The cover image symbolized the attitude of the magazine. More than an illustration, it was an icon, claiming to be the voice of truth and authority that could speak for the nation in the form of the man in the street.

The centre spread carried the only other illustration, a cartoon summarizing the issues of the day, including votes for women, strategy at the Bank of England (the Old Lady of Threadneedle Street) and the competing demands of funding a hospital for disabled children, led by the Lord Mayor of the City of London, Sir William Purdie Treloar, and completing the delayed battleship HMS *Lord Nelson*.

Odhams Press
(217 × 310 mm, stapled, 28 pages)

GRAPHIC (5 September 1885)

THE GRAPHIC

An Amateur Photographer at the Zoo.

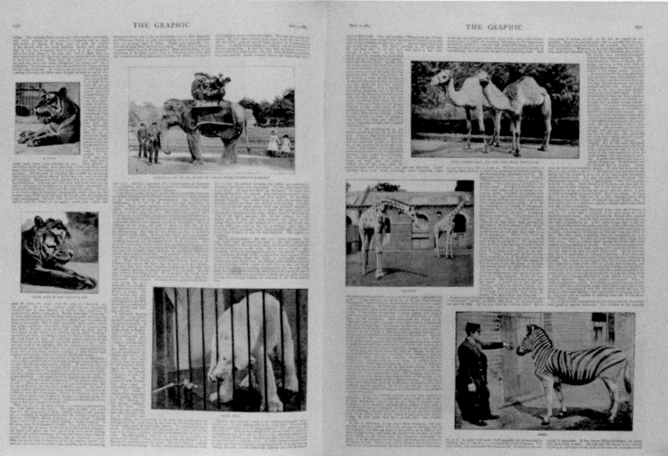

Although photography was well established (the V&A started collecting photographs in 1857), the images could not be directly reproduced in magazines until the advent of the half-tone process. Using this technique, the continuous tones of a photograph are turned into tiny dots that can be etched into a printing plate. The *Graphic* began reproducing half-tones in 1884 and this four-page supplement, 'An amateur photographer at the zoo' by Phil Robinson, is an early example of photographic reportage – a genre that would bloom 50 years later. The 15 shots were by C.J. Hinxman and were reproduced in sizes ranging from 53 × 62 mm to 188 × 112 mm. They were printed using blocks made by George Meisenbach, a German who had patented a half-tone process in England in 1882.

The Graphic Ltd
(298 × 404 mm, stapled, 20 pages)

RAMBLER (19 November 1898)

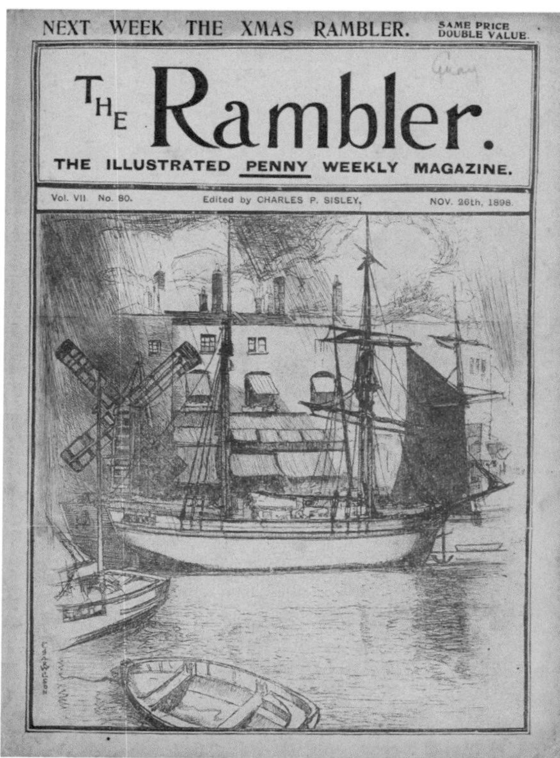

NEXT WEEK THE XMAS RAMBLER. SAME PRICE DOUBLE VALUE.

THE Rambler.

THE ILLUSTRATED PENNY WEEKLY MAGAZINE.

Vol. VII. No. 90. Edited by CHARLES P. SISLEY. NOV. 26th, 1898.

THE RAMBLER. 33

A DRY DIVE.—A PHOTOGRAPHIC FALSITY.

A MORNING DIP FROM HOLBORN BRIDGE.

If the Thames flowed along Farringdon Street, doubtless enthusiastic bathers would take their morning dip from Holborn Viaduct Bridge. Our photographer thinks this is how they would look.

OGDEN'S 'GUINEA-GOLD' CIGARETTES

Are the purest and most fragrant on the market.

BEWARE OF IMITATIONS.

Magazines soon started playing with images and this manipulation shows divers off Holborn Viaduct, about half a mile from the magazine's offices in Carmelite House. The area around Fleet Street was littered with publishers and printers, and remained so for most of the 20th century.

The Cycle Press
(168 × 230 mm, stapled, 36 pages)

STRAND (December 1920)

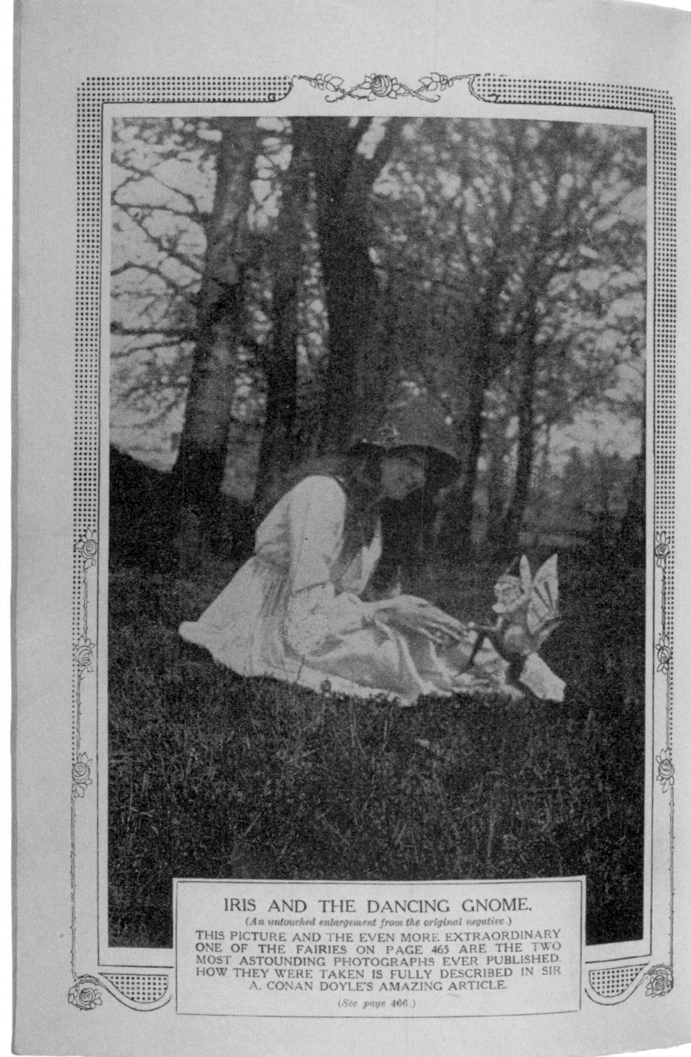

IRIS AND THE DANCING GNOME.

(An untouched enlargement from the original negative.)

THIS PICTURE AND THE EVEN MORE EXTRAORDINARY ONE OF THE FAIRIES ON PAGE 465 ARE THE TWO MOST ASTOUNDING PHOTOGRAPHS EVER PUBLISHED. HOW THEY WERE TAKEN IS FULLY DESCRIBED IN SIR A. CONAN DOYLE'S AMAZING ARTICLE.

(See page 466.)

Fairies Photographed

AN EPOCH-MAKING EVENT .... DESCRIBED BY

A. CONAN DOYLE

SHOULD the incidents here narrated, and the photographs attached, hold their own against the criticism which they will excite, it is no exaggeration to say that they will mark an epoch in human thought. I put them and all the evidence before the public for examination and judgment. If I am myself asked whether I consider the case to be absolutely and finally proved, I should answer that in order to remove the last faint shadow of doubt I should wish to see the result repeated before a disinterested witness. At the same time, I recognize the difficulty of such a request, since rare results must be obtained when and how they can. But short of final and absolute proof, I consider, after carefully going into every possible source of error, that a strong *prima facie* case has been built up. The cry of " fake " is sure to be raised, and will make some impression upon those who have not had the opportunity of knowing the people concerned, or the place. On the photographic side every objection has been considered and adequately met. The pictures stand or fall together. Both are false, or both are true. All the circumstances point to the latter alternative, and yet in a matter involving so tremendous a new departure one needs overpowering evidence before one can say that there is no conceivable loophole for error.

It was about the month of May in this year that I received a letter from Miss Felicia Scatcherd, so well known in several departments of human thought, to the effect that two photographs of fairies had been taken in the North of England under circumstances which seemed to put fraud out of the question. The statement would have appealed to me at any time, but I happened at the moment to be collecting material for an article on fairies, now completed, and I had accumulated a surprising number of cases of people who claimed to be able to see these little creatures. The evidence was so complete and detailed, with such good names attached to it, that it was difficult to believe that it was false; but, being by nature of a somewhat sceptical turn, I felt that something closer was needed before I could feel personal conviction and assure myself that these were not thought-forms conjured up by the imagination or expectation of the seers. The rumour of the photographs interested me deeply, therefore, and following the matter up from one lady informant to another, I came at last upon Mr. Edward L. Gardner, who has been ever since my most efficient collaborator, to whom all credit is due. Mr. Gardner, it may be remarked, is a member of the Executive Committee of the Theosophical Society, and a well-known lecturer upon occult subjects.

He had not himself at that time mastered the whole case, but all he had he placed freely at my disposal. I had already seen prints of the photographs, but I was relieved to find that he had the actual negatives, and that it was from them, and not from the prints, that two expert photographers, especially Mr. Snelling, of 26, The Bridge, Wealdstone, Harrow, had already formed their conclusions in favour of the genuineness of the pictures. Mr. Gardner tells his own story presently, so I will simply say that at that period he had got into direct and friendly touch with the Carpenter family. We are compelled to use a pseudonym and to with-

A simple form of trickery duped Sir Arthur Conan Doyle, who was the world's most famous exponent of spiritualism. The Cottingley fairies were based on photographs taken by two girls in their garden in Yorkshire in 1917. Doyle accepted the photos as genuine and also wrote a book, *The Coming of the Fairies*, based on fairy lore, which is still in print. It was not until 1983 that one of the grown-up girls admitted that the Cottingley fairies were fakes, made using illustrations cut out from books.

George Newnes
(245 × 165 mm)

ILLUSTRATED LONDON NEWS (Christmas issue 1887)

BUBBLES.
From the Original Painting by the late Sir John E. Millais Bt. President of the Royal Academy
in the possession of Messrs. Pears.

PUNCH (26 April 1884)

Illustrated London News owner Sir William Ingram bought several paintings by the Pre-Raphaelite artist John Everett Millais to use in Christmas issues of the magazine, the most famous being *Bubbles*, which was published as a presentation colour print (V&A: E.1660–1931). Ingram then sold *Bubbles* to A. & F. Pears, where managing director Thomas Barratt turned it into an advertisement by adding a bar of soap (V&A: E.227–1942). He used 'artistic' advertising to add respectability to his goods, which were intended for middle-class customers. Chromolithograph colour prints of the painting were given away as part of his marketing. Barratt was described as 'the father of modern advertising' by T.F.G. Coates in an article in *Modern Business*, September 1908.

Illustrated London News Ltd
(400 × 300 mm, 34 pages)

The advertising strategies used by Thomas Barratt sparked this Harry Furniss cartoon. The tramp says: 'I used your soap two years ago; since then I have used no other', a parody of Lillie Langtry's testimonial advertisement for the soap. Barratt bought the rights to the cartoon from *Punch* and used it in Pears' marketing! As a result, an irate Furniss left *Punch* to set up his own humorous weekly, *Lika Joko*, yet he subsequently accepted the Pears' advert on the back cover. *Lika Joko* failed to thrive and Furniss moved to the United States, where he worked in the film industry and pioneered animated cartoons.

Punch Publications
(206 × 270 mm, 12 pages)

RAILWAY MAGAZINE ILLUSTRATED (February 1901)

viii.
ADVERTISEMENTS.
THE . .
Linotype
Composing
Machine.
"It is to the printing business of the present day what the inventions of Gutenburg and Caxton were to the primitive writing systems of the Fifteenth Century."
"A mighty but peaceful Revolution."
"A machine from which I cannot but anticipate effects equally extensive and beneficial to mankind."—The Right Hon. W. E. GLADSTONE, M.P.
NEARLY EVERY LEADING NEWSPAPER printed in the English Language is composed on the Linotype Machine. The Linotype Keyboard has also been adapted to compose in German, Spanish, Italian, Dutch, French, Danish, Swedish and Norwegian.
Magazines, Books, Periodicals, Voters' Lists, Library Catalogues, Directories, Company Prospectuses and Articles of Association, Parliamentary Debates, &c., &c., are being composed by Linotype in ever-increasing number.
THE LINOTYPE COMPANY, LIMITED, 188, Fleet Street, London, E.C.

This advert for the Linotype composing machine appeared on page viii of the *Railway Magazine Illustrated*, which was 'printed from Linotype' by the Century Printing Company in London's Fetter Lane, just off Fleet Street. Joseph Lawrence, founder of the *Railway Magazine*, formed the Linotype Company in 1889, having seen the machines in action on a visit to the US. Three machines were brought to England and a factory was later established in Manchester. The Linotype operator sat at a keyboard with the most frequent letters arranged to the left. The machine would set a whole line of type at once by pouring molten metal into moulds with the characters lined up – 'hot metal' typesetting. This was far faster than the manual assembly process, whereby a compositor would pick out a single pre-cast metal character at a time from a wooden case to make up a line of text. The machine was invented in 1884 by German-born watchmaker Ottmar Mergenthaler in the US and revolutionized typesetting, at first in newspapers. It was not until the advent of phototypesetting, allied to offset litho printing in the 1960s, that hot-metal technology from Linotype – and its rival Monotype, which set up offices at 42 Drury Lane in London in 1897 – was displaced, initially from magazines.

Railway Magazine Illustrated Ltd (174 × 240 mm, side-stabbed, 112 pages plus a colour plate)

STUDIO (April 1893)

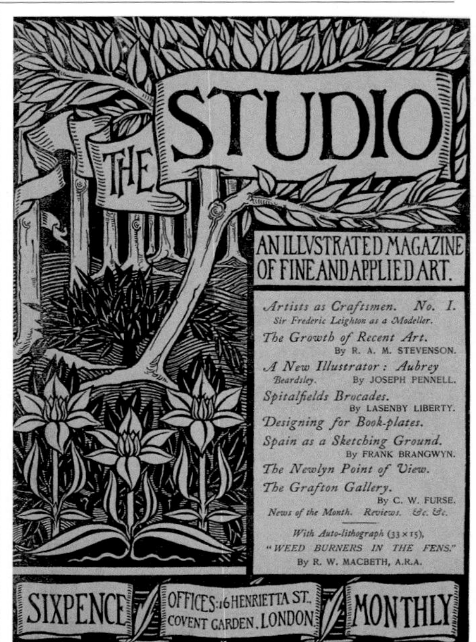

The cover of the first issue of this illustrated magazine of fine and applied art used an Aubrey Beardsley illustration. Inside, it featured the Arts and Crafts movement, the works of the Beggarstaff Brothers[1] and Charles Rennie Mackintosh, so spreading their ideas across Europe. Contributors included Frederic Leighton, R.A.M. Stevenson, Frank Brangwyn and Joseph Pennell. The issue also carried an article by Joseph Pennell about Beardsley, with eight illustrations. A year later, the English edition of Oscar Wilde's *Salomé* was published with Beardsley illustrations. As well as featuring cutting-edge artists, the magazine was printed entirely using a photomechanical process, whereas most magazines still used engravings or a combination of the two.

1 V&A: E.361–1899

The Studio
(285 × 205 mm, side-stabbed)

YELLOW BOOK (April 1894)

The aim of the *Yellow Book* was 'to depart as far as may be possible from the bad old traditions of periodical literature, and to provide an Illustrated Magazine which will be as beautiful as a piece of book-making, modern and distinguished in its letter-press and its pictures, and withal popular in the better sense of the world'. It was part of a movement among private presses to improve the quality of typography and production in publishing. Henry Harland was the literary editor of the letterpress pages and Aubrey Beardsley was art editor of the quarterly, which in form was like a book, with single-column text and yellow cloth binding (partly due to the extent of 300 pages). It was printed by the Ballantyne Press. 'Publishers' announcements' – adverts – were carried at the back. Beardsley's startling, decadent images were controversial and a year later a group of Bodley Head authors demanded his dismissal because of his association with Oscar Wilde. Beardsley went on to work on the *Savoy* magazine. The first issue of the *Savoy* (January 1896) includes a reproduction of *The Abbé*[1] and a version of the cover showed a cherub urinating on a copy of the *Yellow Book*.[2]

1 V&A: E.305–1972
2 Malcolm Easton, *Beardsley and the Dying Lady* (London 1972)

Elkin Mathews & John Lane, The Bodley Head
(book binding, 300 pages)

YELLOW BOOK (January 1895)

The Head of Minos by John Trivett Nettleship was one of 15 images in this issue. They were reproduced by the Swan Electric Engraving Company. Ten different artists, including Walter Sickert, Frederic Leighton and Joseph Pennell, were represented.

Elkin Mathews & John Lane, The Bodley Head
(200 × 150 mm)

POSTER (July 1898)

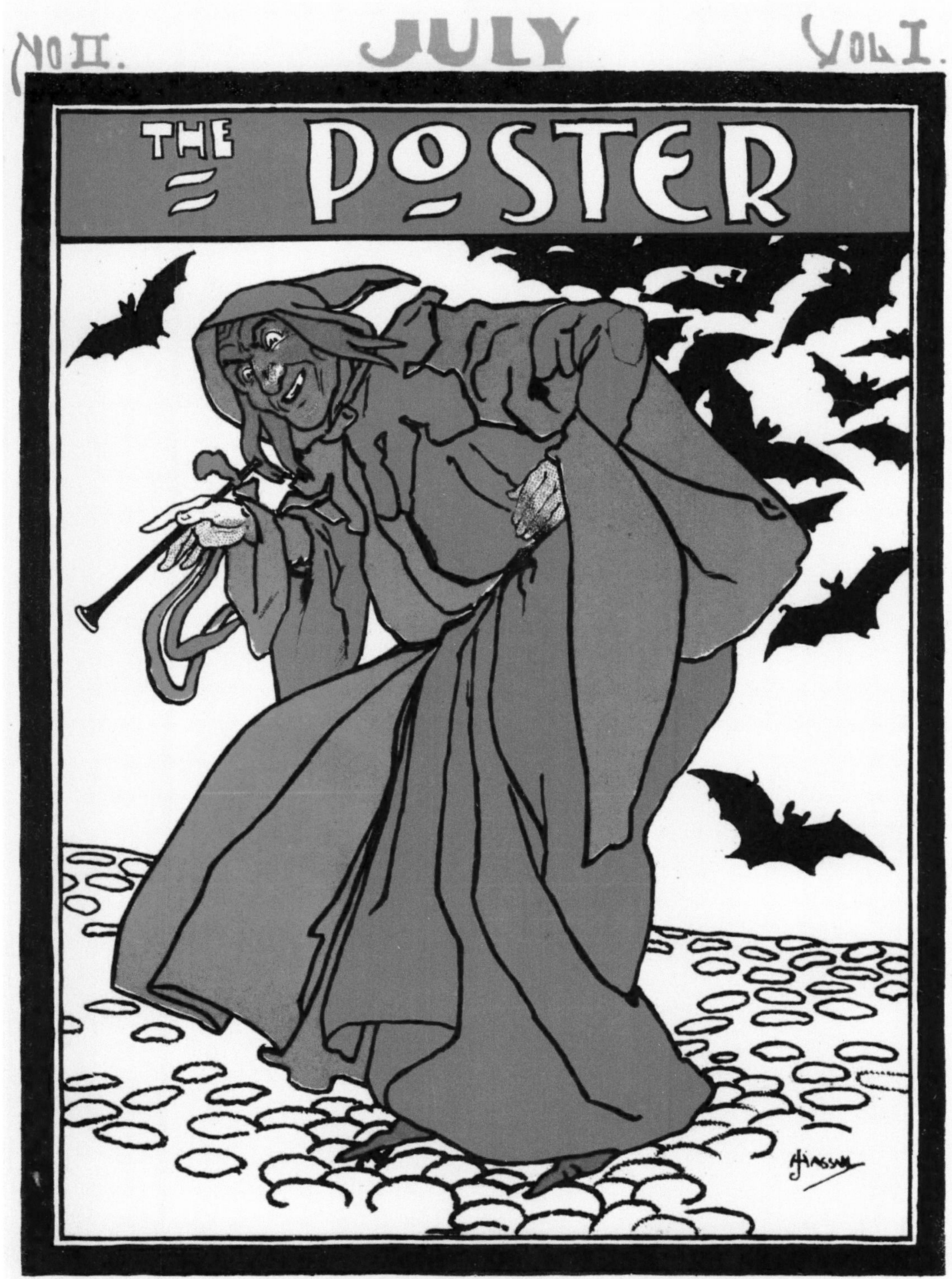

The *Poster*, an 'illustrated monthly chronicle', documented the latest in poster techniques and was edited by Charles Hiatt. This cover, with its flat colours and thick black lines portraying a gruesome piper followed by bats, is by John Hassall. He worked on the *Graphic* and later created the 'Skegness Is So Bracing' poster (1908), which was used for decades by the London and North Eastern Railway.[1]

1 V&A: E.1326–1931

E.R. Alexander & Sons
(238 × 180 mm, 48 pages)

STRAND (January 1891)

THE STRAND MAGAZINE
THE STORY OF THE STRAND.

As with *Punch*, the cover of the *Strand* remained more or less the same for decades. It showed a view by George Charles Haité looking east from the corner of Burleigh Street towards the church of St Mary le Strand. The letters of the title are portrayed as hung from wires across the street.

The first issue included a nine-page article about the Strand, 'the most interesting street in the world'. The Haité illustration shows Burleigh Street, where the magazine shared its office with *Tit-Bits*, hence the rooftop advertising sign. There are no dates on the pages because these would have detracted from the bookish feel once bound. The building shown on the left page housed the offices of Coutts, the bankers. When the magazine moved premises, the cover illustration remained the same but the street sign was changed to Southampton Street. The December 1896 cover claimed that the *Strand* was 'the most profusely illustrated magazine in the world'.

George Newnes
(245 × 165 mm)

STRAND (July 1891)

"I AM DELIGHTED THAT YOU HAVE COME DOWN, MR. HOLMES."

Newnes secured exclusive rights to the Sherlock Holmes short stories by Arthur Conan Doyle. These were instrumental in the success of the magazine and 56 were published, starting in the seventh issue, over a period that lasted until 1927. The strategy began a trend for short stories based around a common character, rather than serialization, in magazines. 'The Adventure of the Silver Blaze' was illustrated by Sidney Paget.

George Newnes
(245 × 165 mm)

STRAND (June 1930)

Although George Charles Haité's street scene was kept for the covers of the bound volumes, it was reworked to accommodate advertising on the magazine wrappers. A poster for Hall's Wines appeared above the Southampton Street sign in December 1897 and this became a permanent feature. A colour version of the scene appeared on the December 1903 cover. In the variant shown here, the scene has been brought into the present day and allows space for prominent cover lines as well as the advertising – Oxo is at the top left. Colour had become a standard on the covers in the early 1920s. Note the advert on the side of the bus for the *Humorist*, a weekly sister title to the *Strand*. From the mid-1930s, the cover scenes roamed away from the Strand to depict other famous places in London, and also people. Many artists were used, including Edward Ardizzone, winner of the first Kate Greenaway Medal in 1955.

George Newnes
(245 × 165 mm)

PALL MALL MAGAZINE (January 1901)

Pall Mall Magazine was launched in 1893 by William Waldorf Astor as a spin-off from the *Pall Mall Gazette*. Like its rival the *Strand*, it included poetry, short stories and extensive artwork. By 1901, photographs were used regularly and each issue was accompanied by a presentation plate, in this case an early photogravure made by Annan & Sons, Glasgow, of a Gainsborough painting of Lady Frances Conway. Other plates with the first four issues of 1901 were a Swantype colour plate of a hunting scene by G.D. Armour, a plate by Swan Electric Engraving Company of Nelly O'Brien by Reynolds, a photo by W. & D. Downey of Queen Victoria reproduced by Swan Electric, a Gainsborough portrait of Mrs Robinson by Swan Electric and a photogravure by T. & R. Annan & Sons, Glasgow, of *The Dairymaid* by Greuze.

Pall Mall Magazine
(240 × 175 mm, 144 pages)

PEARSON'S MAGAZINE (June 1897)

THE WAR OF THE WORLDS
BY H.G. WELLS

"But who shall dwell in these Worlds if they be inhabited? . . . Are we or they Lords of the World? . . . And how are all things made for man?"—(Kepler: quoted in *The Anatomy of Melancholy*.)

I.—THE EVE OF THE WAR.

No one would have believed in the last years of the nineteenth century that human affairs were being watched keenly and closely by intelligences greater than man's and yet as mortal as his own; that as men busied themselves about their affairs they were scrutinised and studied perhaps almost as closely as a man with a microscope might scrutinise the transient creatures that swarm and multiply in a drop of water.

With infinite complacency men went to and fro over this little globe about their affairs, dreaming themselves the highest creatures in the whole vast universe, and serene in their assurance of their empire over matter. It is just possible that the infusoria under the microscope do the same.

No one gave a thought to the Older Worlds of Space, or thought of them only to dismiss the idea of life upon them as impossible or improbable. At most, terrestrial men fancied there might be other men upon Mars, probably inferior to themselves and ready to welcome a missionary enterprise. Yet across the gulf of space minds that are to our minds as ours are to those of the beasts that perish, intellects vast and cool and unsympathetic, regarded this earth with envious eyes, and slowly and surely drew up their plans against us. And early in the twentieth century came the great disillusionment.

The planet Mars, I may remind the reader, revolves about the sun at a mean distance of 140,000,000 miles, and the light and heat it receives from the sun is scarcely half of that received by this world. It must be, if the nebular hypothesis has any truth, older than

Copyright, 1897, by H. G. Wells, in the United States of America.

Vol. III.—April, 1897.—No. 16.

The War of the Worlds by H.G. Wells was first published in *Pearson's*. The serial was illustrated by Warwick Goble, who, as well as providing illustrations for magazines, later worked as a book illustrator for Macmillan.

Pearson
(240 × 170 mm)

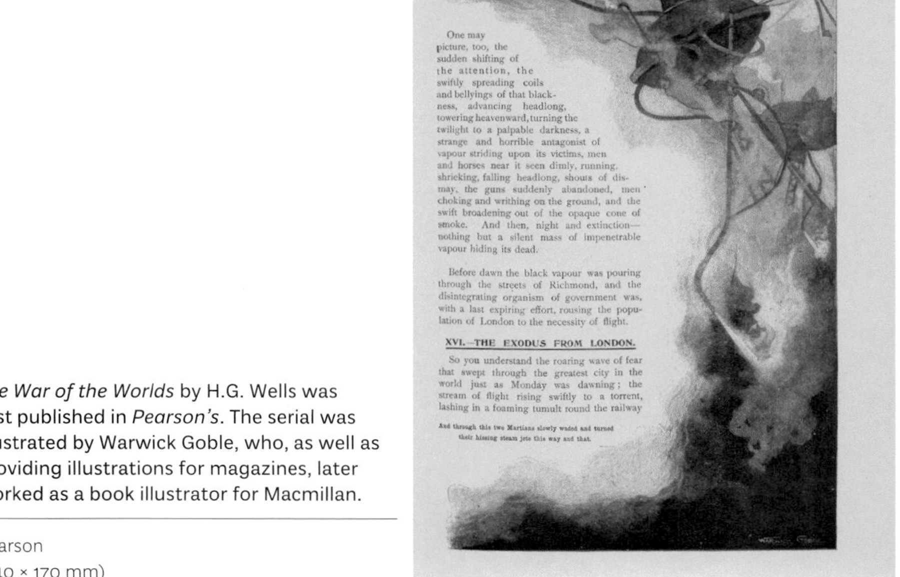

THE WAR OF THE WORLDS.

One may picture, too, the sudden shifting of the attention, the swiftly spreading coils and bellyings of that blackness, advancing headlong, towering heavenward, turning the twilight to a palpable darkness, a strange and horrible antagonist of vapour striding upon its victims, men and horses near it seen dimly, running, shrieking, falling headlong, shouts of dismay, the guns suddenly abandoned, men choking and writhing on the ground, and the swift broadening out of the opaque cone of smoke. And then, night and extinction—nothing but a silent mass of impenetrable vapour hiding its dead.

Before dawn the black vapour was pouring through the streets of Richmond, and the disintegrating organism of government was, with a last expiring effort, rousing the population of London to the necessity of flight.

XVI.—THE EXODUS FROM LONDON.

So you understand the roaring wave of fear that swept through the greatest city in the world just as Monday was dawning; the stream of flight rising swiftly to a torrent, lashing in a foaming tumult round the railway

And through this two Martians slowly waded and turned their hissing steam jets this way and that.

WIDE WORLD ILLUSTRATED (April 1898)

This cover illustrates the vogue for Art Nouveau illustration, with its hand-drawn type. Tales of derring-do fed the hero culture of the Victorians and the Edwardians.

The tales of Louis de Rougemont, the would-be explorer featured on the cover, were later exposed as fiction, and de Rougemont branded 'the greatest liar on Earth'.

In 2009 playwright Donald Margulies, winner of the Pulitzer Prize, penned *Shipwrecked! An Entertainment: The Amazing Adventures of Louis de Rougemont (as Told by Himself).*

George Newnes
(182 × 245 mm, side-stabbed, 132 pages)

BYSTANDER (18 July 1906)

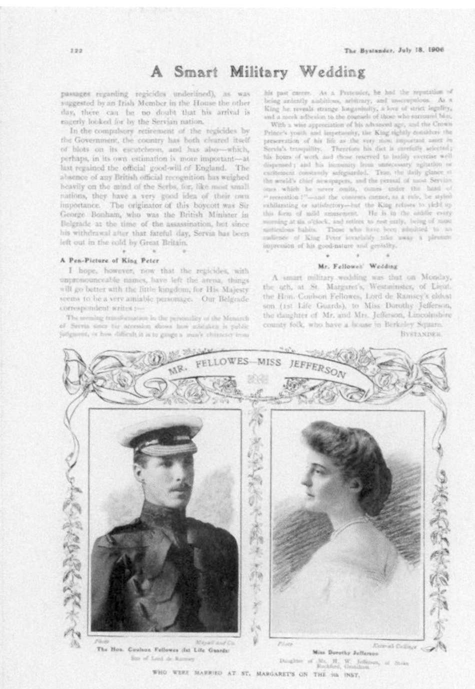

PLAY PICTORIAL (1910)

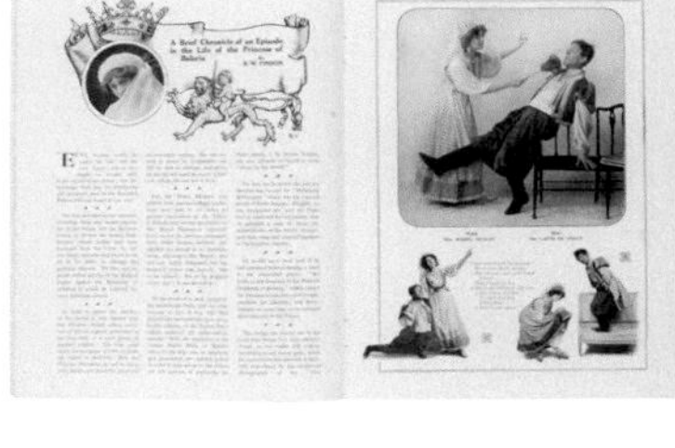

The *Bystander* competed with the *Tatler*, but had a colour illustration for the masthead surrounded by advertising. There was no colour inside. The magazine used high-quality presses based at Tallis Street in the City of London. A coupon on the inside cover promised readers £2,000 if they were killed on a train, hansom cab or omnibus.

Frontispiece photograph by the studio of Alexander Bassano of Victoria Godwin, who raced on her 40-horsepower Ariel Simplex 6-cylinder motorbike.

Photographs of likely readers helped drive sales, while the cartoons of Lawson Wood were popular around the world.

The Bystander Ltd
(206 × 303 mm, stapled, 68 pages)

Gold ink was used as part of this colour cover at a time when it was still rare for covers to be in colour every month.

Inside there were excellent photographs and illustrations, such as this spread with scenes from *The Balkan Princess*.

The Stage Pictorial Publishing Co.
(225 × 295 mm, stapled, 38 pages)

HOME CHAT (18 September 1897)

22 HOME CHAT. September 18, 1897.

Competition on page 5. Two guineas is the prize offered, and, as it will go to the *neatest* correct olution, deft feminine fingers will run a good chance. Everyone may go in for it, so "Selfish" may tell her brothers that here is a competition for them at last.

Remember, too, that ten prizes of books, gloves, &c., are offered in addition to the money prize.

* * *

"Don't you think," asks "Draycot Owl," "that a girl should read solid books as well as novels? So many girls I know never open anything else, and I think they grow silly with never having anything but love to think about. I like to read things that make me want to be brave and noble, and lead an unselfish life, and that make me better for having read them."

You are quite right. Novels are delightful things, like French sweets. But a diet composed entirely of bonbons would be neither satisfying nor beneficial. There must be the solid food to nourish and strengthen the mind as well as the body. Ruskin, Carlyle, Emerson, Macaulay, and the like will help you to long for and to strive after the "worth while" things of life.

THE ASSISTANT-EDITRESS.

THE CYCLISTS' CORNER.

The best gloves to wear for cycling are those of white doeskin, and a large size should be chosen, to admit of a firm grip on the handles. These gloves are pleasanter to wear in hot weather than ordinary kid or suède, and can be washed several times before they are worn out.

A Good Refresher.—One of the finest remedies in the world for cyclists, and one that is little known, is the sustaining power of a tomato. No matter how tired and exhausted the rider may feel, if only a small piece of tomato is eaten it acts like magic, taking all the depressed feeling away and making one feel quite fresh. Cyclists who are travelling a long distance should try this.

When detaching a tyre never *force* it over the rim with the lever. It should be gradually worked over by pressing the wires well into the bed of the rim. If forced over the tyre gets all out of truth, and if the tread be narrow the back tyre will touch the stays at different points, and it will be difficult to get the wheel true again.

When buying a machine, see that the wheels are the same size. The tyre of the hind wheel wears out more quickly than that of the front; and if the wheels are the same size, the tyres can be changed from one wheel to the other, so that they may wear evenly.

Don't give your bicycle too much oil. A well-kept bicycle only needs to be oiled once for every hundred miles you travel. Drop in just a little oil, and, after allowing it to work in carefully, wipe off any that may remain on the machine.

DON'T MISS THIS WEEK'S

"FORGET-ME-NOT."

September 18, 1897. HOME CHAT. 23

THE EXPERIENCES OF A CYCLING CHAPERON.

PART VIII.—A PEEP AT THE ISLE OF WIGHT.

THE profound stillness of the forest lay unbroken, and even our own voices lowered themselves as we sped through on noiseless wheels.

The forest is silent, when one does not stop to listen; when one does, the silence seems alive. There is the hum of a million insects, the stir of leaves, the chatter of squirrels, the murmur of wood pigeons. Suddenly one learns that the atmosphere is full of life, and that, instead of loneliness, one is in the middle of a crowd.

The heath kept on till we reached Lyndhurst, the heart of the forest, and the trees drew away into the distance, and stood about in a kind of dignified reserve.

Up on the crown of the heath there is a high mound, with a beech at the summit, where a vast view can be had on every side.

We did not stop to examine it, for we were all longing for that afternoon tea dear to the heart of the cyclist, and we did not back pedal till we drew up before the picturesque porch of the Crown, prettiest and dearest of forest hotels.

There is more than one sight to be seen in Lyndhurst, but we should be coming back this way, and did not mean to linger now.

Tea was the one subject of our thoughts, and we fully enjoyed it, sitting by the open window of the comfortable coffee-room, with the scent of the flowers in the window-boxes coming in with every breath of breeze. We were out again, and mounted our machines as the church clock opposite chimed five, and the shadows of the great trees lay all across the road as we turned our wheels down the way that led to Brockenhurst and on to Lymington.

This was another beautiful run, full of varied scenery, each turn bringing some new loveliness to sight. We rode up a hill, then a long, long downward slope lay before us, and we ran down it with delight.

Now the trees closed in so tightly that we could hardly see ten yards through their jostling trunks.

Now they sped away back, to leave a green glade, where the tall fern waved airily—then came a common, with red flags to mark the inevitable golf course, and a little bridge across a brook where, Rex told us, the staghound meets were often held.

Stag-hunting still prevails in the forest—nice, kindly sport, where the deer is no longer killed. We rode on through Brockenhurst, where the rail met us again, and almost startled us with a suggestion of nineteenth-century civilisation, which jarred curiously on the calm of the mediæval times the forest suggested. We had almost felt ourselves back again with the Red King, who "loved the tall deer as if they had been his children," as the Saxon chronicle has it; and who harried honest people from their homes, and burnt their cottages, so that he might have a Royal hunting-ground for his pleasures.

We crossed the incongruous railway, and went on past Brockenhurst Church, an antique little edifice, with traces of Saxon work about it, and a vast old spreading yew tree in its churchyard, planted in the days when the parish was bound by law to supply yew long-bows to its villagers.

The road on from here has still its forest characteristics, though they are less wild than those we left behind.

Houses, in their own parks, cottages, and signs of human habitation dotted the way here and there. We were no longer in the heart of the lonely tract where the deer still shelter, and the droves of forest pigs make their home, and the charcoal-burners ply their trade.

When the red roofs of Lymington, with its break-neck High Street, burst upon our view, we were feeling distinctly modern, and had left the Middle Ages well behind us.

There are yachts in the little harbour, and there is a certain stir on market days in the tiny town, whence the boats ply to the Isle of Wight with a fussy importance. We forsook all recollection of the Red King for the contemplation of hats and frocks not six months behind the London fashions, and felt ourselves quite metropolitan again.

The sight of the Isle of Wight boats put a new idea into our minds. Why not create a variation in our tour by getting a glimpse at the island to which we were so close?

We had not contemplated it, it is true; but that made the interlude all the more attractive. We had Saturday at our disposal. We could cross to Yarmouth early to-morrow, or even go to Totland Bay and see a little of the neighbourhood before we returned to Lyndhurst by way of Beaulieu.

We made inquiries about a boat, and found we could get one to suit, so the extension was decided on, and we went to supper at

September 18, 1897. HOME CHAT. 31

EDITORIAL CHIT-CHAT.

The first prize in the "Cycling Proverbs" competition has been awarded to Miss Lewis, 51, Elms Road, Clapham Common, S.W., who sent in the following parodies of well-known proverbs, these forming the best group of six received, though in one or two cases single proverbs sent by other competitors were better:

Never leave loose till to-morrow what you can screw up to-day.

Little drops of oil,
Little bits of rag,
Make the bike run easy,
And save a lot of fag.

Uneasy runs the bike that needs some oil.

A "coaster" and his bike are soon parted.

It is never too late to bike.

Evil roads corrupt good tyres.

The second prize goes to M. R. Heath, 41, Craven Park Road, Willesden, and the third to Mary Byrne, 1, Grafton Street West, Gorton, Manchester.

The following proverbs are selected from the winning and other postcards:

A light in time saves a fine.

Coast in haste, repent in plaister.

Give a dog a wide berth and slang him.

When paraffin gets in at the balls, grit flies out at the bearings.

Too many punctures spoil a spin.

Of two hills, choose the lesser.

Hilly 'tis to him who hilly thinks it.

We know the use of oil when the lamp runs dry.

See a nail and let it lie,
Outfit needed by and by.

Where there's a wheel there's a way.

Don't count your miles before you've ridden them.

Better learn on the old bike before you are on to the new.

When ridden by day, to be cleaned before night,
Keeps a bike ready, useful, and bright.

It's an ill-wind that blows out of a puncture in your tyre.

It's the man without a cyclometer who rides the greatest distance.

* * *

Several correspondents send in short stories and articles, asking me to criticise them in Editorial Chat.

I cannot do this. It would be easy to fill three

"Motor Car" is going with a party of six friends to the North of Ireland next week. "We hope to do a good deal of cycling," she writes, "but unfortunately neither of us has ever mended, or tried to mend, a puncture. Probably we shall be miles away from bicycle shops most of the time, so it is absolutely necessary that we should know how to deal with small breakages. I have a book which describes all the different parts of the bicycle and their functions very well, but the chapter on punctures is quite incomprehensible. Will you very kindly explain the process of mending one?"

It is difficult to describe it clearly without diagrams, and I cannot get these at a moment's notice. However, I am having a little article on the subject prepared, which will appear next week. It will be illustrated by an artist who does a good deal of touring himself, and who knows by experience exactly where the difficulties of puncture-mending come in. This will help you, I hope. But if possible, in addition to reading the article, you should see a puncture mended before you go.

* * *

"E. F. D.," writing from Birmingham, asks if it is absolutely necessary to come to London in order to learn shorthand and typewriting?

Not at all. If you like to send me a stamped, addressed envelope I will give you the address of an office at Birmingham where you can learn.

* * *

"Gussie's" is a question of the same kind: "Where can I learn typewriting?"

Where do you live, "Gussie?" Without knowing that I am afraid I cannot help you much.

Cycling was all the rage at this time and general magazines of course showed images of bicycles to bring in advertising. Cycling magazines were increasingly popular (several editors, including Alfred Harmsworth, cut their journalistic teeth on such titles), so *Home Chat* had a series on cycling and promoted accessories such as gloves and shoes, silk ties, label holders – the railway companies insisted on bikes being labelled when carried – and handy oil cans.

The 'editorial chitchat' page and other features were marked by a small illustration, at this time often in the Art Nouveau style. The articles carried results from a cycling proverbs competition. Among the illustrators were Claude Shepperson, F. Pegram, W. Dewar, Hal Hurst, Warwick Goble and Louis Wain.

Harmsworth Brothers
(154 × 218 mm, stapled, 48 pages)

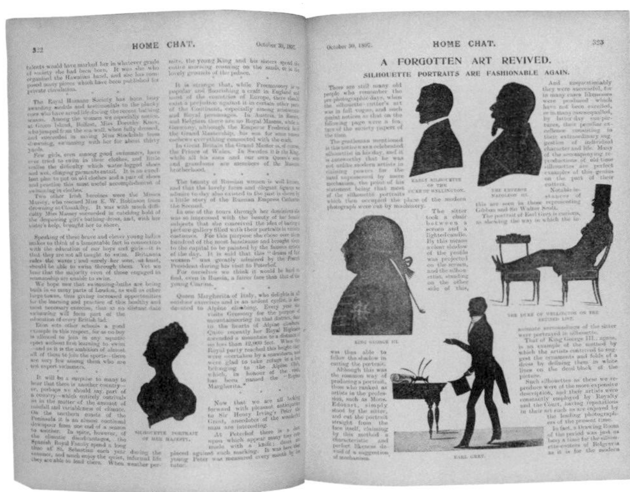

A FORGOTTEN ART REVIVED.

SILHOUETTE PORTRAITS ARE FASHIONABLE AGAIN.

HOME CHAT (30 October 1897)

October 30, 1897. HOME CHAT. 321

SOCIETY SMALL-TALK.

"To speak no slander; no! nor listen to it."

Her Majesty has always delighted in the delicate likenesses which miniature portraits produce, and, even when these pretty pictures were by no means the fashion, continued to have them painted, and always wore one of her youngest grandchild in the bracelet with which we have become familiar through her photographs.

Miss M. H. Carlisle, the eldest daughter of Mrs. Carlisle-Carr, and granddaughter of the late Sir John J. Bissett, by order of the Queen has painted a portrait of her Majesty. It is executed on ivory, and is considered a very good likeness. The Queen has presented it to the Prince of Wales.

* * *

Turquoises have always been a favourite stone with the Royal Family. Witness the very beautiful sets given to various members as wedding-presents. The Queen possesses some fine specimens of these splendid opaque stones. Some are the large, oblong-shaped ones, of the true azure colour so much admired.

Miss Margerita Allanson Winn, who sang before the Queen recently, received from her Majesty a brooch in turquoises and pearls, surmounted by the Imperial Crown.

* * *

What a pity it is that so many women who have a pretty taste in music, singing, and painting often, after marriage, neglect the talents they have been at some pains to cultivate during their girlhood!

The Royal princesses show us an excellent example in this particular. Princess Christian is as keen as ever on her art work; Princess Louise often sketches, and devotes many hours to finishing her work in her studio; Princess Beatrice has just sent one of her own water-colour pictures to the Fine Art Society at Ryde, of which she is president. The subject of the picture is a view of Cimiez.

* * *

There will be considerable interest with regard to the new opera of another clever amateur connected with Royalty, the Marquis of Lorne. Mr. Hamish McCunn is associated with his Royal Highness in connection with the score. The dramatis personæ are of Celtic birth. "Diarmid" is the title of the opera, in which Mademoiselle Cécile Loraine will take the part of the heroine.

This clever young soprano is yet another of Madame Marchesi's talented pupils, and made her début before a critical Parisian audience last year. She is now busy studying the part of the Celtic heroine.

* * *

The ex-Queen Liliuokalani is a distinguished musical amateur in more senses than one. Her

Photo by] [*Lafayette.*
THE MARCHIONESS OF WATERFORD (WHOSE MARRIAGE TOOK PLACE A FEW DAYS AGO).

The frontispiece usually used a photograph, often the only one in the issue at the time. The peacock illustration is by Maud Trelawny.

Silhouette portraits were fashionable in the late 1890s and would pop up again in later decades, as both illustrations and photographs.

Harmsworth Brothers
(154 × 218 mm, stapled, 48 pages)

THE TIMES WOMAN'S SUPPLEMENT (1 October 1910)

The Times.

Woman's Supplement.

No. 1 LONDON, SATURDAY, OCTOBER 1, 1910 *Issued Weekly with The Times*

CONTENTS

Women and The Times

EVERY woman who knows "Ravenshoe," which is one of the things that every ...

Work and Play

NATIONAL UNION OF WOMEN WORKERS

THE LINCOLN CONFERENCE

8 THE TIMES: WOMAN'S SUPPLEMENT [Saturday, October 1, 1910

Coming Fashions

The large-format illustrated magazines often ran supplements, but they were usually devoted to specific topics. This woman's supplement was issued weekly with *The Times* on a Saturday, but lasted only 14 issues. The text is set in 8½ point across 19 picas with 1½-pica gutters. Some advertorial-style articles in the advertising section were leaded out between lines to fill space.

The Times supplement (298 × 452 mm, folded, 8 pages plus 12 pages of advertising)

THE WOMAN'S SUPPLEMENT (early November 1920)

The Woman's Supplement

Early November

Sommaire

Cover by E. Barnard Lintott.

THE RED CLOAK

An introduction to the supplement sets out its aims and states that the first version in 1910 failed because the printing technology was not good enough. This one runs to colour for the cover and several inside pages from the outset, with spot colour on most pages for illuminated capitals and page decoration. The covers were by E. Barnard Lintott and the February issue ran a competition with a £250 prize for cover artists. It was printed by W.H. Smith at the Arden Press in Stamford Street, south of the Thames in Southwark. There were two four-page gravure sections.

The supplement made great play of its illustrators, among them Jean-Gabriel Domergue: 'It is the spirit of fashion which is depicted by the great French artist ... rather than fashion itself ... and JD has caught the elusive charm and grace of the vrai elegante of to-day.' The magazine had also bought exclusive rights to use the drawings of the French artist Soulié. Other illustrators included Bessie Ayscough, Maris Tyrrell and Miss A. Titford.

The contents page was illustrated by Garth Jones. Among the contributors listed was Auguste Escoffier, the Savoy's 'king of chefs and the chef of kings', who was here 'preparing menus not incompatible with the economy which in these days is our duty and our opportunity'. Jones did both editorial and advertising work, including for Selfridges.[1] He was sought after in continental Europe and the US as well as Britain, and built a reputation for decorative work in books, among them a series at the start of the century from George Newnes that included editions of Alfred, Lord Tennyson's *In Memoriam*, *The Booke of Thenseygnementes and Techynge That the Knyght of the Towre Made to His Doughters* and *The Diary of Samuel Pepys*.

The fashion illustration of an opera cape with red as a second colour is signed 'Edouart'.

The Times supplement
(220 × 300 mm, 68 pages)

1 V&A: E.241–1987

SPHERE (6 April 1912)

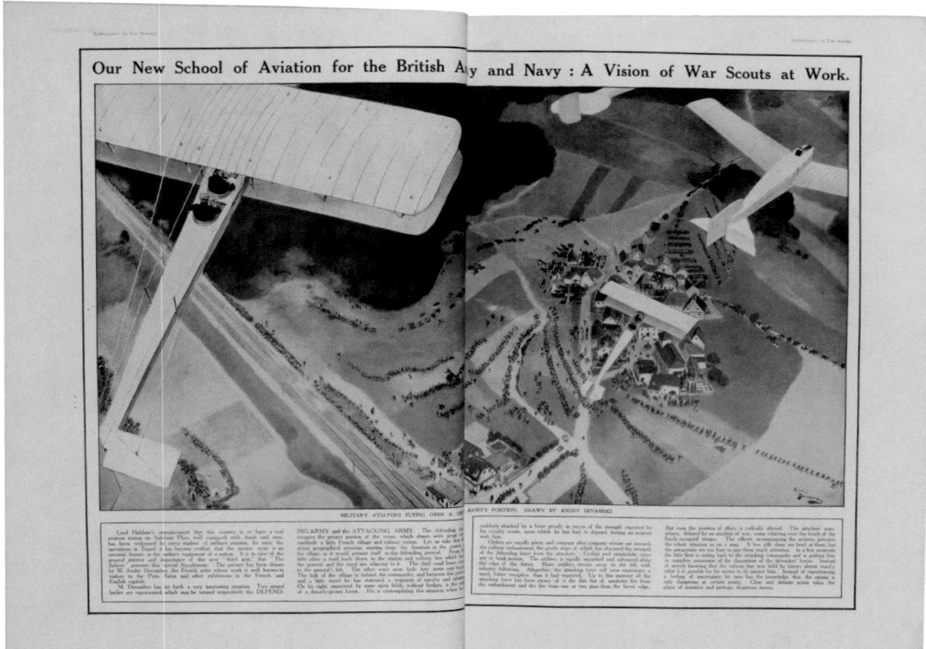

Our New School of Aviation for the British Army and Navy : A Vision of War Scouts at Work.

The flying supplement with this colour spread was numbered separately and inserted after page 8. The airborne vision was 'from the brush of M. André Devambez, the well-known French artist'. In the article, aircraft were seen as scouts rather than as bombers or as being in combat with each other, with the result that 'Clear and definite action takes the place of tentative and perhaps disastrous moves.'

Nineteen Hundred Publishing Syndicate
(348 × 282 mm, 24 pages plus 4-page supplement)

SPHERE (20 April 1912)

THE SPHERE

The *Titanic* disaster on the night of 15 April was a huge news story and the illustrated weeklies devoted many pages to the tragedy over several weeks, covering not only the event but also the inquiries. Wireless communications meant that the news reached the press, and hence the public, quickly. Among the 1,514 people who died was the former editor of the *Pall Mall Gazette* William Thomas Stead, the reforming journalist who exposed the white-slave trade and child sex abuse in London's brothels. There are memorial plaques to Stead on London's Embankment and in New York's Central Park. The *Sphere* cover shows a composite picture of the *Titanic* amid icebergs. Another 12 pages carried photographs of the ship, inside and out, maps, diagrams, pictures of the crew, other ships and past shipwrecks.

Nineteen Hundred Publishing Syndicate
(348 × 282 mm, 34 pages)

SPHERE (27 April 1912)

THE SPHERE

This cover by Fortunino Matania used a technique common among cartoonists and later in films with a newsvendor setting the scene: 'The modern messenger of death'. There were 20 pages on the sinking, including this Matania painting. Other illustrators included John Duncan, G. Torrance Stephenson, G.H. Davis and G. Bron.

Nineteen Hundred Publishing Syndicate
(348 × 282 mm, 34 pages)

SPHERE (4 May 1912)

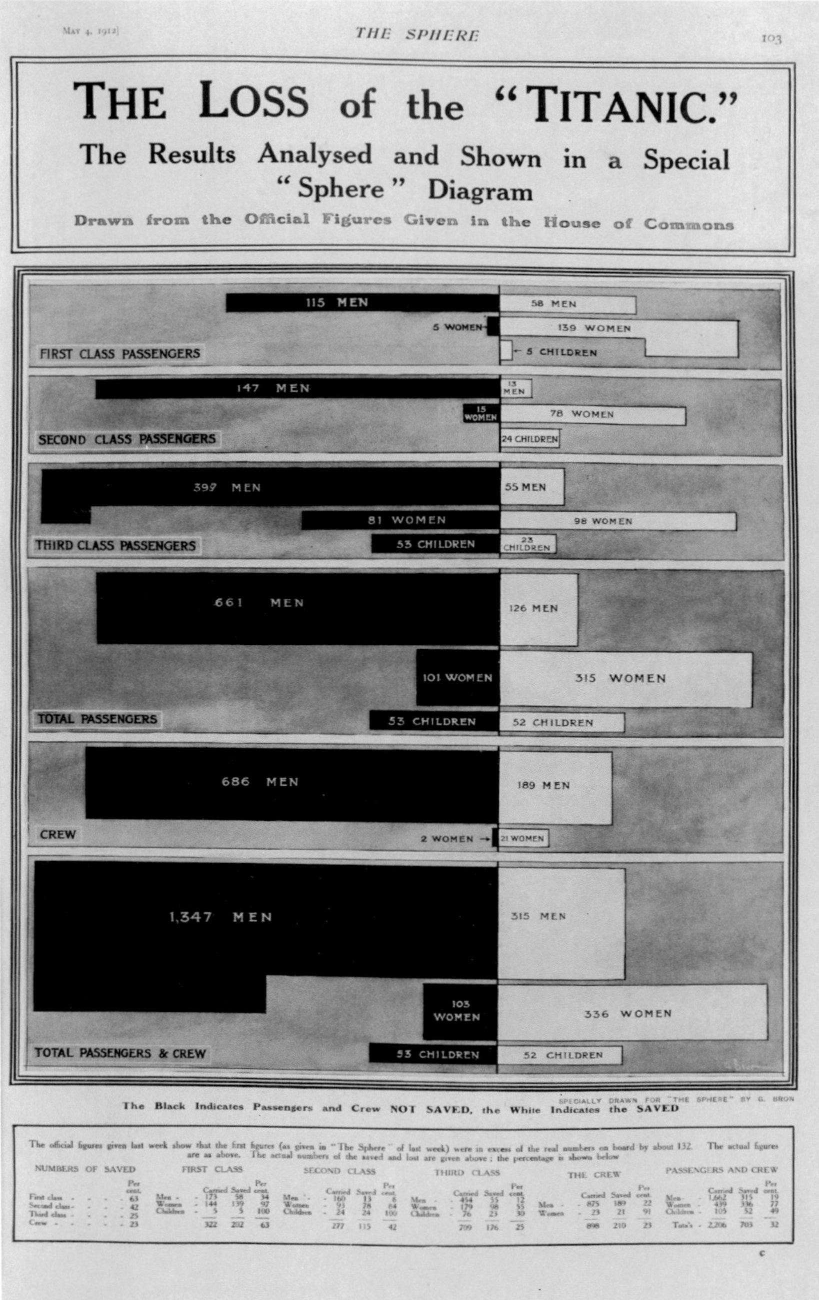

May 4, 1912] THE SPHERE 103

THE LOSS of the "TITANIC."

The Results Analysed and Shown in a Special "Sphere" Diagram

Drawn from the Official Figures Given in the House of Commons

The Black Indicates Passengers and Crew NOT SAVED, the White Indicates the SAVED

The official figures given last week show that the first figures (as given in "The Sphere" of last week) were in excess of the real numbers on board by about 132. The actual figures are as above. The actual numbers of the saved and lost are given above; the percentage is shown below

NUMBERS OF SAVED

	Per cent.
First class	63
Second class	42
Third class	25
Crew	23

FIRST CLASS

	Carried	Saved	Per cent.
Men	173	58	34
Women	144	139	97
Children	5	5	100
	322	202	63

SECOND CLASS

	Carried	Saved	Per cent.
Men	160	13	8
Women	93	78	84
Children	24	24	100
	277	115	42

THIRD CLASS

	Carried	Saved	Per cent.
Men	454	55	12
Women	179	98	55
Children	76	23	30
	709	176	25

THE CREW

	Carried	Saved	Per cent.
Men	875	189	22
Women	23	21	91
	898	210	23

PASSENGERS AND CREW

	Carried	Saved	Per cent.
Men	1,662	315	19
Women	439	336	77
Children	105	52	49
Totals	2,206	703	32

c

Fortunino Matania did a cover for this issue suggesting the need for better regulations covering working hours of wireless operators. Among the 16 *Titanic* pages was this diagram showing the relative losses of men, women and children among the various passengers.

Nineteen Hundred Publishing Syndicate
(348 × 282 mm, 26 pages)

SPHERE (10 May 1912)

THE SPHERE

AN ILLUSTRATED NEWSPAPER FOR THE HOME

With which is incorporated "BLACK & WHITE"

Volume XLIX. No. 642. London, May 11, 1912. [WITH SUPPLEMENT] Price Sixpence.

DRAWN BY F. MATANIA AT WESTMINSTER

"I WAS STANDING THERE, SIR"—A SCENE AT THE WESTMINSTER "TITANIC" INQUIRY

One of the most interesting witnesses before the Wreck Commission now sitting in the Scottish Hall, Westminster, at the beginning of this week was Robert Hitchens, a quartermaster on the "Titanic," who was holding the wheel when the vessel struck. He is here seen pointing out to the court his position at the time of the collision by means of one of the big models and sections placed in the hall. The quartermaster stated that he received the order, "Hard-a-starboard," and the vessel had swung about two points when the crash came.

Fortunino Matania was again the chosen illustrator for the *Titanic* inquiry at Westminster, here showing the helmsman on the night of the sinking, Robert Hichens, answering questions. The inquiry had taken place just three days before the magazine came out.

Nineteen Hundred Publishing Syndicate
(348 × 282 mm, 26 pages)

The Great War and photogravure

Publishers' fears that their businesses would be irrevocably damaged by the First World War proved to be unfounded. Families sent magazines, along with socks, to men at the front and there was an even greater demand for news and pictures. *London Opinion*, a rival to *Punch*, was one of the best-selling magazines of the time and had recently organized *The Laughter Show*, an international exhibition of humorous art, at Holland Park Hall in London. At the start of the war, it published Alfred Leete's Kitchener cover, which was taken up for a government poster campaign for volunteers (conscription was introduced in 1916). Barely a day goes by without this image being reused in some way in Britain. *Picture Post* used the poster as a cover in the Second World War and in 1999 advertising trade weekly *Campaign* identified it as the second-best poster of the century after Saatchi & Saatchi's 'Labour isn't Working' of 1978. In 2002, Leete's poster (with Eric Field identified as the copywriter and Caxton Advertising the agency for the various versions) was nominated as 'the best recruitment advert of all time' by the same magazine.

Cartoonists such as Leete were household names before the war, but other cartoonists became famous during the conflict. Captain Bruce Bairnsfather's mustachioed character Old Bill appeared in the weekly *Bystander*, and lives on as a nickname for a police officer – many demobbed soldiers entered the police sporting moustaches. A 1916 collection of the Old Bill cartoons sold 200,000 copies by the end of March and the character appeared in *Bystander* after the war; the final collection, Volume VIII, was published in 1919 and included editions in Australia, Canada and the United States. Another favourite was Miss Fish (Anne Harriet Fish), who illustrated *Tatler*'s Eve column. Like other 'light' papers, *Tatler* suffered a considerable drop in sales at the outbreak of the war, but countered this by appealing to men in the armed forces. Fish adapted her subjects to reflect the war at home and her unusual style created a 'great vogue': Designers of fashion copied them, and Eve hats, coats and handkerchiefs have been sold in hundreds, while in *Tina*, the popular musical comedy at the Adelphi [1915], a special scene was based on these drawings.[1] The Eve illustrations were published as books and in 1918 Gaumont made a dozen short films based on the drawings, with titles such as *Eve's Burglar* and *Eve Resolves to Do War Work*. Fish also worked for *Vogue* and did 30 covers portraying high society at play for *Vanity Fair*.

The writing was on the wall, however, for caricature and illustration. Edward Huskinson – who himself had been a cartoonist for the Tariff Reform League, producing 1,500 cartoons on the topic between 1904 and 1914 – claimed that *Tatler* was the first weekly paper to rely on snapshots of well-known people, rather than posed photographs taken in studios. He regarded a good snapshot as more indicative of the true looks and characteristics of a person.[2]

Cartoons had great cultural impact – and required appropriate space and printing technology from publishers. Leete began a wartime series in *London Opinion*, 'Schmidt the Spy', which became a silent film. Other characters included George Studdy's Bonzo dog in the *Sketch* – Bonzo was used as an illuminated advertisement in London's Piccadilly Circus – Gran'pop by Lawson Wood and Heath Robinson's contraptions in the *Sketch*, *Tatler* and *Humorist*. And there was always a market for a pretty face, such as William

Barribal's 'Barribal girls' and David Wright's pin-ups in the 1930s and 1940s for the *Sketch*. Outside of appearances in film and on stage, more found their way on to postcards, playing cards, lantern slides and pottery. The market for illustrated gift books never recovered after the war and cartoonists relied on magazines for income – though that outlet diminished as paper was rationed in the Second World War and photographs became more prevalent in print.

In this period, photogravure printing became used more widely, allowing reproduction of continuous tones for photographs and watercolour illustrations. Sun Engraving in Watford gained a near monopoly on fast, rotary photogravure (using cylindrical rather than flat plates) for long-run magazines for the best part of a decade from 1926.

Sun Engraving co-founder Edward Hunter set out to encourage better design across industry by funding the quarterly *Industrial Arts*, which was intended to expose designers to continental and US techniques, as well as the best of British design. The magazine carried articles by leading names such as Eric Gill, Jan Tschichold, Herbert Bayer, Joseph Emberton, Raymond Loewy and László Moholy-Nagy. Around the same time, Austin Cooper, a leading poster designer, co-founded the London branch of the Reimann School of Commercial and Industrial Design, and the Royal Society of Arts founded its Royal Designer for Industry (RDI) scheme. Other periodicals dedicated to typography and the graphic arts included *Typography*, which had a plastic spiral binding, from the Shenval Press under Robert Harling, and *Signature*, under the editorship of Oliver Simon.

Despite the Great Depression of the early 1930s, magazines continued to launch and sales expanded – even if you could not afford one, you could read about new cars each week in *Motor* or *Autocar*, and get the film gossip in *Picturegoer*, or catch up on the latest interiors in *Ideal Home*. But the launches were not just 'lifestyle' titles – *Britannia*, *Everyman*, *Cavalcade* and *News Review* set out to address the demand for news, the latter two within a week of each other in 1936. Alongside these were photo magazines such as *Pictorial Weekly*, *Weekly Illustrated* and *Picture Post*, which relied on new German-built (most famously Leica) cameras and photojournalism techniques.

While the news weeklies stuck to black-and-white reproductions for speed, other magazines with less restrictive deadlines could afford to wait the weeks it took to process colour covers, whether illustrated or photographic. By the mid-1930s full-colour printing had revolutionized the look of women's weeklies in particular, and opened up new markets for magazines such as *World of Wonder*. The Second World War, and consequent paper rationing, changed the landscape again.

1 H. Simonis, *The Street of Ink* (London 1917), p. 256.
2 Ibid., p. 255–6.

LONDON OPINION (5 September 1914)

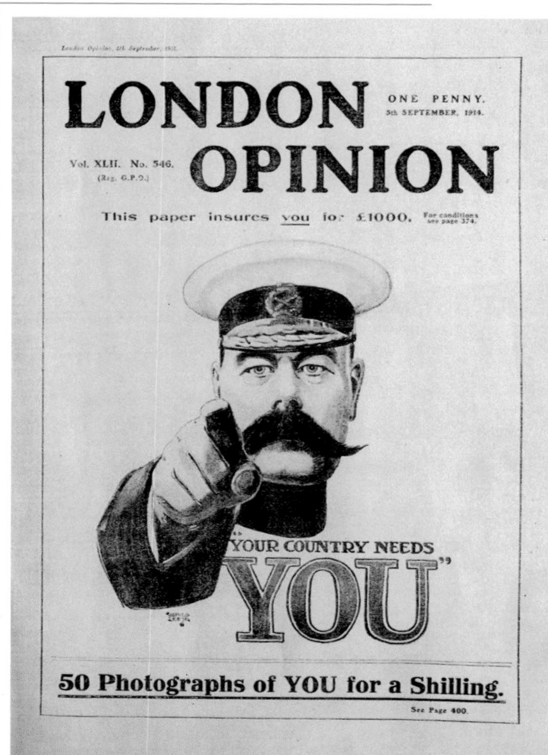

Alfred Leete drew this cover after the First World War was declared – 4 August 1914 – and it remains an iconic image around the globe. James Montgomery Flagg's adaptation, with Uncle Sam replacing Kitchener and the text 'I Want You for the US Army', was first published as the cover of the 6 July 1916 issue of *Leslie's Weekly* with the wordy headline 'What Are You Doing for Preparedness?' Other renditions include the sign for the cult 1960s Carnaby Street boutique I was Lord Kitchener's Valet[1] and a 1998 British Army recruitment poster.[2]

1 V&A: E.1428–2001
2 V&A: E.507–1998

C. Arthur Pearson Ltd
(205 × 290 mm)

RADIO TIMES (27 May 2006)

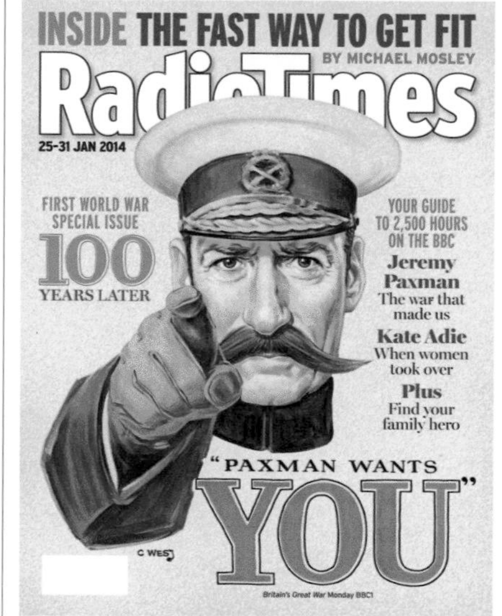

Jeremy Paxman cover echoing Leete's Kitchener drawing.

BBC Magazines
(225 × 300 mm, stapled, 148 pages)

BLAST (20 June 1914)

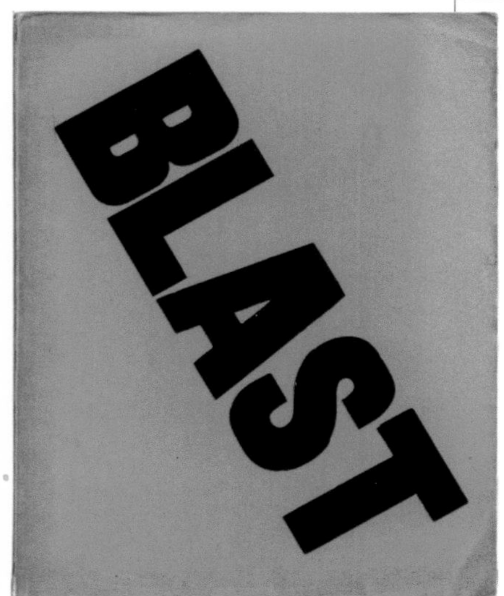

1

BLAST First (from politeness) ENGLAND
CURSE ITS CLIMATE FOR ITS SINS AND INFECTIONS
DISMAL SYMBOL, SET round our bodies,
of effeminate lout within.
VICTORIAN VAMPIRE, the LONDON cloud sucks
the TOWN'S heart.
A 1000 MILE LONG, 2 KILOMETER Deep
BODY OF WATER even, is pushed against us
from the Floridas, TO MAKE US MILD.
OFFICIOUS MOUNTAINS keep back DRASTIC WINDS
SO MUCH VAST MACHINERY TO PRODUCE
THE CURATE of "Eltham"
BRITANNIC ÆSTHETE
WILD NATURE CRANK
DOMESTICATED
POLICEMAN
LONDON COLISEUM
SOCIALIST-PLAYWRIGHT
DALY'S MUSICAL COMEDY
GAIETY CHORUS GIRL
TONKS

Artist Wyndham Lewis was co-founder and editor of this literary magazine, a 'Review of the Great English Vortex', which promoted the agenda of the Vorticist movement – and set a literary bomb under the art establishment. The first issue sported a bright pink cover, summed up by Ezra Pound – Lewis's close friend – as a 'great magenta cover'd opusculus'. The *Sunday Times* reviewed the magazine and compared it with the *Yellow Book* (see page 58). *Blast* was intended to be quarterly, but ran to only two issues, while Lewis went on to produce two other magazines in the 1920s, the *Tyro* and the *Enemy*, both of which had only two or three editions.

Published just before the outbreak of war, *Blast* set out a manifesto that cursed, or blessed, England and France, as well as various people, ideas and institutions. Among those blasted were the artist Frank Brangwyn, National Portrait Gallery director Lionel Cust and the British Academy; the work of Poet Laureate Robert Bridges was condemned as 'drizzle', and Filippo Marinetti, founder of the Futurist movement, had 'limited imagination'. The Commercial Process Co., a lithographic engraver and printer based in Wine Office Court off Fleet Street, was blessed, however. For Lewis, Pound, Henri Gaudier-Brzeska and the other eight signatories, 'The nearest thing in England to a great traditional French artist is a great revolutionary English one.' Lewis, who sold copies of the magazine from the Rebel Art Centre, devised the design and typography based on heavy grotesque type and asymmetrical layouts.

John Lane, The Bodley Head
(305 × 248 mm, 212 pages)

WOMAN'S OWN (24 April 1915)

8 PAGES OF LAUNDRY HINTS INSIDE
WOMAN'S OWN
FREE LAUNDRY SUPPLEMENT
GIL
No. 104, Vol. 4 April 24th, 1915 One Penny

BLAST (July 1915)

On the way to the Trenches. Nevinson.

COLD WATCH FREE
WOMAN'S OWN
Honour for the Housewife
THE MILL-GIRL ARMY NURSE

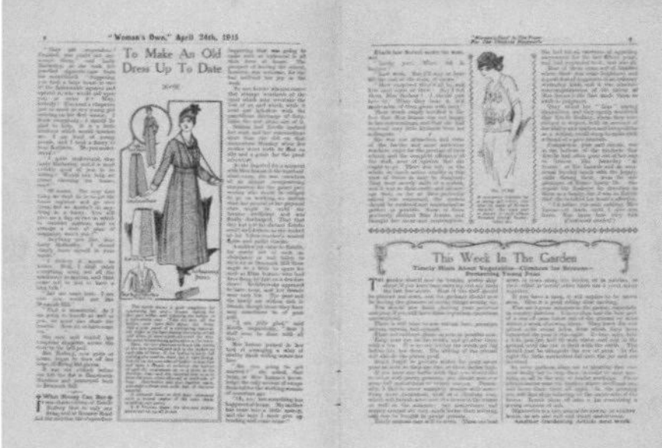
To Make An Old Dress Up To Date
The Week In The Garden

The second and final issue became a War Number and announced the death of Henri Gaudier-Brzeska, one of the original Vorticists, who was killed in the trenches. The page here shows 'On the Way to the Trenches' by Richard (C.R.W.) Nevinson. Like many of those whose work appeared in *Blast*, Nevinson went off to war and later became a war artist. Illustrations were reproduced from other avant-garde artists, including Edward Wadsworth, Spencer Gore, Frederick Etchells, William Roberts and Jacob Kramer.

John Lane, The Bodley Head
(305 × 248 mm, 112 pages)

Silhouette cover design by GIL to promote the magazine's laundry supplement. This use of the name *Woman's Own* by the publisher W.B. Horner pre-dates today's magazine, which was launched in 1932 by George Newnes.

The rose-framed editorial 'Honour for the Housewife' by Jeannie Maitland quotes John Ruskin and writes in praise of the woman's role in the home: 'What task can there be so wonderful and beautiful as to make our household feel nested in the home, safe and cosy?' Maitland wrote several other articles for the issue, including 'Recollections of a Minister's Wife', which included the only photograph in the magazine, her portrait. Many of the pages ran marketing slogans across the top: in this case, '*Woman's Own* – The Helper Over Life's Rough Places'. Another made interesting use of social marketing: 'Let your neighbours know that we are giving another free knitting supplement next week.'

This spread has a typical decorated border around the images and the lower-right headline (pp. 6–7). Many of the articles encouraged helping the war effort.

W.B. Horner
(168 × 240 mm, stapled, 44 pages)

THE SPHERE (24 June 1916)

276 THE SPHERE June 24, 1916

• WITH THE GUNS ON THE WESTERN FRONT. •

Copyrighted in the U.S.A. DRAWN BY F. MATANIA, 1916

"GOOD-BYE, OLD MAN"

An incident on the road to a battery position in Southern Flanders

Fortunino Matania was one of the most popular illustrators of the era. This double-page image, of a Tommy comforting his dying horse, will have been framed and pinned to the walls of homes all over Britain. *Punch* ran a cartoon three months later of an inept rider slung round the neck of his horse and being castigated that appears to refer to the cartoon: 'You needn't say a fond good-bye to that 'orse. You ain't seen the last of 'im by no means.' In Matania's painting, the soldier has removed the horse's harness, but note that a rider in the background is whipping one of the horses pulling the artillery gun. Magazines of the time regularly carried advertising for animal charities that helped such war horses.

London Illustrated Newspapers Ltd
(348 × 282 mm, 20 pages)

JOHN BULL (25 September 1915)

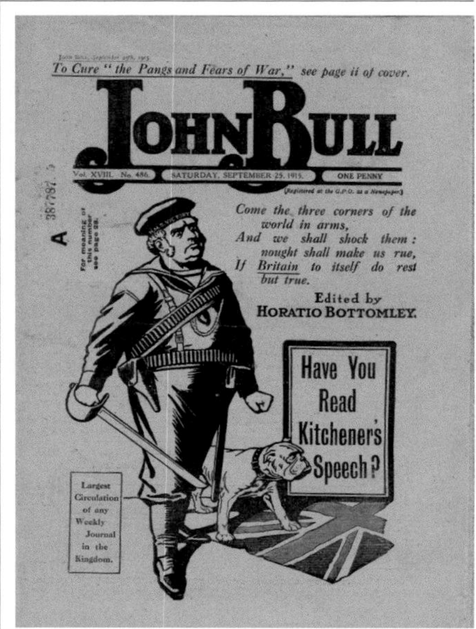

To Cure "the Pangs and Fears of War," see page ii of cover.

JOHN BULL

Vol. XVIII. No. 486. SATURDAY, SEPTEMBER 25, 1915. ONE PENNY

(Registered at the G.P.O. as a Newspaper)

A 387787

For meaning of this number see page 28.

Come the three corners of the world in arms,
And we shall shock them: nought shall make us rue,
If Britain to itself do rest but true.

Edited by
HORATIO BOTTOMLEY.

Have You Read Kitchener's Speech?

Largest Circulation of any Weekly Journal in the Kingdom.

Editor Horatio Bottomley maintained the magazine's unique look among the weeklies during the war, but replaced the country-squire style in favour of military garb – a costume composed of elements from both army and navy uniforms – and gave the bulldog a belligerent stare. The quotation is taken from Shakespeare's *King John*, but with 'England' replaced in the final line. The magazine claimed a circulation of 3.1 million copies a week – the largest of any weekly – but the figure was probably exaggerated. Note the number stamped on the left of the cover: the 'A' signified that a million should be added to the number printed above. Fifty of these numbers were printed on a page inside the issue, and matching a cover number to one of those inside would win a lucky reader a prize of a guinea from the publishers. Later in the war, the John Bull character was much reduced in size, advertising was introduced and the cover was used more frequently to promote Bottomley's editorship.

Odhams Ltd
(222 × 314 mm, stapled, 36 pages)

FRAGMENTS FROM FRANCE (No.7, 1919)

Captain Bruce Bairnsfather's Old Bill was one of the most popular creations of the war and boosted the popularity of *Bystander* magazine. Here the cartoon has been reprinted and pasted on to the cover of a collection from the magazine. The caption reads 'How Old Bill escaped being shot in 1914'.

The Bystander
(205 × 275 mm, stapled, 36 pages)

VOGUE (15 September 1916)

The launch of a British *Vogue*, nicknamed 'Brogue', was sparked by the threat to copies imported from America from Germany's U-boats and shipping restrictions. It was a landmark in Condé Nast's development as an international publisher. The cover was by Helen Thurlow. *Vogue* dated back to 1892 as a weekly society magazine, but Nast focused on women's fashion and published twice-monthly. He sought to attract an affluent audience with high editorial standards, and gained a reputation for using the best illustrators and photographers – specifically appealing to upmarket advertisers willing to pay a premium. Nast was influenced by *La Gazette du Bon Ton*, a French fashion magazine founded in 1912 by Lucien Vogel that treated fashion as an art form. He built up a relationship with Vogel, gaining access to the leading illustrators – such as Georges Lepape and Eduardo Benito – and subsequently bought up, and closed, *La Gazette du Bon Ton* in 1925, having established French *Vogue* in 1920.

Condé Nast UK
(185 × 260 mm)

BLIGHTY (Summer 1917)

Blighty was launched as a free magazine for the armed forces. Modelled on weekly humour titles, it came into being as paper grew scarce and publishing companies no longer had unsold copies to send to the troops. The enterprise was funded partly by the sale of special issues such as this one – 'every copy sold sends three to the trenches' – back in Britain. The cover illustration by Arthur Ferrier was based on an image by F.W. Popson, who was probably a serving soldier. *Blighty* was revived in October 1939 under Lord Nuffield.

The Committee of Blighty
(226 × 230 mm, stapled, 48 pages)

PASSING SHOW (26 April 1919)

Punch was the leading humorous weekly, but the *Passing Show*, *London Opinion* and the *Humorist* (George Newnes) were fierce rivals. The latter three would go through dramatic changes in the next two decades, driven by improvements in printing technology and then the encroachment of photography; only *Punch* retained a constant look. The Irish-born cartoonist David Wilson, who provided this cover, was a prolific contributor to the weeklies.

This spread is typical of the cartoon weeklies, which used hand-drawn logos for regular features. This is an early instance of the 'Man About Town' title.

Odhams Press
(200 × 280 mm, stapled, 32 pages)

PASSING SHOW (7 September 1935)

Odhams relaunched the gravure-printed weekly in a larger format enhanced by a colour cover – here by Gilbert Wilkinson, the regular cover artist. Spot colour was used for the 'Laughter!' 'smile section' inside, which carried cartoon strips by Bruce Bairnsfather ('Old Bill's Boy') and Mabel Lucie Attwell ('Wot a Life').

Excellent gravure reproductions were exploited by advertisers, here advancing a cigarette 'made specially to prevent sore throats'.

This episode of the science fiction serial 'The Secret People', credited to John Benyon, is accompanied by a Fortunino Matania illustration. Beynon's full name was John Wyndham Parkes Lucas Beynon Harris and he opted for another variation when publishing his novel *The Day of the Triffids*.

Odhams Press
(270 × 360 mm, stapled, 32 pages)

ILLUSTRATED (11 March 1939)

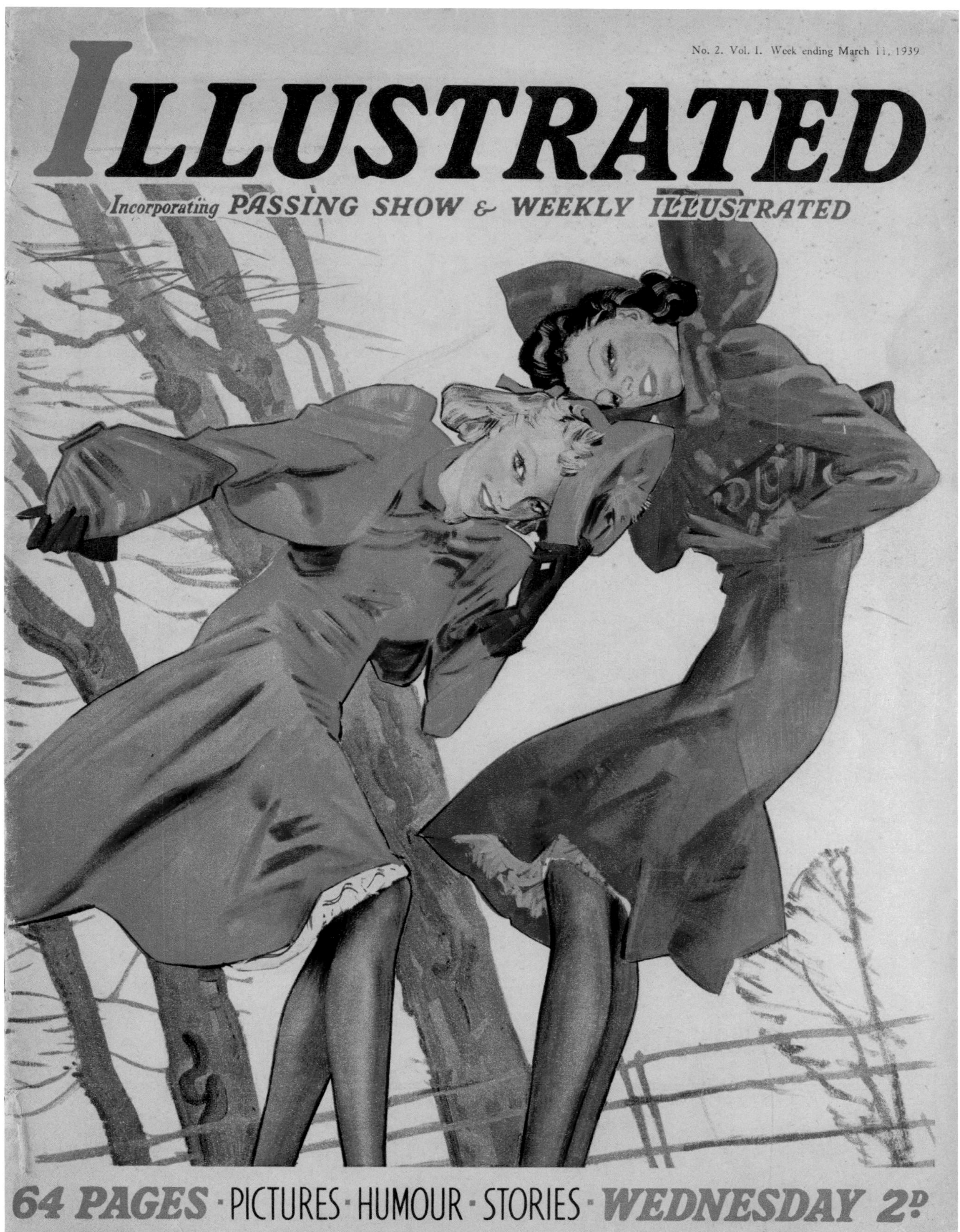

Passing Show and *Weekly Illustrated* combined to form *Illustrated*. The cover style is that of the former, sporting a Gilbert Wilkinson painting, and the centre eight pages, devoted to the 'Laughter!' section, included a colour cartoon in the 'Gran'pop' series by Lawson Wood. Possibly unexpectedly given the new title, the front half of the issue is dominated by large photographs, which are not credited. The work of illustrators including Clive Uptton, Miguel Mackinlay, Clixby Watson and Ronald Lampitt appears only in the second half. *Illustrated* switched to pure photography during the war as the most direct rival to *Picture Post*.

Odhams Press
(270 × 355 mm, stapled, 64 pages)

WOMAN'S LIFE (6 February 1926)

A 3d letterpress mid-format weekly that makes use of two colours, sky blue and warm red, to give the impression of a full-colour cover. The black-and-white photograph of the baby has been cut out and retouched (a tint of red gives skin tone, with more for the lips and cheeks, plus blue on the eyes). The deep blue background is produced by combining the red and blue inks. Note the outline added to the text sitting over the baby's shoulder to improve legibility. Newsprint paper is used inside the magazine and the cover stock has been calendered (rolled and compressed to give a smooth finish).

Photographs throughout the issue are cut out against a paper background and sometimes placed in a decorative frame. As was typical for the time, the headline is hand-drawn.

George Newnes
(176 × 225 mm, stapled, 52 pages)

MY HOME (November 1930)

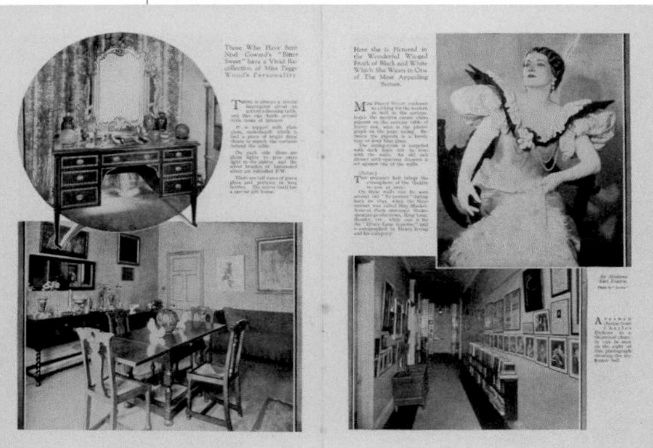

The cover painting on this monthly promotes the free gift, a cardboard 'Faerishade'.

Inside, an eight-page gravure section is used in the first half of the magazine for an article about the actress Peggy Wood. She was playing in Noël Coward's *Bitter Sweet* and living in the 'Beauty home of a favourite actress', Constance Collier, who had gone to Hollywood. The photographs were by Peter North and 'Sasha'.

Apart from the covers, only the centre four pages – illustrated by Watson Charlton – were in colour.

Amalgamated Press
(218 × 295 mm, stapled, 112 pages)

WOMAN'S WORLD (20 February 1932)

THE "BEST WAY" SUPPLEMENT

A COAT-FROCK FOR THE MATRON and A SPRING COAT FOR GIRLIE

THE CECIL CAP and A DAINTY CURVED EDGING

THE "BEST WAY" SUPPLEMENT

"OURS is a HAPPY HOME"

HOW TO SOW SEEDS

Two-colour printing, with the cover devoted to promoting free hairgrips as used by Hollywood actress Bebe Daniels, who later starred in the wartime BBC radio series *Hi Gang!*

Line illustration was favoured for letterpress printing and uncalendered paper. White rules are cut through the 'Happy Home' typeface. The text is set dense, 7 point type across 12 picas with narrow gutters, with many words on each page. The centred cross-heads on the right-hand page of hints and tips from the Dene family are part of the running text – a way of relieving large blocks of text without losing paper space for words.

Amalgamated Press
(187 × 268 mm, stapled, 44 pages)

WOMAN'S LIFE (17 September 1932)

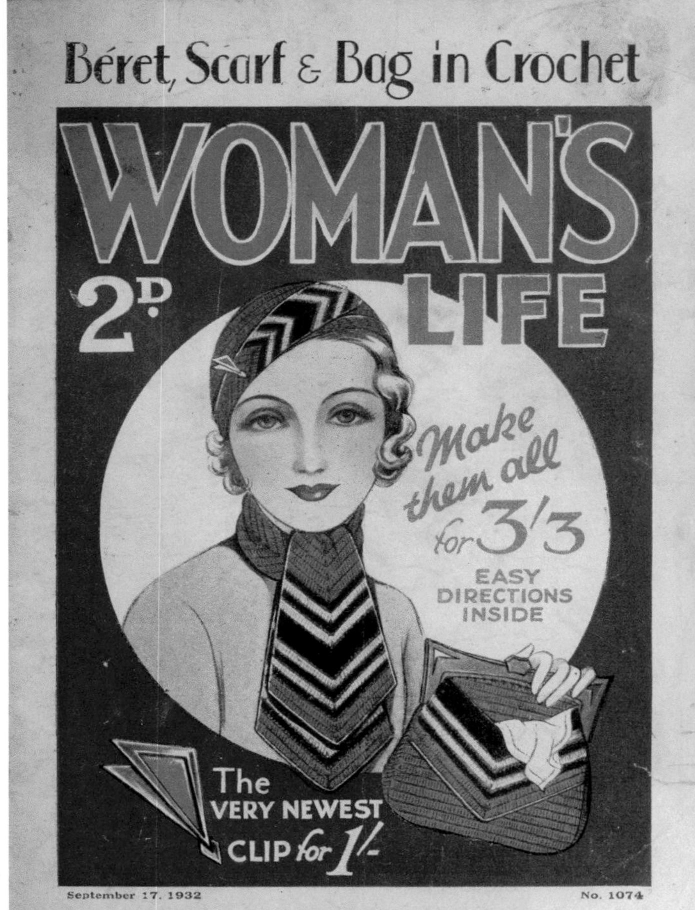

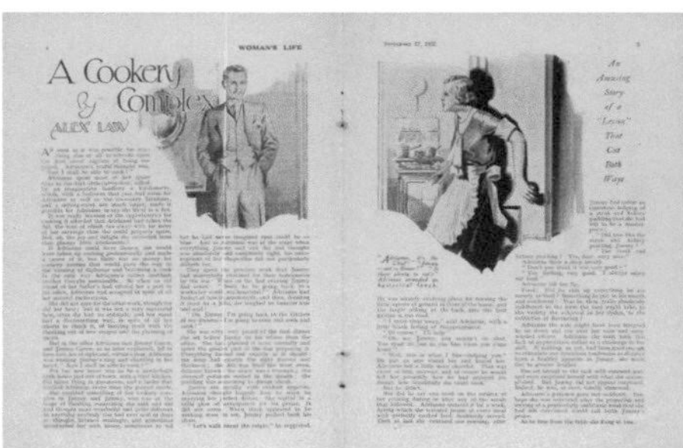

By 1932 *Woman's Life* had narrowed its page width, turned to poorer-quality cover paper (illustrated, rather than using a more expensive photograph) and cut its cover price to 2d. It retained two-colour printing.

Inside, better presses have enabled it to move to illustration with tones, rather than pure line, for fiction. The type size is 8 point across 15 picas. Punctuation spaces are used before exclamation marks and colons, and double spaces between sentences.

George Newnes
(167 × 228 mm, stapled, 52 pages)

WOMAN'S OWN (16 September 1933)

Newnes launched *Woman's Own* in 1932 with photographic covers from the start. It was printed by Sun Engraving using photogravure (for the cover and central eight-page section) and letterpress (which produced clearer type) for the other pages. The covers used a mono photograph of a model (the woman shown here was used frequently) with a spot-colour background. The image was usually 'framed', as here, or cut out. Note the cover line – 'Jobs for the youngsters' – a sign of the depressed times. Pages between issues were numbered consecutively, with roman numerals for the covers, suggesting that the publishers expected the magazines to be bound into annual volumes, or felt that to give that impression took the publication upmarket.

The fiction spread shown here, for 'Kind Cruelty' by Monica Ewer, was illustrated by Leslie Otway, a *Woman's Own* regular. The fiction pages were printed letterpress for better legibility, but these presses were not able to print across the magazine gutter (where the pages meet), or bleed images off the page. Also, the half-tone reproduction process for images could not match photogravure's subtlety of tone. Each article headline has its own unique typeface, drawn by hand. Text from the story is pulled out in a box and the captions are set in italic. The text is in 8 point type across 14-pica columns, with a bastard (or non-standard) measure used to run the text – efficiently, but not beautifully – around the illustrations.

The hair-care spread and the other gravure pages made extensive use of cut-outs and decorative rules to frame the pictures. The gravure presses could also print images bleeding off the page.

George Newnes
(216 × 297 mm, stapled, 36 pages)

HOME JOURNAL (28 September 1935)

HOME JOURNAL
Every Wednesday September 28th. 1935 Vol. 4. No. 82.
3d
Inside FREE PATTERN to make this PRETTY DAY FROCK in SILK or WOOL
Brilliant New Serial Begins in this Issue

Amalgamated took a different tack to its Newnes rival *Woman's Own* in designing *Home Journal*, using monthly production values on a weekly. It adopted a glossy weekly format, though it used the same page size as Newnes and the same printer, Sun. At 3d, it cost 1d more than its rival, but ran to twice as many pages and used gravure printing on a better paper stock. Several publishers would try to make the glossy weekly format work, but none succeeded until *Grazia* in 2005.

Amalgamated Press
(216 × 298 mm, stapled, 60 pages)

HOME JOURNAL
SEPTEMBER 28, 1935
EVERY WEDNESDAY
Dorothy Wilding
LADY ALICE MONTAGU-DOUGLAS-SCOTT.
Happy bride-to-be of the Duke of Gloucester, whose wedding will take place almost exactly a year after the Duke and Duchess of Kent's.

Page 3 was a frontispiece in the style of the society weeklies, in this case of Lady Alice Montagu-Douglas-Scott. The photograph was taken by Dorothy Wilding, who later took the portrait of Elizabeth Bowes-Lyon, Queen Consort of King George VI, used in the double portrait for the 1937 Coronation postage stamp.[1] Wilding was awarded a royal warrant as official photographer, and also took the portrait of the new Queen Elizabeth used on postage stamps between 1953 and 1967.

1 V&A: 1000LM1283-01

RADIO TIMES (28 September 1923)

Radio Times, September 28, 1923.

THE RADIO TIMES

THE OFFICIAL ORGAN OF THE B.B.C.

Vol. 1. No. 1. [Registered at the G.P.O. as a Newspaper.] EVERY FRIDAY. Two Pence.

OFFICIAL PROGRAMMES OF THE BRITISH BROADCASTING COMPANY.

For the Week Commencing SUNDAY, SEPTEMBER 30th.

LONDON CARDIFF
BIRMINGHAM NEWCASTLE
MANCHESTER GLASGOW

SPECIAL CONTENTS:

LORD GAINFORD'S MESSAGE TO LISTENERS.

P. P. ECKERSLEY ON "SIMULTANEOUS BROADCASTING."

A SONG OF ANCIENT CHINA.

GOSSIP ABOUT ARTISTES.

WIRELESS HUMOUR.

THE "UNCLES'" CORNER.

LETTERS FROM LISTENERS.

WHAT'S IN THE AIR?

By ARTHUR R. BURROWS, Director of Programmes.

HULLO, EVERYONE!

We will now give you *The Radio Times*. The good *new* times. The Bradshaw of Broadcasting.

May you never be late for your favourite wave-train.

Speed 186,000 miles per second; five-hour non-stops.

Family season ticket: First Class, 10s. per year.

* * * *

[*All this, presumably, is "by the way" not "In the Air."*—EDITOR.]

* * * *

So I am instructed to write about programmes and not "talk like an Uncle"!

* * * *

Let me tell you all about our plans.

Wait, though! I—I'm just a little bit uneasy. My predecessor in the broadcasting business made a mistake of this character with painful consequences.

You probably remember the incident.

A Company, with distinguished Directors, having lofty ambitions, established a power-station at Westminster. Despite quite a stirring programme there were no oscillations, owing to Government intervention. The Director (Guido Fawkes) and his colleagues somehow lost their heads, and the long-anticipated report failed to materialize.

When WE broadcast Parliament—and it's bound to happen this century or next—the process will be a more dignified one than that planned in 1605. The fate of the culprits may be another matter.

* * * *

Perhaps, after all, it is by stepping clear of the pitfalls of ancient and modern history that British broadcasting has got so far without any serious mishap. (Touch wood!)

* * * *

Do you know that from November 14th last year until now, with only six out of eight projected stations in operation, and despite opposition from some of the "Big Noises" in the entertainment industry, we have shaken the ether of Great Britain for approximately 8,000 hours and have transmitted roughly 1,700 distinct evening programmes. How this ether-shaking process has been carried through so uninterruptedly is for my unrepentant colleague, Captain Eckersley, to tell (possibly with Morse and reactive obligato). The fact remains that if our plans for the next twelve months go through, even in their present basic form, we shall add to this record 2,500 other distinct programmes, consisting of 16,500 hours of ever-changing musical, dramatic, and instructive entertainment.

Photo] [Foulsham & Banfield.
Mr. ARTHUR R. BURROWS.

* * * *

Two thousand five hundred distinct programmes!

[*Perhaps it IS as well that your comments are inaudible.*]

And some folk pressing for a six-hour day!

* * * *

Have you ever played jigsaw?

At 2, Savoy Hill, London, W.C.2, is the biggest jigsaw puzzle yet invented, railway time-tables *not* excepted. It goes by the name of simultaneous broadcasting, a process which comes into existence so far as our musical programmes are concerned on Monday next, October 1st. For some weeks now the writer and others of the same Department, all in varying states of mental distress, have pored over this latest brain-teaser, trying to coax a refractory twiddly-bit into some time-space for which it was never intended.

(Continued in column 3, page 2)

'The Official Organ of the BBC' was published under contract by George Newnes, with *Tit-Bits* chief Leonard Crocombe as editor. The title was drawn by hand, with the typography based on *John O'London's Weekly* and listings in the style of a theatre programme. The poor paper and letterpress that *Radio Times* stuck with until the 1960s meant that line illustrations reproduced better than photographs. In 1929, one issue devoted eight pages to 'The Art of Etching', an article by James Laver, Keeper of Prints, Drawings and Paintings for the Victoria and Albert Museum from 1938 to 1959.[1] From the 7 January 1937 issue, photogravure television supplements with large photographs were included for readers in the London area. Television broadcasts started in 1936 and carried on until the outbreak of the Second World War.

1 James Laver, *A History of British and American Etching* (London 1929)

BBC/George Newnes
(230 × 280 mm, stapled, 96 pages)

By 1934, *Radio Times*, with sales of 2 million a week, had overtaken *John Bull* as the biggest-selling magazine, a position it held until 1993. Maurice Gorham became the magazine's art editor in 1928 and then editor (1933–41). He ran special issues, many with colour covers, and topics such as 'Woman's Broadcasting' and 'Home' joined the Christmas edition. The 'Humour' cover of a grinning cat was by John Gilroy, best known for his Guinness advertising.

BBC
(167 × 228 mm, stapled, 96 pages)

RADIO TIMES (9 October 1936)

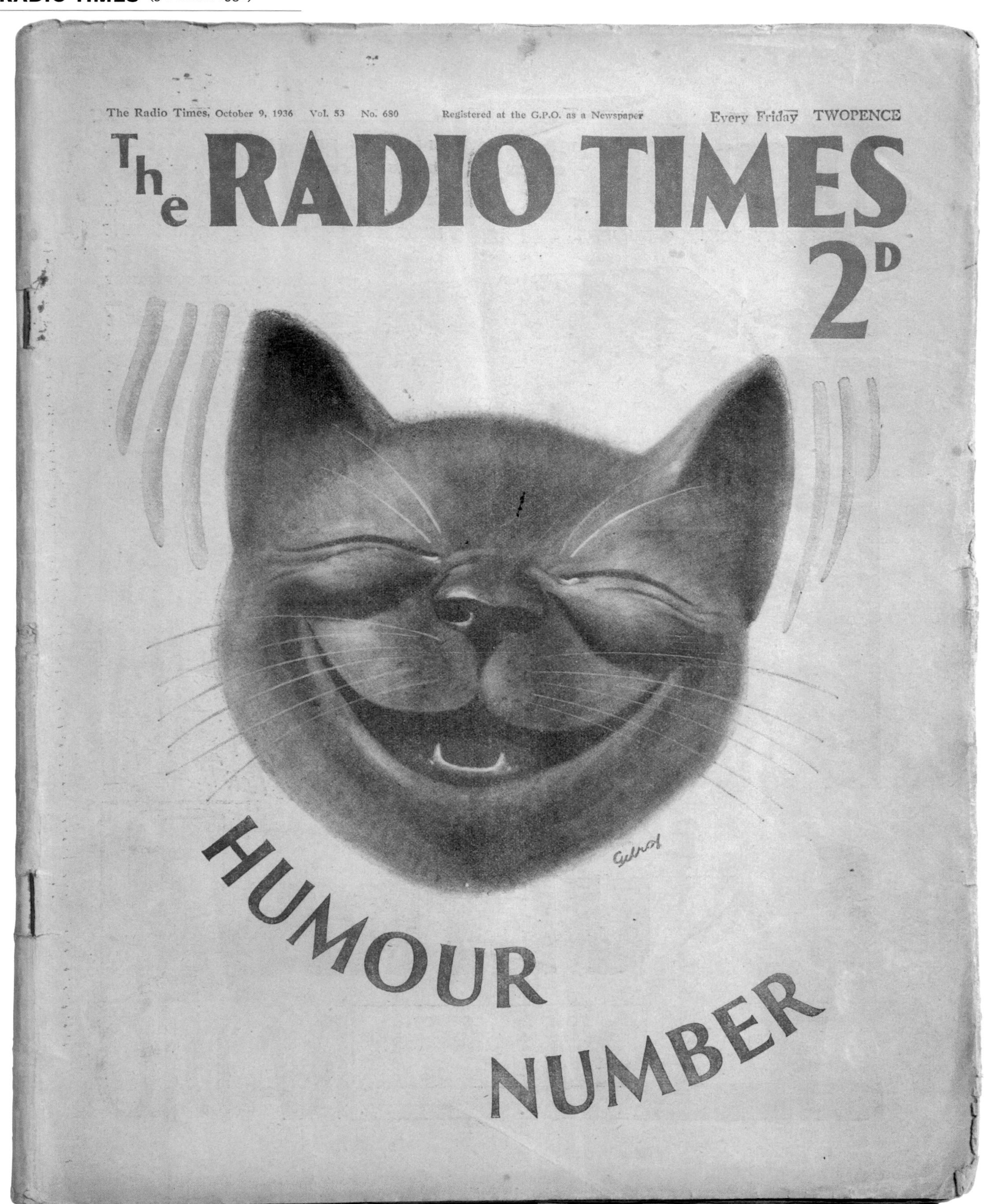
The Radio Times, October 9, 1936 Vol. 53 No. 680 Registered at the G.P.O. as a Newspaper Every Friday TWOPENCE

The RADIO TIMES 2D

HUMOUR NUMBER

PEARSON'S WEEKLY (27 February 1926)

In the 1920s and 1930s, three of the four mass-media weeklies used cheap 2d formats barely distinguishable apart from the colour of their covers – red for *Pearson's Weekly*, pink for *Answers* and green for *Tit-Bits*. Note the pun below the title – 'Is read wherever the map is red', a reference to the colour shown on maps for the British Empire. *Pearson's* relaunched in the mid-1930s as a photo weekly with gravure covers and centre pages, but it lacked the visual power of its rivals and closed at the start of the Second World War, a move that would have allowed C. Arthur Pearson (owned by Newnes) to assign its paper ration to other magazines.

C. Arthur Pearson
(252 × 320 mm, stapled, 32 pages)

ANSWERS (12 July 1930)

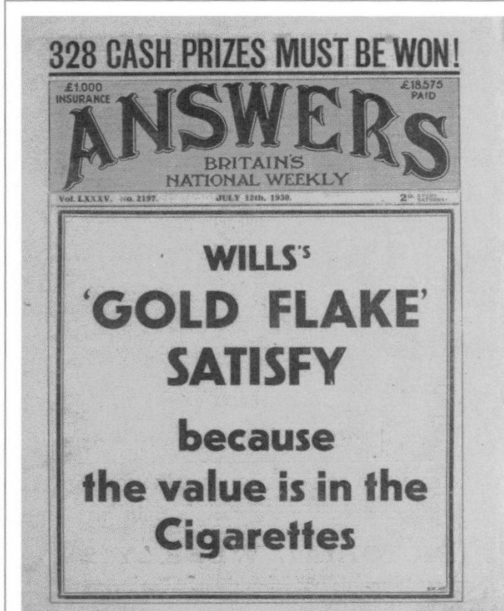

'Britain's National Weekly' also marketed itself as 'the popular journal for home and train', showing the importance of commuting readers. The cover is dominated by advertising and promotions – cash prizes and life insurance. In 1925, *Answers* offered £20 a week for life in a competition that was won by a girl living in Spain. She did not die until 1996, claiming the prize for 71 years.

Hand-drawn type used with the fiction illustration. Every other page ran some kind of competition. There were also lines at the foot of the pages, many promoting features in coming issues.

Amalgamated Press
(252 × 320 mm, stapled, 28 pages)

JOHN BULL (14 December 1935)

JOHN BULL, DECEMBER 14, 1935

B.B.C.'S REPLY TO US — SEE PAGE 11

TWOPENCE.
Vol. LVIII.
1539.

JOHN BULL

"My job and home were on the Brink of DISASTER"

"P.S.: If any other wife ever has the experience that we've been through.."

A once-ailing husband tells his own story of how a miracle of health saved his happy family from ruin

I used to shudder when I read the news of unemployment in the paper. I had a good job and prayed I'd never lose it. But one can never tell. How near I came to disaster, and to what depths of despair I dragged my wife and myself, only she and I know.

We were married shortly after the war. My post in the bank paid a good salary, and after our three children came we moved to Surrey, paying for our home bit by bit. Time rolled happily by—our lives seemed consummate.

Clouds gather

That was two years ago. Then my health failed. I became irritable, tired, down in the dumps. I had been wounded in the war, and put down my condition to this old trouble. Worse yet, my work suffered. I was slowing up, often had to work overtime to finish the day's assignment. And I made several stupid mistakes in balance sheets.

One day the manager said, "Smith, you are next in the line for promotion. But I am moving one of your juniors over your head. Your work has not been up to standard for many months. You are a sick man. I suggest," he continued, "that you take an extended holiday until you are fit again." I felt faint, but managed to protest that I was perfectly fit. What if I lost my job, our home!

I grasp at a straw

That same day I lunched with Gregson, my closest friend at the bank, and poured out my whole miserable story to him. What he told me gave me back my health and saved our home.

"Hazel and I lost our first child at birth," he said, "and I nearly lost her, too. After the ordeal, she wasted away: doctor said she was suffering from nervous disorder and anæmia, and recommended Wincarnis. He explained that Wincarnis is a fine tonic wine that builds and restores strong new red corpuscles in the blood. It contains, he said, beef extract, and the benefits of rich, red wine from sunny Spain. By the time she had taken three bottles, I thought a miracle had taken place. She was her normal, lively self again." I drank in Gregson's words thirstily. Maybe his words would be my salvation.

I am saved

I took Wincarnis home with me that very night. I drank a glass before dinner. It tasted good. It seemed to perk up my appetite and I ate a good meal. My nerves had settled and I slept better than for months. I continued my Wincarnis and in several weeks I felt like a man twenty years younger. What was wrong with me may be wrong with thousands of hard-working men—just run-down and tired-out, a weakened and anæmic condition of the blood.

Helen Writes

My wife, Helen, is by my side, and she wants to add a few words. Here they are:—"I knew that John was ill. I only wish I'd known of Wincarnis sooner. If any other wife should experience what we've been through, I hope these words may catch her eye and be the means of restoring health and happiness to other homes than ours."

This story was suggested by testimonials in our files. Names and places have been altered out of courtesy to our friends who have been kind enough to write to us about their wonderful experiences with Wincarnis.

Give Wincarnis a trial; it's free

Thousands of men, as well as women, suffer from some form of debility or other. If your nerves jangle easily; if your head aches often and nervous pains shoot through your body; if you lack appetite, pep and zest for life, give Wincarnis a trial. Give the combined benefits of the beef, malt, and rich red wine in this fine tonic the chance to build up strong red corpuscles in your blood. You're only as young as your blood; young blood is the sap of life. Wincarnis is sold at all wine merchants, licensed chemists and grocers, two sizes, 5/6d. and 3/3d.

POST THIS COUPON FOR FREE SAMPLE

To: Coleman & Co., Ltd., Dept. 5-R, Wincarnis Works, Norwich.

I enclose 4½d. in stamps. Please send me a free sample of Wincarnis.

NAME ....

ADDRESS ....

....

The weekly exception, in terms of format, was the idiosyncratic *John Bull*, which used a larger format and better paper than its rivals. However, the cover is dominated by advertising and the editorial matter did not begin until page 9.

Newspaper-style layouts with crude picture cut-outs support this centre-spread campaigning article on road safety. Transport minister Leslie Hore-Belisha is shown on one of the pedestrian crossings introduced in 1934.

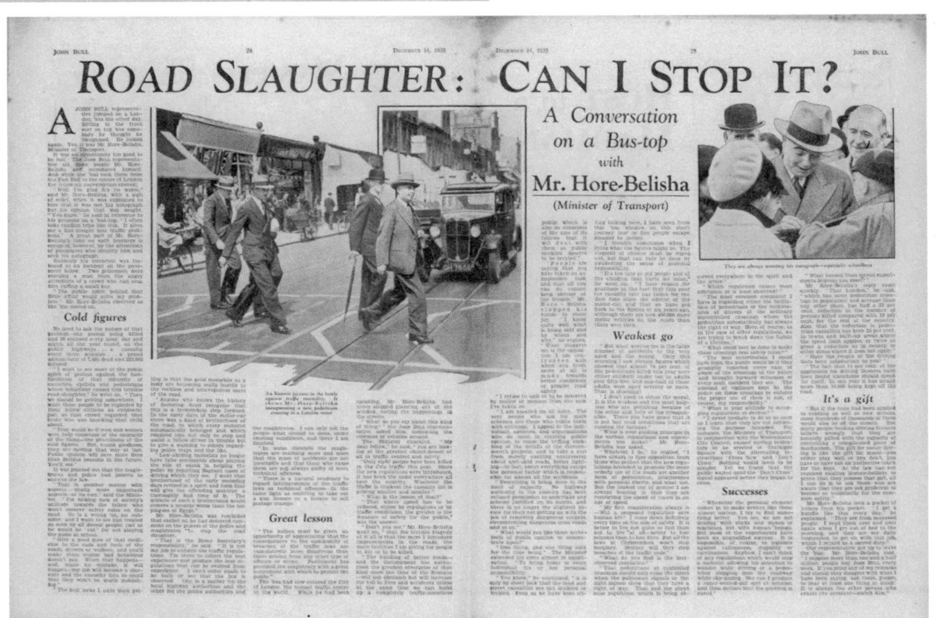

ROAD SLAUGHTER: CAN I STOP IT?

A Conversation on a Bus-top with **Mr. Hore-Belisha** (*Minister of Transport*)

Cold figures

Great lesson

Weakest go

It's a gift

Successes

Odhams Press
(270 × 360 mm, stapled, 48 pages)

VOGUE (early May 1926)

Eduardo Benito was one of a group of illustrators Condé Nast gained access to when he took over the pioneering French fashion magazine *La Gazette du Bon Ton*. Benito produced covers for *Vogue* and *Vanity Fair* until the war. This issue included photographs by Maurice Beck and Helen Macgregor, who were chief photographers for British *Vogue*. Members of staff were not credited.

Condé Nast
(230 × 310 mm, perfect bound, 84 pages)

VOGUE (19 October 1927)

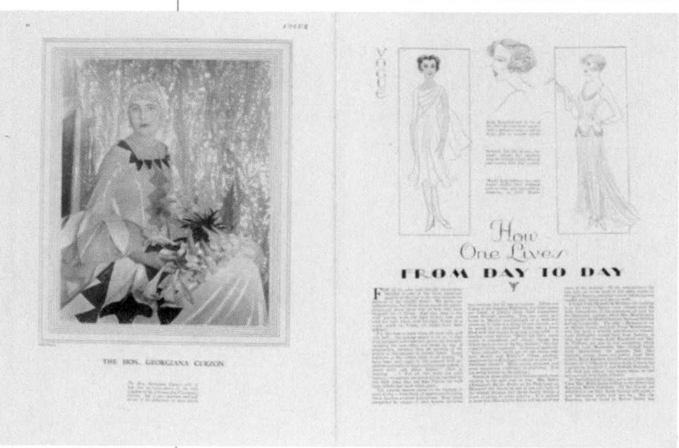

Vogue was still structured to be bound into volumes, so the first editorial was not seen until page 41 and the adverts began again on page 81. The photograph on the left is of Georgiana Curzon and is one of two portraits in the issue by Cecil Beaton, who started working at *Vogue* the year this edition was published. This was the start of the era of the 'bright young things', who were documented by Beaton. The links between Beaton, George Hoyningen-Huene, photographer for French *Vogue*, and Horst (Paul Albert Bohrmann) in the US sparked the sophisticated transatlantic style of the 1930s. Horst's breakthrough in British *Vogue* was in the 30 March 1932 issue, which carried his fashion studies and a portrait of the daughter of Sir James Dunn, a patron of Surrealism.

Condé Nast
(247 × 320 mm, perfect bound, 100 pages)

VOGUE (20 July 1932)

This was the magazine's first photographic cover, taken by Edward Steichen, later director of photography at New York's Museum of Modern Art. The covers reverted to illustration for most of the next decade. Steichen worked for Condé Nast from 1923 to 1938. Nast is said to have told him: 'Every woman [Baron] de Meyer photographs looks like a model. You make every model look like a woman.'

Condé Nast
(240 × 315 mm, perfect bound)

THE SKETCH (29 April 1936)

No. 2257.—Vol. CLXXIV. WEDNESDAY, APRIL 29, 1936. ONE SHILLING.

PHOTOGRAPH BY ANGUS MCBEAN.

IVOR NOVELLO *plays Lord George Hell, the wicked Regency buck, in the stage version of "The Happy Hypocrite," at His Majesty's, and achieves an alarmingly dissolute countenance by means of elaborate make-up. Lord George Hell, as everyone knows, wore a beautiful mask in order to win the love of an innocent girl, and, eventually, his features took the mould of the mask. This mask is a reproduction of Ivor Novello's own features.*

LORD GEORGE HELL AND HIS HEAVENLY MASK—IN "THE HAPPY HYPOCRITE."

The *Sketch*, *Bystander* and *Tatler* commissioned photographic prints of strongly lit subjects that were well processed for reproduction. Max Beerbohm's short story 'The Happy Hypocrite' first appeared in the *Yellow Book* in 1897 and was produced as a play in 1936 starring Ivor Novello and Vivien Leigh. This *Sketch* cover shows Novello as the play's anti-hero George Hell holding a mask made by Angus McBean. The mask-maker turned to 'surrealized' photography and his images from the play really made a mark.

Illustrated London News and Sketch Ltd
(240 × 315 mm, stapled, 108 pages)

'All five of the weekly "shinies" which devoted space to the theatre – *The Sketch*, *Tatler*, *Bystander*, *Illustrated London News* and *Britannia and Eve* [actually a monthly] – carried a properly credited McBean photograph from the show as a frontispiece. The veteran publicity man [William 'Popie' Macqueen Pope] believed, correctly, that this had never been achieved by any West End show before.'[1] McBean's pictures of Leigh helped her secure the role of Scarlett O'Hara in *Gone with the Wind*. Editor Stefan Lorant championed McBean in both *Lilliput* and *Picture Post*. The latter's issue of 17 February 1940 commissioned a cover article about taking a portrait of Diana Churchill, with the actress's head lying on a floor under a chair.[2] McBean also shot the cover for the Beatles' *Please Please Me*.[3]

1 Adrian Woodhouse, 'Angus McBean: Face-maker' (London 2006), p. 87
2 V&A: S.4191–2013
3 V&A: E.2101:1–1992

BRITANNIA (28 September 1928)

BRITANNIA

Miss Britannia's Present from Yarmouth Conference

THE FLARE of THE TORCHES

By GILBERT FRANKAU

SOFT ROES OR HARD FACTS

ZERO

Gilbert Frankau, a popular novelist, 'directed' this short-lived right-wing weekly, which covered politics, foreign affairs, technology, women's fashion and sport. Most of the issue consisted of advertising on the left pages and editorial matter on the right. It later merged with the woman's monthly *Eve* to form *Britannia and Eve*. The cover showed a spot-red silhouette of Britannia in a similar pose to that on a penny coin of the time. The frontispiece cartoon by Brien shown here has a youthful Britannia spearing Conservative prime minister Stanley Baldwin at the party's conference in Great Yarmouth while other political fish flounder. Liberal leader David Lloyd George is portrayed as a crab. The issues carried an advert for the Fultograph, a device for receiving pictures transmitted by the BBC over the radio. Another half-page advert for Wright's Coal Tar Soap offered a first prize of a Morris Oxford car in a crossword competition.

Gilbert Frankau's 'The Flare of the Torches' column, with the phrase in Greek on the opening spread, was expected to shed light on topical debate. The page was set in 9 on 9½ point Century across 16 picas. Illustrated logos for features were used throughout the issue.

British National Newspapers
(246 × 355 mm, stapled, 100 pages)

EVERYMAN (15 September 1933)

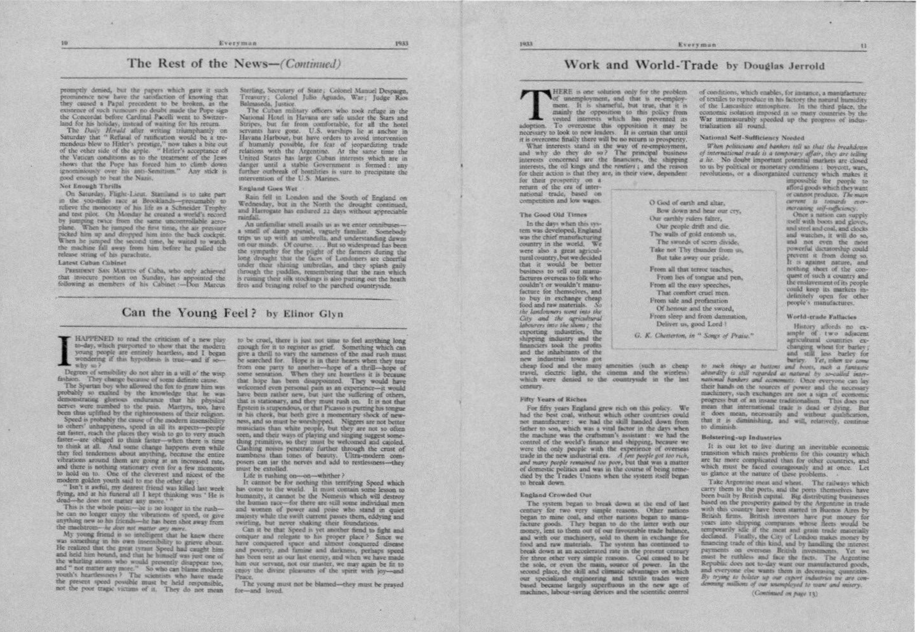
The Rest of the News—(*Continued*)

Can the Young Feel? by Elinor Glyn

Work and World-Trade by Douglas Jerrold

Everyman

THE WORLD NEWS WEEKLY

Trial Issue | Price Twopence | Friday, September 15th, 1933

Contributors this week: | Edited by F. Yeats-Brown

Elinor Glyn | André Maurois | Douglas Jerrold

Trial Issue—Not for Publication

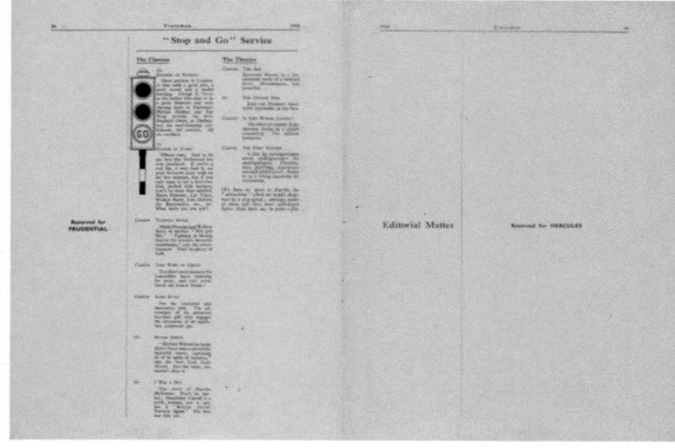
"Stop and Go" Service

Reserved for PRUDENTIAL

Editorial Matter

Reserved for HERCULES

This was a trial issue of 'The World News Weekly' aimed at advertisers to promote the relaunch of a weekly arts review founded in 1929, so most of the pages were not complete. The dummy cover has red and blue spot colour frames. Note the graphic device for the price – the front and back of a 1933 penny; this is one of the rarest British coins, because only seven were made. Editor Francis Yeats-Brown said the issue was designed to hold 30,000 words and be read in an hour. Contributor Elinor Glyn was one of the most famous authors and screenwriters of the day, having coined the term 'It girl' to describe Hollywood actress Clara Bow.

A typical two-column spread with the headlines and bylines framed within rules. The page was set in 10 on 10½ point Plantin across 21 picas.

A partly made-up spread with advertising space reserved for the Prudential insurance company and – probably – Hercules bicycles (two-thirds, outside right page). The review page uses the metaphor of the traffic light, a relatively new development, with films and plays marked as 'Go' or 'Caution'.

Everyman Publications
(245 × 246 mm, stapled, 36 pages)

CAVALCADE (7 August 1937)

Two news magazines were launched in February 1936: *News Review* (Cosmopolitan Press) and *Cavalcade*. The former adopted the US cover design model popularized by *Time* (which introduced its red border in 1927, having experimented with red and green strips down the left side). *Cavalcade* was printed gravure by Sun Engraving. It ran pages promoting the concept of advertising: 'The manufacturer knows that his product must be good, before he can advertise ... That is why advertised goods are the best and cheapest. Study the advertisements in this paper therefore, and remember that Advertised Goods have got to be good.' The magazine set out its editorial philosophy on the cover: 'accurate, brisk, complete'. The cover photograph of Chili Bouchier, an early sex symbol on the silver screen, is not credited and is probably a publicity shot. Inside, the magazine averages two pictures a page, though the largest was 110 × 140 mm. This issue claimed an audited net sale of 50,000 copies a week. In March 1938, *Cavalcade* relaunched as a tabloid weekly on newsprint under the auspices of Illustrated Publications; it launched again after the war as the *New Cavalcade* but, like *News Review*, closed in 1957.

A regular feature was a centre-spread map of the world with captions summarizing international news.

News Periodicals
(215 × 280 mm, stapled, 48 pages)

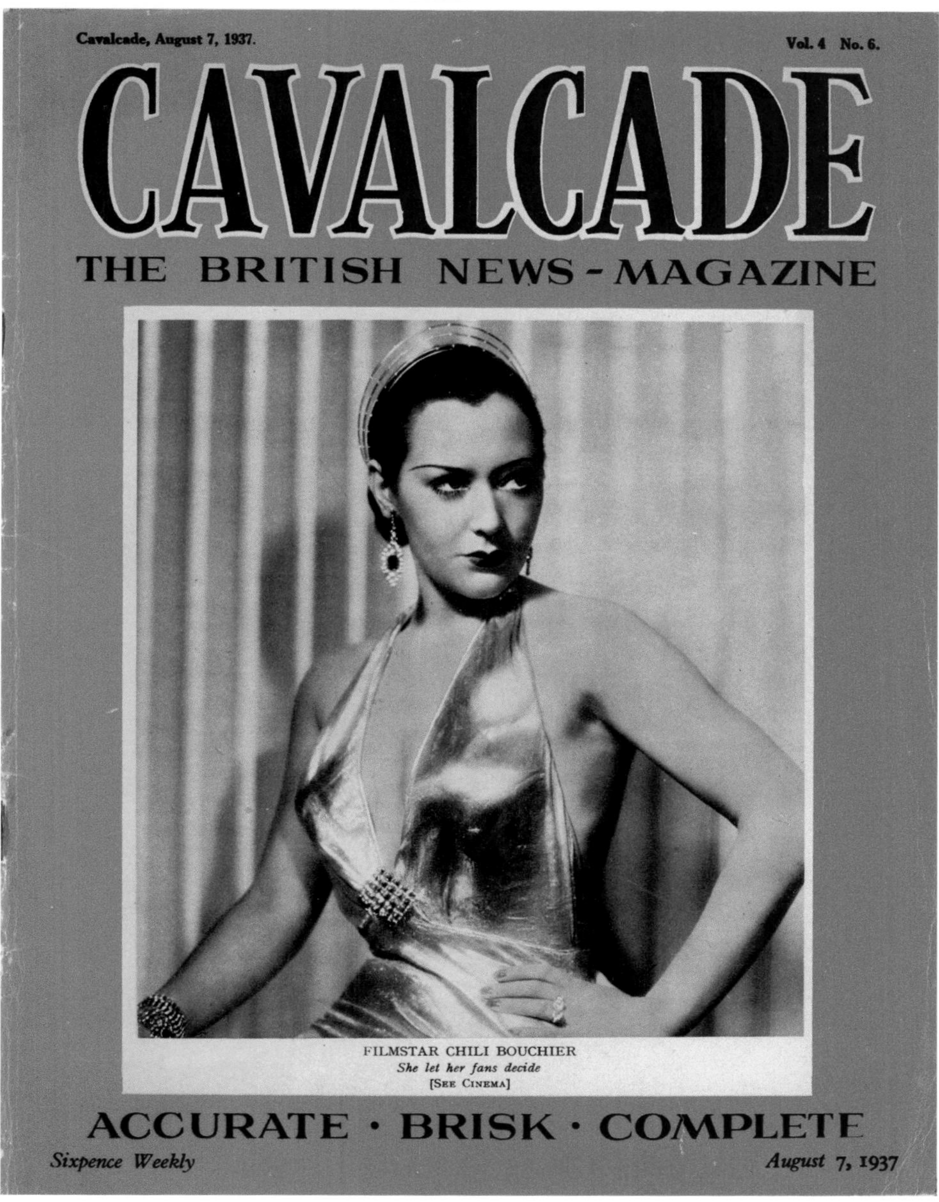

Cavalcade, August 7, 1937.
Vol. 4 No. 6.
CAVALCADE
THE BRITISH NEWS-MAGAZINE
FILMSTAR CHILI BOUCHIER
She let her fans decide
[See Cinema]
ACCURATE · BRISK · COMPLETE
Sixpence Weekly
August 7, 1937

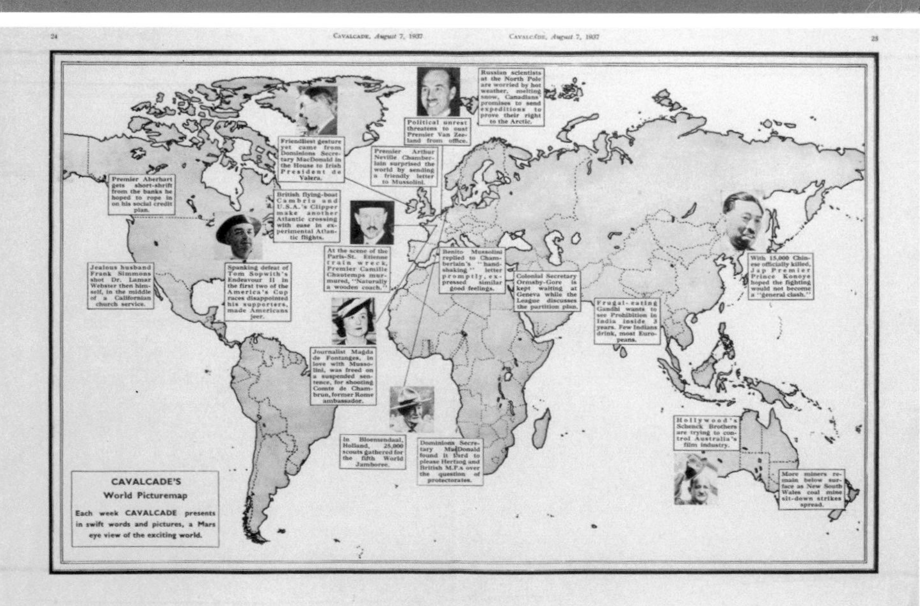

PICTORIAL WEEKLY (2 December 1933)

Pictorial Weekly switched from letterpress to a larger format and gravure two-colour printing for this cover. It was in the vanguard of the photo-led weeklies and was printed on Amalgamated's own presses.

Pictorial Weekly displays many complex layout techniques in these spreads, with a sweeping layout for 'Can Trenchard Do It?' The move to gravure means images can be printed across the central gutter.

Amalgamated Press
(215 × 280 mm, stapled, 48 pages)

WEEKLY ILLUSTRATED (26 September 1936)

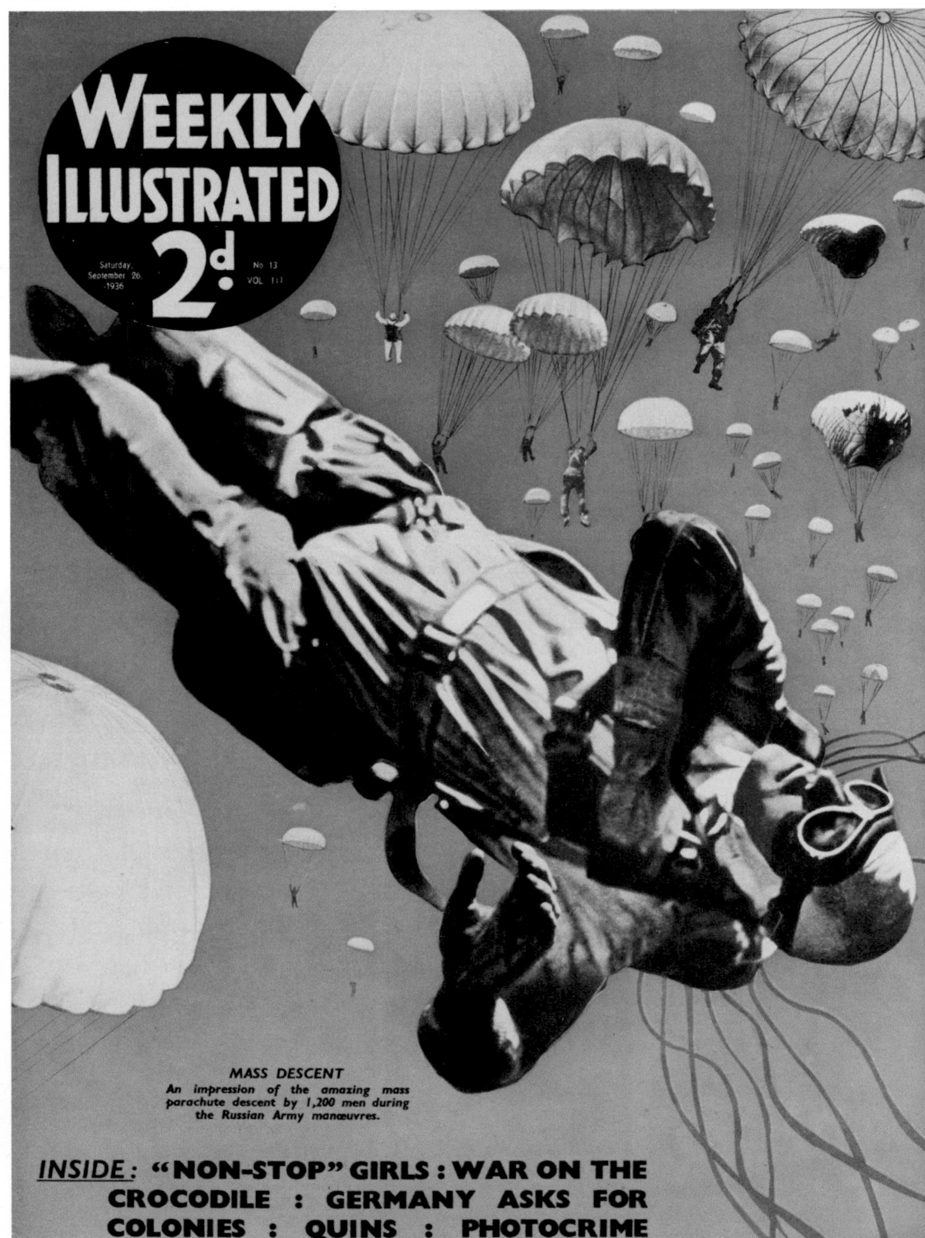

WEEKLY ILLUSTRATED
2d
Saturday, September 26, 1936
No 13 VOL III
MASS DESCENT
An impression of the amazing mass parachute descent by 1,200 men during the Russian Army manœuvres.
INSIDE: "NON-STOP" GIRLS : WAR ON THE CROCODILE : GERMANY ASKS FOR COLONIES : QUINS : PHOTOCRIME

Weekly Illustrated was a relaunch of a Victorian magazine, *Clarion*, by Hungarian-born editor Stefan Lorant, who had fled Hitler's Germany. Lorant had worked on the left-wing weekly *AIZ* (*Arbeiter-Illustrierte-Zeitung*) and brought German techniques – and photographers – to the UK. Tom Hopkinson, a freelance journalist, joined the magazine before Lorant left at the end of the year to publish his book *I was Hitler's Prisoner*, and then founded *Lilliput*; the two men were eventually reunited on *Picture Post*. George Brassai, Tim Gidal and Bill Brandt[1] were among the photographers who contributed to *Weekly Illustrated*. Here, a dramatic cover has been assembled from a blurry photograph of Russian paratroopers using spot-colour background and photomontage – a technique developed as an art form by both the Dada movement in Berlin and the Russian Constructivists.

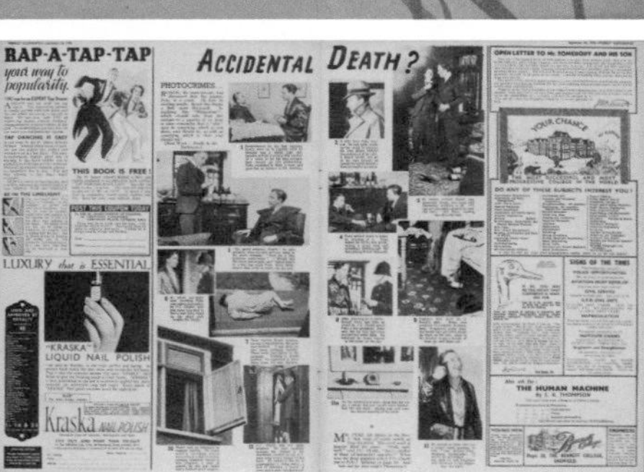

Mileson Horton developed the 'Photocrime' feature, in which readers had to solve a mystery through spotting clues in the photographs. It was taken up as a BBC television series in 1938 and again when the service resumed after the war. Tom Hopkinson also contributed.

1 V&A: PH.84–1978

Odhams Press
(290 × 400 mm, stapled, 28 pages)

WEEKLY ILLUSTRATED (12 December 1936)

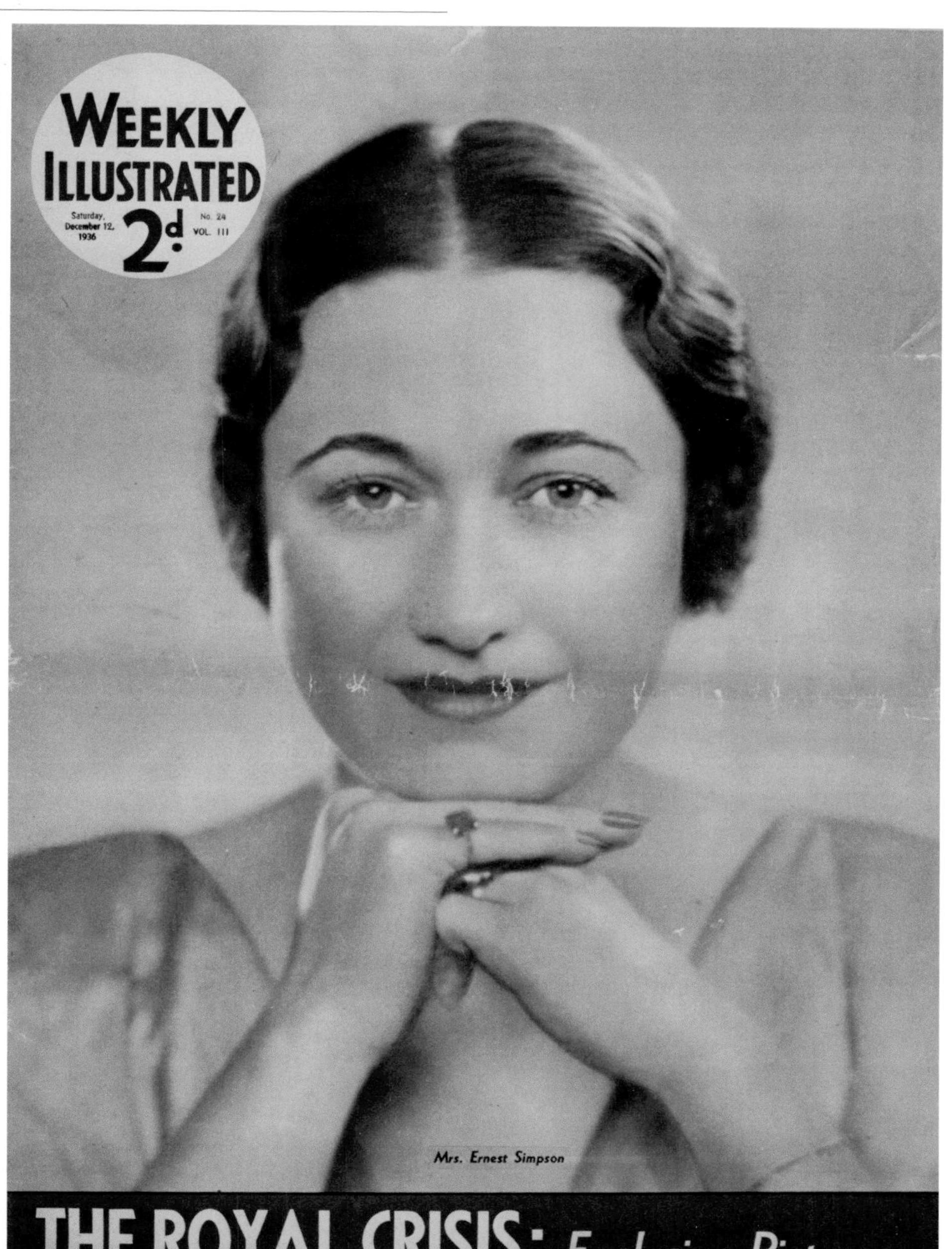

Ten pages, as well as full-page pictures on front and back covers, were devoted to the abdication crisis caused by Edward VIII's desire to marry divorcee Wallis Simpson. None of the images were credited.

Odhams Press
(292 × 404 mm, stapled, 28 pages)

WEEKLY ILLUSTRATED (1 December 1934)

Duotone – two-colour printing – adds night-time drama to this spread of pictures by George Brassai, whose book *Paris de Nuit* (*Paris by Night*) was published in 1933.

Odhams Press
(298 × 404 mm, stapled, 28 pages)

LILLIPUT (November 1946)

In 1937, Stefan Lorant set up his own publishing company with backing from friends in order to launch *Lilliput*, a pocket-format monthly with an anti-totalitarian stance. Up until September 1949 the covers were painted by Walter Trier, who had come to Britain from Germany in 1936. They always featured a man, a woman and a dog. The first of Ronald Searle's St Trinian's cartoons was published in the magazine and he also did several covers, the first in December 1949, just after Trier's run ended.

Pocket Publications
(137 × 196 mm, stapled, 124 pages)

From the start, *Lilliput* ran photo-essays by such photographers as Bill Brandt over several pages. It also ran 'juxtapositions', picture comparisons where two photographs were printed on opposite pages with captions that drew comparisons. In 1940, Lorant compiled many of these in *101 Best Picture Comparisons from Lilliput: Or Chamberlain and the Beautiful Llama*.[1] The book's introduction describes how a picture of Rockefeller as a poor old man and another of a happy peasant triggered the idea for the first issue: 'We found that what people liked most in the magazine were just these few photographic jokes.' The 'idea behind the idea' became to debunk, 'to show how stupid pomposity, how silly self-importance is'. Note the eclectic sources for the photographs in this example – New York (left) and Prague (right).

1 National Art Library General Collection 602.AM.0001

PICTURE POST (1 October 1938)

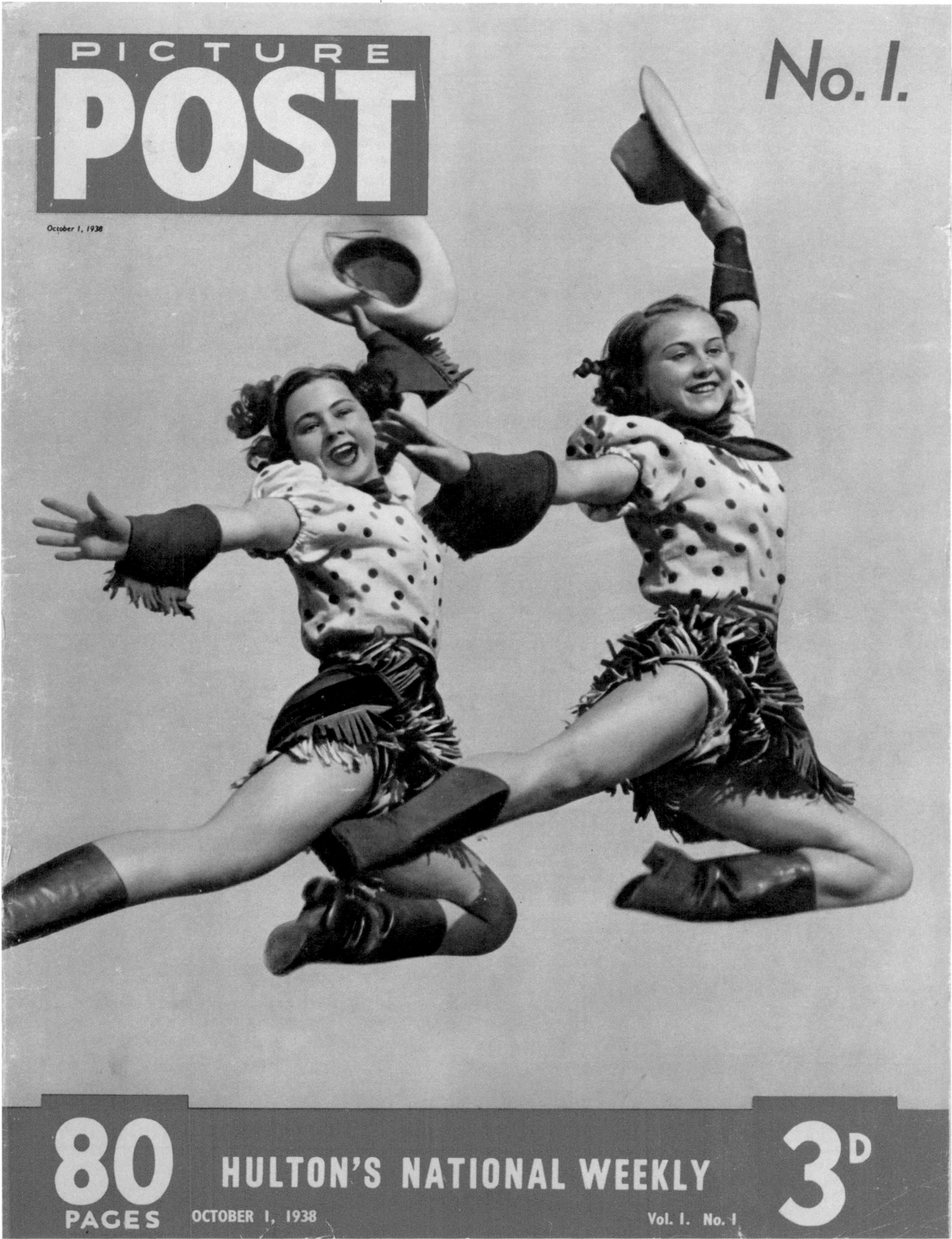

Picture Post developed the idea of the photomagazine and was a spectacular success from the start, with a weekly circulation topping 1.6 million at its height. Sir Edward Hulton bought up Stefan Lorant's *Lilliput* to secure his services and Tom Hopkinson joined him. Hopkinson founded the Centre for Journalism Studies at Cardiff University in 1970. The cover photograph of the dancers jumping was repeated for the last issue (1 June 1957).

Hulton
(262 × 348 mm, stapled, 80 pages)

INDUSTRIAL ARTS (Spring 1936)

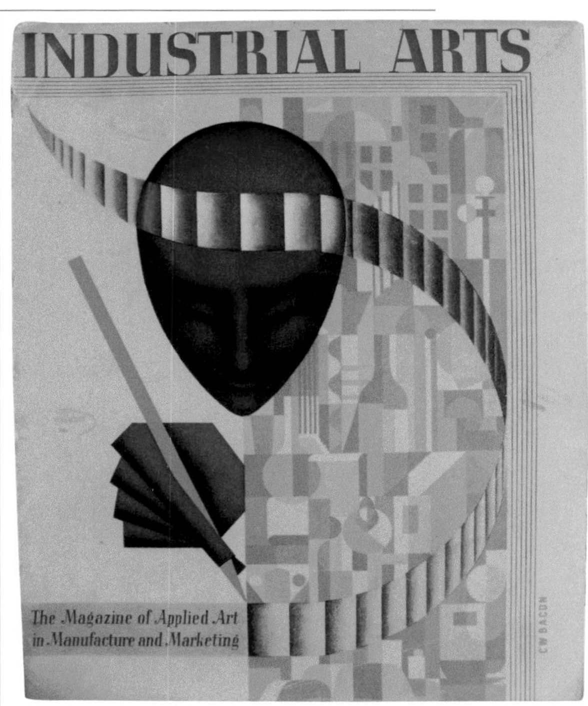

This 'Magazine of Applied Art in Manufacture and Marketing' was launched with the backing of Edward Hunter, co-founder of Sun Engraving (where the magazine was printed). It ran for only four issues, possibly because Odhams opened its own printing plant in Watford using the Speedry Gravure Process for colour printing. Not only was this competition for Sun, but Odhams had been a big customer. *Industrial Arts* set out to improve the standard of design in industry – Sun itself employed Max Gill (brother of Eric), who drew the Wonderground map of the London Underground, to design its brochures around this time. Alongside Hunter on its board were Joseph Emberton, the modernist architect; David Greenhill, who developed rotary high-speed colour printing for Sun Engraving in 1926; L.D. Greenhill, Sun Engraving manager; Eileen Hunter, Edward Hunter's eldest daughter and a fabric designer; Bernard E. Jones (owner of the publishing company); and Tom Purvis, graphic artist. At the front of the first issue was a statue by Alexander Archipenko under the heading 'Let Beauty Abound'. The magazine was something of a showcase for Sun Engraving, using several papers, metallic ink and double-gatefold pages. Sun would print Arthur Szyk's *Haggadah*, regarded as one of the most beautiful books ever produced, in 1940. The cover of this issue was by Cyril Bacon, who had started producing scraperboard images for the *Radio Times* in 1935 and carried on doing so until 1968. The next two covers were by Tom Purvis and Austin Cooper, the poster artist, six of whose works were exhibited in the V&A's 1931 international poster exhibition and who supplied the catalogue cover.

This colour spread of English furnishing fabrics illustrated an article by Eileen Hunter. The issues mixed sans and serif types for the text, mostly across two columns with wide margins and gutters. László Moholy-Nagy also wrote for this issue.

Bernard Jones Publications
(250 × 308 mm, 92 pages)

ILLUSTRATION (*c.*1919)

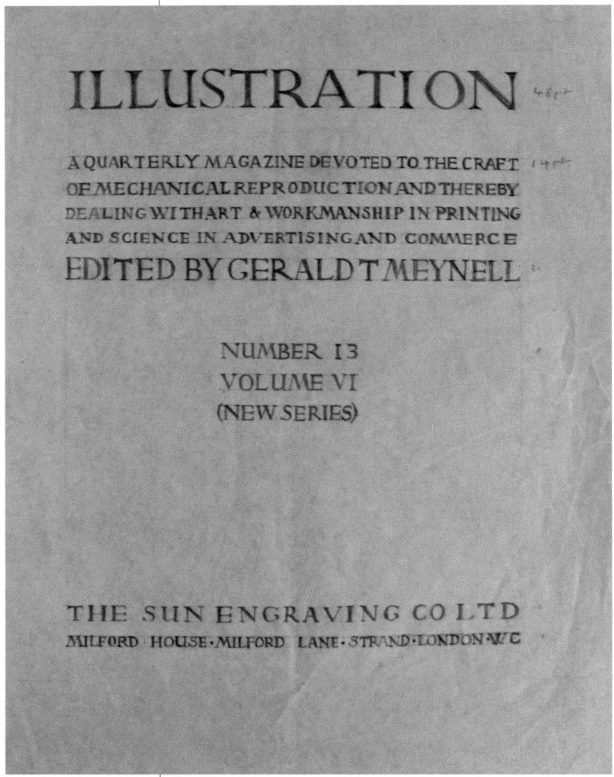

ILLUSTRATION

A QUARTERLY MAGAZINE DEVOTED TO THE CRAFT OF MECHANICAL REPRODUCTION AND THEREBY DEALING WITH ART & WORKMANSHIP IN PRINTING AND SCIENCE IN ADVERTISING AND COMMERCE

EDITED BY GERALD T MEYNELL

NUMBER 13
VOLUME VI
(NEW SERIES)

THE SUN ENGRAVING CO LTD
MILFORD HOUSE·MILFORD LANE·STRAND·LONDON W C

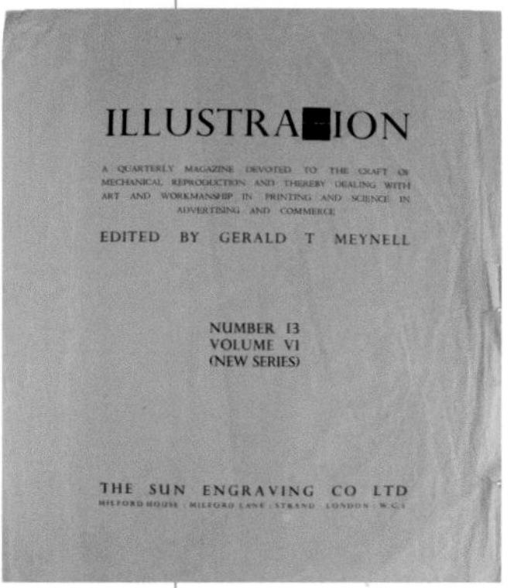

ILLUSTRA■ION

EDITED BY GERALD T MEYNELL

NUMBER 13
VOLUME VI
(NEW SERIES)

THE SUN ENGRAVING CO LTD

This title page is from *Illustration*, forerunner of Sun Engraving's *Industrial Arts*. The type was set out by Edward Johnston, one of the most influential practitioners of lettering and calligraphy, who designed the sans-serif alphabet for the London Underground and taught Eric Gill.[1] Ruari McLean has credited Johnston as a vital influence on Jan Tschichold, saying the German designer and author of *Die Neue Typographie* had studied Johnston's textbooks, in particular *Writing and Illuminating and Lettering* since the age of 15.[2] Another German typographer, Hermann Zapf, taught himself calligraphy using Johnston's books and was honorary president of the Edward Johnston Foundation. Shown above the magazine page is the hand-drawn lettering by Johnston (held by the St Bride Printing Library). The National Art Library holds the manuscript of Johnston's *Writing and Illuminating*, as well as working papers and diaries.

1 V&A: E.48–1936

2 Ruari McLean, 'Jan Tschichold' in *The Penrose Annual*, vol. 63 (1970), p. 89

Bernard Jones Publications
(250 × 308 mm, 92 pages)

INDUSTRIAL ARTS (Spring 1936)

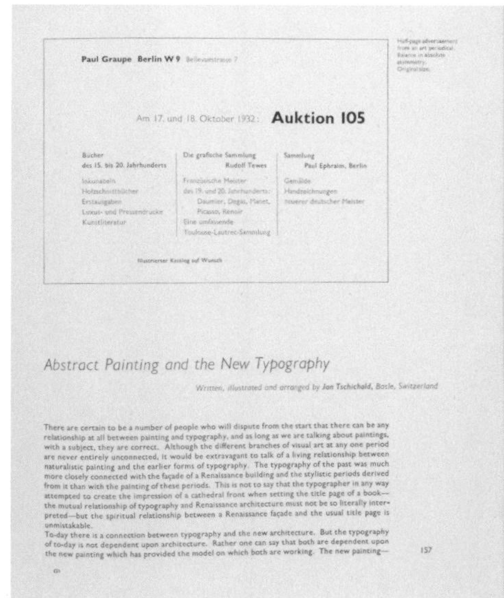

Paul Graupe Berlin W 9

Am 17. und 18. Oktober 1932: **Auktion 105**

Abstract Painting and the New Typography

Written, illustrated and arranged by **Jan Tschichold**, *Basle, Switzerland*

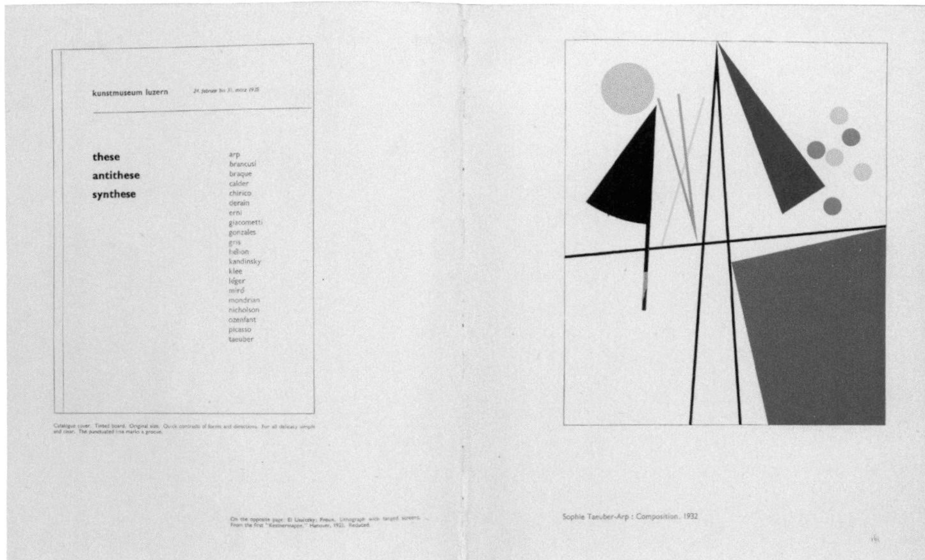

kunstmuseum luzern

these
antithese
synthese

arp
brancusi
braque
calder
chirico
derain
ernst
giacometti
gonzales
gris
hélion
kandinsky
klee
léger
miró
mondrian
nicholson
ozenfant
picasso
taeuber

Sophie Taeuber-Arp : Composition. 1932

This eight-page article, 'Abstract Painting and the New Typography', was written, illustrated and arranged by Jan Tschichold, giving the German typographer an unusual level of control over its presentation. Tschichold visited England in 1935 and 1937–8 as a guest of Lund Humphries and designed *The Penrose Annual*, in 1938 and again in 1947–9, when he worked with Ruari McLean at Penguin. Eric Gill also wrote for this issue.

Bernard Jones Publications
(250 × 308 mm, 92 pages)

INDUSTRIAL ARTS (Autumn 1936)

TOWARDS A UNIVERSAL TYPE

HERBERT BAYER

Neue Erdölbohrung
Geknotete Schnüre
Frühling in der Sch
LUGANO GENF LUZ
Banken
Nachtleben
Hamburger Sender
SETZMASCHINEN

The opening spread of a seven-page article, 'Towards a Universal Type', by Herbert Bayer concludes: 'In England the most familiar type of this order [sans serif] is commonly known as "Gill-Sans", after the name of its designer, Eric Gill. Sans-serif type is the child of our period. It is in complete harmony with other visible forms and phenomena of modern life. We welcome it as our most modern type.' Bayer studied at the Bauhaus until 1928, when he became art director at *Vogue*'s office in Berlin. He fled Germany for the US in 1937. Other contributors in this issue included the French-born American industrial designer Raymond Loewy.

Bernard Jones Publications
(250 × 308 mm, 92 pages)

INDUSTRIAL ARTS (Winter 1936)

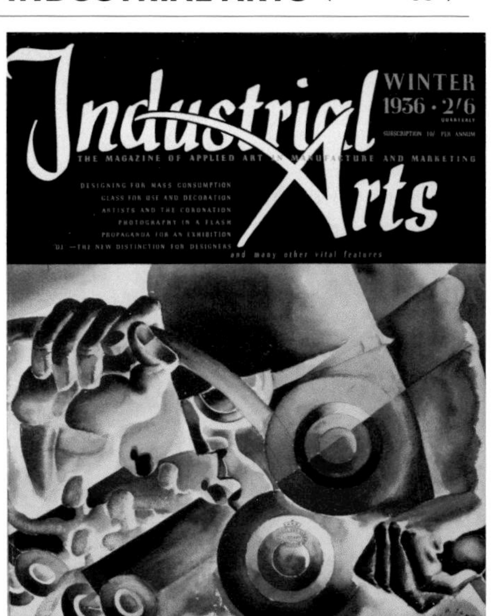

The cover is by R.W. James. The issue included an article by Sir Henry McMahon about the new Designer for Industry award, which would become the Royal Designer for Industry, from the Royal Society of Arts. Among the 10 recipients were Tom Purvis, Eric Gill, J.H. Mason, Fred Taylor and E. McKnight Kauffer. Purvis was a member of the Society of Industrial Artists, which lobbied for better training for graphic designers in industry.

Bernard Jones Publications
(250 × 308 mm, 92 pages)

ARTIST (January 1933)

The cover price of 2s reflects the cost of heavy, coated paper, a short run and colour printing. Many of the adverts were for commercial drawing schools – including correspondence courses – for people looking to draw for newspapers and magazines.

The headlines and titles on magazines were still drawn by hand at this time, demanding original thinking and fast throughput week after week. This article on lettering and layout was by Cecil Wade, author of *Modern Lettering from A to Z* (1932)[1] and one of the most influential lettering artists and typographers of his generation. Two Letraset faces released in 2000, Collins and Comedy, were inspired by Wade and developed by Dave Farey and Richard Dawson. Wade recommended a Joseph Gillott No. 303 fine steel pen for copperplate writing. Elsewhere, an article by Balliol Salmon discussed fiction illustration using Russian charcoal, and showed drawings he had done for *Woman's Journal*. Salmon also drew for the *Graphic* and opened his own drawing school.

1 National Art Library General Collection G.29.EE.41

The Artist Publishing Company
(270 × 328 mm, stapled, 40 pages)

PRACTICAL MOTORIST (19 May 1934)

The second issue of this letterpress weekly claimed to have sold 'over 150,000 copies of No. 1'. Such claims are dubious because the magazine will have gone to press while the first issue was still on sale, so unsold copies were yet to have been returned to the publisher. Spot red was used to frame the title and cover image, with a strip of advertising below. The issues were liberally illustrated with small photographs of cars and diagrams explaining car maintenance and technology.

The only byline in the magazine was for the editor, F.W. Camm, but 'Eve's Driving Mirror' was by 'Cylinda'. Cutaway drawings quickly became an established part of both motoring and aircraft magazines.

George Newnes
(210 × 282 mm, stapled, 60 pages)

FLYING (July 1939)

This cutaway drawing of a Handley Page Hampden was by James H.Stevens Jr. The drawing is self-contained, with its own captions and title; areas are left for typesetting in boxes. Early cutaways were done for the cycling press; Edward Iliffe's *Cyclist* (Iliffe Press) and Edmund Dangerfield's *Cycling* (Temple Press) used them to show technical advancements.[1] Techniques developed as Iliffe Press launched *Autocar* and *Motorcycle*, while Temple competed with the *Aeroplane*. The artists used pen and ink on art board, though some drew on linen – which explains why some lines look slightly jagged on close inspection.

1 Science Museum, *Beneath the Skin: A History of Aviation Cutaway Drawings from Flight International* (London 1998)

George Newnes
(242 × 304 mm, stapled, 32 pages)

SUPERMAN (March 1939)

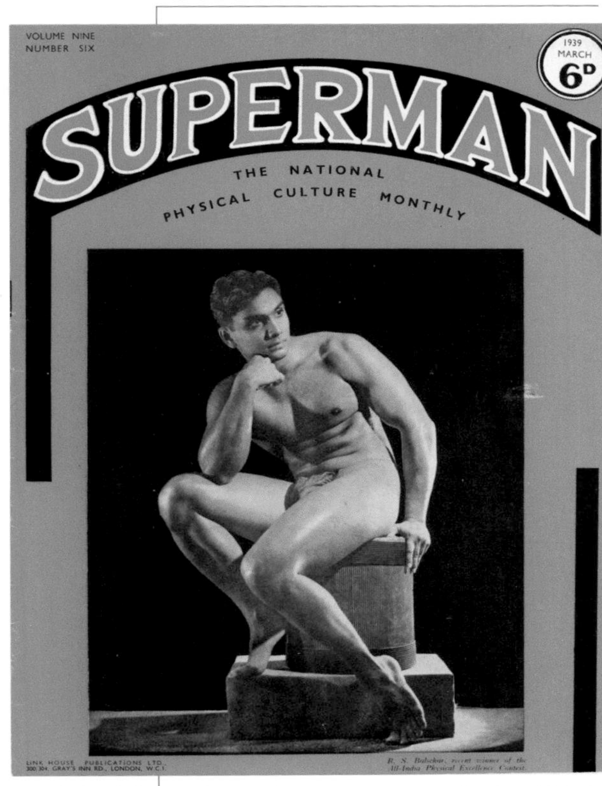

FLIGHT (24 May 1945)

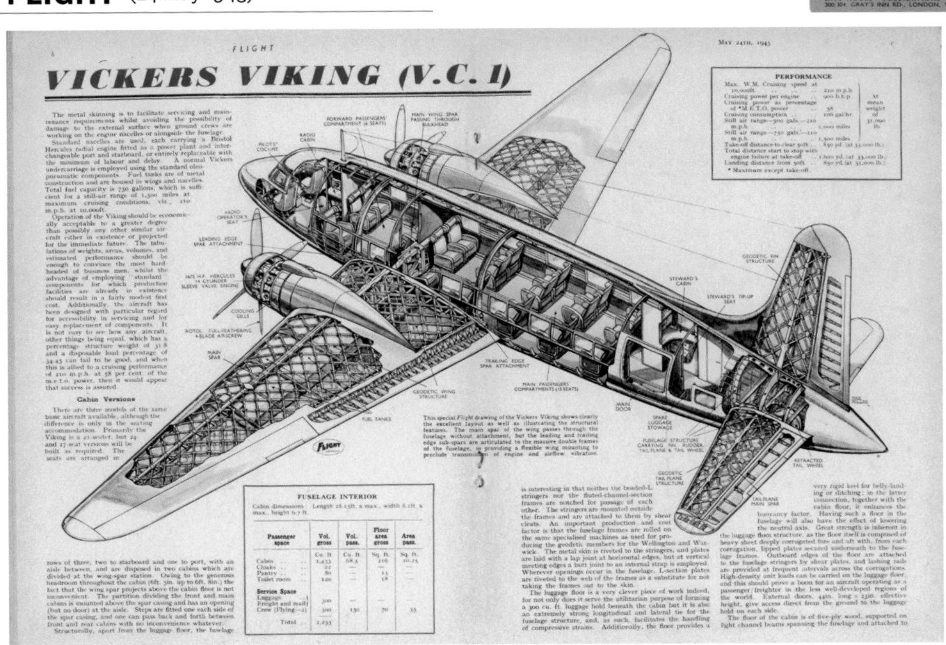

FLIGHT

VICKERS VIKING (V.C. 1)

PERFORMANCE

Cabin Versions

FUSELAGE INTERIOR

Max Millar, one of the pioneers of cutaways, typeset the captions on this drawing. He did his first drawings for *Flight* in 1912 as a freelance and started the art department at Iliffe in 1920. Other technical artists included Peter Endsleigh Castle, Jimmy Clark, Arthur Bowbeer, Frank Munger, G.W. Heumann, John Marsden, Lawrie Watts, Ira Epton, Michael Badrocke, Tim Hall, David Hatchard and Giuseppe Picarella; each of them adopted a different style. Munger has been credited with more than 250 cutaways in a 40-year career, with the most complex taking more than 300 hours to complete. During the war, Endsleigh Castle worked for MI6 on air intelligence, studying crashed enemy bombers to make illustrations for classified documents. Some of his work remained secret for decades.

Flight Publishing
(210 × 287 mm, stapled, 32 pages)

Don't be Whipped by Heredity

L. E. EUBANKS

Many magazines were launched based on naturism, health and fitness crazes – the most famous, *Health & Efficiency*, has been continuously published since 1900 – and these topics were a frequent inspiration for cartoonists. This 'National Physical Culture Monthly' printed the cover and centre four pages gravure to aid reproduction of pictures of posing bodybuilders. The cover shows R.S. Balsekar, winner of the All-India Physical Excellence Contest. Balsekar, a graduate of the London School of Economics, became general manager of the Bank of India in Bombay and then a guru and spiritual adviser to, among others, singer/songwriter Leonard Cohen. The back cover was an advert for Shredded Wheat as a general fitness food. Link House also published a weekly, *Health and Strength*, the official organ of the Health & Strength League, which claimed 153,241 members.

The idea of eugenics – improving the abilities of the human race through breeding – spread in the 1920s and saw its worst excesses in the ideas of the Nazi party in Germany, which also distorted the concept of the Übermensch (Superman) espoused by the philosopher Friedrich Nietzsche in his 1883 book *Thus Spoke Zarathustra*. The article here discusses ways of getting round the limitations of someone's genetic make-up through exercise and diet.

Link House Publications
(218 × 278 mm, stapled, 32 pages)

MEN ONLY (July 1937)

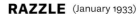

Men Only arrived in an unusual book-like pocket format with a plain, bright orange cover and the title written in a script style suggesting a rope. One reader commented in a letter in a later issue: 'It looks like a guide-book to the British Museum.' However, the pocket size was also adopted by humour weeklies *London Opinion* and the *Humorist* (when they turned themselves into monthlies at the start of the Second World War), and later the *Strand* and *Razzle*. Within a few issues line drawings of a pair of men chatting were introduced on the cover and then a caricature for this 'permanently enlarged' July 1937 issue. Although the cover illustrations – by Edward Hynes – became more colourful, the format stayed the same until 1954, showing servicemen, and the occasional woman, and their leaders during the early war years, then historical figures, then politicians and celebrities. The covers were slightly larger than the inside pages ('yapped' in book-binding terminology), which helped to protect the pages when carried by commuters. The advert inside the front cover in this issue was for Leica cameras.

The small size dictated a book-like layout (it was printed by Hazell, Watson and Viney). Interspersed between the 16-page black-and-white sections were four-page sections of colour or mono cartoons on coated paper.

The uncalendered paper and letterpress printing favoured line illustrations.

Pearson/George Newnes
(128 × 190 mm, stitched book binding, 164 pages)

RAZZLE (January 1933)

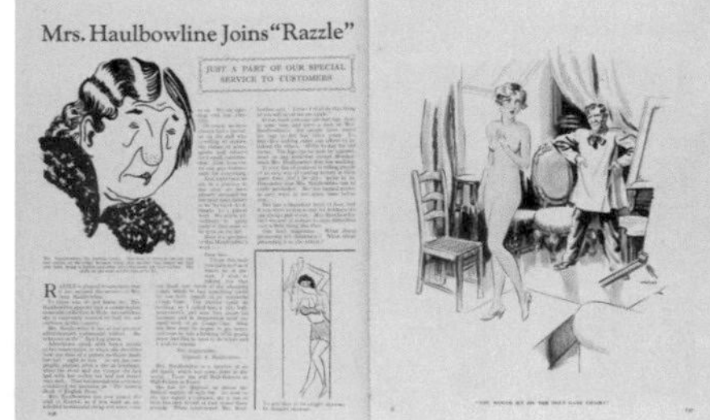

Razzle initially used a large format similar to the humour magazines the *Humorist* and *London Opinion*. It switched to a pocket format after the war when it was relaunched, but it retained the Art Deco title. Note that this copy has been cut down because it was bound into a volume at some stage.

A typical spread consisted of timeless single-page articles facing a whole-page cartoon.

Ritz Publishing
(230 × 300 mm, stapled, 36 pages)

LONDON LIFE
Once again we are delighted to present the wonder face of MARLENE DIETRICH. Here she is in her latest film, "The Blonde Venus" (Paramount).
January 20, 1934.
Price Sixpence

The cover image of Marlene Dietrich was a retouched version of a black-and-white publicity photograph from the 1932 film *Blonde Venus*. *London Life* relied on such images – there were 11 full-page pin-ups in this issue. It was very well produced and cost 6d – three times the cost of *Woman's Own* at the time. The magazine changed its cover title typography every week and often used strong graphic shapes with cut-outs on the cover. As well as being a lesson in inventive typography, its letters pages encompassed the world of bizarre erotica; discussions of high-heeled shoes, boots, corsets, human ponies and amputated limbs led to a ban in Ireland. Readers sent in their own sketches and photographs and special issues were devoted to readers' letters. During the war, it reduced its page size, becoming a monthly pocket title in 1942.

Most pages used 7 point type with 1 point leading over two, three or four columns. Each page layout and headline style was unique; only the page straps at the top provided visual unity.

"LONDON LIFE" A MAGAZINE OF

Which Race are the Greatest Lovers?

GENTLEMEN'S CORSETS

FICTION FILMS AND FUTURE FASHIONS

Losing Lester

Written by "Ad Astra."

New Picture Press
(240 × 315 mm, staple, 28 pages)

WOMAN'S OWN (27 February 1937)

February 27, 1937 WOMAN'S OWN 3

Listen In

A SERIAL YOU WILL NEVER FORGET

George Newnes relaunched *Woman's Own* as 'No. 1 of the World's Finest Weekly Paper' with a full-colour cover, larger page size and greater extent than before. The self-referential cover illustration was by Van Jones. The editor justified the cover's claims with the words 'our big new *Woman's Own* makes me feel all "new" ... and also because stepping on to this gay page is rather like pulling up the blind to let in the sunlight'. At 64 pages, it was a big issue featuring extensive use of a single spot colour on editorial and advertising – and there was full colour on the centre spread and outside cover. The text size was increased to 9 point type across 16-pica columns, with non-standard line lengths around the illustrations. Despite the increase in page size, there was no increase in the number of words on a page. The colour centre pages featured fashion designs that readers could make; most of them required the further purchase of a pattern for 1s, meaning this was a lucrative business for the publisher.

Under the relaunch, the editor's 'Listen In' feature was pushed back two pages to allow for spot-colour advertising on page 3. A sans-serif face was introduced for drop capitals throughout the issue.

George Newnes
(258 × 320 mm, stapled, 64 pages)

WOMAN (11 September 1937)

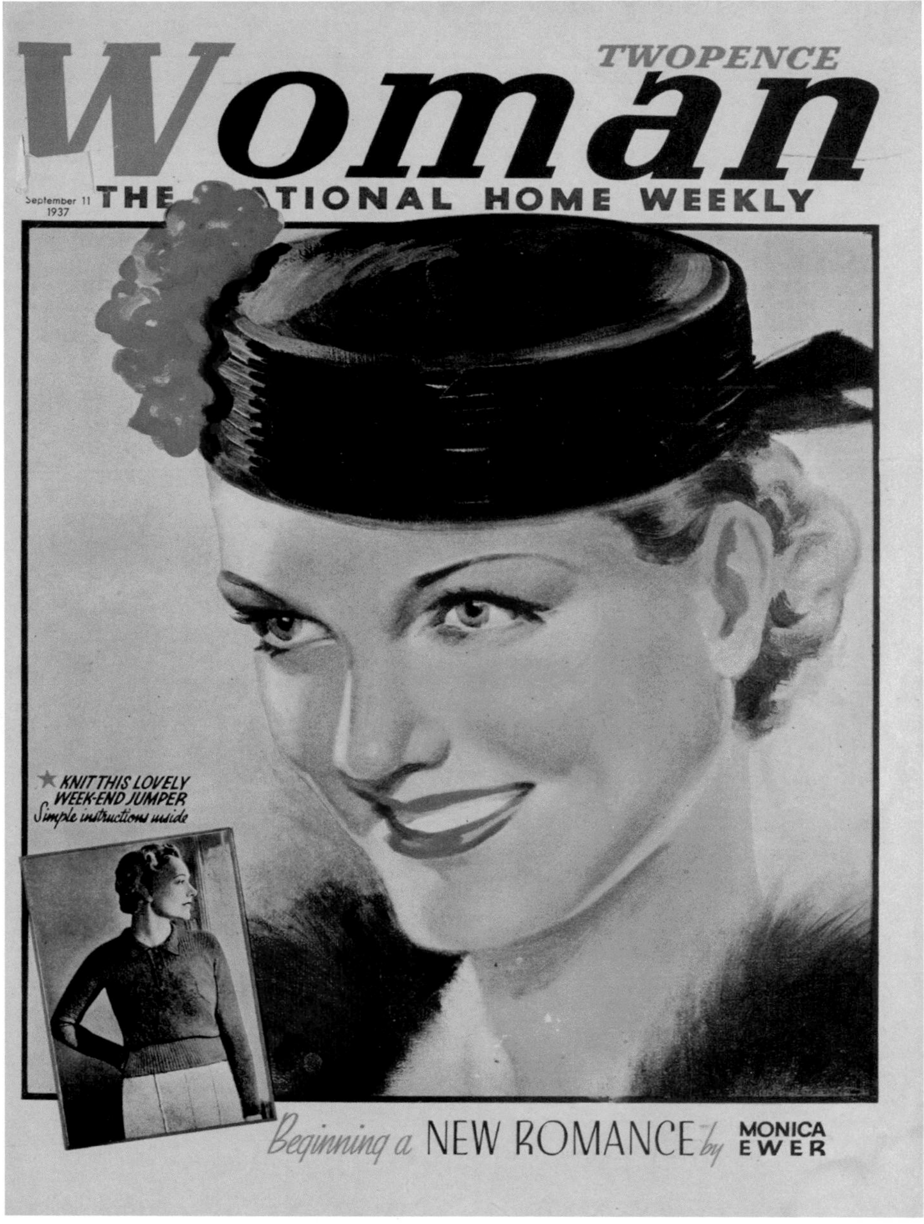

From its first issue in August 1937, *Woman* set out to distinguish itself from the market leader, *Woman's Own*, using illustration for its covers and a larger format. It was printed using the Speedry presses, which were housed in Odhams' new Art Deco building on the other side of Watford from Sun Engraving, where *Woman's Own* was printed. As with *Woman's Own*, full colour was reserved for the outer covers and the centre spread, where the focus again was on selling dress patterns. There was also spot colour on some editorial and advertising. The issue number has been cut from just below the 'W' of the title – these, or small vouchers on the inside back covers of some magazines, were collected to qualify for reader offers.

Odhams Press
(265 × 360 mm, stapled, 48 pages)

WOMAN (11 December 1937)

This centre spread for the short story 'Luck for a Bride' by Lady Troubridge is used to spectacular effect by Gilbert Wilkinson, who also did covers for *Passing Show* and *Illustrated*. Troubridge was the partner of Marguerite 'John' Radclyffe-Hall, author of the 1928 lesbian novel *The Well of Loneliness*. Other illustrators in this issue included Van Jones, Treyer Evans and T. Grainger Jeffrey.

Odhams Press
(265 × 360 mm, stapled, 52 pages)

WOMAN (12 February 1938)

"WOMAN" • MARTLETT HOUSE • MARTLETT COURT • LONDON • W.C.2

Woman to Woman

★ This is your page as well as ours—the page where we meet to exchange views, ideas and information. Whatever you have to say, why not say it here?

Royal Housewives

"R" in the Months

WOMAN (12 February 1938)

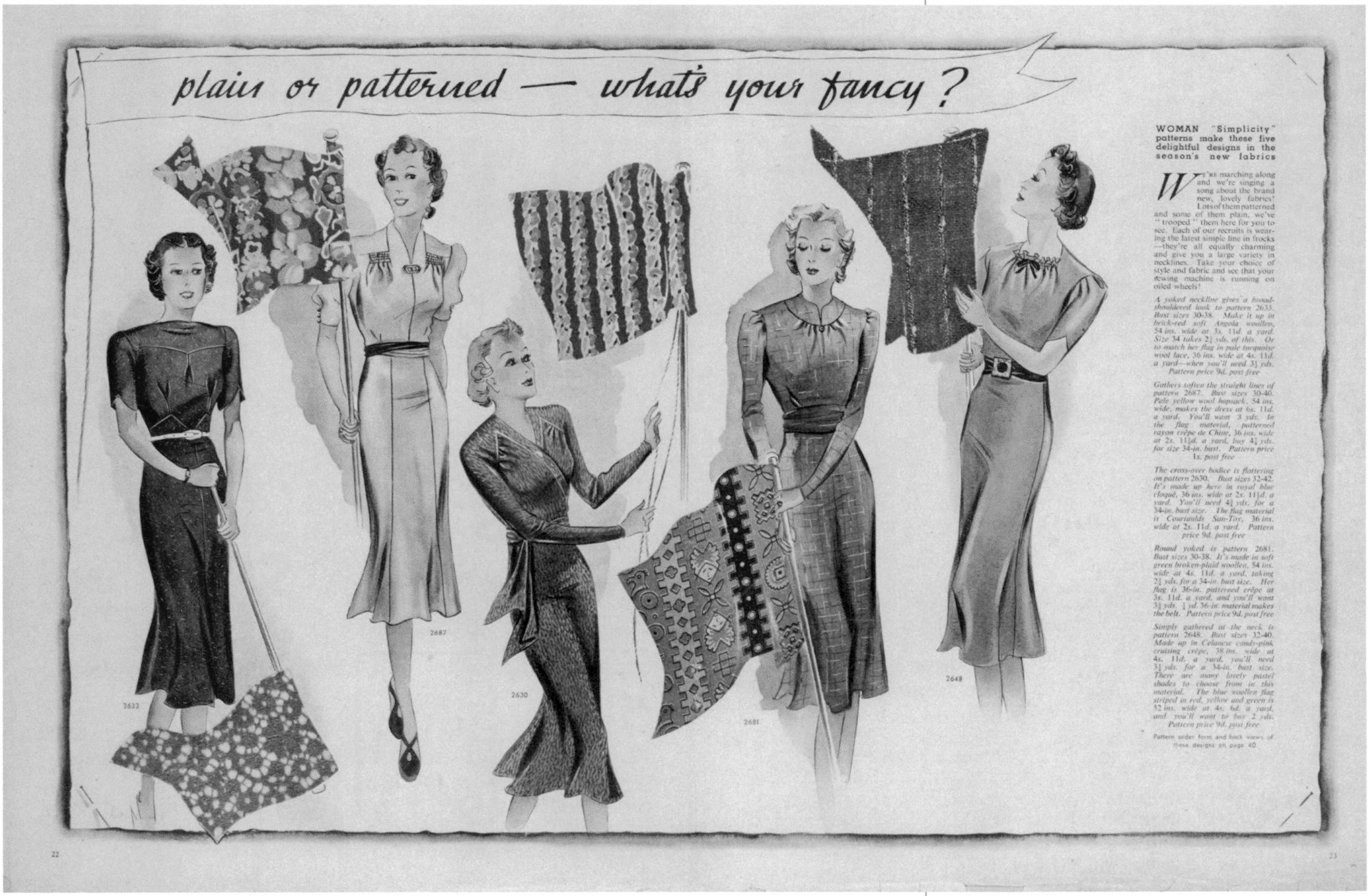

plain or patterned — what's your fancy?

WOMAN "Simplicity" patterns make these five delightful designs in the season's new fabrics

We're marching along and we're singing a song about the brand new, lovely fabrics! Lots of them patterned and some of them plain, we've "trooped" them here for you to see. Each of our recruits is wearing the latest simple line in frocks—they're all equally charming and give you a large variety in necklines. Take your choice of style and fabric and see that your sewing machine is running on oiled wheels!

A yoked neckline gives a broad-shouldered look to pattern 2633. Bust sizes 30-38. Make it up in brick-red soft Angola woollen, 54 ins. wide at 3s. 11d. a yard. Size 34 takes 2¼ yds. of this. Or to match her flag in pale turquoise wool lace, 36 ins. wide at 4s. 11d. a yard—when you'll need 3¼ yds. Pattern price 9d. post free

Gathers soften the straight lines of pattern 2687. Bust sizes 30-40. Pale yellow wool hopsack, 54 ins. wide, makes the dress at 6s. 11d. a yard. You'll want 3 yds. In the flag material, patterned rayon crêpe de Chine, 36 ins. wide at 2s. 11½d. a yard, buy 4¾ yds. for size 34-in. bust. Pattern price 1s. post free

The cross-over bodice is flattering on pattern 2630. Bust sizes 32-42. It's made up here in royal blue cloqué, 36 ins. wide at 2s. 11½d. a yard. You'll need 4¼ yds. for a 34-in. bust size. The flag material is Courtaulds San-Toy, 36 ins. wide at 2s. 11d. a yard. Pattern price 9d. post free

Round yoked is pattern 2681. Bust sizes 30-38. It's made in soft green broken-plaid woollen, 54 ins. wide at 4s. 11d. a yard, taking 2¼ yds. for a 34-in. bust size. Her flag is 36-in. patterned crêpe at 3s. 11d. a yard, and you'll want 3½ yds. ¼ yd. 36-in. material makes the belt. Pattern price 9d. post free

Simply gathered at the neck is pattern 2648. Bust sizes 32-40. Made up in Celanese candy-pink cruising crêpe, 38 ins. wide at 4s. 11d. a yard, you'll need 3¼ yds. for a 34-in. bust size. There are many lovely pastel shades to choose from in this material. The blue woollen flag striped in red, yellow and green is 52 ins. wide at 4s. 6d. a yard, and you'll want to buy 2 yds. Pattern price 9d. post free

Pattern order form and back views of these designs on page 40

This centre spread devoted to dress patterns uses a more active style than *Woman's Own*, with the pages presented using a trompe l'oeil effect as an illustration pinned to the page.

Odhams Press
(265 × 360 mm, stapled, 44 pages)

The 'Woman to Woman' column was on the last page facing the back cover (the horoscope had occupied that place in earlier issues). The portrait of the princesses Elizabeth and Margaret from a sitting in November 1934 was by Marcus Adams. A later photograph of the princesses by Adams was used on the cover of the relaunched *Woman's Own* in 1950 (see page 120).

Odhams Press
(265 × 360 mm, stapled, 44 pages)

MODERN WONDER (24 July 1937)

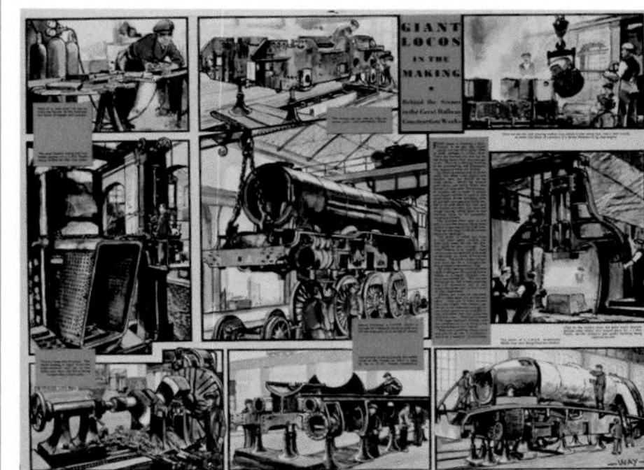

Bryan de Grineau drew the cover of this weekly, containing illustrated science articles and action true life and science fiction stories for boys and young men. Some of the illustrations and stories were republished from other magazines, such as *Illustrated London News* and John Benyon sci-fi from Odhams' *Passing Show*. *Modern Wonder* closed with wartime paper rationing, but some of the ideas and illustrators – particularly the cutaway drawings of Leslie Ashwell Wood – would feature again with the launch of the *Eagle* in the 1950s, and *TV21* and *Look and Learn* in the 1960s. Odhams printed *Modern Wonder* on its presses in Watford.

Odhams
(267 × 407 mm, stapled, 16 pages)

Along with the covers, the centre spread was in colour, a pattern common among the weekly magazines. The fact that the centre pages were a single sheet meant artwork could be used large and could run across the gutter. Also, there was no problem with variations in the ink colour or plate registration, both potential problems when an image was printed across a spread when the two sides were in different printing sections.

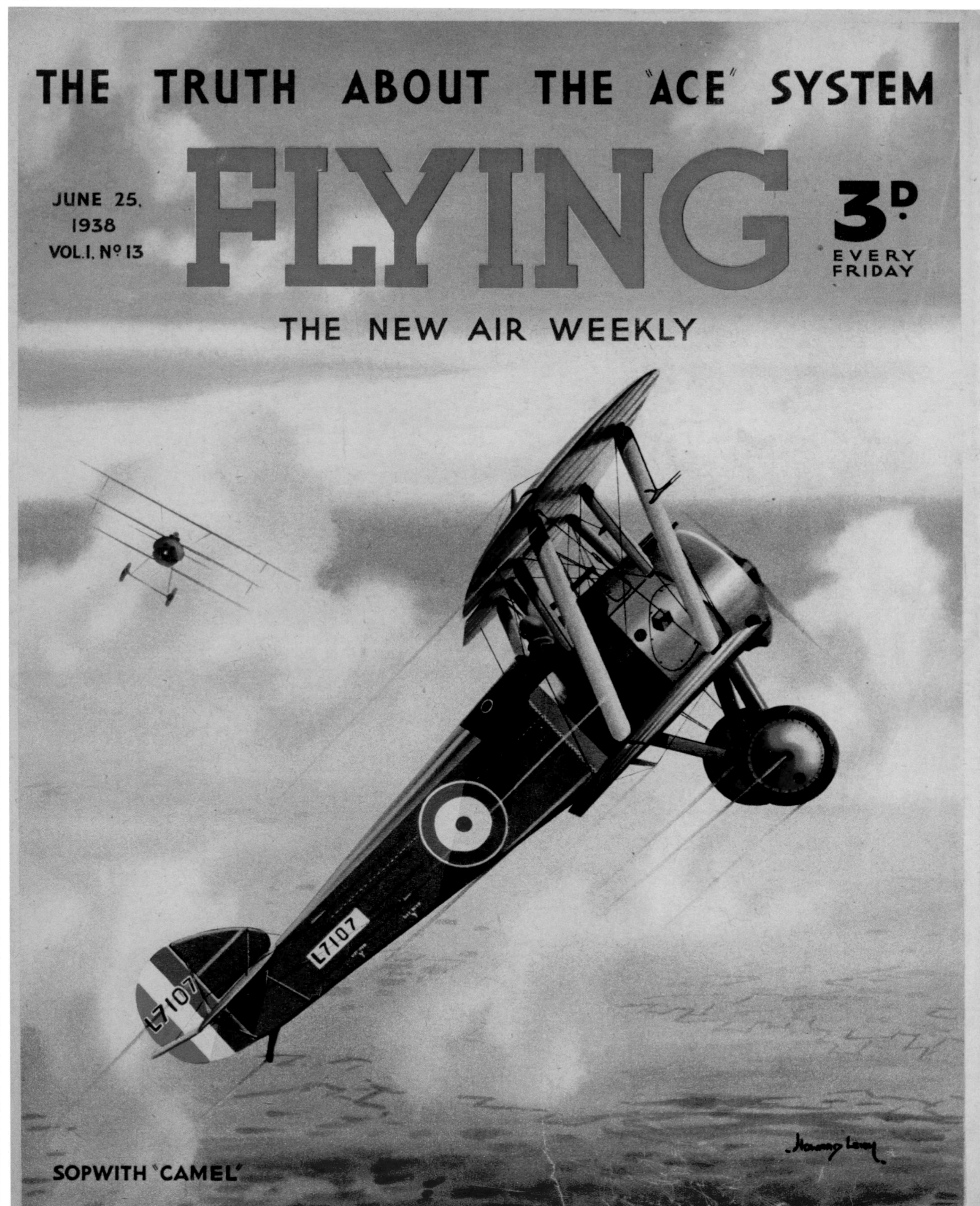

The editor was *Biggles* author W.E. Johns, whose friend Howard Leigh painted the cover's Sopwith Camel. This issue included a feature, 'Mastering the Stratosphere', by Clarence Ebey; this was bought in from the Ledger Syndicate, which distributed features that had appeared in the US publications the *Saturday Evening Post* and *Ladies' Home Journal*. It was printed by Sun Engraving, Watford.

George Newnes
(248 × 318 mm, stapled, 32 pages)

IMAGE MANIPULATION IN THE 1950S

The sequence here demonstrates how photographs could be manipulated in the 1950s. The history of such techniques is as old as photography itself, and magazines would always 'retouch' photographic negatives and prints to remove blemishes such as dust, or the hairs on a woman's face, or to whiten eyeballs and teeth.

The repro department at Sun Engraving in particular took these skills to a high level. During the war, the company turned over much of its production to military purposes, such as printing maps and documentation. A 2015 exhibition at the Science Museum in London, 'Churchill's Scientists', detailed a less likely activity – Sun's work for 'Tube Alloys', Britain's top secret atomic bomb project. Churchill had written in 1924: 'Might not a bomb no bigger than an orange be found to possess a secret power to … blast a township at a stroke?'[1] In 1941, Sun was asked to adapt the screens it made to produce printing films from colour photographs and illustrations and develop them into ultra-fine screens that could 'enrich' uranium by a process called gas diffusion. The screens progressively concentrated the proportion of uranium-235, the lighter isotope of the metal that is essential to a nuclear explosion, from the 1 per cent found in ores towards the 85 per cent needed for weapons-grade material.

These pictures were preserved by former Sun Engraving workers and their families, including Shirley Greenman, Basil Boden and Peter Greenhill.

1 'Shall we all commit suicide', *Nash's Pall Mall*, September 1924

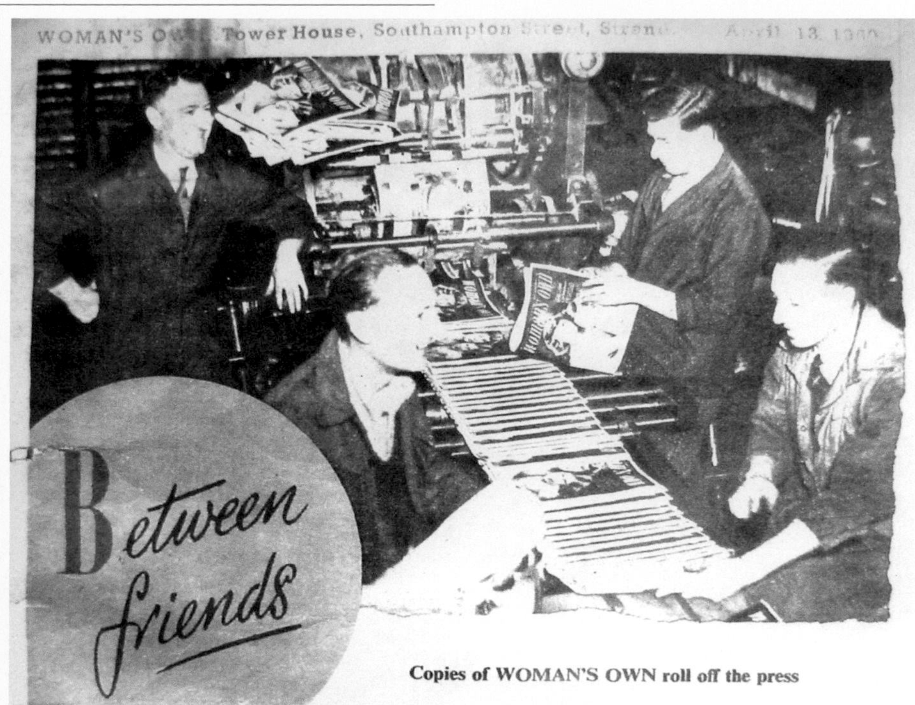

A cutting from *Woman's Own* (13 April 1950) showing a photograph of John 'Jack' Priestley, front left, and press minders at Sun with copies of *Woman's Own* dated 2 March 1950. This was the first issue printed after paper rationing ended. It ran to 48 pages, whereas wartime issues had been half that size or less.

Press photograph of the actor (and former Lieutenant Commander in the US Navy during the Second World War) Douglas Fairbanks signing the visitors' book in the office of Mary Edith Bridger, mayor of Watford. Fairbanks visited the Sun printing works, where he recognized aerial photographs used during the lead-up to D-Day that had been printed by Sun.

Intermediate composite image: the photograph of Fairbanks with the mayor was resized. He was cut out of the print and the pen in his hand replaced with a cut-out of the *Woman's Own* magazine originally held by a Sun employee.

The image was rephotographed and Fairbanks with magazine inserted into the original press picture, then the background was touched up and again rephotographed. Notice the 'smudged' area behind the actor where one of the press operators has been removed.

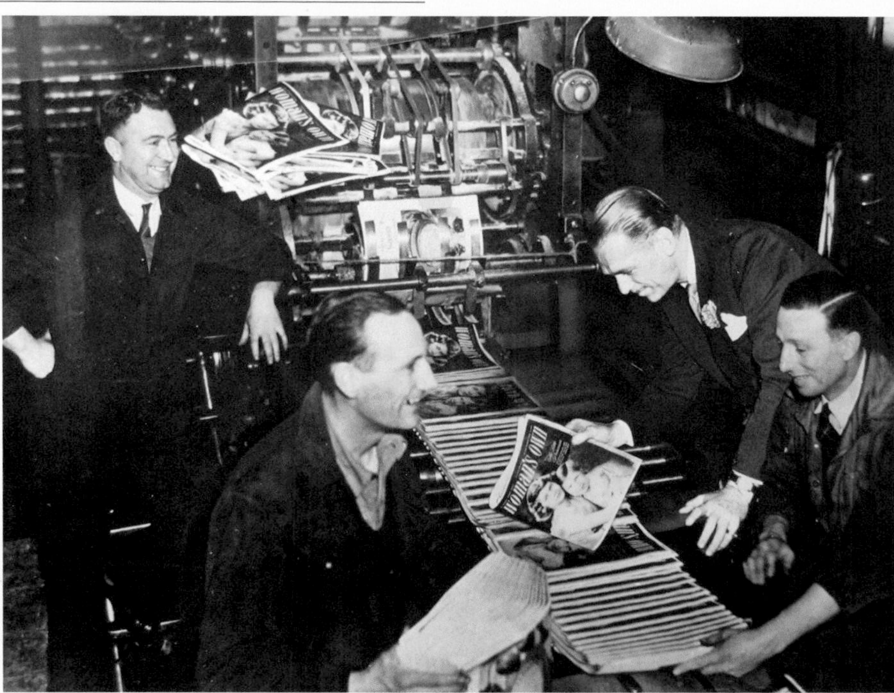

The final photograph shows Fairbanks appearing to hold a copy of *Woman's Own* that has just come off the presses. This final image was used in a Sun staff magazine.

War and austerity

War brought deprivation and seemed to change the look of magazines overnight. Yet two of the biggest-selling titles, *Lilliput* and *Picture Post*, had been on a war footing since their inception. Their founder, Stefan Lorant, was imprisoned by the Nazis and fled to Britain from Germany. The war imagery that Lorant had carried on his pages since founding *Weekly Illustrated* in 1934 was soon everywhere. *Woman* put its models in uniform as air raid wardens or working on production lines. Illustrators at *London Opinion* and *Men Only* turned their minds to martial themes, and even Walter Trier's escapist covers for *Lilliput* showed his man, woman and dog appearing in uniform.

An early challenge was the loss of staff. Although, in retrospect, the war years were glory days for *Picture Post*, 1940 saw the magazine in dire straits. Tom Hopkinson took over when Lorant left Britain. Hopkinson wrote: '[My] situation was: the editor had left for the US; our two chief cameramen [German-born Felix Man (Hans Baumann) and Kurt Hutton (Kurt Hubschmann)] had been interned in the Isle of Man as "enemy aliens"; the three or four most experienced staff writers [Sydney Jacobson, Lionel Birch and Richard Bennett] had joined the armed forces. I was a one-man band, desperate as to how I could keep the magazine alive.' Over at *Woman*, editor John Gammie went to war, as did Bert Hardy from *Picture Post*. Peter Endsleigh Castle, who specialized in cutaway drawings of aircraft, became vital to the intelligence services.

The summer of 1940 saw the Battle of Britain, after which came the Blitz, and publishers' warehouses around Fleet Street and St Paul's Cathedral were prime targets for the Luftwaffe. Since 1481, when William Caxton died and his apprentice Wynkyn de Worde took England's first printing press with movable type from Westminster Abbey to be housed next to St Bride's Church, printers and publishers had clustered in the area – a tradition that is kept alive today in the St Bride Printing Library. Alfred Harmsworth's *Answers* had its first offices in Paternoster Square, then moved around the corner to Farringdon Road. Newnes's *Strand* was near the west end of Fleet Street. *London Life* was based in Wine Office Court, between the Olde Cheshire Cheese pub and Dr Johnson's House. In 1940, such offices and their warehouses were filled with magazines, newspapers, books and their printing plants with paper and oil-based inks. From Covent Garden to St Paul's, the lanes were littered with printers, as was Southwark on the opposite side of the river. Famously, St Paul's Cathedral survived the bombing, but many printers' and publishers' premises fell victim to the bombs.

In the spring of 1941 another blow fell: rationing of both ink and paper. Costs had already shot up, causing monthlies such as *Lilliput* and *London Opinion* to raise their prices from 6d at the outbreak of the war to 9d. The merchant ships that brought supplies from Canada were being sunk by U-boats. Paper was rationed – to 18½ per cent of pre-war levels. *Picture Post* cut its pagination from its peak of 104 pages before the war to 28 pages for the duration. Constance Holt, *Woman's Own* editor, recalled: 'We had to know immediately of any impending shortages of things like sugar. Our recipes were already tailored to fit into rationing constrictions, and if ships carrying particular commodities were sunk, we quickly had to change the recipes accordingly.'

The weekly *London Life* started the war larger than A4 but was cut down to a smaller format in 1941. In October that year the cover carried a warning that paper controls meant it had to reduce further to a 'magazine size', in this case pocket size, and go fortnightly. Furthermore, its offices just off Fleet Street were bombed and it moved out to Reading, though it later returned to the Strand. After the war, it adopted a slightly larger pocket format, with spot-colour and then four-colour covers; however, it never regained the standards of its pre-war days. *London Opinion*, the *Strand* and *Good Housekeeping* were among many other titles that reduced their page size and took on a bookish look.

Many recent launches, such as *Modern Wonder*, were simply closed. Since 1879, the *Boy's Own Paper* had published an annual of the year's issues, but this was another practice that rationing curtailed: the 1940–41 edition was the last.

The editorial in the May 1941 issue of *Men Only* complained about paper shortages: 'Owing to increased demand and to this paper rationing, there are not enough copies of *Men Only* to go round ... We are sorry for those subscribers who cannot get their copies, but we are also a little sorry for ourselves. We have worked hard for success, and now that it has come we are robbed of it by this paper shortage. Believe us, we are properly browned off.'

This feeling spread, as magazines that would not toe the government's line were censored, a stance *Picture Post* fought by printing blacked-out photographs. Others were more conciliatory, as designers squeezed more copy on to pages and, in the case of *Woman's Own*, started articles on its front cover.

Yet the war gave many magazines a focus. According to Mary Grieve, who took over at *Woman* when Gammie left: 'War forced us into practical services for our readers. It was right up our street, really, and *Woman* was built on triumph over adversity. We didn't carry articles on celebrities – they simply aggravated readers.' Women were shown in uniform or working on the land; generals and admirals dominated the men's monthlies. The diktats of war even influenced the typefaces: 'The day came when we had to use smaller type and the price of the magazine had to rise,' recalled Holt at *Woman's Own*. When paper rationing ended in 1950 *Woman's Own* (2 March) ran a celebratory 48-page issue (wartime copies had been 20 or 24 pages).

For some, though, war's end brought new problems. Britons had seen large-format, colourful US magazines, which suffered no rationing and also pushed new glamorous personalities, products and graphic approaches. Tom Cottrell, who had been producing cartoons for *Punch*, *Blighty* and other papers since 1914, complained about the 'Americanization' of the cartoon market, with highly finished pen and wash drawings on board being replaced by a relentless stream of simple one-line gags drawn on typing paper. He saw this as driving down prices and increasing his workload. The November 1946 issue of *Men Only* discussed the change in humour as a battle between older illustrators, who prided themselves on the quality of their drawings, and younger ones, for whom the drawing was likely to be 'a little slap-dash in execution'. The editor came down on the side of the modern, more inclusive manner: 'Humour being equal, the better the drawing, the better the result. But humour comes first.' And editors at the big women's weeklies seemed to agree. Such was the transatlantic ingress that by 1960 some issues of *Woman's Own* had all their colour fiction spreads provided by Americans such as Andy Virgil, John McClelland and Coby Whitmore, even for quintessentially English works such as *When the Green Woods Laugh* by H.E. Bates. Ironically, in 2013, the American TV series *Mad Men* turned to Brian Sanders, a leading British illustrator of the 1960s, to evoke that era in Madison Avenue advertising agencies.

Luckily, the coronation, the Festival of Britain and the comings and goings of the royal family provided magazines with upbeat fare, from images of the young Queen Elizabeth dominating the women's weeklies to *Men Only* putting a serialized biography of Prince Philip on its cover.

In an article for *The Times Printing Supplement* of July 1955, *Picture Post* owner Edward Hulton described how all periodicals were sharing in the 'general buoyancy' of the economy, but, he warned, 'at least one big bogy is a real and imminent one – commercial television'. The advent of commercial television would be a blow in two ways: it took away from magazines and newspapers their role as the nation's main advertising medium; and it eroded the mass-market readership as people spent more time goggling at the box. At first, however, the impact was not great. Although *Picture Post* was in decline, in 1954 *John Bull* and *Illustrated* were both selling a million copies a week. In 1955 the *Radio Times* was able to take out a page of advertising in *The Economist* to announce sales of 8,832,579 copies – 'the largest sale of any weekly magazine in the world' (10 September, p. 821). As a comparison, the American photographic weekly *Life* was selling 5.6 million copies. The Independent Television commercial network started broadcasting 12 days after that *Economist* issue and the commercial broadcasting companies launched their own listings magazine, *TV Times*, on 22 September. The cover images were of Patricia Dainton from *Sixpenny Corner*, a home-made daily serial, and American import Lucille Ball from *I Love Lucy*, together framed by the shape of a TV screen. It was printed letterpress on calendered newsprint, with spot magenta on the cover, a basic production standard very similar to the *Radio Times*.

Mainstream magazines responded with even more colour, larger formats and bigger pictures – many from the Hollywood publicity machine – and yet more sensationalist fare, again much of it from US syndicates. Men's monthly *Razzle* gives a feeling of the threat from television (issue 97) with its 'Tittle-Tattle' section seeing in the New Year:

> And as 1957 limps in we, your humble recorders of the Fourth Estate, are pledged.
>
> We swear on the things we hold most dear to report only the truth, the whole truth and nothing but the truth ... as we see it ... so help us. And can we help it if we suffer from astigmatism? The editor's decision is final.
>
> Then as one man – which isn't difficult when you're on your own! – we doff our caps, remove our hands from the pile of expense sheets and place them palms upwards on RAZZLE. With one accord we shout: 'Death to TV! The spoken word shall never oust the written word.'

Many titles foundered. Great name such as the *Strand*, *Picture Post*, *Illustrated*, *Everybody's*, *John Bull* and *Lilliput* were among the big-sellers that lost their way and all were closed by the end of 1960.

Vogue, which had had a good war, being seen by the government as a morale booster, continued to excel as photography dominated illustration. Joining Cecil Beaton and Norman Parkinson was John Deakin, a denizen of Soho who rubbed shoulders in the Colony Room drinking club with the likes of Francis Bacon, George Melly, Jeffrey Bernard, Henrietta Moraes and Lucian Freud. Deakin's portrait was painted by Freud and his photographs were described in the *Daily Telegraph* under the headline 'Studies of Compelling Nastiness'.[1] Photography was gaining recognition in the art world and Deakin's work was hung by Bruce Bernard, Jeffrey's older brother, in the Parton Gallery in Soho's Greek Street in 1956. Four years later, Ida Kar became the first photographer to have a retrospective exhibition at a major gallery, the Whitechapel Art Gallery. Bruce Bernard was picture editor for Purnell's *History of the 20th Century* part-work, and later at the *Sunday Times Magazine* and *Independent Magazine*. His collection of 100 photographs from the 1840s to the 1990s was exhibited at the V&A.

1 Quoted in Kevin Jackson, 'Through the Eye of the Beholder', *Independent*, 30 March 2002, p. 8; see also V&A: PH.100–1984

PICTURE POST (9 September 1939)

This photomontage by John Heartfield was on the cover of *Picture Post* a week after the declaration of war. Editor Stefan Lorant had already used the image in *Lilliput*, along with other examples of Heartfield's work. Heartfield was a Dadaist who had anglicized his name from Helmut Herzfeld in protest at German militarism during the First World War. Between 1930 and 1938 he contributed hundreds of photomontages to *AIZ* (*Arbeiter-Illustrierte-Zeitung*), a left-wing weekly in Germany, including this one, 'His Majesty Adolf. I lead you towards splendid bankruptcies!' Like Lorant, Heartfield fled Germany to escape persecution by the Nazis. In a May 1939 article, 'A Master of Political Art', *Lilliput* profiled Heartfield and published 'Hurrah, die Butter ist alle!' ('Hurrah, the butter is finished!'). It was inspired by a quote from Hermann Goering: 'Iron always made a nation strong, butter and lard only made the people fat.'

Odhams
(260 × 346 mm, stapled, 64 pages)

PICTURE POST (1 June 1940)

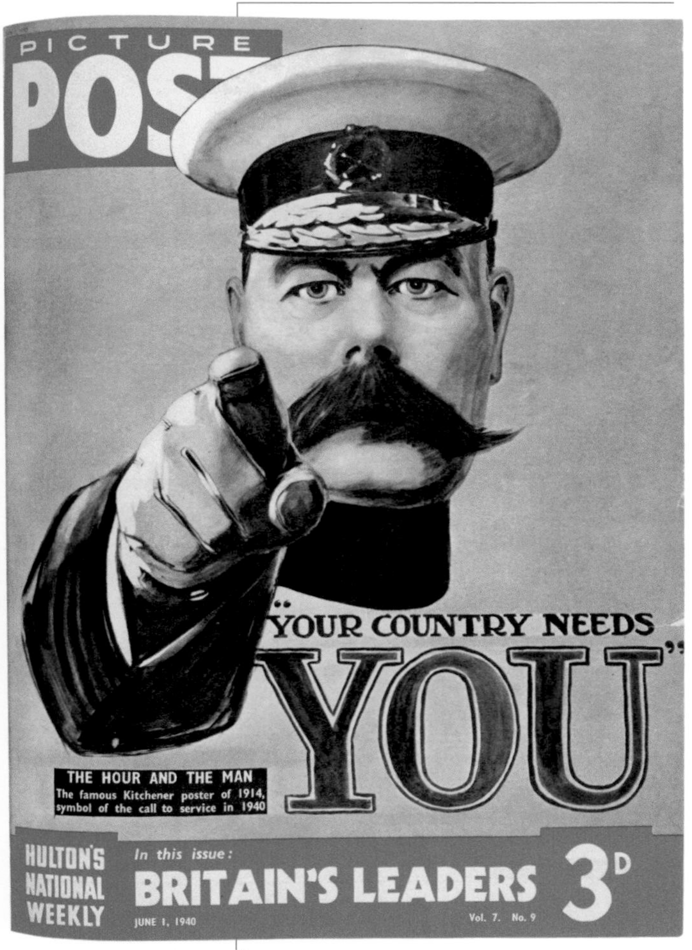

Stefan Lorant dusted off the artwork for the 1914 Kitchener poster by Alfred Leete – originally a *London Opinion* cover – for an issue about Britain's leaders. In total, 32 pages were devoted to government members: one page started with photographs comparing a 'grimly determined' Churchill in 1914 with him 'grimly determined again' in 1940.

A similar approach was taken by *About Town* for the Macmillan government in March 1961 and the *Sunday Times Magazine* for Margaret Thatcher's first administration in 1980.

Odhams
(260 × 346 mm, stapled, 64 pages)

PICTURE POST (26 November 1938)

The four guardians of German culture today: they shield its purity from the "contaminated race."

BACK TO THE MIDDLE AGES

Stefan Lorant used images laid out in striking ways to put across complex ideas – and with an initial print run of 750,000 and weekly sales peaking at 1,750,000 in 1939, a large part of the nation must have been reading *Picture Post*. Tom Hopkinson, who took over as editor after Lorant fled to the US in 1940, identified this article (which continued for another five pages) as 'the finest example of the use of photographs for political effect'. He describes how Lorant – a Hungarian Jew – drew up the pages to hit back at 'This bloody Hitler. These bloody pogroms!'

Odhams
(260 × 346 mm, stapled, 64 pages)

ILLUSTRATED LONDON NEWS (8 June 1940)

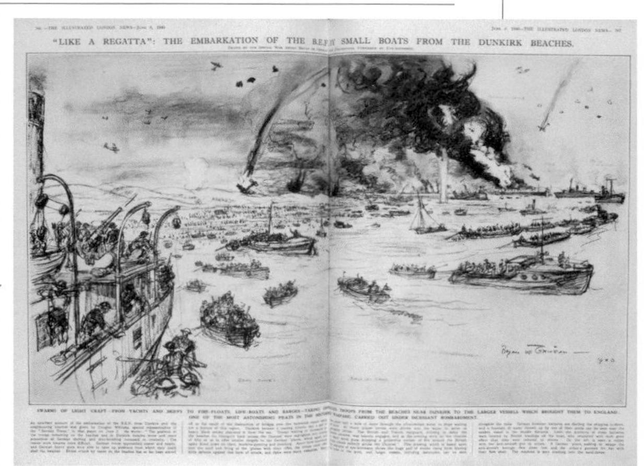
"LIKE A REGATTA": THE EMBARKATION OF THE B.E.F. IN SMALL BOATS FROM THE DUNKIRK BEACHES.

PICTURE POST (1 February 1941)

PICTURE POST

FIRE-FIGHTERS!

The *Illustrated London News* reported the evacuation at Dunkirk with this image by 'special war artist' Bryan de Grineau 'from descriptions furnished by eye-witnesses'. De Grineau also drew for Temple Press's *Motor* and did many covers for *Modern Wonder*. Rationing required a low-key celebration for the *ILN*'s 100th anniversary on 16 May 1942 – the magazine's offices were damaged in the bombing – with the cover title printed in spot red. The price rose from 1s to 1s 6d between 1939 and 1942.

Illustrated Newspapers
(260 × 370 mm, 34 pages)

This photo-essay about Blitz-stressed firefighters by Bert Hardy was the first to be given a named credit in *Picture Post*. Lorant did not usually name photographers in *Weekly Illustrated* and *Picture Post* because so many of them – for example, Felix H. Man (Hans Baumann), Kurt Hutton (Kurt Hubschmann) and Tim N. Gidal – were German refugees who had no work permits. By this time, Man and Hutton had been interned as enemy aliens. Paper rationing saw *Picture Post* issue sizes cut from 104 pages to just 28.

Odhams
(260 × 346 mm, stapled, 36 pages)

BLIGHTY (3 May 1941)

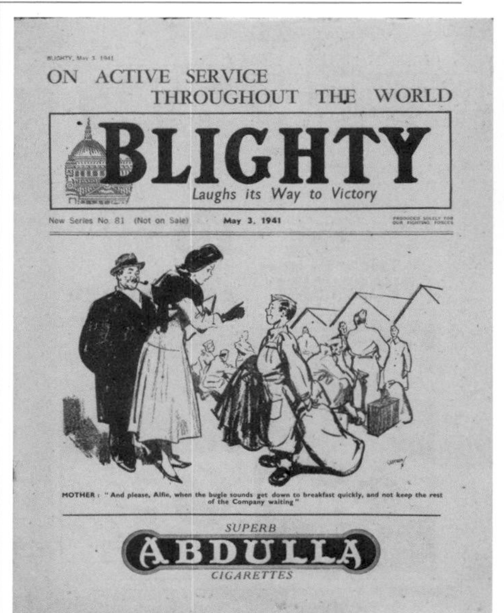

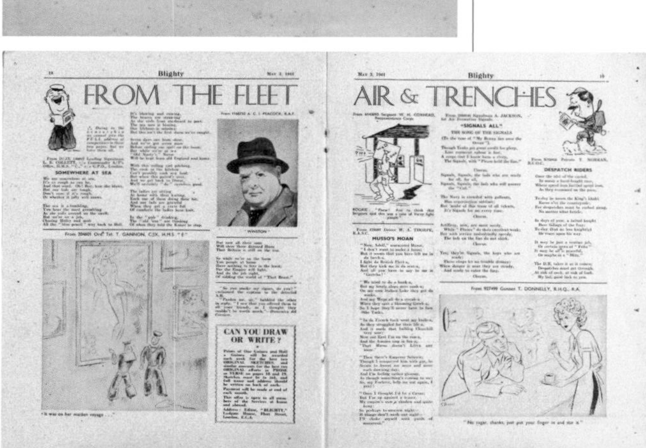

Blighty was resurrected to be 'the free paper for our fighting forces', with a list of patrons that included Churchill. It followed a format similar to that in the First World War, with costs subsidized by advertising. Paper restrictions meant that by 1943 it was sent only to troops abroad. There was a regular quota of 31,500 copies a week, averaging 1.6 million copies a year. The cover cartoonist here is Horace C. Gaffron, who had fought with the Gordon Highlanders in the Great War and drew *Good Housekeeping* covers in the 1930s. Arthur Ferrier supplied the regular page 3 cartoon, which later moved to the front cover.

Prizes were offered for sketches and prose published on the fleet, air and trenches pages.

Blighty Ltd
(238 × 310 mm, stapled, 32 pages)

EVERYWOMAN (May 1940)

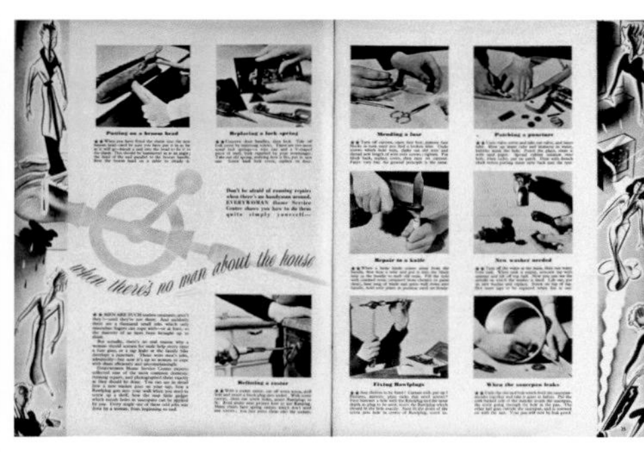

The Odhams monthly *Everyman* had been launched in 1937 with an aggressive cover price – 7d, compared with a society weekly such as *Tatler* for 1s. However, the cheaper paper used to keep the price down now shows; the wood pulp has degraded over the years, while the art paper used for other titles still maintains its gloss. Illustrators used for the fiction in this issue included Clixby Watson and Eric Earnshaw.

A utility spread: 'When there's no man about the house' by the *Everywoman* home service. The gravure presses at Odhams' Watford printworks allow illustrations to bleed off both outside edges.

Odhams Press
(226 × 300 mm, stapled, 96 pages)

WOMAN (23 October 1943)

Women readers are regularly portrayed in uniform or doing manual jobs. This cover is presented as a poster with minimal cover lines and the title positioned out of the way to suit the image. The designers did not have to worry about recognition on a crowded news-stand because by this stage of the rationing process magazines had to be ordered and every copy was pre-sold. The covers were not credited.

Odhams Press
(260 × 302 mm, stapled, 24 pages)

WOMAN'S OWN (27 August 1943)

WOMAN'S OWN

3d

ON SALE FRIDAY, AUGUST 27th, 1943

WINNING JOBS

VICTORIA STEVENSON talks to the "back-room" girls

YOU don't wear a uniform. You just work behind the noise, bustle and glamour of a nation at war, maybe quietly typing invoices, making up pay packets, filing correspondence or even checking laundry lists. At times you kick against the pricks. "Not much of a war job," writes the confidential secretary to an engineering director. "I'm doing the same old job that I did in peacetime. We work longer hours, it's true, but there's the same quiet atmosphere, the same old routine. I wish I could be de-reserved and an older woman take my place!"

I know just how you feel, but no one can take your place or they would have done so long ago. You're the power behind the job. But you're never in the limelight! Whenever I've been shown round a factory with its thousands of women workers, I've never met the manager's confidential clerk or the host of typists and book-keepers who are at the back of any modern business concern. The women in the news are the women who are tackling unusual jobs. But where would the works be if the office staff disappeared? It is essential.

The great clerical army behind the workshops, the coal mines, the shipyards of Britain, is every bit as necessary as the metal workers, the miners and the sailors.

Finance, too, plays its part in winning the fight. Every War Savings campaign needs clerical help. The banks, the big insurance firms, the post office, have already released hundreds of men and women. The girls left behind who wield a pen instead of a precision instrument, who tap a typewriter in a humdrum office instead of a lively orderly room, are key women who cannot be dispensed with.

There are the smaller concerns, too—contractors, builders, timber yards—all indirectly connected with the war effort, and, of course, laundries. I often get a groan from girls in laundries who have tried again and again for their release for the Forces. "Surely someone else can do my job. It's so simple," wrote one girl. "It would release me for a worthwhile job." But laundry work *is* a worthwhile job, otherwise the Ministry of Labour would never have reserved the workers. Many laundries are now doing soldiers' washing, or laundering for the busy housewife who herself is doing two jobs.

Any girl who has been granted deferment can have the satisfaction of knowing that her individual case has been thoroughly scrutinized by her Employment Exchange and, however trivial her job may seem to her, it looms big in the eyes of the authorities. If she is left to march with the great army of civilians, she can rest assured she is an important cog in the great war machine because she is irreplaceable.

Write to me, enclosing a stamped, addressed envelope, if you have a war-job problem. You know my address? It is: c/o "Woman's Own," Tower House, Southampton Street, London, W.C.2.

★ ★ FOUR COMPLETE STORIES IN THIS ISSUE ★ ★

Not her war

By MONICA EWER

LOVE makes you vulnerable—or it makes you strong just as you choose

Shortage of paper saw *Woman's Own* putting text on the covers right up until 23 June 1944. 'Winning Jobs', a series by Victoria Stevenson which often appeared there, usually discussed jobs in the services – in this case, the 'back-room girls' who did essential jobs but might be overlooked because they were not in uniform. Notice the time on the clock: 7.40. She's either in early or very late.

The colour centre spread was the short story 'Not Her War' by Monica Ewer. It was illustrated by Hookway Cowles, celebrated for his jackets for the books by H. Rider Haggard and *Unfinished Portrait*, Agatha Christie's semi-autobiographical novel.

George Newnes
(270 × 358 mm, stapled, 24 pages)

TIT-BITS (19 June 1942)

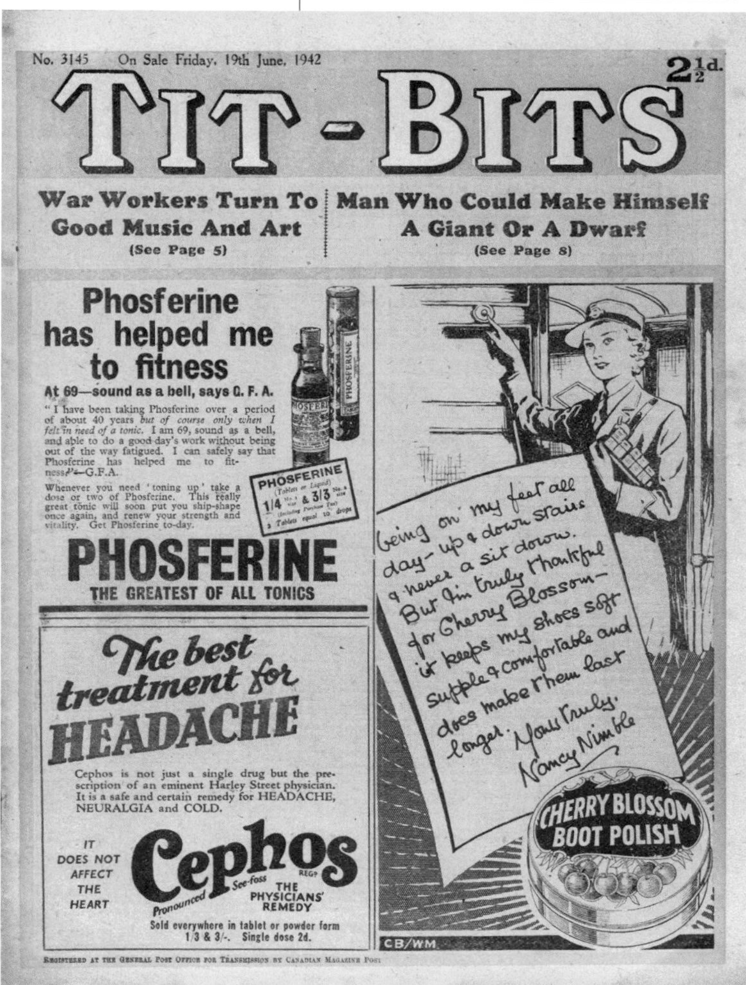

No. 3145 On Sale Friday, 19th June, 1942

TIT-BITS

$2\frac{1}{2}$d.

War Workers Turn To Good Music And Art (See Page 5)

Man Who Could Make Himself A Giant Or A Dwarf (See Page 8)

Phosferine has helped me to fitness

At 69—sound as a bell, says G. F. A.

"I have been taking Phosferine over a period of about 40 years *but of course only when I felt in need of a tonic.* I am 69, sound as a bell, and able to do a good day's work without being out of the way fatigued. I can safely say that Phosferine has helped me to fitness."—G.F.A.

Whenever you need 'toning up' take a dose or two of Phosferine. This really great tonic will soon put you ship-shape once again, and renew your strength and vitality. Get Phosferine to-day.

PHOSFERINE (Tablets or Liquid) 1/4 & 3/3

PHOSFERINE

THE GREATEST OF ALL TONICS

The best treatment for **HEADACHE**

Cephos is not just a single drug but the prescription of an eminent Harley Street physician. It is a safe and certain remedy for HEADACHE, NEURALGIA and COLD.

IT DOES NOT AFFECT THE HEART

Cephos REGD

Pronounced See-foss

THE PHYSICIANS' REMEDY

Sold everywhere in tablet or powder form 1/3 & 3/-. Single dose 2d.

Being on my feet all day – up & down stairs & never a sit down. But I'm truly thankful for Cherry Blossom – it keeps my shoes soft supple & comfortable and does make them last longer. Yours truly, Nancy Nimble

CHERRY BLOSSOM BOOT POLISH

CB/WM

REGISTERED AT THE GENERAL POST OFFICE FOR TRANSMISSION BY CANADIAN MAGAZINE POST

Have You Ever Eaten Calabrese Or Scorzonera?

Seven Stars of Hollywood

Tell TIT-BITS Their Funniest Stories

What The Future Holds For Us

The cover is dominated by semi-display advertising, dictated by wartime paper rationing, which also forced *Tit-Bits* to drop its frequency – it came out on alternate Fridays at this time. The design makes use of the green adopted by the magazine as its corporate colour, though as a tint to preserve ink. The angled title design has been dropped.

The original *Tit-Bits* layout approach is maintained, with short items in three or four columns, but longer articles have now been introduced, along with cartoons and photographs. The typography has a newspaper feel. Lots of short items suited the wartime restrictions, as more subjects could be covered in the same space, and Hollywood publicity shots will have been cost-effective.

George Newnes
(230 × 298 mm, stapled, 16 pages)

VOGUE (June 1942)

VOGUE
INCLUDING VOGUE PATTERN BOOK
Summer Fashions
JUNE, 1942 (6)
PRICE 3/-

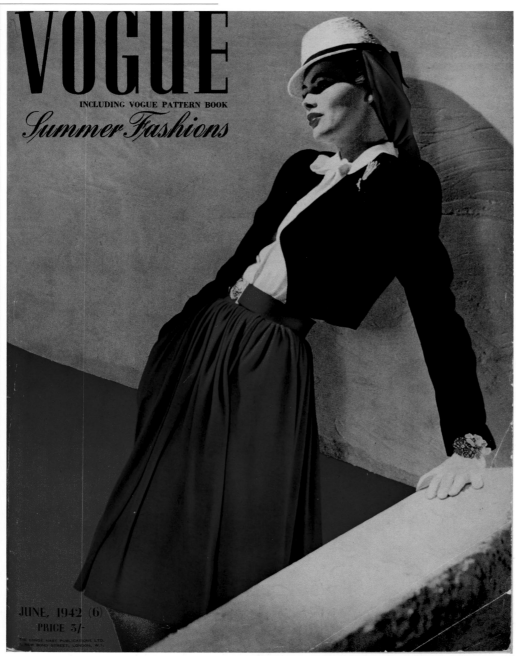

This cover was printed by Edmund Evans in London and subsequently combined with the inside pages, which were printed by Sun Engraving in Watford. At the outbreak of war, the fortnightly *Vogue* cut its frequency to monthly and incorporated *Vogue Pattern Book*, *Vogue Beauty Book* and *Vogue House and Garden Book*. The magazine maintained a strict 'editorial well', with 18 pages of advertising followed by editorial and the *Vogue* pattern book (eight pages) and then another 14 pages of advertising. At the end of 1942, Amalgamated Press took control of Condé Nast Publications after Nast's death, selling the company to Samuel Newhouse (of the Advance newspaper empire) in 1959.

At this time, colour printing was typically limited to the front cover and perhaps a single internal four-page section. This spread on US fashion was by Lee Miller and the German-born Horst P. Horst, who worked for *Vogue* for 60 years.

Condé Nast
(240 × 315 mm, side-stabbed, 80 pages)

VOGUE (July 1942)

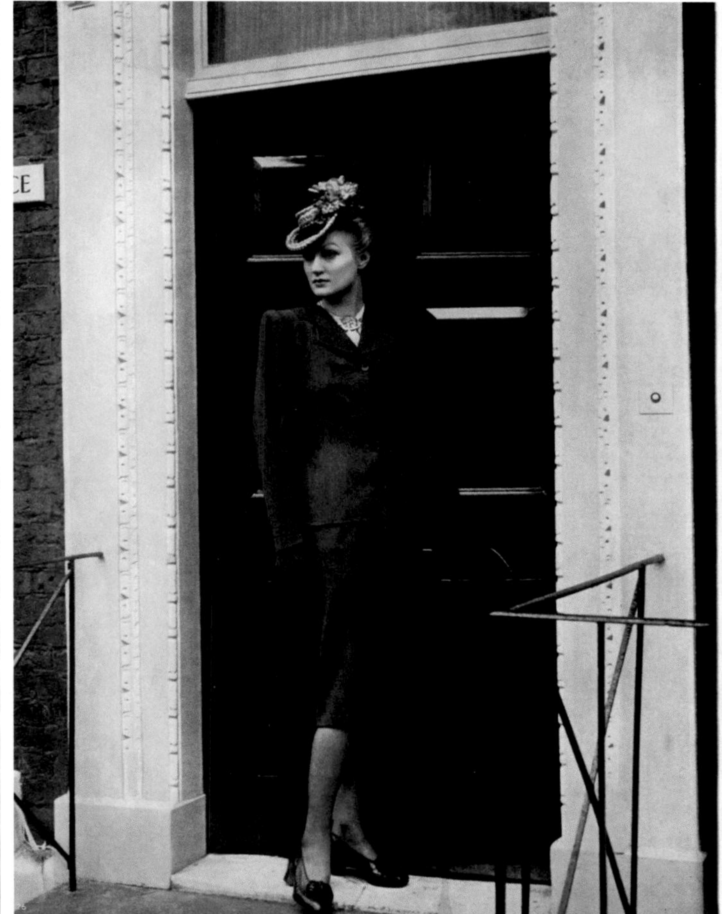

Fighting Trim

DRESS RESTRICTIONS simply pare away superfluities, but leave basic elegance

Fashion is undergoing a compulsory course of slimming and simplification; and is emerging from those reducing rollers, the new dress restrictions, in fine shape. Not that it was really self-indulgent before; it was simple and charming. But the progress of the war has made it necessary to prohibit all superfluous material and superfluous labour; and modern eyes, apt to approve slimness, rest appreciatively on the spare elegance that results from this decree ...

It is a great opportunity for the couture. They, by sheer skill of cut, sheer interest of fabric, can turn negative restrictions into positive triumphs. See here some indication of the range that can be achieved. At right, a high cardigan closing; opposite, a classic tailormade: only similarity the fitted line of the jacket.

OUTDOORS, austere elegance: Angèle Delanghe's grey-green suit, with diamond inlets accentuating the waistline. Erik's straw hat. Delman crocodile shoes and bag

The editorial in this issue yearns for things past – holidays abroad and petrol to spare – but ends with 'Holidays are not where you take them, but what you make them'. The austerity feel continues with an article about Land Girls (photographs by Norman Parkinson) and then this 'Fighting Trim' fashion article with typewritten text and hand-drawn headlines. The photographs are by Lee Miller.

Condé Nast
(240 × 315 mm, side-stabbed, 80 pages)

VOGUE (October 1942)

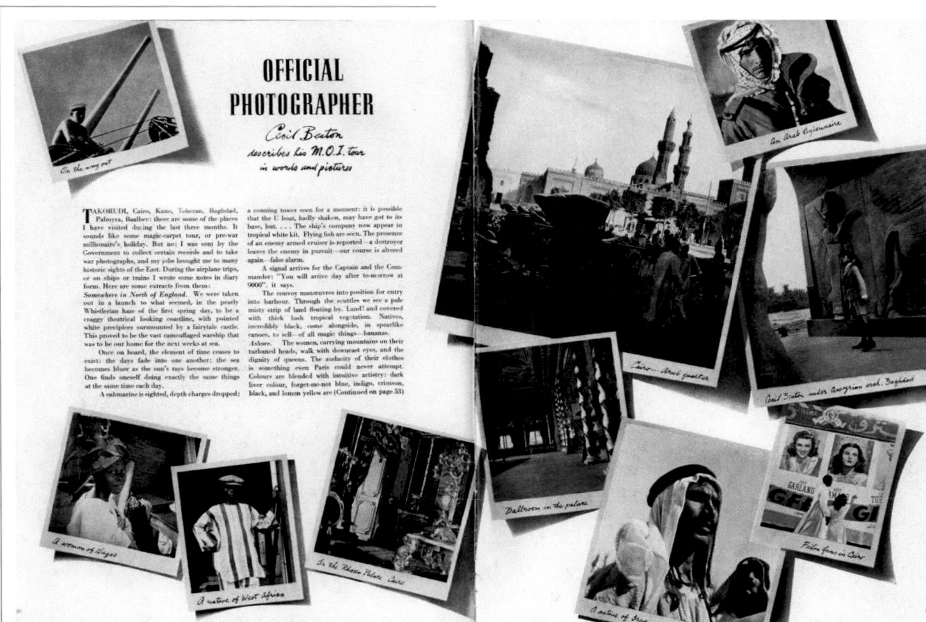

OFFICIAL PHOTOGRAPHER

Cecil Beaton describes his M.O.I. tour in words and pictures

Even fashion photographers were sent off to war. This spread uses photographs and an essay by Cecil Beaton about his three-month stint as a Ministry of Information photographer in the Middle East. The right-most picture on the right-hand page shows him standing under the Assyrian arch in Baghdad. The following pages carried an article about Noël Coward and his recent morale-boosting film *In Which We Serve*, again with a Beaton portrait. Beaton was written about in magazines as well as contributing to them; his social affairs were reported in the likes of the *Sketch*, the society weekly, and his life story was told in several parts by *Woman and Home* in 1949.

Condé Nast
(240 × 315 mm, side-stabbed, 92 pages)

WOMAN'S OWN (1 December 1944)

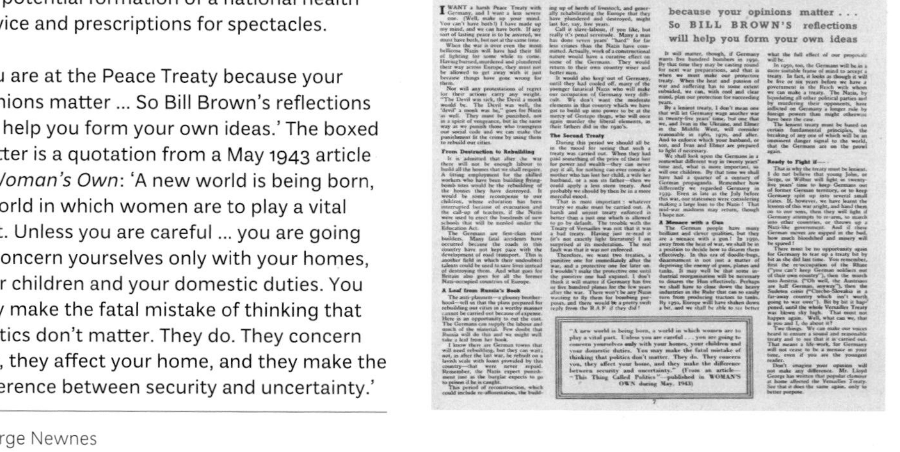

You are at the Peace Treaty

because your opinions matter ... So BILL BROWN'S reflections will help you form your own ideas

A Menace with a Gun

"A new world is being born, a world in which women are to play a vital part. Unless you are careful . . . you are going to concern yourselves **only** with your homes, your children and your domestic duties. You may make the fatal mistake of thinking that politics don't matter. They do. They concern you, they affect your home, and they make the difference between security and uncertainty." (From an article—"This Thing Called Politics"—published in WOMAN'S OWN during May, 1943)

7

One of the rarer sights on the front cover of a woman's magazine: the model is wearing glasses. With the end of the war in sight, thoughts turned to the future and, in this case, the potential formation of a national health service and prescriptions for spectacles.

'You are at the Peace Treaty because your opinions matter ... So Bill Brown's reflections will help you form your own ideas.' The boxed matter is a quotation from a May 1943 article in *Woman's Own*: 'A new world is being born, a world in which women are to play a vital part. Unless you are careful ... you are going to concern yourselves only with your homes, your children and your domestic duties. You may make the fatal mistake of thinking that politics don't matter. They do. They concern you, they affect your home, and they make the difference between security and uncertainty.'

George Newnes
(240 × 334 mm, stapled, 20 pages)

WOMAN (27 November 1943)

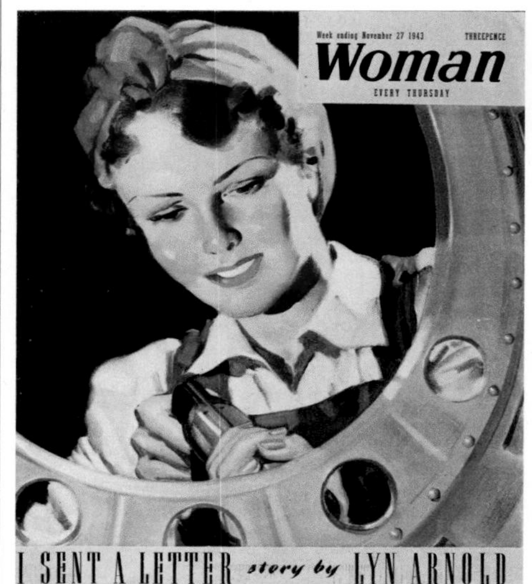

Many weeklies in wartime portrayed women doing what had been seen as men's jobs in factories, on the land or in laboratories, wielding spanners, test tubes or, in this case, a riveter. As always, the woman is well made-up, with plucked eyebrows, lipstick and nail varnish.

Odhams
(260 × 300 mm, stapled, 24 pages)

No other love

Julie burned her bridges—and like many women tried not to show she was swimming back…

BY LEONIE MASON

COMPLETE

ILLUSTRATED BY KOOLMAN: CARLTON

WOMAN (2 February 1945)

WOMAN'S OWN

THE NATIONAL WOMEN'S WEEKLY

3d

ON SALE FRIDAY, FEBRUARY 2nd. 1945

Another rare sight: a cover showing a woman with a lit cigarette. The centre-spread illustration is credited to 'Koolman: Carlton'. One woman is in uniform with the designation 'Official War Correspondent' on her shoulder. On the table is a packet of Lucky Strike cigarettes – a US brand that adopted this packaging design (by industrial designer Raymond Loewy) in 1942 to appeal more to women. The concept of the female war correspondent dates back at least to Sarah Wilson and Elizabeth Charlotte Briggs, who reported on the Boer Wars for the *Daily Mail* and *Morning Post* respectively. In the Second World War, both Lee Miller and Martha Gellhorn covered the conflict for the US. Miller was a freelance photographer and from 1940 war correspondent for *Vogue*. After the war, she married artist Roland Penrose and settled in Britain. Gellhorn wrote short stories in the 1950s that were published in both *Woman's Own* (see page 121) and, in the US, the *Saturday Evening Post*.

George Newnes
(240 × 334 mm, stapled, 20 pages)

JOHN BULL (16 February 1946)

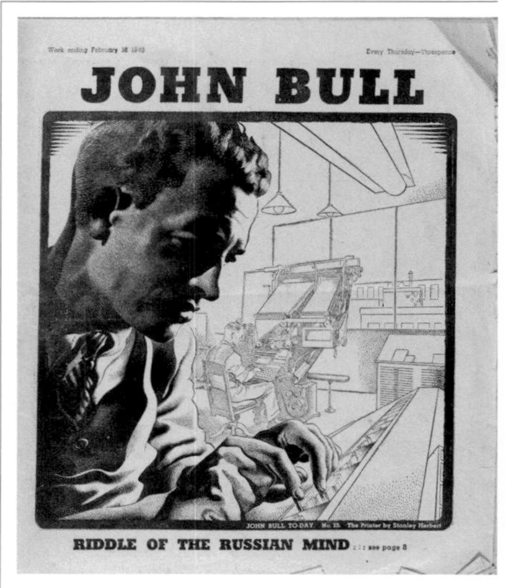

The cover by Stanley Herbert is entitled 'The Printer' and is No. 15 in a series, '*John Bull* To-day', that began before the war but was suspended because of a switch to cover advertising. On page 3 Hannen Swaffer describes how 25,000 of the 200,000 workers in the printing trade are compositors, half of whom went to war and are now coming back. However, Swaffer warns, they face unemployment because of the lack of paper for newspapers, books and general printing. Herbert's scraperboard image shows a compositor examining cast lines of type while a hot-metal Linotype composing machine is operated behind him. Inside is an illustration by Alfred Sindall, who drew the radio-inspired Paul Temple strips in the *London Evening News* in the 1950s.

Odhams Press
(264 × 325 mm, stapled, 24 pages)

JOHN BULL (19 October 1946)

After the war, best-seller *John Bull* was quick to switch to Odhams' full-colour presses in Watford, adopting the same page size as *Woman*. Albert Bailey painted this picture of a boy with his dog, braces and toy boat watching the *Queen Elizabeth*, the world's largest and fastest liner, on her maiden voyage across the Atlantic.

Odhams Press
(264 × 325 mm, stapled, 20 pages)

WOMAN'S OWN (4 August 1949)

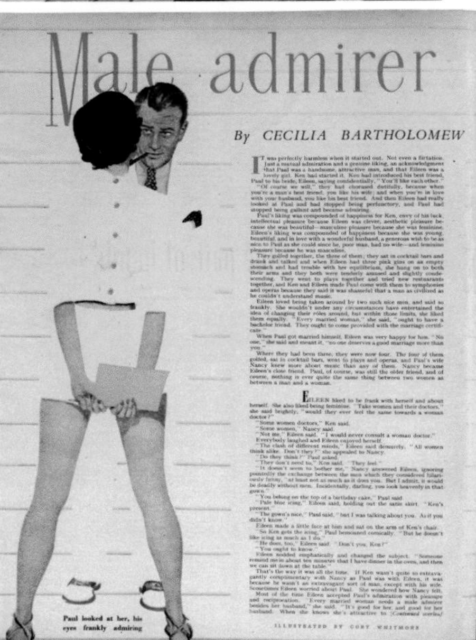

Rival *Woman* switched to cover photography and *Woman's Own* tried that route (using photos of film stars such as Bette Davis), but eventually settled on the illustrations of Aubrey Rix. His stylish portrayals of confident, aspirational young couples dominated the magazine's covers for five years. In this case, the couple are packing a suitcase that carries labels from the Swiss resort of Wengen, where Britons had developed downhill skiing in the early 1920s, and a hotel in Cannes. Slight variations of the capitalized serif title were used until a 1950 relaunch, when it switched to an italic lower case.

An American, Cecilia Bartholomew, wrote the short story 'Male Admirer', which was illustrated by Coby Whitmore, one of the leading US commercial artists.

The centre spread by *Daily Express* fashion illustrator Andrew Robb focuses on Dior's 'floating panel'. Two years before, Dior's 'New Look' had caused a minor crisis when Harold Wilson, president of the Board of Trade, warned journalists against covering extravagant Paris fashions; cloth rationing meant any extra internal demand for fabric thwarted Britain's attempt to export as much as it could to improve the balance of payments after the high levels of debt incurred by buying weapons from the US.

George Newnes
(240 × 334 mm, stapled, 20 pages)

WOMAN AND HOME (September 1949)

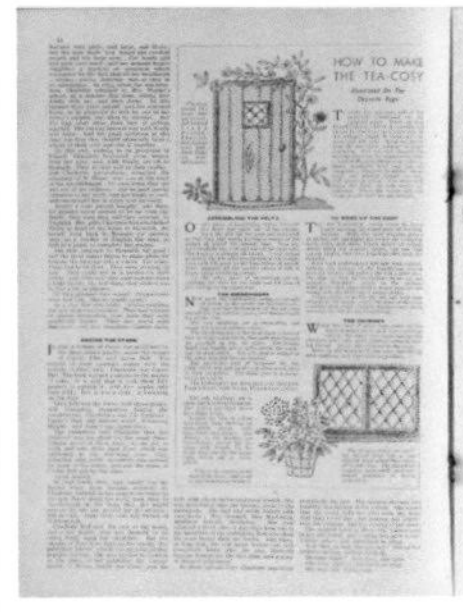

The Amalgamated group concentrated on keeping its prices low. This issue cost 9d, compared with 2s for *Britannia and Eve*. The results of this cost-conscious approach included poorer-quality paper and minimal use of colour.

The fiction spread by Margaret Dale was illustrated by US artist Edwin Georgi. The magazine was printed letterpress, so none of the images bleed off the page or over gutters.

The four centre pages were in colour and devoted to crafts. The pattern for this cottage tea cosy in felt – complete with rain butt – cost 1s 1d from the magazine's transfer department in Bear Alley, which was by its Farringdon Street offices in London.

Amalgamated Press
(220 × 300 mm, stapled, 76 pages)

TATLER & BYSTANDER

(20 April 1949)

Complications in a Lounge. *Author Nigel Wainwright (Frank Lawton) has succeeded so well in enshrining the past happiness of Widow French (Rosalyn Boulter) in a short story that she decides he can guarantee her future tranquillity as well. Reacting curiously to this happy ending are the hotel's femme fatale, Rowena Smith (Shelagh Furley), Judy Holmes (Daphne Arthur), who had half an eye to Nigel herself, small Angela Kingsley (Ann Stephens) and (right) the irrepressible henchwoman Effie as interpreted by Irene Handl*

Anthony Cookman

[Illustration by Tom Titt]

At The Theatre

"Summer in December" (Comedy)

A MILD spring has produced quite a spread of mild little comedies. They are not in the least bit original nor do they profess to be, but they make their points lightly and appeal with gentle confidence to the large playgoing public which comes enviably fresh to their familiar themes.

A stage M.P. satisfactorily rearranges his indispensable secretary's marriage at the Vaudeville; Mr. R. F. Delderfield knowledgeably explores the humour and pathos of late-Victorian shop assistants at the Duke of York's; and Mr. Philip King at the Embassy makes a whole play out of a dress rehearsal by a provincial repertory company and contrives to make it amazingly like the real thing. In each case much is owing to the chief actors—Mr. Leslie Banks, Miss Thora Hird and Mr. Henry Kendall. The theme may be familiar, but acting can still endow it with perennial freshness.

QUITE the best of this group of spring comedies is Mr. James Liggat's comic and sentimental evocation of what happened in the lounge of a seaside hotel one sunny summer. He reassembles familiar types of visitor, but the danger here is less the familiarity of these old friends and their affairs than the absence of any one affair which might concentrate interest.

AGAIN the actor comes to the rescue of his author. Mr. Frank Lawton is the visitor whose chief mission in life is to bring back to the present a lady whose bereaved mind insists on dwelling in the past. It is for her sake that he revives in a short story for a Christmas annual the life of the summer that has passed. It is a very successful short story, stirring the editor's aged heart to youthful enthusiasm and, what is more, achieving its ulterior purpose. But though this affair is started in a prologue, it is by no means strongly developed in the play itself and the epilogue winds it up quite perfunctorily.

This narrative flaw might well have fatal consequences. The truth is that it passes almost unnoticed. Mr. Lawton busies himself jauntily and sympathetically with all the other affairs that come to their crises in the lounge, and his cheerful presence somehow tautens what is slack and tones up what is lacking in comic energy.

He has a great deal on hand, this unobtrusively benevolent busybody. There is a young wife who must be taught the hard lesson that she had better not seem to pursue a husband showing signs of taking flight. There is a shy boy left by Anglo-Indian parents at the mercy of an uncle who is as tough with the young as he is indulgent to himself. There is the usual hotel siren to be discomfited. There is a pleasant little girl who must be protected from shocks and put in the way of reconciling erring parents.

And there is, of course, the beautiful hotel manageress who, when she is not helping her admirer to play providence among the guests, prefers to walk alone with her grief.

MR. LAWTON presents himself as the life and soul of the hotel in such a way that he completely alters our conception of that holy horror. He is always there when wanted, never at any other time, and when there never fails to find the happy phrase, whether benign or satirical, which puts us all in good humour with the latest turn of events. Miss Rosalyn Boulter makes a discreet display of her grief and Mr. Reginald Dyson of the horrid uncle's brutalities. Ann Stephens and Brian Weske are admirable as the children who comfort each other in their distress. And Miss Irene Handl, as the skittish and privileged old servant, is, as always in this part, a steady source of innocent mirth.

Photographed by Angus McBean

SHEILA BURRELL AND DAVID GREENE as Barbara Allen and Marvin Hudgens at a moment of crisis in *Dark of the Moon* at the Ambassadors, the eerie U.S. play of a mortal girl loved by a witch-boy. London-born Sheila Burrell originated the part of Bathsheba in Alan Melville's *Jonathan* at the Embassy, and went to Dublin a few months ago to play a part in *Abdication*. She is married to Laurence Payne, who played Romeo in last season's Stratford-on-Avon festival. David Greene is a Dubliner who spent two and a half years with the Oxford Rep., then toured the Far East with John Gielgud in *Hamlet* and more recently returned from Italy, where he had been filming in *The Golden Madonna* with Phyllis Calvert. In an interval between engagements he became, in turn, crime reporter, barman and trawler fisherman. In 1937 he was the boy swimming champion of England

Freda Bruce Lockhart

[Decorations by Hoffnung]

At The Pictures

The Wizard's Wand

"Young love is not a new discovery"

CLIVE BROOK, who poses for this latest and last of the series of Emmwood sketches of theatre personalities, has recently returned from a much-needed holiday in the Bahamas following his outstanding success in the Aldous Huxley play *The Gioconda Smile*, which he left at Christmas. Mr. Brook has, in addition to playing frequently in the West End, done much film work, both here and in Hollywood, and it is well worth recording his opinion about which medium, film or stage, is the more difficult—that good acting is good acting in either. For eleven years he lived in the U.S., and of it he says, "I loved it and I love Americans. And so would anyone who had lived there as long as that." His son Lyndon and daughter Faith have inherited a full measure of their father's acting talent and are among the most promising of the younger generation of players

The centre 20 pages of this issue were printed in gravure and the outer section letterpress. This spread incorporates both printing techniques. The gravure of the right-hand page shows the detail in Angus McBean's surreal photograph of Sheila Burrell and David Greene to its best effect. The theatre caricatures on the opposite page are by Tom Titt – his monogram is on the far left.

On the next spread is a portrait of Clive Brook by Emmwood (John Musgrave-Wood), who had joined the magazine the previous year. Musgrave-Wood also drew for *Punch*, the *Sunday Express* and the US title *Life*. From 1957 to 1975, he was a political cartoonist on the *Daily Mail*.

Illustrated Newspapers
(222 × 302 mm, stapled, 40 pages)

LILLIPUT (December 1949)

According to Russell Davies, his biographer, Ronald Searle's first national cartoon was in the July 1940 issue of *London Opinion*. He introduced St Trinian's to the world in the October 1941 issue of *Lilliput* and the cartoons began again after the war. In 1949, Walter Trier's series of covers for *Lilliput* – which had run since the launch of the pocket monthly – ended and various different artists were used each month. Searle's scratchy style influenced many later caricaturists; he was made a Royal Designer for Industry in 1988. The cartoons led to the film *Belles of St Trinian's* in 1954, with other films based on the cartoon following in the 1950s, 1960s, 1980s and 2000s.

Hulton
(138 × 198 mm, stapled, 124 pages)

LILLIPUT (December 1949)

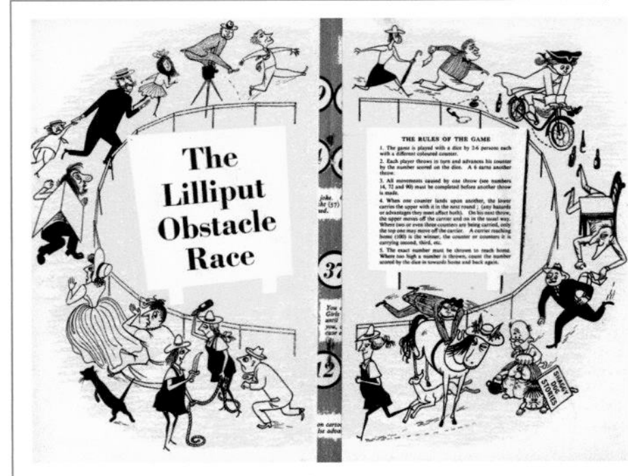

Ronald Searle produced this Obstacle Race dice game as a pull-out centrefold.

Hulton
(138 × 198 mm, stapled, 124 pages)

WOMAN'S OWN (2 March 1950)

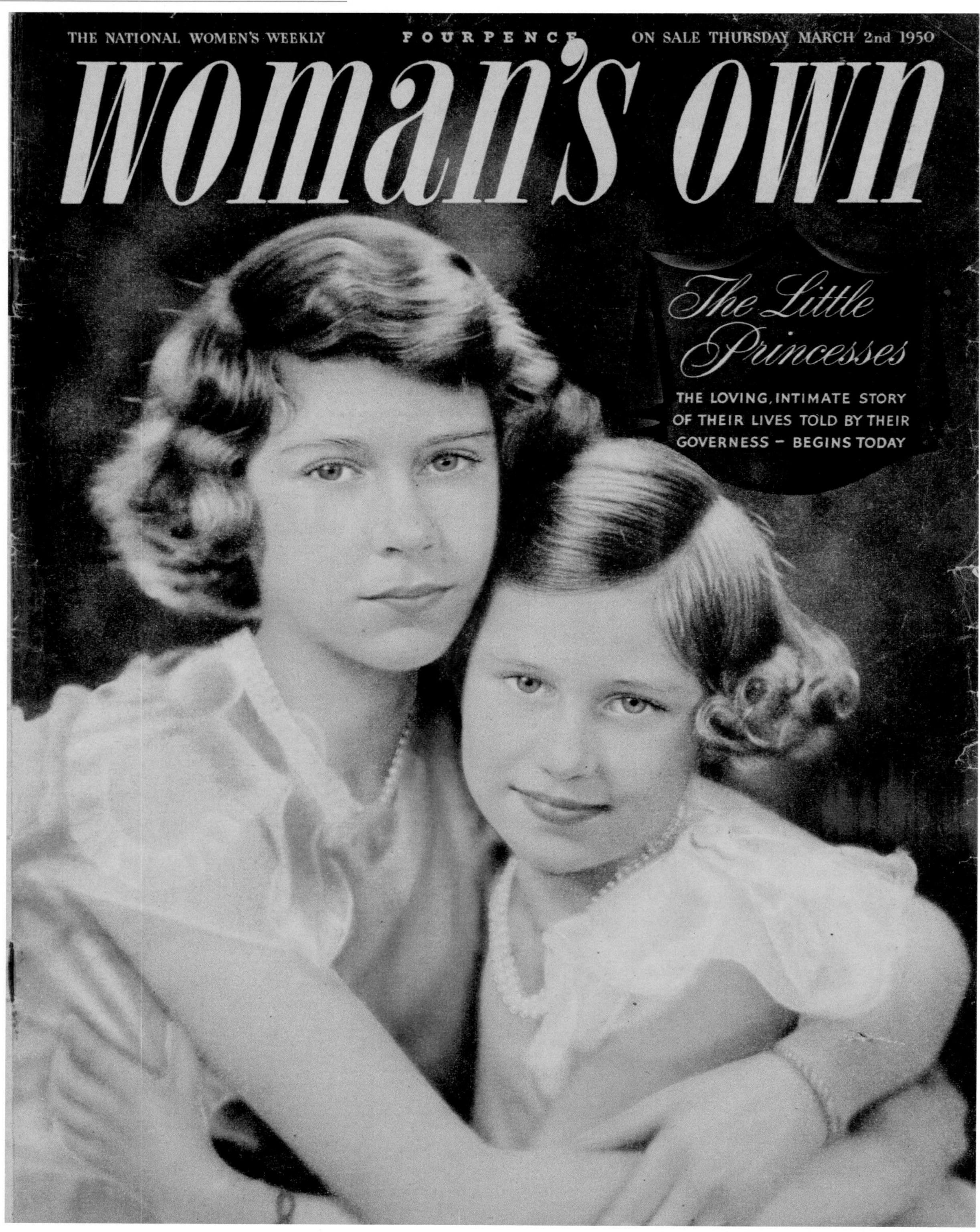

Woman's Own celebrated the end of paper rationing for magazines with 48 pages in this issue (wartime copies had been 20 or 24 pages). This retouched photographic cover – of the two princesses, Elizabeth and Margaret, taken in black and white by Marcus Adams in February 1939 (see an earlier example on page 101) – set the tone for women's weeklies over the next decade, as stories about the young royal family became vital to their circulation.

The issue also marked an important watershed: where the illustrations of Aubrey Rix had dominated covers for the previous five years, from now on photography was the first choice. The advertising reminds us, however, that some products were still rationed. A half-page advert includes the copy: 'The Bigger Size Mars is the most you can get in a chocolate bar for 2 [ration card] points'.

George Newnes
(255 × 330 mm, stapled, 48 pages)

WOMAN'S OWN (4 December 1952)

Robb's Fashion News...

Party DRESSES are brighter than ever . . . in colours and materials which catch the mood of a party. This winter it is gay colours for gay times—pinks, blue, reds and soft greens which brighten and flatter your complexion and bring a sparkle to your eyes.

New this season is the emphasis on the boat-shaped and chemise neckline, the shoulder collar, the halter neck and the soft shoulder stole. **Here are the clothes** to give you the look of the perfect party girl.

SUZANNE GREY

Warm red, velvet and separates (top and short skirt) are three fashion pointers which are certain for success this winter. The top is 59s. 6d. and the skirt is 4½ gns. Made in many colours by Estrava.

A full evening dress of spot-printed net in milk-maid blue. The top of the bodice and edges of the stole are appliqued with white pique outlined in blue. By Acquer, price 15½ gns.

Photographed above are two long evening dresses. The taffeta dress trimmed with roses, from Bijou price £5 14s. 8d. The halter-necked dress in two shades of net from Roecliffe and Chapman, price 11 gns.

Black net with brilliantly coloured laced cummerbund. The skirt is very full and the bodice stiffened and boned. In a large range of different colours with contrast cummerbund. By Acquer, price 11 gns.

White, black and red are the colours in these party separates by Lady in Black. The jet trimmed chemise top is in grosgrain price £6 12s. 6d. The short velvet skirt with fringed pockets is £8 18s.

Green faille dress with full flared skirt of mid-calf length. The huge ruff collar is very flattering to pretty shoulders. The perfect dress for a special party by Lady in Black price 8 gns.

24

25

This centre spread by fashion illustrator Andrew Robb, who also worked for the *Daily Express*, merges his bold, minimal line with a washed-out photograph which is used as a background. Robb regularly illustrated the fashion news by Suzanne Grey and provided a centre-spread painting of the coronation for the magazine; he also sketched for Norman Hartnell, who designed the Queen's gown. This issue carried a short story, 'The Long Journey', by Martha Gellhorn, who was war correspondent for the US weekly magazine *Collier's* and had been married to Ernest Hemingway from 1940 to 1945. The story had featured in the US *Good Housekeeping* in June. The artist was Ben Ostrick, a magazine regular who also illustrated book covers, including James Bond thrillers, for the publisher Pan using the pen name J. Oval.

George Newnes
(255 × 330 mm, stapled, 48 pages)

ILLUSTRATED LONDON NEWS (12 May 1951)

No. 5847—Volume 218
PRICE THREE SHILLINGS

The Illustrated London News,
May 12, 1951

THE ILLUSTRATED LONDON NEWS
FESTIVAL OF BRITAIN

CUNEO 1951

THE EXHIBITION'S OPENING–SPECIAL NUMBER

PRICE 3s. : BY INLAND POST, 3s. 3d.
Canada, 1½d. Foreign, 4d.

REGISTERED AS A NEWSPAPER FOR TRANSMISSION IN THE UNITED KINGDOM.

PUBLISHING OFFICE : COMMONWEALTH HOUSE,
1, NEW OXFORD STREET, LONDON, W.C.1.

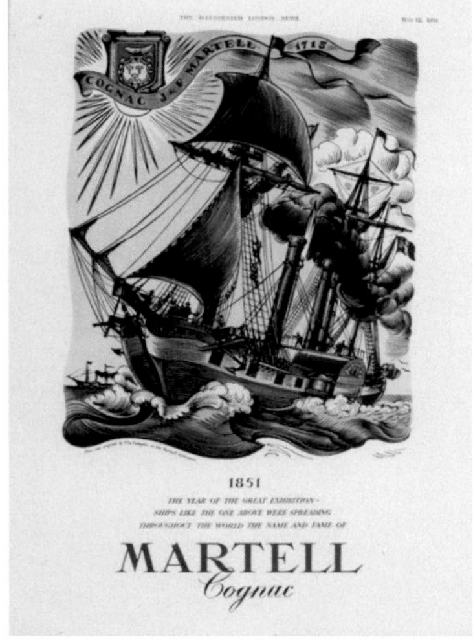

Terence Cuneo, a renowned military and railway painter who was appointed as the official artist for the coronation in 1953, chose an Olympian scene to mark the Festival of Britain for the *Illustrated London News*. The Dome of Discovery can be seen clearly on the South Bank, with the Skylon tower to the left.

There appears to be no sign of a mouse, which Cuneo later adopted as a trademark in his paintings. Inside were eight colour pages on the same paper stock as the cover; four for the centre pages devoted to the festival and four for advertising, including a Martell cognac advert that used a special gold ink.

Illustrated News and Sketch Ltd
(260 × 367 mm, stapled, 74 pages)

RADIO TIMES (31 May 1953)

BBC SOUND AND TELEVISION PROGRAMMES..MAY 31—JUNE 6 3D

RADIO TIMES

EIIR

1953

eric fraser

CORONATION NUMBER

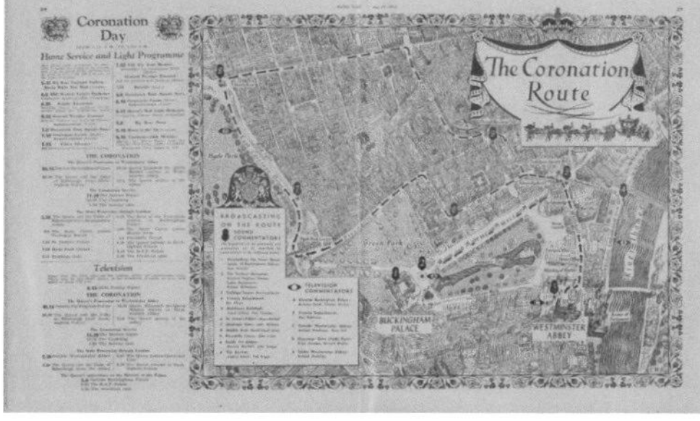

The *Radio Times* commissioned an unusual cover for the coronation in that Eric Fraser drew not only the heraldic illustration on the front, but also the back cover advertisement for Batchelors Foods in a similar style. The yellow/gold background with crowns picked out in a darker tint continued across the back and marked the first time the BBC's listings weekly had used colour since before the war. The Batchelors advert was also used on the back of the BBC's *Listener* (28 May 1953). Fraser drew for the *Radio Times* from 1926 until 1982, the year before his death.

The opening spread featured an advertisement for Shell, 'The Crowning of a British Queen', by Dick Hart. This showed the royal procession from the gates of Buckingham Palace to Westminster Abbey framing a poem with the verses detailing the journey through 'London's brave historic streets'. For the opening editorial page, the Queen's portrait was framed by Norman Mansbridge (NM), a *Punch* favourite who drew its main political cartoon on alternate weeks in the late 1950s.

The centre spread showed the procession route marked with the positions of the BBC's 16 sound commentators and eight television commentators for the event. The illustration was by Cecil W. Bacon (CWB).

The listings spread was framed with illustrations of modern and Elizabethan fireworks by C. Walter Hodges. Decorative borders and boxes were a feature of the magazine. Elsewhere in the issue were images by Hodges, as well as by Robert Stewart Sherriffs (who took over *Men Only*'s cover caricatures from Edward S. Hynes – Hynes – in 1956), Robin Jacques (another long-time contributor, from 1946 to 1995) and David Knight.

In 1954, the *Radio Times* began to use photographic covers, following the approach of the commercial stations' listing magazine, *TV Times*. Both tended to display cover photographs in a TV-shaped frame. The *Radio Times* carried on using illustration for its Christmas specials.

BBC
(250 × 314 mm, stapled, 52 pages)

MOTOR SPORT (March 1952)

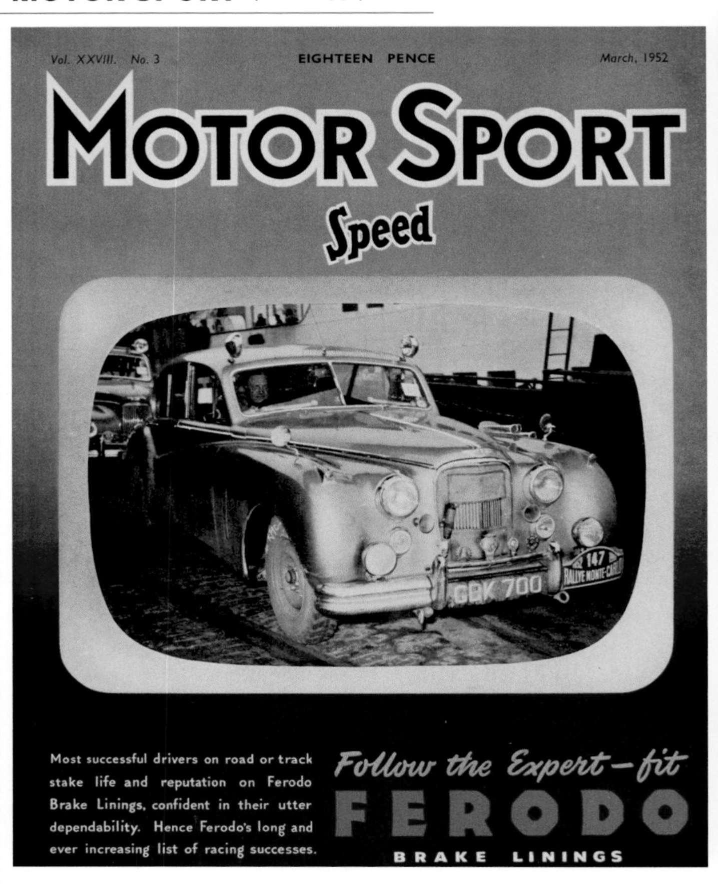

The temptation to carry advertising on the front cover can be difficult for magazine publishers to resist. Some trade publications – particularly in the motoring and aviation sectors – commissioned illustrated or photographic covers in cooperation with advertisers, and around this time *Motor Sport* ran photographic covers with the image framed as if on a television set. The Jaguar, a winner in one of the Monte Carlo rally classes, is credited in the contents panel inside as using Ferodo brake linings and clutch, reflecting the fact that Ferodo was the regular cover advertiser. *Motor Sport* carried on with cover advertisers until late 1953. Inside, the pages used three columns throughout, with single- or double-column pictures. The centre four pages, printed on better paper, were used for advertising and a photographic centre spread. There was no colour apart from on the covers.

Teesdale Publishing
(214 × 280 mm, stapled, 56 pages)

PICTUREGOER (26 April 1952)

A dancing Rita Hayworth provides the glamour for this cover of the film weekly. *Picturegoer*'s covers were printed using a spot colour or, as in this case, duotone – a second colour printed over the black, giving a rich look. Cinema audiences were on a slow decline after the war, but magazines such as this thrived on photographic publicity handouts from the film studios until the late 1950s (ABC Cinema launched its own magazine, *ABC Film Review*, in 1950 based on free studio publicity stills). Elizabeth Taylor promotes Lux soap on the inside cover of this issue.

Odhams Press
(230 × 300 mm, stapled, 24 pages)

PUNCH (13 June 1956)

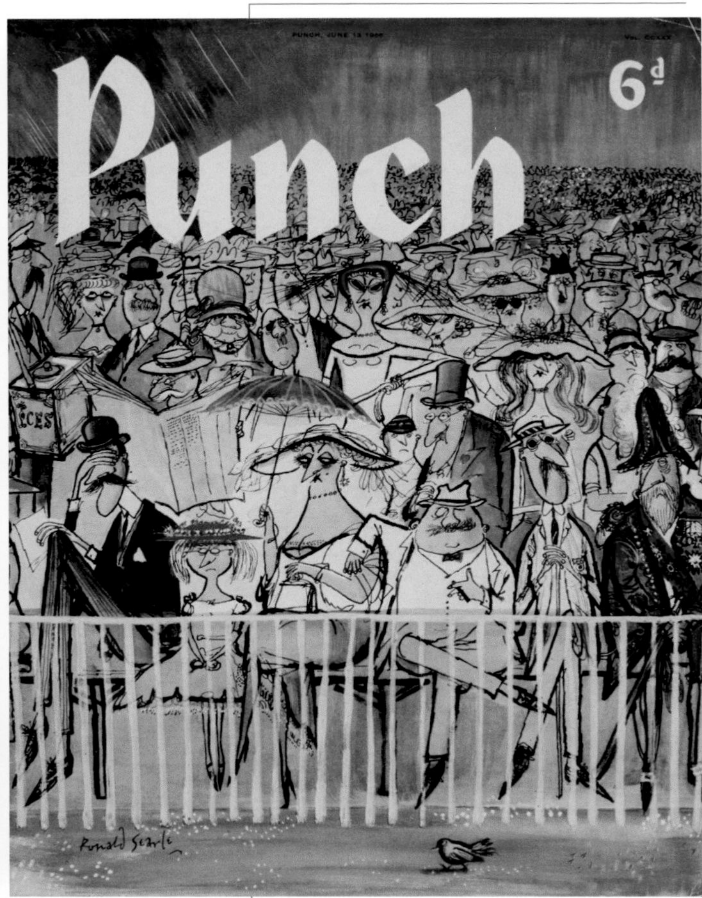

Malcolm Muggeridge became editor of *Punch* in 1953 with a brief to increase its sales. Seen as having lost its edge, it faced strong competition as many magazines relaunched with colour printing, larger formats and pepped-up design to try to cement their attractiveness with advertisers. At *Punch*, Richard Doyle's century-old illustration was still the standard cover, with commissioned colour illustrations for issues that attracted more advertising, such as those that coincided with motor shows, seasonal specials (such as the Summer Number) and the almanacs. Muggeridge introduced variants on the Doyle cover by *Punch* regulars, and colour covers gradually ousted Doyle's creation – though it was still used into 1957 and there were later parodies of it. The 21 December 1977 issue resurrected Doyle's drawing for a Nostalgia Number. This racing-crowd cover – coinciding with Royal Ascot – is by Ronald Searle and features a new title style that remained more or less the same for a decade. Searle also did one of the first weekly *Punch* colour covers for the 24 October 1954 issue, a parody of Picasso's style in celebration of the artist's birthday.

Bradbury, Agnew & Co.
(224 × 285 mm, stapled, 60 pages)

PICTURE POST (20 April 1957)

Picture Post, April 20, 1957

Picture Post, April 20, 1957

Swords glint in the myriad lights; Paris's smartest set crowds the balconies; then, [illegible] a procession eclipsing the glamour of any Opéra performance, the Queen mounts the broad [illegible] to the Royal Box. The first day of Paris's Royal visit is reaching the climax of its [illegible]

18

19

Bert Hardy took 15 photos of Queen Elizabeth's entrance to the Paris Opéra for this montage, which was assembled by the magazine's technicians. Some of the joins can be seen on close scrutiny, if one follows the lens distortion at the edges of the original images. Also, note that several of the Republican Guard in polished helmets lining the staircase have not drawn their sabres, suggesting that those parts of the montage were taken before the Queen entered the room. *Picture Post* had colour on its covers at this stage as well as for the centre four pages. However, it closed soon after this issue. Hardy went on to a career in advertising and to cement his reputation as Britain's most popular photographer.

Hulton
(250 × 330 mm, stapled, 80 pages)

RAZZLE (April 1950)

Razzle closed during the war but reappeared in a pocket format, keeping its Art Deco title. Its main selling point was a colour centre spread that featured the '*Razzle* dream girl' by George Davies, who also drew strip cartoons for the *Daily Express* and *Sunday Pictorial* newspapers. The cover and centre pages were printed on slightly better stock. The rest of the magazine consisted of cartoons, timeless short articles and a couple of photographs of topless women. As the 1950s progressed, such magazines were able to gain access to a free, plentiful supply of pin-up photographs in the form of publicity handouts. The issues were numbered, not dated.

Ritz Publishing (1935)/Gaywood Press
(133 × 212 mm, stapled, 72 pages)

TIT-BITS (10 November 1951)

Tit-Bits dropped advertising from its covers after the war in favour of photographs of actresses, sportsmen and TV personalities, but maintained an A4-ish size. Then in 1950 it moved to a tabloid format with pin-up covers, sensational topical stories and newspaper-style layout and typography – note the bastard measure intro paragraph to the splash in a larger bold type. These issues can be seen as a forerunner of the red-top tabloids in the 1980s. The *Tit-Bits* green is still used. Inside, the cover feature gushed: 'Eighteen-year-old Joan Collins, our Cover Girl this week and who specially posed for these pictures, is now playing an important part in *One Sinner*, now filming at Ealing Studios. She is a young star of the future, sparkling with vivacity and good health – and with beautiful posture.' This formula was the essence of the *Sun*'s 'Page 3' girl from 1970. Rupert Murdoch was at university in Oxford in the early 1950s, where he managed Oxford Student Publications before becoming a subeditor on the *Daily Express*. *Tit-Bits* was still a general-interest magazine, however, running fashion and women's features. Here there are five pages devoted to football pools, horse-racing and prize competitions, which were heavily promoted.

Newnes
(225 × 300 mm, stapled, 24 pages)

MEN ONLY (May 1954)

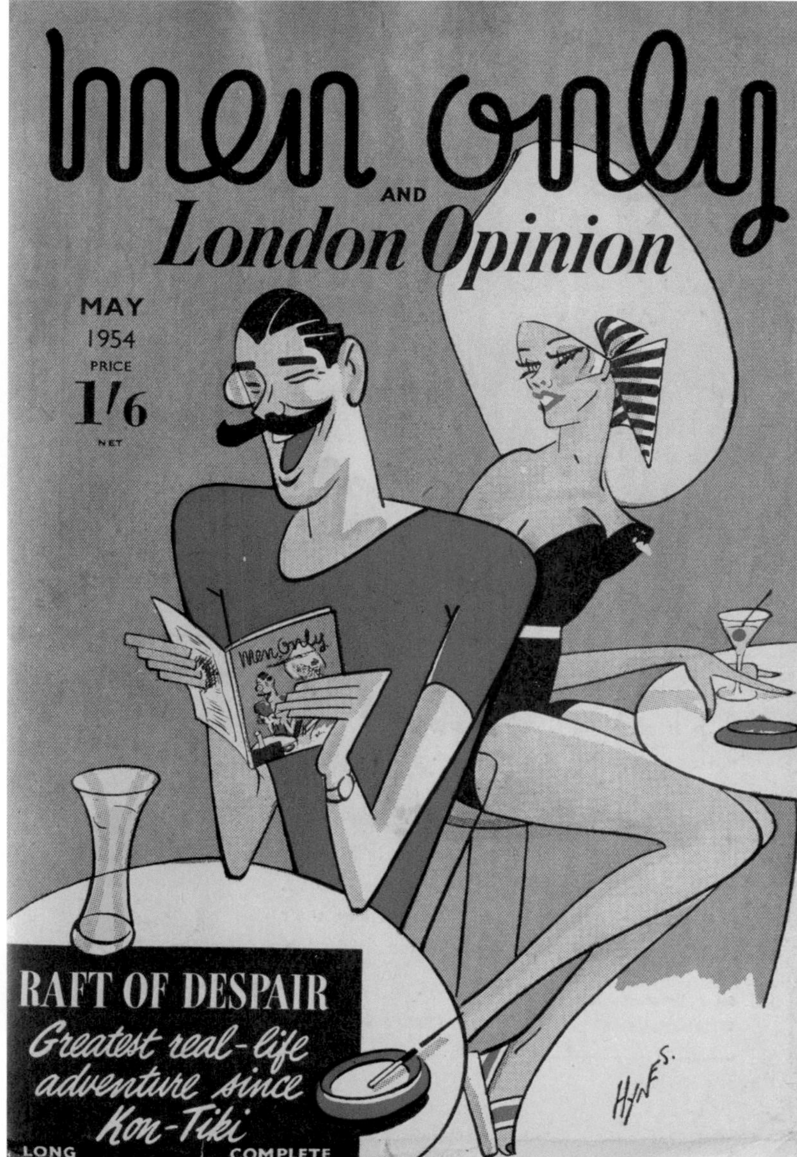

Having taken over both the *Strand* and *London Opinion* (which had in turn bought the *Humorist*), *Men Only* had a monopoly of the men's lifestyle monthlies – except for *Lilliput*. This issue was the first after the takeover of *London Opinion*. It adopted a racier cover style with the Edward S. Hynes cartoons portraying the leery activities of a mustachioed man about town, rather than showing caricatures of the great and the good. Inside, the pages were still bookish, in a single- or double-column setting. Two sets of four pages of photographs were interspersed between standard printing sections; there were also whole-page cartoons that used spot colour. The 30-page 'Raft of Despair' real-life adventure story was set across two columns with two half-page illustrations, with raised capitals on each spread. The pin-up on a 'Let's Join the Ladies' page was a colour illustration by the Peruvian artist Alberto Vargas, who made his name on *Esquire* in the US. Later contributors to the page, which as a concept mirrors *Razzle*'s strategy, included Archie Dickens and the US artist Joyce Ballantyne.

C. Arthur Pearson (128 × 192 mm, though the cover was 4 mm larger, book binding, 158 pages)

BLIGHTY (7 August 1954)

Blighty went through many redesigns in the 1950s and changed its name, first to *Blighty Parade*, then to *Parade & Blighty* and finally, after the *Blighty* part of the title had got smaller and smaller, to *Parade*. Cover designs changed from full-page cartoons with a military theme to leggy women by Arthur Ferrier, and on to black-and-white pin-ups in 1954. The covers went colour in the second half of the year, and this portrait of US actress and singer Abbe Lane is typical. Arthur Ferrier's cartoons were then carried on page 3. Later issues used various devices on the cover to promote articles, such as rag-outs (where a piece of text is made to look as if it has been torn from another publication), starbursts, corner slashes, text reversed out of, or printed black-over, coloured rectangles, and circles and strips presented along the bottom. The magazine saw itself as a humorous weekly, but evolved into a men's top-shelf title in the 1960s.

City Magazines
(204 × 286 mm, stapled, 36 pages)

SPAN (September 1954)

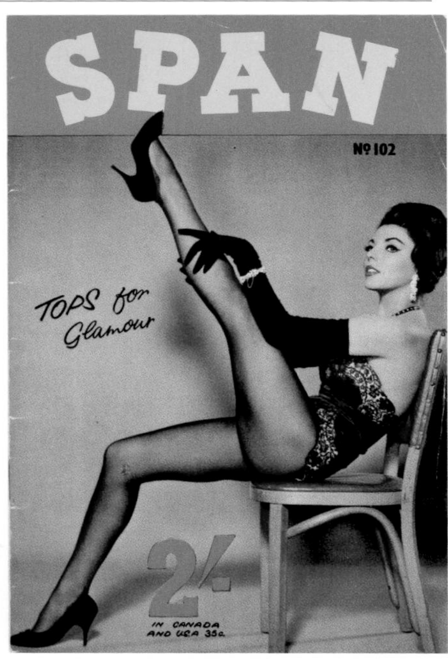

Spick and *Span* were pocket-format pin-up titles launched at about the same time as *Playboy* in the US. However, the content was much more geared to 'girl next door in her underwear' photographs, with little text and low costs. *Span* did show some film stars, and a third title from the same publisher, *66*, was based around that number of photographs of a single star for each issue – Diana Dors, Sabrina, Sophia Loren and Joan Collins were featured. Dozens of cheap titles were launched in this pocket format, initially in mono, but with colour covers and some colour inside as the 1950s progressed. In 1957, photographer George Harrison Marks and model Pamela Green launched the larger-format *Kamera*, which showed topless women on its colour covers from the start, and claims to have sold 150,000 copies of its first issue after several reprints. Photographs were retouched to comply with obscenity laws (removing pubic hair, for example). Most of the pocket titles folded in the face of larger-format titles in the 1960s, but both *Spick* and *Span* lasted into the mid-1970s.

Town & Country Publications
(117 × 176 mm, stapled, 44 pages)

WOMAN'S REALM (22 February 1958)

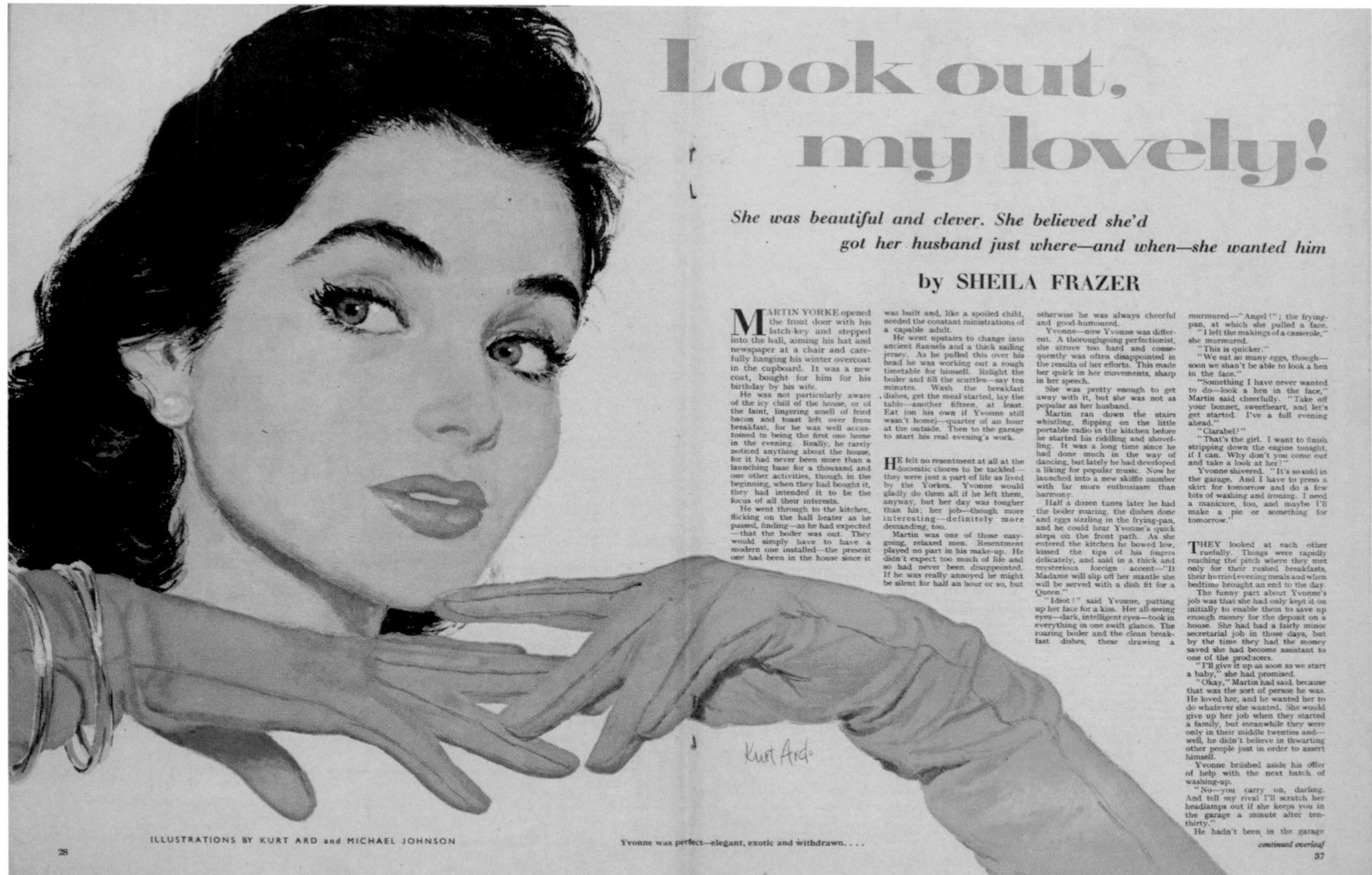

Look out, my lovely!

She was beautiful and clever. She believed she'd got her husband just where—and when—she wanted him

by SHEILA FRAZER

MARTIN YORKE opened the front door with his latch-key and stepped into the hall, aiming his hat and newspaper at a chair and carefully hanging his winter overcoat in the cupboard. It was a new coat, bought for him for his birthday by his wife.

He was not particularly aware of the icy chill of the house, or of the faint, lingering smell of fried bacon and toast left over from breakfast, for he was well accustomed to being the first one home in the evening. Really, he rarely noticed anything about the house, for it had never been more than a launching base for a thousand and one other activities, though in the beginning, when they had bought it, they had intended it to be the focus of all their interests.

He went through to the kitchen, flicking on the hall heater as he passed, finding—as he had expected—that the boiler was out. They would simply have to have a modern one installed—the present one had been in the house since it was built and, like a spoiled child, needed the constant ministrations of a capable adult.

He went upstairs to change into ancient flannels and a thick sailing jersey. As he pulled this over his head he was working out a rough timetable for himself. Relight the boiler and fill the scuttles—say ten minutes. Wash the breakfast dishes, get the meal started, lay the table—another fifteen, at least. Eat (on his own if Yvonne still wasn't home)—quarter of an hour at the outside. Then to the garage to start his real evening's work.

HE felt no resentment at all at the domestic chores to be tackled—they were just a part of life as lived by the Yorkes. Yvonne would gladly do them all if he left them, anyway, but her day was tougher than his; her job—though more interesting—definitely more demanding, too.

Martin was one of those easy-going, relaxed men. Resentment played no part in his make-up. He didn't expect too much of life and so had never been disappointed. If he was really annoyed he might be silent for half an hour or so, but otherwise he was always cheerful and good-humoured.

Yvonne—now Yvonne was different. A thoroughgoing perfectionist, she strove too hard and consequently was often disappointed in the results of her efforts. This made her quick in her movements, sharp in her speech.

She was pretty enough to get away with it, but she was not as popular as her husband.

Martin ran down the stairs whistling, flipping on the little portable radio in the kitchen before he started his riddling and shovelling. It was a long time since he had done much in the way of dancing, but lately he had developed a liking for popular music. Now he launched into a new skiffle number with far more enthusiasm than harmony.

Half a dozen tunes later he had the boiler roaring, the dishes done and eggs sizzling in the frying-pan, and he could hear Yvonne's quick steps on the front path. As she entered the kitchen he bowed low, kissed the tips of his fingers delicately, and said in a thick and mysterious foreign accent—"It Madame will slip off her mantle she will be served with a dish fit for a Queen."

"Idiot!" said Yvonne, putting up her face for a kiss. Her all-seeing eyes—dark, intelligent eyes—took in everything in one swift glance. The roaring boiler and the clean breakfast dishes, these drawing a murmured—"Angel!"; the frying-pan, at which she pulled a face.

"I left the makings of a casserole," she murmured.

"This is quicker."

"We eat so many eggs, though—soon we shan't be able to look a hen in the face."

"Something I have never wanted to do—look a hen in the face," Martin said cheerfully. "Take off your bonnet, sweetheart, and let's get started. I've a full evening ahead."

"Clarabel?"

"That's the girl. I want to finish stripping down the engine tonight, if I can. Why don't you come out and take a look at her?"

Yvonne shivered. "It's so cold in the garage. And I have to press a skirt for tomorrow and do a few bits of washing and ironing. I need a manicure, too, and maybe I'll make a pie or something for tomorrow."

THEY looked at each other ruefully. Things were rapidly reaching the pitch where they met only for their rushed breakfasts, their hurried evening meals and when bedtime brought an end to the day.

The funny part about Yvonne's job was that she had only kept it on initially to enable them to save up enough money for the deposit on a house. She had had a fairly minor secretarial job in those days, but by the time they had the money saved she had become assistant to one of the producers.

"I'll give it up as soon as we start a baby," she had promised.

"Okay," Martin had said, because that was the sort of person he was. He loved her, and he wanted her to do whatever she wanted. She would give up her job when they started a family, but meanwhile they were only in their middle twenties and—well, he didn't believe in thwarting other people just in order to assert himself.

Yvonne brushed aside his offer of help with the next batch of washing-up.

"No—you carry on, darling. And tell my rival I'll scratch her headlamps out if she keeps you in the garage a minute after ten-thirty."

He hadn't been in the garage

continued overleaf

Kurt Ard

ILLUSTRATIONS BY KURT ARD and MICHAEL JOHNSON

28

Yvonne was perfect—elegant, exotic and withdrawn. . . .

37

Colour coordination between gloves, lips and headline mark this confident centre spread for the first issue of *Woman's Realm* by Danish artist Kurt Ard, who trained in the US. Illustration in the 1950s was noted for the popularity of large areas of flat colour (toned with black). Michael Johnson provided a second drawing for the next page of the story. Despite the visual pull of Ard's image now, it would have been muted on first sight by an eight-page knitting pull-out bound into the centre of the magazine. Other illustrators for fiction pieces included Douglas Hills and Kenneth Kirkland.

Odhams Press
(226 × 300 mm, stapled, 64 pages)

MAN ABOUT TOWN (Spring 1956)

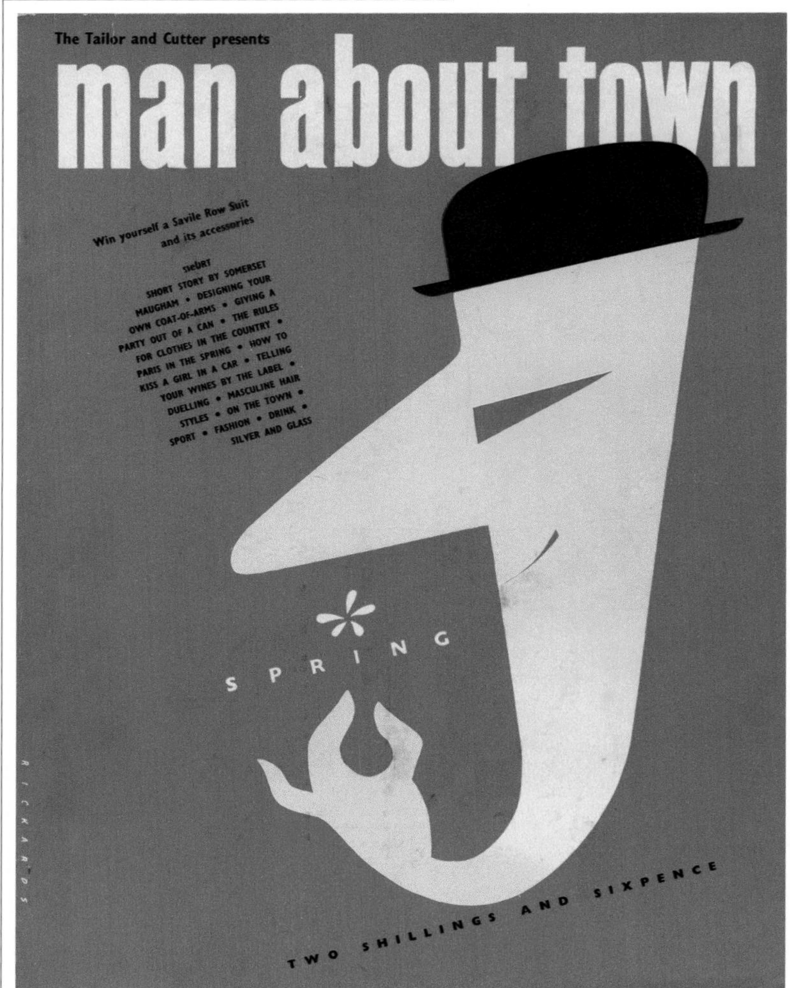

John Taylor launched *Man About Town* as an offshoot of trade magazine *Tailor & Cutter*, which, according to *The Times*, he had made into 'the most quoted trade paper in the world', a statement echoed by both the *Guardian* and *Time*. *Man About Town* was distributed through tailors' shops, but it was a tough market, as shown by the fact that a UK edition of US men's monthly *Esquire* failed to establish itself. *Man About Town* was personified by a mustachioed man in a dinner suit or a louche-looking stick figure who appeared on the first issue cover by *Eagle* artist Frank Bellamy. Maurice Rickards – who later popularized the study of ephemera – worked as a designer on *Man About Town* and produced this poster-style cover. Elsewhere in the issue were cartoons by Young Turks Marc (Mark Boxer) and Michael Heath, Bill Taylor and Polish-born Franciszka Themerson, who with her husband, Stefan, had founded avant-garde book publisher Gaberbocchus Press in 1948. Beresford Egan illustrated the 1927 short story 'The Closed Shop' by W. Somerset Maugham.

Tailor and Cutter Ltd
(216 × 280 mm, side-stabbed, 108 pages)

MAN ABOUT TOWN (Summer 1957)

TRAVEL

HOW TO GET INTO OTHER PEOPLE'S HOUSES

The Art of the P.G.

A few friendly instructions about current methods of getting fat and fit and feeding off the native population.

IF this is the age of anything it is surely the age of the "Gimmick", the search of novelty for its own sake—and the trend applies to holidays as much as it does to anything else.

The idea of going away for a holiday at all is relatively modern, only commencing with the coming of the railways and the sudden accessibility of the seaside to those who once lived their whole life without moving out of the parish they were born in.

For a while the idea behind a holiday was to spend your time doing exactly the opposite of what you did during the other fifty weeks. So the busman's holiday was yachting, the Banker's was hiking or camping, the rich man "roughed it" and the poorer man saved up all year for a fortnight of relative luxury.

The new trend is to live a normal life in different surroundings.

At last it has got through to the population that hotel life is much the same all over the world. Whether you stop at the Savoy, or Shepherds, the Bar Au Lac, or the Splendide, hotel service, hotel meals and hotel decor follow an international mean once you get above the acceptable line. To the Briton all waiters are foreign anyway—so he is not faintly tickled to have his lunch served by a man with a broken accent. The menu is French whether or not the hotel is—and the business executive used to a reasonable amount of hotel life finds that foreign hotels do not really give him a foreign holiday. He spends all that money on his train or air fare and finds that, apart from the fact that the sun is shining outside, he might well have taken a cab to the Strand Palace.

Doubtless this is the psychological reason for the boom in "home holidays"—where the visitors stay with a native family and live, eat, and talk and behave as they would themselves in the normal way.

Not so long ago this idea of going

MAN ABOUT TOWN, SUMMER, 1957

33

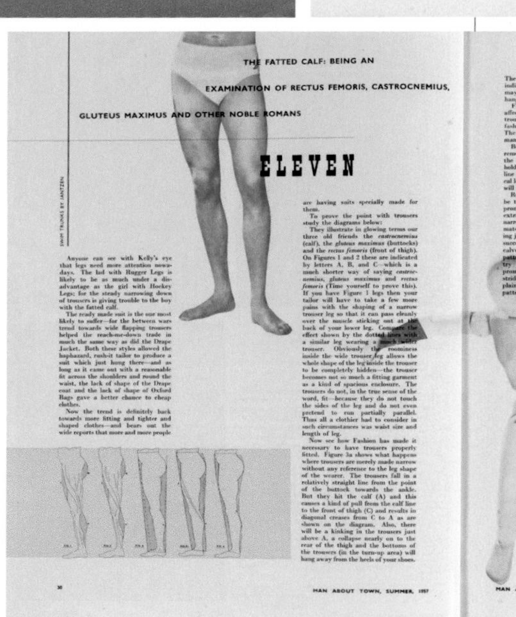

THE FATTED CALF: BEING AN EXAMINATION OF RECTUS FEMORIS, CASTROCNEMIUS, GLUTEUS MAXIMUS AND OTHER NOBLE ROMANS

ELEVEN

MAN ABOUT TOWN, SUMMER, 1957

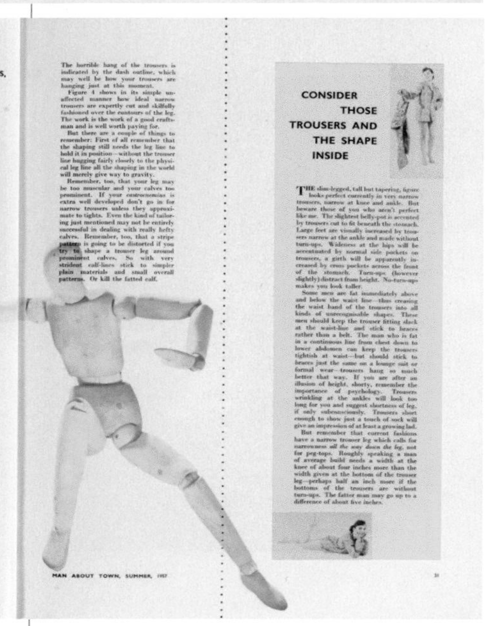

CONSIDER THOSE TROUSERS AND THE SHAPE INSIDE

MAN ABOUT TOWN, SUMMER, 1957

Each feature was designed with extensive use of spot-colour panels, decorative rules, drop capitals and illustrated letters.

Tailor and Cutter Ltd
(216 × 280 mm, side-stabbed, 104 pages)

MAN ABOUT TOWN (Autumn 1958)

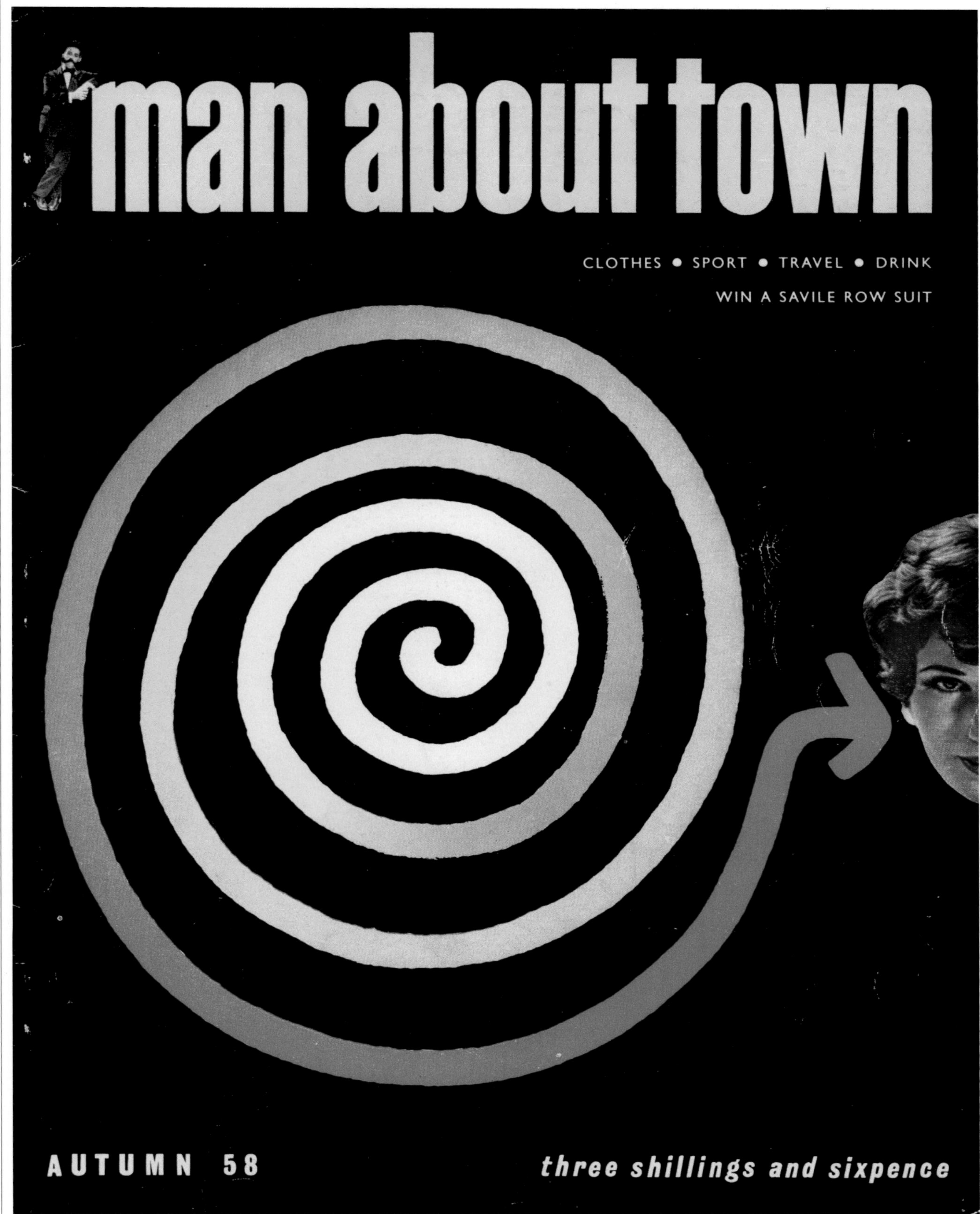

This squiggle cover has no individual cover lines for features but lists the topics: clothes, sport, travel and drink, plus a competition to win a Savile Row suit. Other covers had added 'women and various other bad habits', an example of the humorous approach of editor John Taylor, of whom the magazine was a personification. The magazine's mascot, a mustachioed man in a dinner suit, can be seen leaning against the masthead in the top left corner. He also appeared on the contents page. The cover is another example by ephemerist Maurice Rickards. Illustrators included Michael Heath and Franciszka Themerson.

Tailor and Cutter Ltd
(216 × 280 mm, side-stabbed, 124 pages)

HOMES AND GARDENS (November 1956)

SUCH AN ORDINARY WOMAN . . .

perhaps . . . but once she was the sole guardian of a deadly secret!

By ANTHONY GILBERT

LAST YEAR, for health reasons, I spent some weeks at a small hotel on the Italian Riviera. It was "off-season" and there were not more than half-a-dozen people staying there, among them an old couple who were obviously fellow-countrymen. As a rule, I am very satisfied with my own company when I am abroad, and I certainly had not come to Italy to meet other Englishmen, but from the first this pair engaged my interest.

I had a strange feeling that, though I was sure I had never met him before, I ought to know who the old man was. I racked my brains, but without result. He must have been extraordinarily handsome once; even now, there was a fineness of bone structure, a kind of courtly arrogance about him that was impressive. His wife was a little younger, a sweet and gentle woman, obviously devoted to him, but so ordinary in appearance and manner that I found myself wondering what had led this striking personality to marry anyone so undistinguished. I supposed she had once been his nurse or secretary whom he had married, mainly for convenience, fairly late in life.

It was he who made the first move by offering me his copy of *The Times*, which was flown out to him each day; his last extravagance, he said with an odd smile, as if I should know what he meant. I learned that their name was

ILLUSTRATED BY JOHN WARD

Most British magazines designed each opening spread to suit the flavour of the article; these, within 14 pages of each other, demonstrate the variation in design that could result. 'Such an ordinary woman' by Anthony Gilbert was illustrated by John Ward. Ward worked as an illustrator for *Vogue* for four years until 1952, when he went freelance and later illustrated dust jackets for Laurie Lee's *Cider with Rosie* and H.E. Bates's *The Darling Buds of May*. In the 1980s, he gave painting lessons to the Prince of Wales.

George Newnes
(222 × 290 mm, side-stabbed, 248 pages)

Travelling Light

BY MERVYN JONES

Strange, unexpected things can happen on board ship!

"ONLY THESE two cases, sir?"

"That's all, thank you."

The steward allowed himself a glance of surprise. People who crossed the Atlantic in an "A" Deck stateroom were not often in the habit of travelling light. No business of his, though. He put the expensive but rather worn pigskin suitcases down carefully, accepted a more than adequate tip, and retired, grateful for his luck.

With deft movements of his long, supple fingers, Ralph Blakeney put the mirror and the ashtray where he wanted them.

"Here we are, then," he said. "Thanks so much for driving me over, Tom."

Tom Woods gave his cheerful grin. "I enjoyed the run," he asserted. "And getting aboard before the boat train people saves a lot of pushing and shoving. Jolly good plan. What I'd expect from such an experienced traveller."

Ralph wasn't listening. Tom was used to that and not in the least offended. As far back as when they'd been schoolboys together, he had learned to know that withdrawn, abstracted look in the keen grey eyes. It didn't mean that Ralph was bored with him, or tired of their friendship—that was unthinkable—only that there were certain realms of thought to which he could not follow. He couldn't, as he was fond of saying, compete. Nor had he ever wanted to compete—for Ralph, the honours degree, the gold medals, the swift emergence as the country's most brilliant surgeon; for Tom, the satisfying task of keeping some acres in Sussex in good heart and delivering a quota of good milk. If Ralph occasionally invited himself for a night at the farm—even if only because it was handy for Southampton, as on this occasion—Tom was sincerely delighted.

Ralph unpacked his books, which were fat and medical, or paper-bound and criminological, and said: "You push along, then. No need to wave the ship good-bye."

"Oh, it's hours yet before the visitors have to go ashore. Let's find the bar."

"All right, then."

Tom's mind worked slowly, but it worked well. He knew that Ralph didn't want a drink, didn't want to talk—hadn't wanted to sit round the log fire with the brandy last night, and indeed had gone to bed as soon as he decently could. Once again, no offence taken. But there was something the matter, and he knew quite well what it was. And since old Ralph had no closer friend, it was up to him to do anything he could to help.

So when they were settled at a corner table of the still

To his amazement Linda was dressing in his cabin. "You might shut the door," she said.

ILLUSTRATED BY FRANCIS MARSHALL

MY MEMORIES OF SIX REIGNS

The Autobiography of Her Highness Princess Marie Louise, V.A., C.I., G.C.V.O., G.B.E., R.R.C.

PART TWO

The decorated borders used here conjure up the Victorian era with a strictly symmetrical layout for 'My Memories of Six Reigns' by Princess Marie Louise. By the 1970s, 'holly borders' had become a term of derision in the industry for an over-decorative design.

In between these two spreads was a feature entitled 'Is Television a Menace?' The asymmetrical layout and illustration by Francis Marshall for 'Travelling Light' by Mervyn Jones would probably have shocked Princess Marie Louise ...

NEW SCIENTIST (19 June 1958)

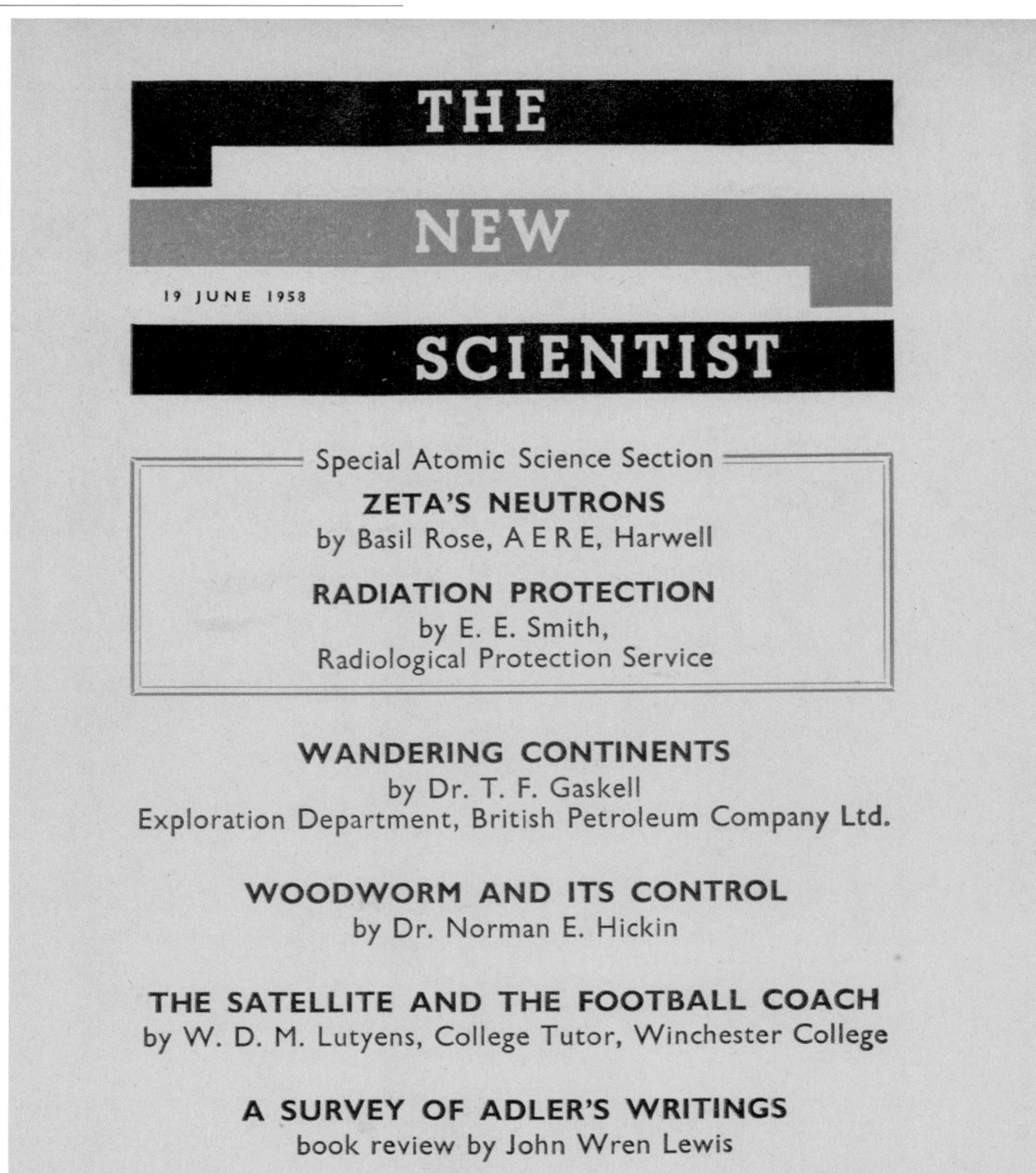

THE NEW SCIENTIST

19 JUNE 1958

Special Atomic Science Section

ZETA'S NEUTRONS
by Basil Rose, A E R E, Harwell

RADIATION PROTECTION
by E. E. Smith, Radiological Protection Service

WANDERING CONTINENTS
by Dr. T. F. Gaskell
Exploration Department, British Petroleum Company Ltd.

WOODWORM AND ITS CONTROL
by Dr. Norman E. Hickin

THE SATELLITE AND THE FOOTBALL COACH
by W. D. M. Lutyens, College Tutor, Winchester College

A SURVEY OF ADLER'S WRITINGS
book review by John Wren Lewis

VOLUME 4 NUMBER 83

ONE SHILLING WEEKLY

The *New Scientist* was launched on 22 November 1956 'for all those men and women who are interested in scientific discovery, and in its industrial, commercial and social consequences'. Its design maintained the authoritative look of an academic journal rather than a magazine, but it attracted a substantial news-stand readership. From the outset, Percy Cudlipp, a former editor of the *Daily Herald*, was at the helm and insisted: 'Nothing goes to press until I have read it and understood it.' Despite its journal-leaning look, the layout was always open and there was a budget for cartoons and illustrations to enliven the pages, placed alongside the scientific diagrams. Despite these innovations it lost money as advertising dried up amid an economic recession and in the aftermath of the Suez Crisis. The launching of Sputnik on 4 October 1957 boosted interest in science and technology and the magazine survived. The spot blue on the cover was the only colour used. Maxwell Raison – who was semi-retired, but had worked on *Farmer's Weekly*, *Picture Post*, *Housewife* and the *Leader* – conceived the magazine after hearing a speech by Churchill about the importance of science and technology to the future of Britain.

Harrison, Raison & Co.
(216 × 284 mm, stapled, 48 pages)

THE ECONOMIST (22 August 1959)

The Economist

AUGUST 22, 1959

FOUNDED 1843

One Shilling and Sixpence

THE RADCLIFFE REPORT

First impressions of a major economic policy document are given in a leading article on page 553. On pages 507 to 509 appears the first instalment of a commentary on its many important sections.

A Summit in Paris

What Mr Eisenhower has to discuss with General de Gaulle (page 509).

Tough on Labour

In the United States Congress is arguing about trade union reform (page 538).

Independent People

What the Icelanders are like, and why (page 545).

ROSTOW ON GROWTH

The concluding articles of the Rostow analysis put western relations with Soviet Russia, actual and possible, in a new light, page 524 (editorial comment, page 511).

World Politics and Business

The Economist had brightened up its design in the late 1930s with a red title. However, paper restrictions during the war led it to drop a separate cover – not bringing one back until 1952. The covers were based solely around type and listed the main contents. In August 1959 the magazine's title began to be shown in a red box with the name reversed out in white. This was designed by Reynolds Stone, appointed a Royal Designer for Industry in 1956 for his work on lettering.

Cover illustrations were also introduced, generally sketches of leading figures in politics and business. Stone's concept survives to this day, although the typeface has been tweaked to suit changing printing techniques. From this time, *The Economist* and the *New Scientist* began to think about how to present the ideas they discussed on their covers, and their changes encouraged other trade and professional magazines to do the same.

Economist Newspaper Ltd
(220 × 302 mm, stapled)

Magazines for swingers

In the world of magazines, the Swinging Sixties began in 1957 when Jocelyn Stevens used his inheritance to buy *Queen*, the 'Ladies' Newspaper and Court Chronicle' since 1861, and turned it into *Queen*, a magazine for 'Caroline', an imaginary, 'ambitious, intelligent bachelor girl – or the same girl married to a young executive on the way up – who wants all the material things in life'.[1] Stevens, a nephew of *Lilliput* and *Picture Post* owner Sir Edward Hulton, had worked for his uncle and spent a year in training at the London College of Printing. He set up shop at *Queen* with Mark Boxer handling the design and another contact, Antony Armstrong-Jones, among those providing the avant-garde photographs. Although never a big-seller, *Queen* was influential and Stevens would go on to bankroll Radio Caroline, the pirate radio station. Terry Mansfield, then an advertising salesman and later president of the National Magazine Company, has described how programmes would be recorded in the attic of the *Queen* building in Fetter Lane off Fleet Street.

What Stevens did for women at *Queen*, Michael Heseltine and Clive Labovitch did for men at *Man About Town*. Their designer of choice was Tom Wolsey, who came from Crawford's, one of the leading advertising agencies, and brought with him an enthusiasm for continental and US layout techniques. A particular influence was Willy Fleckhaus, whose German youth bible *Twen* inspired both *Man About Town* and later *Nova*.

At the *Sunday Times*, the Edwardian idea of the magazine supplement was revived to give the paper a way of attracting colour advertising and Boxer was plucked from *Queen* to run it. The idea worked and soon the *Observer* and the *Telegraph* had their own supplements. Without the demands of the news-stand, the supplement designers could be more experimental, and they often had the budgets to commission the best photographers and illustrators. Fleet Street looked down on magazines and masthead lists crediting a publication's staff were dubbed 'flannel panels'. The white space lauded by modernist designers was 'art holes'. A conversation in John le Carré's *The Honourable Schoolboy*, in which a newspaper's managing editor corrects a freelance writer, sums up the attitude: '[The newspaper's] not a comic, it's a rag. Comic's a colour supplement.'

The agenda for modernist design had been set out by Jan Tschichold with his austere New Typography – first espoused in Britain before the war in Sun Engraving's *Industrial Arts* and *The Penrose Annual* – but had yet to gain traction. However, there had been a battle raging over the merits of symmetry and asymmetry and the use of decoration in design. As John Biggs wrote in *The Use of Type* (1954):

> The words 'static' and 'dynamic' have been used to denote respectively these two kinds of design ... the word 'static' suggests stillness, almost lifelessness and lack of vitality, whereas the best symmetrical designs are far from lifeless and can suggest strength, vigour and discipline of mind. The word 'dynamic' suggests energy and forcefulness, whereas it is evident that many asymmetrical designs are feeble.[2]

Yet the proponents of modernist design were gaining ascendancy and they were encouraged by Ruari McLean at *Motif* and Willy Fleckhaus at *Twen*, as well as the larger, more colourful titles in the US that had not been subject to austerity budgets. So, alongside imports such as Italian scooters and rock and roll, in came the sans-serif typefaces Helvetica, Optima, Folio, Univers and Microgramma/Eurostile. In 1962, the Fletcher Forbes Gill design agency was formed, Design & Art Direction (D&AD) was set up to promote excellence in graphic design and the Kynoch Press in Birmingham published a series of essays to promote modern ideas. Contributors to the A4 Kynoch booklets included *Town*'s Wolsey and the photographer William Klein, photographer Terence Donovan, Derek Birdsall of BDMW Associates, typographer Anthony Froshaug, John Donegan, who was the art director behind the early issues of the *Sunday Times Colour Supplement*, graphic designer Bob Gill and animator Richard Williams.

However, other designers rallied around a reaction against the 'high-pitched scream of consumer selling' and advertising. Ken Garland, who was art editor of *Design* magazine from 1956 until setting up his own design studio in 1962, published *First Things First*, which was backed by 22 graphic designers, photographers and students. This 1964 manifesto sought 'a reversal of priorities in favour of the more useful and more lasting forms of communication'.

Many of these ideas were spread through the new colleges, such as the Watford School of Printing, founded in 1953, the London College of Printing, which combined the St Bride Foundation (founded in 1891) and other printing schools at a new campus at Elephant and Castle in 1962, and a rejuvenated Royal College of Art.

Women's monthly *Nova* had the resources of George Newnes behind it – his company had been merged with the two other largest publishers, Odhams and Fleetway/Amalgamated, to form the giant

International Publishing Corporation. Dennis Hackett took over after six months (having been editor at Jocelyn Stevens's *Queen*) to create a groundbreaking magazine with designer and photographer Harri Peccinotti, who moved from the world of advertising. For Fleet Street editor Eve Pollard: '*Nova* was the first glossy with serious words.'[3] Peter Crookston from the *Sunday Times Magazine* took over in 1969 and David Hillman joined him as art director. Such was its legendary status that IPC tried to revive the title in 2000. While *Nova* is regarded as a high point in magazine design, its page size was reduced twice as the publishers tried to cut costs before it closed in 1975. Meanwhile, in 1970 *Queen* merged into *Harper's* and *Town* (see pages 146–7) closed.

Debate about design approaches was sparked by the 1969 publication of Ruari McLean's *Magazine Design*, the first book to address the topic. A *Times Literary Supplement* review gave voice to concerns that art editors were becoming dominant and that text was being subjugated by images:

> For most art editors, words seem to be merely elements in the graphic patterns which they seek to impose on each spread ... The unintentional message of Mr McLean's book seems to be that magazine art editors seem almost as big a menace to the freedom of the printed word as Irish priests and Greek colonels.[4]

One of the magazines the *TLS* reviewer cited as exemplifying the problem was *Nova*. The critical storm was summed up by the eminent newspaper designer Allen Hutt, who also quoted *Nova* editor Dennis Hackett attacking the book for having 'too little background and analysis' and not reflecting the 'mood of the times'.[5]

Town's demise was not a total loss for its publisher, Haymarket. The title made the company's reputation, and art director Roland Schenk brought the same design values to a weekly journalism and advertising trade magazine it bought in 1967, *World's Press News*. The editorial strategy was to focus on advertising and marketing, with a large page size to help present the news and, crucially, glossy paper rather than newsprint; the paper allowed Schenk to develop dramatic features. The name was changed to *Campaign* and the magazine eschewed PR handout photographs, working instead with 'a talented photographer called Keith McMillan who took all the news pictures, most often of people on fire escapes looking wind-blown and worried, but at least real'.[6] Although Haymarket failed to succeed on the news-stand with *Topic* and *Town*, trade magazines have been the foundation of a company that thrives to this day.

By the early 1960s most magazines had become tightly focused on their niche, to the point where they could provide a shorthand for writers wanting to conjure up a sense of character or place. For Len Deighton in *The Billion-Dollar Brain* (1966), a woman 'held her hands as though she'd seen too many copies of *Vogue*, picking up one hand with the other and holding it against her face and nursing it as if it was a sick canary'. In a room, 'There was an inlaid desk upon which silver ornaments had been placed in that carefully posed look that photos in *House and Garden* have.'

But while magazines could provide an identity for their readers, they were also used frequently to attack established personalities and social norms. The satire of the early 1960s, of *That Was the Week That Was* and *Private Eye*, relied on new technical developments as much as new ways of thinking. *Private Eye* notably exploited the latest technology in the form of Letraset dry-transfer lettering and offset lithographic printing to keep down production costs. Fibre-tip pens were a new tool for sketch artists and illustrators, and phototypesetting was in its infancy.

The do-it-yourself techniques that made *Private Eye* possible also enabled an underground press in the form of magazines such as *International Times* (1966–72), *Oz* (1967–73), *Time Out* (1968–) and *Friends*. Only *Time Out* survives, though it has lost its radical roots and in 2012 decided it would become a free weekly. The fame of *Oz* is guaranteed by the obscenity trials of 1971 over the May 1970 'Schoolkids' issue. These magazines encouraged experimentation and enabled designers and illustrators such as Pearce Marchbank and Peter Brookes (cartoonist at *The Times*) to thrive, as well as Felix Dennis, who would jump on the computer boom of the 1980s and go on to launch *Maxim* and the *Week*. The underground theme was taken up by the punk movement, which could turn to photocopiers for short-run fanzines such as *Sniffin' Glue*, *Strangled* and *Barbed Wire*.

1 'Brash Young Giant', *Time*, 23 February 1962
2 John R. Biggs, *The Use of Type: The Practice of Typography* (London 1954), p. 132
3 Eve Pollard, quoted in Meg Carter, 'Happening All Nova Again', *Independent on Sunday*, 16 April 2000
4 'Poor Old Words', *Times Literary Supplement*, 24 July 1969, p. 802
5 'The First Word on Magazine Design', *The Penrose Annual*, 1970, vol. 63, p. 224
6 Lindsay Masters, 'How We Launched Campaign', *Campaign*, 26 October 2007, p. 58

MOTIF (November 1958)

Motif was published three times a year in a large book format, edited by the graphic designer Ruari McLean. It set out to 'record and investigate a few aspects of the visible world and certain activities in the visual arts', with painting and sculpture covered alongside its typographical content. The cover and endpapers for each issue were unique, designed by such people as Laurence Scarfe, Richard Guyatt, Hans Unger, Charles Mozley and Robert Stewart. There were articles and book and type reviews by typographers, designers and illustrators at the height of their careers (for example, Reynolds Stone) and those starting out (for example, Matthew Carter and Roger Law). At £1 1s 8d it was a specialist journal and listed *Typography*, *Alphabet & Image* and *Image* as its predecessors. Charles Mozley drew the binding for the first issue.

Shenval Press (238 × 302 mm, book binding, 88 pages plus endpapers and hardcover)

MOTIF (March 1960)

AaBbCcDdEeFfGgHhIi
JjKkLlMmNnOoPpQq
RrSsTtUuVvWwXxYyZz

A DESIGN FOR A NEW TYPEFACE

The third designer approached was Matthew Carter, aged 22, son of Harry Carter, who trained as a punchcutter at Enschedés. After leaving Haarlem he worked for a short time under his father at the University Press, Oxford, and is now freelancing as punch-cutter, engraver, letter-cutter and designer. He drew 'MOTIF' on the title page of this issue and is preparing an article on the types of Pierre Haultin (a contemporary of Garamond) for a future issue of MOTIF. He was recently commissioned by the Westerham Press to cut a set of new and more appropriate Roman figures for 'Monotype' Van Dijck (1 2 3 4 5 6 7 8 9 0). These are now available from the Monotype Corporation on 10, 11, 12 and 16 pts. (F 1487).

He is also working on a commissioned design for a new book-face. The alphabet shown here for the first time could go, we think, directly into production as a typeface, and is a remarkable achievement. Matthew Carter describes below the problem he set himself.

This design has been neither commissioned nor christened; it is in fact still a rough, and is reproduced here from pasted-up photographs of freehand drawings. It was started as an experiment with the legibility of Sanserifs, and since it seemed logical to follow as much as possible the details and proportions of types of proven legibility, I traced over a Garalde* Roman leaving out the serifs. For a model I used a type of sixteenth-century French inspiration drawn originally for punchcutting practice. The result was hopeless, the letters had an unmistakably pollarded look, and their relative proportions had gone haywire. However, adjusting them was a fascinating exercise, and although not much of the Garalde has survived the redrawing intact, various atavistic traits of pen lettering seemed worth keeping, such as the oblique emphasis of a few round-bowled forms (b, c, d) and the thick-and-thin stress. Among some simplifications that I drew experimentally and decided to keep are p, d, a and u, in which the bowls or arches carry on from the main stroke instead of branching from it. The x-height is fairly large; the capitals rather small and of much the same weight as the lower-case. I have tried to keep the design practicable and disciplined by avoiding kerns and mannerisms, and by imagining that I was going to have to cut it in steel myself.

As the problem of devising a type of this character has already been solved so completely by Hermann Zapf in Optima, an explanation of my temerity in trying a similar thing is perhaps necessary. The fact is that 'Stressed Sanserif Romans' are an unhackneyed type family, attractive because they are capable of further exploration; and although they are admittedly hybrids, the crossbreeding combines some of the freshness of Grots (which I like) with a hint of the solid merits of Old Style Romans (which I respect). Now that the main incentive to designing new types has passed from book-production to publicity and advertising, this is one interesting form that belongs to the class of broadly self-effacing types intended as vehicles rather than eye-catchers.

MATTHEW CARTER

* The 'Vox Classification' name for types related to those of Aldus and Garamond.

96

24 Every young Beginner should then be taught by Rules because Letter-cutting depends as much upon Rule and Compass as any other Trade does. You may in other places where you find most Convenience make a Square which may stand you in stead for

24 ABCDEFGHIJKLMNOPQRSTUV
abcdefghijklmnopqrstuvwxyz

18 ABCDEFGHIJKLMNOPQRSTUVWXYZ
abcdefghijklmnopqrstuvwxyz

14 ABCDEFGHIJKLMNOPQRSTUVWXYZ
abcdefghijklmnopqrstuvwxyz

12 ABCDEFGHIJKLMNOPQRSTUVWXYZ
abcdefghijklmnopqrstuvwxyz

10 ABCDEFGHIJKLMNOPQRSTUVWXYZ abcdefghijklmnopqrstuvwxyz

Every young Beginner should then be ta 18
Letter-cutting depends as much upon Rul

Every young Beginner should then be taught by Rule 14
Letter-cutting depends as much upon Rule and Comp

Every young Beginner should then be taught by Rules because 12
Letter-cutting depends as much upon Rule and Compass as any other Trade does. You may in other places where you find most Convenience make a Square which may stand you in stead for

agdbqpRu

AaBbCcDdEeFfGgHhIi
JjKkLlMmNnOoPpQq
RrSsTtUuVvWwXxYyZz

SAPIENTIA SCRIBAE IN TEMPORE VACUITATIS

97

MOTIF (September 1959)

Some Grotesque Type Faces

VENUS

AND EXTENDED

Folio-Grotesk

Annonce

ABCDEFGHIJKLMNOP
QRSTUVWXYZ&
abcdefghijklmnopqrs
tuvwxyz1234567890

This spread of grotesque (also called grot or early sans-serif) typefaces includes in its commentary the point that good grots were scarce in Britain. The article states: 'To those who have been watching typographic trends in America and on the Continent since 1945 the current enthusiasm in this country for Grotesque types will not seem so surprising; what is remarkable is that it has been so long in coming.' McLean had been promoting the New Typography of Jan Tschichold since before the war. The autumn 1960 issue carried an article, 'Palette for Printers' by P.M. Handover, about Adam Frutiger's Univers, with its 21 numbered weights and widths, from the normal 55 to the light extra condensed 49 and expanded heavy 83.

Shenval Press (238 × 302 mm, book binding, 108 pages plus endpapers and hardcover)

Ruari McLean commissioned three young British designers to design alphabets: John Woodcock, Michael Harvey and Matthew Carter, then aged 22. Carter's face had no name and was reproduced from pasted-up photographs of freehand drawings. He commented: 'The main incentive to designing new types has passed from book-production to publicity and advertising.' Carter also provided the *Motif* logo on the contents page.

Shenval Press (238 × 302 mm, book binding, 104 pages plus endpapers and hardcover)

QUEEN (27 March 1962)

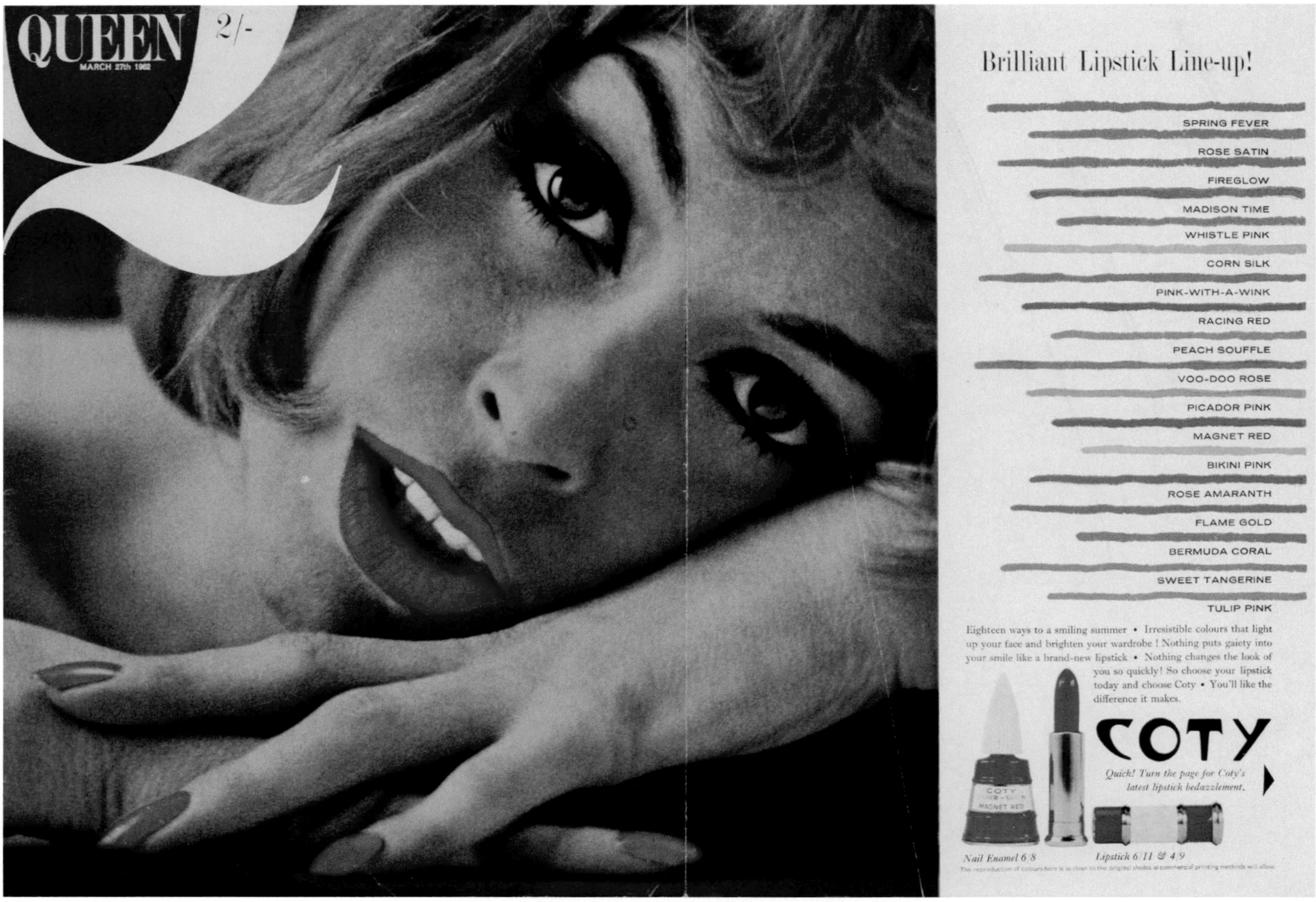

QUEEN 2/-

MARCH 27th 1962

Brilliant Lipstick Line-up!

SPRING FEVER

ROSE SATIN

FIREGLOW

MADISON TIME

WHISTLE PINK

CORN SILK

PINK-WITH-A-WINK

RACING RED

PEACH SOUFFLE

VOO-DOO ROSE

PICADOR PINK

MAGNET RED

BIKINI PINK

ROSE AMARANTH

FLAME GOLD

BERMUDA CORAL

SWEET TANGERINE

TULIP PINK

Eighteen ways to a smiling summer • Irresistible colours that light up your face and brighten your wardrobe ! Nothing puts gaiety into your smile like a brand-new lipstick • Nothing changes the look of you so quickly! So choose your lipstick today and choose Coty • You'll like the difference it makes.

COTY

Quick! Turn the page for Coty's latest lipstick bedazzlement.

Nail Enamel 6/8 *Lipstick 6/11 & 4/9*

A VERY PERSONAL VIEW OF THE BRITISH FOURTH STORY

THE LONELINESS OF THE WIDOW GRUBB

THE

On her first visit to England the American photographer EVE ARNOLD was struck by the picture of English individuality shown in the Personal Columns of THE TIMES. She has been investigating the stories behind five of these advertisements: in this article, the fourth in this series, she photographs and describes a farmer's widow, who is deeply rooted in country life.

Jocelyn Stevens bought the once-pioneering society magazine *Queen* and relaunched it with an irreverent edge. Mark Boxer handled the design before Tom Wolsey arrived from *Town*. A typical cover in the 1950s would have been a floral display, but this cover photograph by Sandra Lousada folds out to reveal it is really an advertisement for Coty, with the cosmetics company's Spring Fever lipstick and nail varnish punched out on the cover. David Hamilton was art director for the issue. Playing with the 'Q' of the title was a regular feature.

Stevens Press
(235 × 318 mm, perfect bound, 102 pages)

The series 'A Very Personal View of the British' by US photographer Eve Arnold was inspired by her reading adverts in the personal columns of *The Times*. Note the very tight page margins. Other photographers in the issue included theatre specialist Zoë Dominic and Patrick Ward.

The 'Last Word' cartoon by Niky, who also drew for the *New Statesman*, gave an editorial lead into the magazine for people who read from the back. It will also have increased the value of the inside back cover position, because publishers charge more for adverts facing editorial matter.

ABOUT TOWN (March 1961)

about town
2/6 March 1961
The Tories scrutinised

Michael Heseltine and Clive Labovitch rechristened *Man About Town* after buying the magazine from Tailor and Cutter Ltd and increasing its frequency. It called itself 'Britain's only luxury magazine for men'. Heseltine was lampooned in a limerick by the *Observer* newspaper as a 'Beau' – and considered suing because he felt it portrayed him as a homosexual and he feared being labelled as a pornographer.[1] *Private Eye* parodied *About Town* as *about* (for Pseuds' Corner) and suggested that 'Clive Brilliantine' was one of the pacesetters of 1962. Art editor Tom Wolsey switched from illustrated to photographic covers and introduced an international design approach influenced by magazines such as Willy Flekhaus's *Twen* in Germany and *Look* in the US. White space – a luxury to an industry still expecting to squeeze text on pages in a style dictated by post-war paper rationing – was used copiously on the features pages. Terence Donovan took the cover photograph of prime minister Harold Macmillan.

Type is used to spectacular effect for this opening spread of interviews with the Tory leadership by Godfrey Smith. Heseltine stood for Parliament in 1958 and 1964, and eventually became an MP in 1966, despite receiving criticism because of his relationship with *Town*. One selection committee questioned him about an article they saw as attacking the royal family; in reply he said he would act like *Sunday Times* owner Lord Thomson and appoint an editor 'and let him get on with it' (rather than *Express* owner Lord Beaverbrook's approach, 'appoint someone and do the job yourself'). Heseltine appointed directors to run the company and took his name as publisher off the masthead.

1 Michael Crick, *Michael Heseltine: A Biography* (London 1997), pp. 112–3

Cornmarket Press
(234 × 318 mm, perfect bound, 82 pages)

TOWN (December 1962)

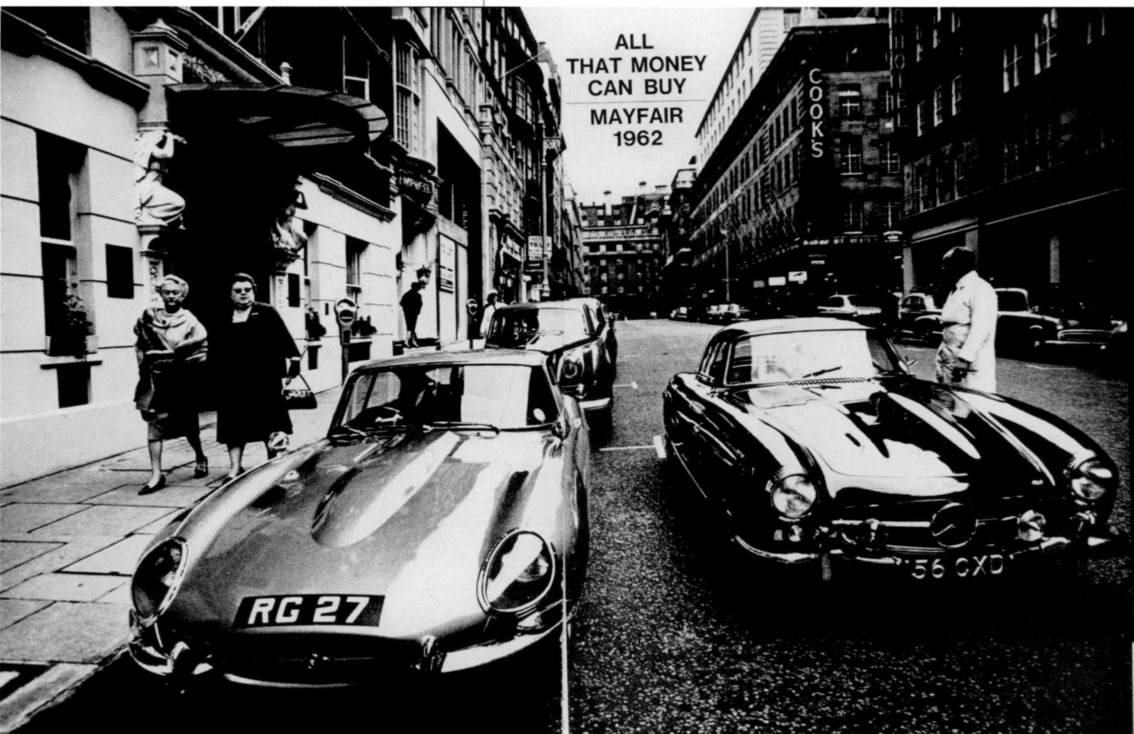

TOPIC (14 July 1962)

TOPIC 14 July 1962

Focus on Hate

It started quietly enough. And at first it all looked a little ridiculous. The strutting members of the Nationalist Socialist Movement, swastikas in their lapels, could have come straight out of one of those untidy 1930 movies. The police were grimly good-humoured. The anger and the hatred grew slowly – and inevitably – as the speakers expounded the thesis 'Free Britain from Jewish Control'.

It exploded with bursting eggs and tomatoes and flying pennies. A man cried 'Lynch them', a woman's voice, shrill and clear, screamed 'Break their necks'. The police held the crowd back while some members of the movement escaped in a truck, bearing a shattered banner, raising their arms defiantly in the Nazi salute. It ended swiftly, but there was still the reckoning: the appearances in court, the questions in Parliament, the reassessment of the boundaries of free speech. Above all was left the thought that hate, from whatever side of a police cordon, is a distasteful and frightening thing.

TOWN (May 1963)

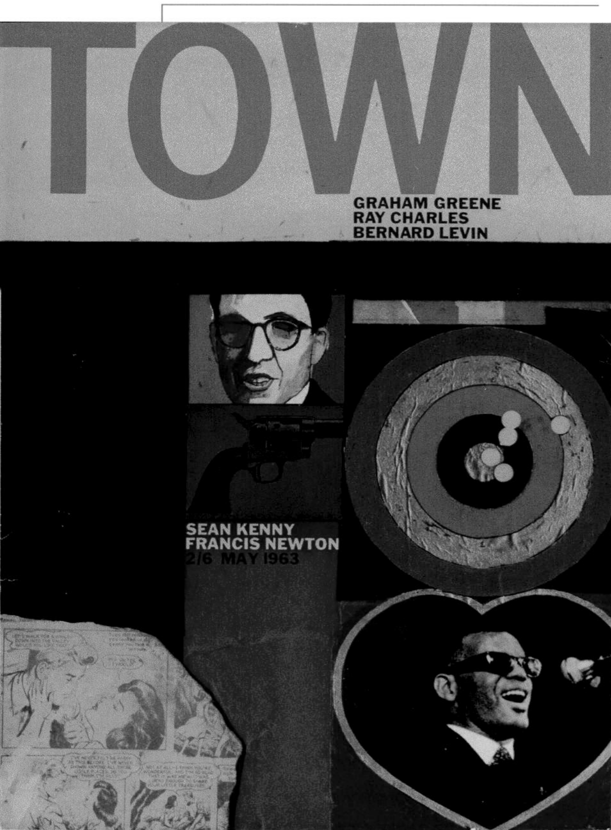

Tom Wolsey applied his international approach to the British news weekly *Topic*, which Cornmarket took over in 1962. The main spread, for a photographic feature by Don McCullin about protests in Trafalgar Square against the 'strutting members of the Nationalist Socialist Movement', frames the single picture on the left with white strips down each side. The right-hand page uses a dynamic modular layout, with white space reinforcing a classic 'Catherine wheel' effect. The page numbers were placed about 3 cm down from the top outside edges of the pages, where a reader's thumb might be when flicking through.

Cornmarket Magazines
(206 × 275 mm, stapled, 44 pages)

About Town rebranded – once more losing a word from its name. This is the opening spread by McCullin for a feature on Britain's affluent society. James Gilbert took pictures for the cover and inside of aerobatic pilots wearing suits and goggles.

Cornmarket Press
(234 × 318 mm, perfect bound, 124 pages)

The Pop art cover by is Barry Fantoni, who would become a comic-strip cartoonist and poet-in-residence E.J. Thribb for *Private Eye*. The feature inside identifies 1954 as the year Pop art was first cited as a real movement by a group of critics at the Institute of Contemporary Art. Thomas Wolsey was the art editor.

Cornmarket Press
(234 × 318 mm, perfect bound, 82 pages)

TOWN (March 1967)

The Bridges

by Rolf Schneider

N. yelled: 'No. Not me! His name is van Gogh!' And as he shouted the tears ran into his mouth; tears of happiness because at last he had found the name; tears at a miracle, but the miracle dried up ...

It's the name of the publishing company that has now changed, with printers Hazell, Watson and Viney taking a stake in Cornmarket in lieu of debts. However, *Town* closed at the end of the year: 'It was too expensive to survive,' said Heseltine. Even so Haymarket thrived by applying the visual style of *Town* to trade publishing, with *Management Today* and *Campaign* as early successes under art director Roland Schenk. Harry Gordon was art director for this issue. 'The Bridges' by Rolf Schneider was illustrated by Bob Gill. Just six editorial pages inside the magazine were in colour.

Haymarket Press
(234 × 318 mm, perfect bound, 72 pages)

NOVA (March 1965)

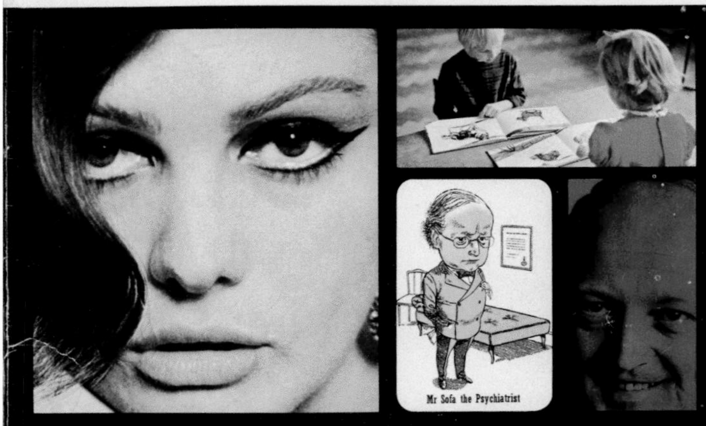

Mr Sofa the Psychiatrist
This is No. 1 of the British monthly with the 1965 approach. What's the isometric system? Mary Rand figures it out. What does Christopher Booker say about Miss Cardinale? (That's her above.) Who's Mr. Blond? Pages & pages of answers, plus Jill Butterfield, Robert Robinson, Elizabeth David, Irwin Shaw—and Paris fashion. And where's 'Terra Nova'? Explore inside

'A new kind of magazine for the new kind of woman' with 'the 1965 approach' was launched by editor Harry Fieldhouse with Harri Peccinotti as art editor (Dennis Hackett, deputy editor of *Queen*, took over as editor in September). Sixteen editorial pages were in colour. Microgramma Extended, a typeface dating from 1952 by Alessandro Butti and Aldo Novarese, was used for the title.

Terence Donovan took the photograph of Vidal Sassoon with some of his clients, including Grace Coddington (later fashion director at *Vogue* in both the UK and US), models Jill Kennington (who would appear in Antonioni's *Blow-Up*, set in London's fashion photography scene of the 1960s) and Paulene Stone, miniskirt and hot-pants pioneer Mary Quant and actress Nyree Dawn Porter. Sassoon is reckoned to have created his Five Point Cut on Coddington, who modelled before going to *Vogue* in 1968.

George Newnes
(260 × 334 mm, perfect bound, 188 pages)

NOVA (March 1965)

Brian Duffy took the photographs reproduced as whole-bleed pages, or spreads like this one, for a 10-page article by fashion editor Molly Parkin. Harri Peccinotti was art director. French couturier André Courrèges, who had launched his Space Age collection the year before, was renowned for trouser suits with boots and goggles and for introducing the miniskirt to France.

George Newnes
(260 × 340 mm, perfect bound, 154 pages)

NOVA (July 1968)

For the feature 'What Paris Could Do for the Queen' by Brigid Keenan, photographs of the 'most written about, most photographed woman in the world' were retouched and manipulated to show her wearing designs by the House of Courrèges and shoes by Roger Vivier, with hair by Alexandre and make-up by Carita. According to the book *Nova 1965–75*, the article caused an uproar in official circles – it was Fleet Street lore that photographs of the Queen were never manipulated: 'The pictures were retouched in New York and promptly impounded in Britain on their return. They were finally released only with further retouching to lower the hemline and the sanction of Buckingham Palace.'[1] The consultant art director was Derek Birdsall.

1 D. Hillman, H. Peccinotti and D. Gibbs, *Nova 1965–75: The Style Bible of the 60s and 70s* (London 1993)

George Newnes
(260 × 340 mm, perfect bound, 100 pages)

NOVA (August 1968)

The magazine was not afraid to tackle contentious issues such as racism, contraception and religion. The cover photograph was by Harri Peccinotti and the consultant art director was Derek Birdsall. The Microgramma title has been dropped in favour of a tightly spaced Windsor Extra Bold Condensed inspired by a woodblock type Peccinotti found in a garage. Sixteen editorial pages inside were in colour and the issue was printed by Sun in Watford.

George Newnes
(260 × 340 mm, perfect bound, 92 pages)

NOVA (March 1971)

A Harri Peccinotti cover linked to a 10-page Caroline Baker feature on blue fashions. The art director was David Hillman. Black models were a rare sight in (or, particularly, on) fashion magazines at the time. This issue was printed in Italy. Baker has been credited for starting a vogue for army surplus chic and street fashion. 'I was a 24-year-old with a Vidal Sassoon haircut, totally obsessed with fashion,' Baker has said. 'You have to remember that everyone looked like the Queen back then so we were intent on liberating women. Our fashion stories tended to be rather shocking – pictures of models on the toilet, that sort of thing. We had no idea that you had to please the advertisers as well as the readers.'[1] IPC revived the *Nova* name in 2000 but the appearance was short-lived.

1 Simon Mills, 'Super Nova', *Scotland on Sunday*, 30 April 2000

IPC Magazines
(260 × 334 mm, perfect bound, 100 pages)

NOVA (May 1971)

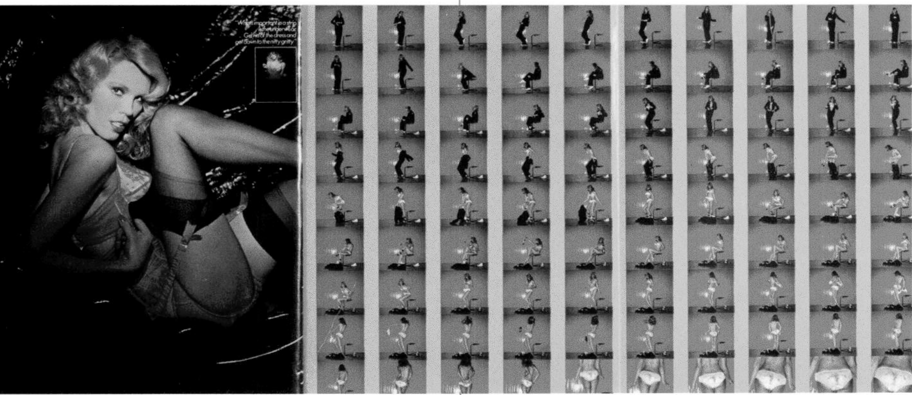

Amanda Lear was the model for the 'How to Undress in Front of Your Husband' feature and a tipped-in gatefold that could be cut up to make a 'flick book' held in a bulldog clip. The photographs by Brian Duffy were for art director David Hillman. *Nova* used 'interactive' ideas in several issues, such as holes cut in pages to reveal part of an image and images printed over several pages that could be cut out and assembled into a poster (which cleverly required the reader to buy several copies). The book *Nova 1965–75* refers to rumours that Lear is a transsexual with a caption: 'Duffy photographed the enigmatic Amanda Lear (the clue is buried in her name)'.[1] She was also a cover model for *Town* (August 1967).

1 D. Hillman, H. Peccinotti and D. Gibbs, *Nova 1965–75: The Style Bible of the 60s and 70s* (London 1993), p. 116

IPC Magazines
(260 × 334 mm, perfect bound, 100 pages)

LONDON LIFE (6 November 1965)

London Life was launched by editor Mark Boxer as a reworking of the 60-year-old *Tatler*. Boxer assembled a high-profile editorial team that included David Hillman and model Jean Shrimpton alongside less-established names such as David Puttnam, but the high-rolling budget – paid for by Lord Thomson, who ultimately owned both the *Sunday Times* and *Tatler* – bankrupted the title after six months. Its stated aim was to be a 'comprehensive guide to the entertainment scene: films, theatre, restaurants, night life, music, sport', but at 2s 6d it was expensive.

The cover of Tony Bennett for a profile by Benny Green was by Ian Dury (who later became famous with his band the Blockheads), who was studying at the Royal College of Art. The cover style was carried through to a spread inside with a joint illustration by Alison Armstrong, Ian Dury and Stan Steel. Alison (now Alison Chapman Andrews) explained: 'Ian, Stan Steel and I studied together at Walthamstow Art School and went to the RCA at the same time to study painting. The final-year painting studio was divided into individual spaces; Ian and I shared a space, Stan was the next one. Because Ian worked at home, Elgin Avenue in Maida Vale, this wasn't a problem. He did the *London Life* cover and other work for Mark Boxer from home. The costumes [on the spread] are in coloured pencil, as is the background in Tony Bennett, but Ian got very strong colours from them. The heads are in black pencil and the background may have been paint.'

This issue was held together by three staples and structured with an outer 16 pages of letterpress on newsprint to carry listings for the week at the front and classified adverts at the back; 24 pages of gloss coated paper, eight in colour, mainly used for advertising; a middle 16 pages on matt stock devoted to features, half in colour. The centre spread in this issue was a colour photograph poster by Terence Donovan, the '*London Life* pin-up', of Barbara Windsor, in a Plantagenet dress for Lionel Bart's musical *Twang!!*

Illustrated Newspapers
(240 × 316 mm, stapled, 60 pages)

VOGUE (April 1962)

David Bailey's New York shoot with Jean Shrimpton established him as an international fashion photographer. He had been catapulted into the public eye in 1960 by his *Daily Express* photograph of the model Paulene Stone – who had won a 1958 *Woman's Own* competition to find a cover girl – kneeling down to kiss a squirrel. The contents page on issues of this size would be on something like page 95, with a 'well' of editorial content in the middle of the magazine. *Vogue* also ran cut-out-and-keep recipe cards by Robert Carrier.

Condé Nast
(220 × 288 mm, perfect bound, 210 pages)

VOGUE (June 1962)

David Bailey's first cover for the monthly fashion glossy with his muse and supermodel Jean Shrimpton. The term 'supermodel' did not come into general use until the 1970s; in fact, 'mannequin' was the preferred term until the 1950s, when the wasp-waisted Barbara Goalen was the leading choice for the general weeklies such as *Illustrated* and *Picture Post* and glossies such as *Vogue*. Models were rarely credited before the 1920s, when women such as Daisy Fellowes, Marion Morehouse, Ludmila 'Lud' Fedoseyeva, the exiled Romanov princess Natalia Paley and Toto Koopman became famous through the pages of *Vogue* and *Harper's Bazaar*.

Condé Nast
(220 × 288 mm, perfect bound, 142 pages)

VOGUE (October 1967)

This issue featured Twiggy (by Ronald Traeger) on the cover for the first time, though she had been a regular on shoots for a year and was following in the footsteps of Jean Shrimpton as a supermodel. Twiggy also appeared inside the magazine, photographed by Cecil Beaton posing in his house as 'Cosmic Ariel'. Fashion journalist Deidre McSharry – who had worked on *Woman's Own* and would go on to help launch *Cosmopolitan* and then take over as editor for 13 years – had christened Twiggy 'The face of 1966' in the *Daily Express* (23 February) with a Barry Lategan photograph. Twiggy was just 16 years old and painted her eyelashes on.

Condé Nast
(230 × 308 mm, perfect bound, 144 pages)

WOMAN (16 July 1960)

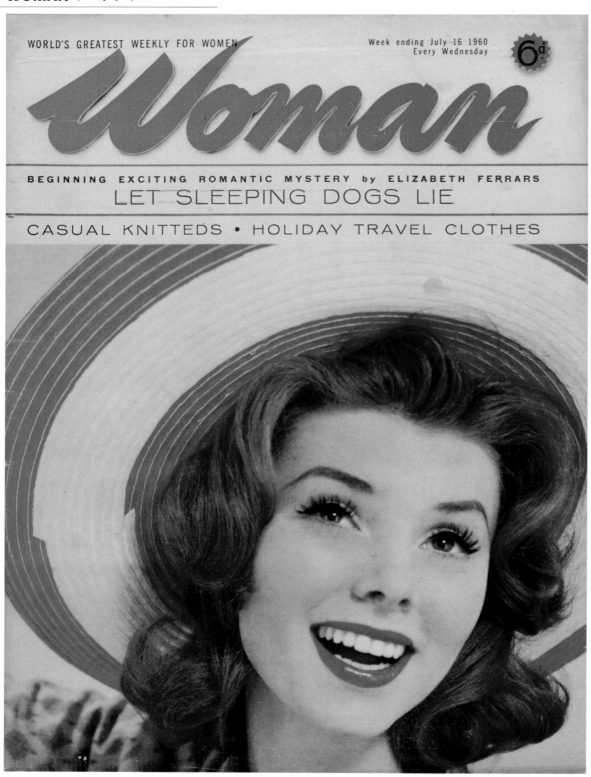

WORLD'S GREATEST WEEKLY FOR WOMEN

Week ending July 16 1960
Every Wednesday

6d

Woman

BEGINNING EXCITING ROMANTIC MYSTERY by ELIZABETH FERRARS

LET SLEEPING DOGS LIE

CASUAL KNITTEDS • HOLIDAY TRAVEL CLOTHES

By now most magazine covers were photographic. The title here is drawn with a shadow to give a three-dimensional effect. As the decade progressed, the influence of international design became clear in such women's weeklies, with white space and extensive use of sans-serif type, for both headlines and text, prevalent.

A dramatic spread of a bohemian Soho street by Liverpool-born Oliver Brabbins makes use of colour (only available on the right-hand page) for a serial thriller by crime writer Elizabeth Ferrars, who penned some 80 books. *Woman*'s large format and excellent colour printing allowed it to show off such graphic work – Michael Johnson illustrated another colour spread and there were black-and-white pages by Alex Ross and Tanat Jones. The spread reflects a trend towards grittier subjects in magazines' editorial content, in terms of both fiction and features.

BEGINNING A THRILLING STORY OF LOVE AND INTRIGUE
by ELIZABETH FERRARS
Let Sleeping Dogs Lie

Odhams Press
(255 × 345 mm, stapled, 76 pages)

WOMAN'S MIRROR (1 October 1960)

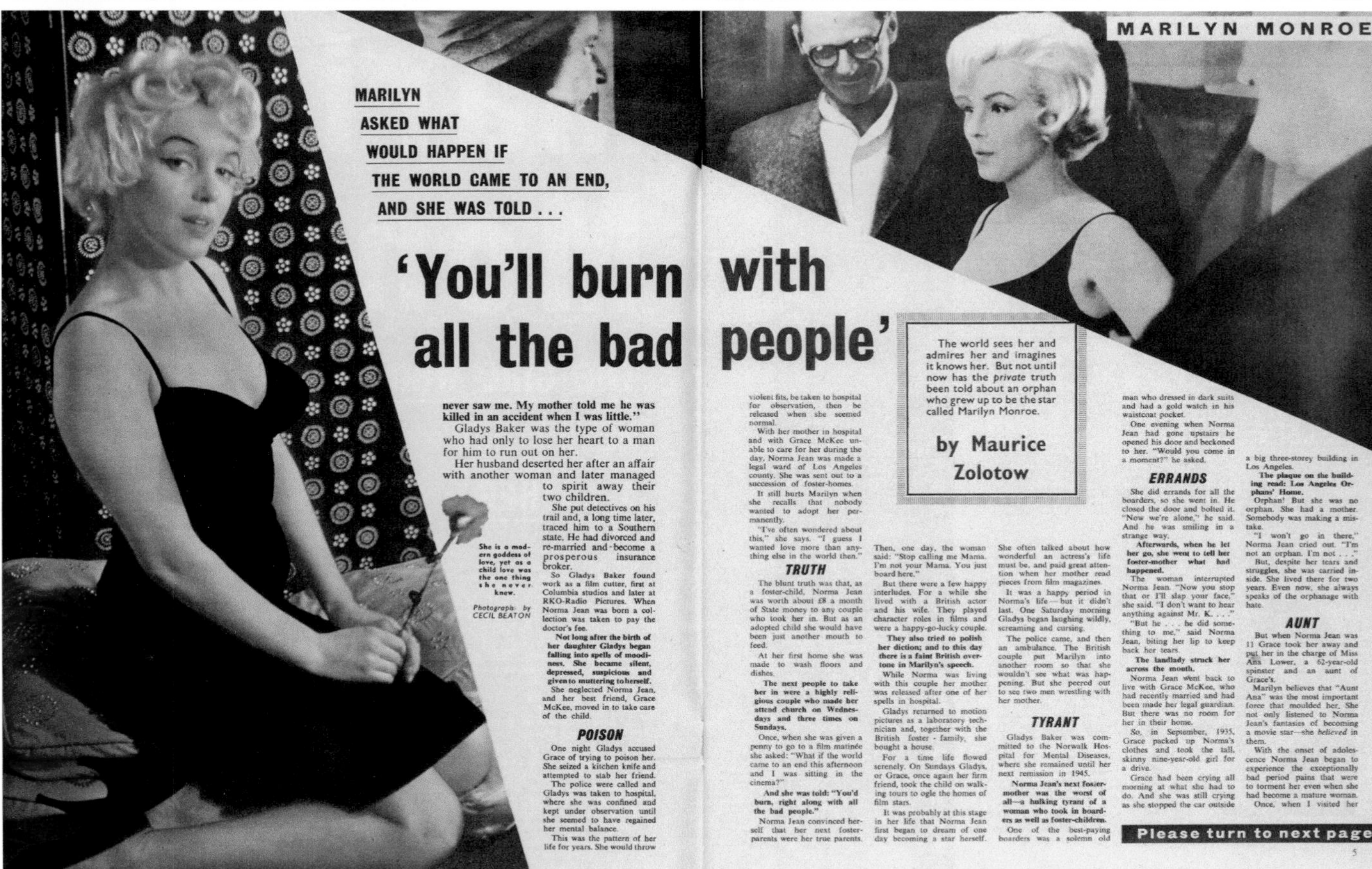

MARILYN MONROE

MARILYN ASKED WHAT WOULD HAPPEN IF THE WORLD CAME TO AN END, AND SHE WAS TOLD . . .

'You'll burn with all the bad people'

The world sees her and admires her and imagines it knows her. But not until now has the private truth been told about an orphan who grew up to be the star called Marilyn Monroe.

by Maurice Zolotow

She is a modern goddess of love, yet as a child love was the one thing she never knew.

Photograph by CECIL BEATON

never saw me. My mother told me he was killed in an accident when I was little."

Gladys Baker was the type of woman who had only to lose her heart to a man for him to run out on her.

Her husband deserted her after an affair with another woman and later managed to spirit away their two children.

She put detectives on his trail and, a long time later, traced him to a Southern state. He had divorced and re-married and become a prosperous insurance broker.

So Gladys Baker found work as a film cutter, first at Columbia studios and later at RKO-Radio Pictures. When Norma Jean was born a collection was taken to pay the doctor's fee.

Not long after the birth of her daughter Gladys began falling into spells of moodiness. She became silent, depressed, suspicious and given to muttering to herself.

She neglected Norma Jean, and her best friend, Grace McKee, moved in to take care of the child.

POISON

One night Gladys accused Grace of trying to poison her. She seized a kitchen knife and attempted to stab her friend.

The police were called and Gladys was taken to hospital, where she was confined and kept under observation until she seemed to have regained her mental balance.

This was the pattern of her life for years. She would throw violent fits, be taken to hospital for observation, then be released when she seemed normal.

With her mother in hospital and with Grace McKee unable to care for her during the day, Norma Jean was made a legal ward of Los Angeles county. She was sent out to a succession of foster-homes.

It still hurts Marilyn when she recalls that nobody wanted to adopt her permanently.

"I've often wondered about this," she says. "I guess I wanted love more than anything else in the world then."

TRUTH

The blunt truth was that, as a foster-child, Norma Jean was worth about £8 a month of State money to any couple who took her in. But as an adopted child she would have been just another mouth to feed.

At her first home she was made to wash floors and dishes.

The next people to take her in were a highly religious couple who made her attend church on Wednesdays and three times on Sundays.

Once, when she was given a penny to go to a film *matinée* she asked: "What if the world came to an end this afternoon and I was sitting in the cinema?"

And she was told: "You'd burn, right along with all the bad people."

Norma Jean convinced herself that her next foster-parents were her true parents.

Then, one day, the woman said: "Stop calling me Mama. I'm not your Mama. You just board here."

But there were a few happy interludes. For a while she lived with a British actor and his wife. They played character roles in films and were a happy-go-lucky couple.

They also tried to polish her diction; and to this day there is a faint British overtone in Marilyn's speech.

While Norma was living with this couple her mother was released after one of her spells in hospital.

Gladys returned to motion pictures as a laboratory technician and, together with the British foster - family, she bought a house.

For a time life flowed serenely. On Sundays Gladys, or Grace, once again her firm friend, took the child on walking tours to ogle the homes of film stars.

It was probably at this stage in her life that Norma Jean first began to dream of one day becoming a star herself.

She often talked about how wonderful an actress's life must be, and paid great attention when her mother read pieces from film magazines.

It was a happy period in Norma's life — but it didn't last. One Saturday morning Gladys began laughing wildly, screaming and cursing.

The police came, and then an ambulance. The British couple put Marilyn into another room so that she wouldn't see what was happening. But she peered out to see two men wrestling with her mother.

TYRANT

Gladys Baker was committed to the Norwalk Hospital for Mental Diseases, where she remained until her next remission in 1945.

Norma Jean's next foster-mother was the worst of all—a hulking tyrant of a woman who took in boarders as well as foster-children.

One of the best-paying boarders was a solemn old man who dressed in dark suits and had a gold watch in his waistcoat pocket.

One evening when Norma Jean had gone upstairs he opened his door and beckoned to her. "Would you come in a moment?" he asked.

ERRANDS

She did errands for all the boarders, so she went in. He closed the door and bolted it. "Now we're alone," he said. And he was smiling in a strange way.

Afterwards, when he let her go, she went to tell her foster-mother what had happened.

The woman interrupted Norma Jean. "Now you stop that or I'll slap your face," she said. "I don't want to hear anything against Mr. K. . . ."

"But he . . . he did something to me," said Norma Jean, biting her lip to keep back her tears.

The landlady struck her across the mouth.

Norma Jean went back to live with Grace McKee, who had recently married and had been made her legal guardian. But there was no room for her in their home.

So, in September, 1935, Grace packed up Norma's clothes and took the tall, skinny nine-year-old girl for a drive.

Grace had been crying all morning at what she had to do. And she was still crying as she stopped the car outside a big three-storey building in Los Angeles.

The plaque on the building read: Los Angeles Orphans' Home.

Orphan! But she was no orphan. She had a mother. Somebody was making a mistake.

"I won't go in there," Norma Jean cried out. "I'm not an orphan. I'm not . . ."

But, despite her tears and struggles, she was carried inside. She lived there for two years. Even now, she always speaks of the orphanage with hate.

AUNT

But when Norma Jean was 11 Grace took her away and put her in the charge of Miss Ana Lower, a 62-year-old spinster and an aunt of Grace's.

Marilyn believes that "Aunt Ana" was the most important force that moulded her. She not only listened to Norma Jean's fantasies of becoming a movie star—she *believed* in them.

With the onset of adolescence Norma Jean began to experience the exceptionally bad period pains that were to torment her even when she had become a mature woman.

Once, when I visited her

Please turn to next page

5

Woman's Mirror was launched in 1955 as a black-and-white tabloid newspaper and switched its format to become a news magazine to reflect what it saw as the 'winds of change' in the country: 'The colour and richness which surrounds the Woman of the Sixties will now be mirrored, as never before, in the colour and richness we bring into your homes.' The title was redesigned in 1962, abbreviated to *WM* in 1965 and then *wm* in 1967, before the magazine was merged with *Woman.*

Fleetway
(250 × 330 mm, stapled, 72 pages)

As befits its heritage and tagline – 'The News Magazine for Women' – *Woman's Mirror* brought a more topical pace, in terms of both content and layout, to the weeklies. Fleetway had bought the serialization rights to the biography of Marilyn Monroe by US show-business writer Maurice Zolotow and gave it the full treatment, opening on page 3. The knitting pattern in the issue was for a jumper like Monroe's. Following newspaper practice, there is no contents page and no staff list.

The photograph on page 4 of the spread is by Cecil Beaton. The black edge around Monroe's bosom is sharp compared with the rest of the image, suggesting it may have been altered.

Pages 8 and 9 run newspaper-style advertising shapes and layouts.

SUNDAY TIMES (4 February 1962)

Colour supplements changed the nature of the magazine industry, taking advertising in particular from magazines and ultimately helping to kill off general-interest weekly magazines such as *Weekend* and *Tit-Bits*. The art director here was John Donegan, who had worked in advertising and later became a cartoonist for *Punch* and the *Sunday Express*. The first-issue cover shows a sequence of fashion photographs taken on Chelsea Pier by David Bailey of Jean Shrimpton wearing a Mary Quant dress. They are broken up by Burnley footballer Jimmy McIlroy taken by John Bulmer, who, unlike most photojournalists, shot in colour. The issue published the Ian Fleming short story 'The Living Daylights', but overall was seen as disappointing. The next two issues were considered 'a crashing bore' by a former *Daily Express* executive in the news weekly *Topic*.

Editor Mark Boxer said he had had only seven weeks to produce the first issue and was 'amazed by its success'. He wanted to change the name to *Sunday Times Colour Magazine* but was told that this might be interpreted as a sign of losing confidence; also, they were not allowed to publish a magazine on a Sunday. 'The supplement,' he added, 'is still not being taken seriously. It is like the toy in the cornflake packet.'[1] The *Observer* brought out its Sunday magazine on 6 September 1964 with a cover portrait of Lord Mountbatten by John Hedgecoe, who established the Photography Department at the Royal College of Art the next year. It aimed to compete with the *Sunday Times* supplement as well as illustrated titles such as *Life* and *Paris Match* (British photojournalism pioneers *Picture Post* and *Illustrated* had closed in the late 1950s).

1 Mark Boxer, quoted in *Topic*, 21 April 1962

Sunday Times supplement
(253 × 330 mm, stapled)

SUNDAY TIMES (16 November 1969)

Michael Rand, who was art director between 1963 and 1993, has said: 'I never attempted a style for the magazine. I just wanted it busy but simply laid out, and there had to be tension there: grit and glamour. I realise now my unconscious influence was *Picture Post*. It had those great covers and was unashamedly a picture magazine. And I used a lot of illustration – David Hockney, Peter Blake and Ian Dury did front covers. There was a feeling that, creatively, you could do anything.'[1] *Eagle* and *TV21* artist Frank Bellamy illustrated this comic-style 'Playwright's Progress' spread based on the experiences of writer Frank Norman. Bellamy did similar work for many magazines, including *Doctor Who* covers for the *Radio Times*. Elsewhere in this issue was an article on wartime images by Henri Cartier-Bresson for 'Paris Takes Its Revenge'. David King, David Hillman, Roger Law (who developed model caricatures with Peter Fluck, which led to the TV series *Spitting Image*), Clive Crook (later creative director for the launch of *Elle* in the UK), John Tennant and Tony Chambers all worked for the supplement.

1 'Michael Rand', *Sunday Times*, 5 February 2012, p. 31

Sunday Times supplement
(252 × 326 mm, stapled, 96 pages)

SUNDAY TIMES (5 September 1971)

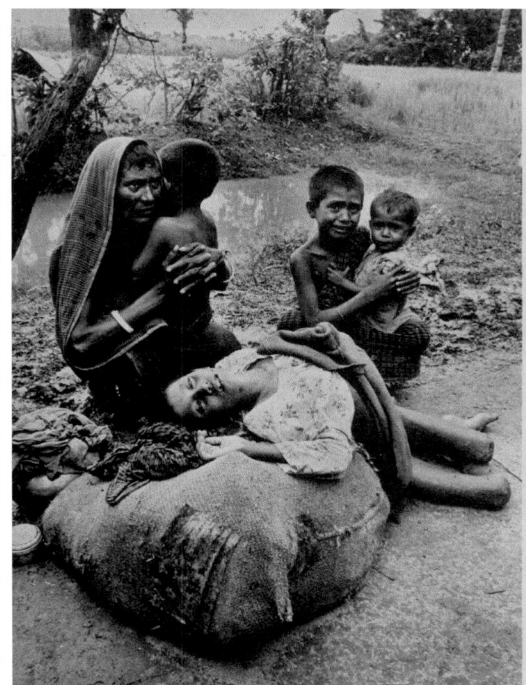

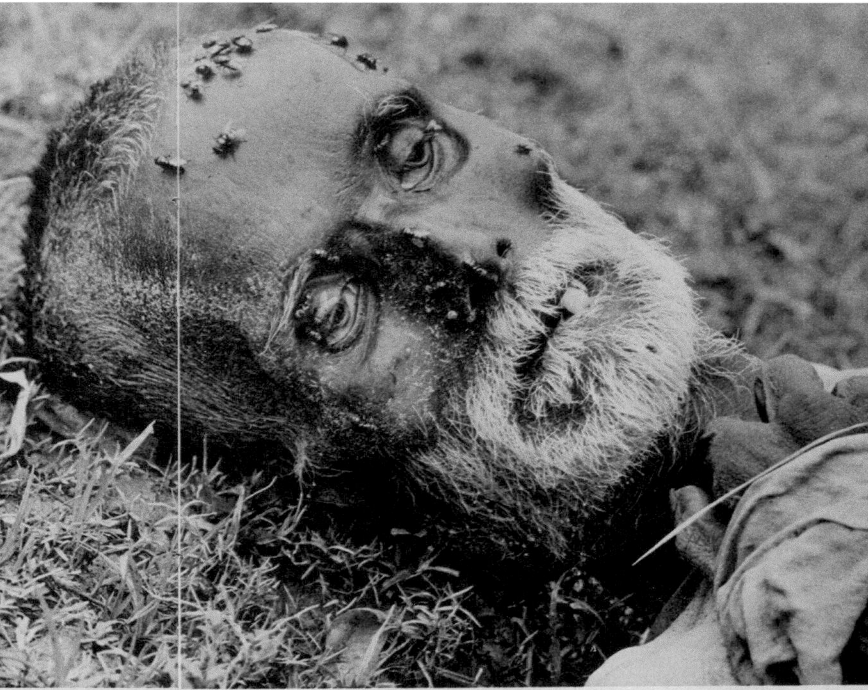

Above: a typical roadside casualty, this mother sits disconsolate with her dying child on her knees. Right: West Bengal is filled with the sound of crying children. The child on the cover has its mother to soothe it, but this starving baby girl is alone. Perpetually hungry, bewildered and frightened, they are an easy prey to exhaustion and disease. The ceaseless rains bring the danger of bronchial pneumonia which by July had succeeded cholera and starvation as the biggest threat to survival; while the swelling of the stagnant pools by flood water breeds bacteria

38

Above: this old man had been on the road for two or three weeks, making very slow mileage by day and sleeping by the roadside at night. His aim was to cross the border in safety – and he had achieved it, only to be denied life as soon as he had done so. The smell of his decaying body did not deter other refugees from camping, in tents made out of leaves, beside his corpse, because space was so scarce at Banaswar Pur. Railway stations near the border are so packed with refugees (or "evacuees" as the local Indians prefer to call them, implying that their stay is temporary) that to board a train one has to clamber over hundreds of sleeping bodies, past crying children covered in flies, amid constant squabbles occasioned by would-be travellers who can't afford tickets, or refugees claiming territorial rights to a few inches of ground. Yet, ironically, the Ladies' First and Third Class waiting-rooms at these railway stations are swept clean and always locked

'A Land Beyond Comfort': photo reportage about West Bengal by Don McCullin, who was the consummate war photographer of the era. *Tatler* trumpeted his first fashion shoot in its April 1981 issue. McCullin told BBC Radio that when he came back from a job he put his cameras away, so he rarely took photos at home: 'Those cameras are just as contaminated as my mind.'[1] In 1982, he was forbidden to cover the Falklands War by the British government. This photograph showing a corpse was pushing at the limits of acceptability.

1 Don McCullin, *Front Row*, BBC Radio 4, 12 October 2011

Sunday Times supplement
(238 × 298 mm, stapled, 80 pages)

Cecil Beaton's dream wardrobe was based on a V&A exhibition, *Fashion*, he had organized. From the left, a vamp cut in satin by Charles James from 1935; Dior's New Look from 1948 (V&A: T.116–1974); organdie appliquéd Schiaparelli from 1950 (V&A: T.397–1974); silk flamenco by Balenciaga from 1961 (V&A: T.26–1974). Beaton had won three Oscars for his costume designs, one for *Gigi* and two for *My Fair Lady* (V&A: S.773–1982). The backgrounds were illustrations from the Mary Evans Picture Library.

Sunday Times supplement
(238 × 298 mm, stapled, 80 pages)

PRIVATE EYE (7 August 1964)

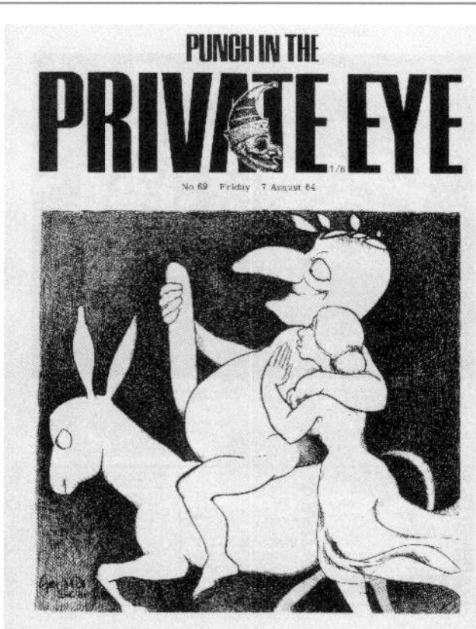

8

Anyone who has been editor of Punch knows that the office in Bouverie Street where it is edited would have made Edgar Allan Poe consider scrapping his "Tales of Mystery and Imagination" and beginning again. I never even now pass it without a shiver.

I first went in there some twelve years ago at the request of the Agnews, who own the place. It was a clandestine visit. Talking with them in their downstairs office, I could hear people upstairs, moving about, as it seemed, on tiptoe, and occasionally whispering together. Clearly something was going on there. It was. They were bringing out the magazine.

The impression the Agnews made on me was of dispirited men who had been cast by fate in an unsuitable role. Laughter seemed very far away from them; to say that there was no twinkle in their eye is an understatement.

I myself, as it happened, had scarcely ever read Punch; at most two or three issues picked up by chance. Everyone will be expecting me to add "At the dentist's." Not so. Waiting to see a dentist, I have always preferred the Tatler or the Queen; any magazine, in fact, which can be relied on, as Punch cannot, to have in it a photograph of Lord Snowden, or at any rate of Jocelyn Stephens.

The only sure memory I had of the magazine's contents was of parliamentarians portrayed as birds. I also seemed to remember, with decided distaste, that it had first published A. A. Milne's Christopher Robin verses.

Nonetheless, the Agnews appeared eager that I should become editor. I propounded a sum, by way of salary and expenses, that I hoped would prove exorbitant. Now, like Clive, I stand amazed at my own moderation. The Agnews, not notable for a readiness to unbelt, seemed unabashed.

It was, I realised disconsolately, as good as settled, and I returned to the Daily Telegraph round the corner, where I was then working. This newspaper, God knows, is not among the liveliest of man's productions, but somehow on that dismal December afternoon it had a sudden glory. In the same sort of way, a whore who has agreed, for money, to become the steady companion of some tedious old privy-counsellor or man-of-letters will see with new eyes the striptease joint where she has hitherto operated.

The institution round which Punch revolved was, as I soon discovered, the Table. Upon it, the initials of past editors, artists and writers had been carved; round it, we gathered weekly over luncheon to consider our cartoon. I sat opposite the Agnews. Looking across at them was like staring into the face of a slow-moving clock at St. Pancras Station while waiting for a train.

On the occasion of my first appearance at the Table someone asked me whether I was interested in cricket. I answered laconically: "No!" It was, I realised, one of those tremendously meaningful exchanges after which nothing is ever quite the same again. Like Luther I could do no other. So help me God.

Our deliberations on the week's cartoon were lengthy and confused. Usually someone would suggest showing President Eisenhower as Humpty Dumpty, or General de Gaulle as Alice. Usually we did. Our attitude throughout was informed by the dilute liberal-humanitarianism which (apart from Senator Goldwater, Mao Tse-tung, Dr. Verwoerd, and a few other sturdy swimmers against the stream) has now become pretty well universal.

In my own room I sat opposite a portrait of Sir Owen Seaman, Bart, who edited Punch from 1906 to 1932. He obviously did not care for me. Nor I for him. I tried moving him to the side and putting Mark Lemon in his place, but the Bart's fleshy, complacent countenance continued to be oppressive.

The only alternative was to look out of my window into the office of the News of the World; to watch the great rolls of newsprint being hoisted up, with the cheerful prospect that they would soon be recording the doings of West-End Majors, of Scout-Masters on Serious Charges, to which that estimable newspaper was then still dedicated.

Bringing ou a humorous publication is, in any case, a sombre undertaking. I gives you the feeling, as Thurber put it when writing about Ross and the New Yorker, that nothing funny ever has happened, or ever can happen, in the world.

Occasional visits to the Agnews provided no alleviation. They kept in the top drawer on one side of their desk a paper showing the magazine's circulation, and in the top drawer on the other side a paper showing the advertising coming in. What they kept in the middle drawer I have no idea, but it was certainly not jokes.

To add to my difficulties advertisers were always making trouble, either about some particular drawing or article, or about the magazine as a whole. The advertising manager had to bear the brunt of this. He came to have a crucified air, wearing his bowler like a crown of thorns, and swallowing his Veuve Cliquot as though it were vinegar.

9

Newspaper proprietors and higher paid journalists often declaim, with their hands on their hearts, that never, never, never has advertising matter been permitted etc., etc. Other newspaper proprietors and higher paid journalists present on the occasion warmly applaud, wreathed in brandy fumes and cigar smoke; as do also archbishops, sheriffs, lord-lieutenants and aldermen, ready at the drop of a hat to get up and proclaim that the British press is the best and most honest, etc. etc. Lower paid journalists know that the press is about as independent of advertisers as M. P's are of their party whips.

Sometimes, in an effort to appease advertisers, I was taken to lunch with one or other of them – the B.M.C. man or the Gilette man - at some tremendously expensive place like the Belfry. They were mournful and unproductive occasions. The smoked salmon entered into my soul.

Perhaps the biggest row came over a cartoon of Churchill, then Prime Minister, suggesting that it was time he went. This was so obviously true, had been so frequently remarked, especially among Churchill's closest associates, that it enfuriated everyone. Angry letters poured in; the Agnews winced, especially when they received protests from their numerous share-holding relatives scattered about the Home Counties. I myself was honoured by a communication from Farmer Soames.

Thenceforth I began to lose interest. The final break came over some mildly facetious verses on the Prince of Wales' preparatory school which the Agnews decided to remove without reference to me. I then resigned, to their and my intense relief. Shortly afterwards other verses expressing a proper love of the monarchy appeared in the magazine. The Duke of Edinburgh came to the Table, the ads rolled in, and peace was restored.

Malcolm Muggeridge

The unsophisticated typesetting and layout of the satirical fortnightly were a key part of its anti-establishment image. But the crude look disguised the fact that *Private Eye* used the latest technology – Letraset rub-down type for headlines, IBM golfball typewriters for typesetting and offset litho printing. All this avoided the expense of letterpress typesetting and printing; typed strips of text were pasted on to boards to be photographed for printing film. The same techniques would be used by underground magazines later in the decade, by the punk fanzines of the 1970s and early issues of *i-D*. The title design was by Matthew Carter and saw its first outing on 18 May 1962. Carter later moved to the US and designed type for *Time*, *Newsweek* and *Wired*. His influence on the look of newspapers and magazines is immeasurable, whether they were published on paper or online, especially after he designed the fonts Georgia and Verdana for Microsoft. The Gerald Scarfe cover for issue 69 parodies *Punch*, as a naked Mr Punch 'rides' a donkey while hugging a female admirer – a detail from the 'Dickie' Doyle cover that fronted *Punch* for a century. From this issue on, the 'Rabelaisian gnome' was adopted as a mascot on the Lord Gnome page.

Malcolm Muggeridge, editor of *Punch* from 1953 to 1957, was guest editor for this 'Punch in the Private Eye' issue, which argued that the old, radical incarnation of *Punch* magazine – which *Private Eye* once admired – was dead. Muggeridge writes that he never read *Punch*, even in the dentist's: 'Waiting to see a dentist, I have always preferred the *Tatler* or the *Queen*; any magazine, in fact, which can be relied on, as *Punch* cannot, to have in it a photograph of [photographer and husband to Princess Margaret] Lord Snowden, or at any rate of [*Queen* owner] Jocelyn Stephens.' Both surnames are misspelt, deliberately, in order to irritate their subjects. The article's crude typesetting, in which there are many real typing errors ('enfuriated'), bears evidence of letters having been corrected. Publication names are underlined because the typewriter could not reproduce italics. The byline is in Letraset Clarendon medium, with a broken serif on the second 'g' of Muggeridge. Ronald Searle illustrated the article and did the Mr Punch skull superimposed on the front cover. Elsewhere, his *Rake's Progress* cartoon denoted the six ages of *Punch*. Searle was a regular *Punch* contributor and did many covers, both adaptations of the Doyle cover in the mid-1950s and then full-colour covers.

Pressdram
(224 × 288 mm, stapled, 16 pages)

OZ (October/November 1967)

This psychedelic Bob Dylan cover was by Martin Sharp, one of the magazine's founders. Many designers and illustrators worked on *Oz* at various times, including Barney Bubbles, Peter Brookes and Pearce Marchbank, bringing a range of visual influences. The magazines used more colour than most mainstream magazines and combined it with edgy illustration that was often based on graphics from other magazines, together with anarchic layouts. The magazine used the production techniques pioneered by *Private Eye*.

Oz Publications
(210 × 298 mm, stapled, 48 pages)

This spread is typical of the experimental approaches seen in the magazine. This issue could be read from either end with two covers: a World of Young Love (portraying sex and drugs and rock and roll) or Angry Oz. The latter was a reaction to the verdicts over the 'Schoolkids' issue (May 1970), which had led to a long obscenity trial and the initial conviction of editors Richard Neville, Jim Anderson and Felix Dennis, verdicts that were overturned on appeal. The 'Young Love' cover, signed by Peter 'Hack' Brookes, was based on a Peter Driben cover for US pulp title *Beauty Parade* from February 1949.

Oz Publications
(210 × 298 mm, stapled, 48 pages)

TIME OUT (12 August 1968)

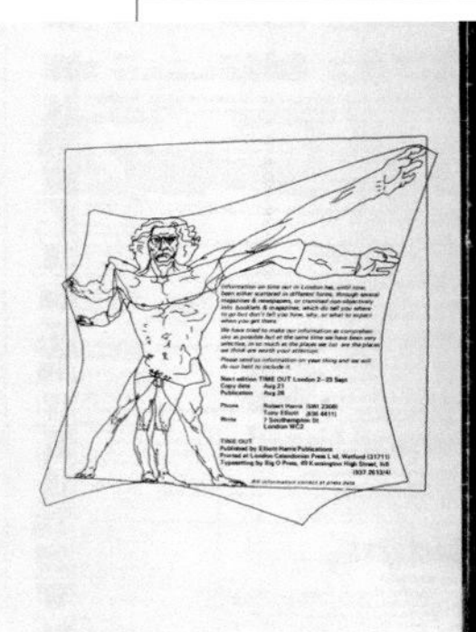

The first issues of *Time Out* were fold-out posters with small pages produced by Tony Elliott and Bob Harris ('Whispering Bob' of BBC TV's *The Old Grey Whistle Test*).

Elliott-Harris Publications
(152 × 214 mm, 16-page foldout)

MEN ONLY (November 1964)

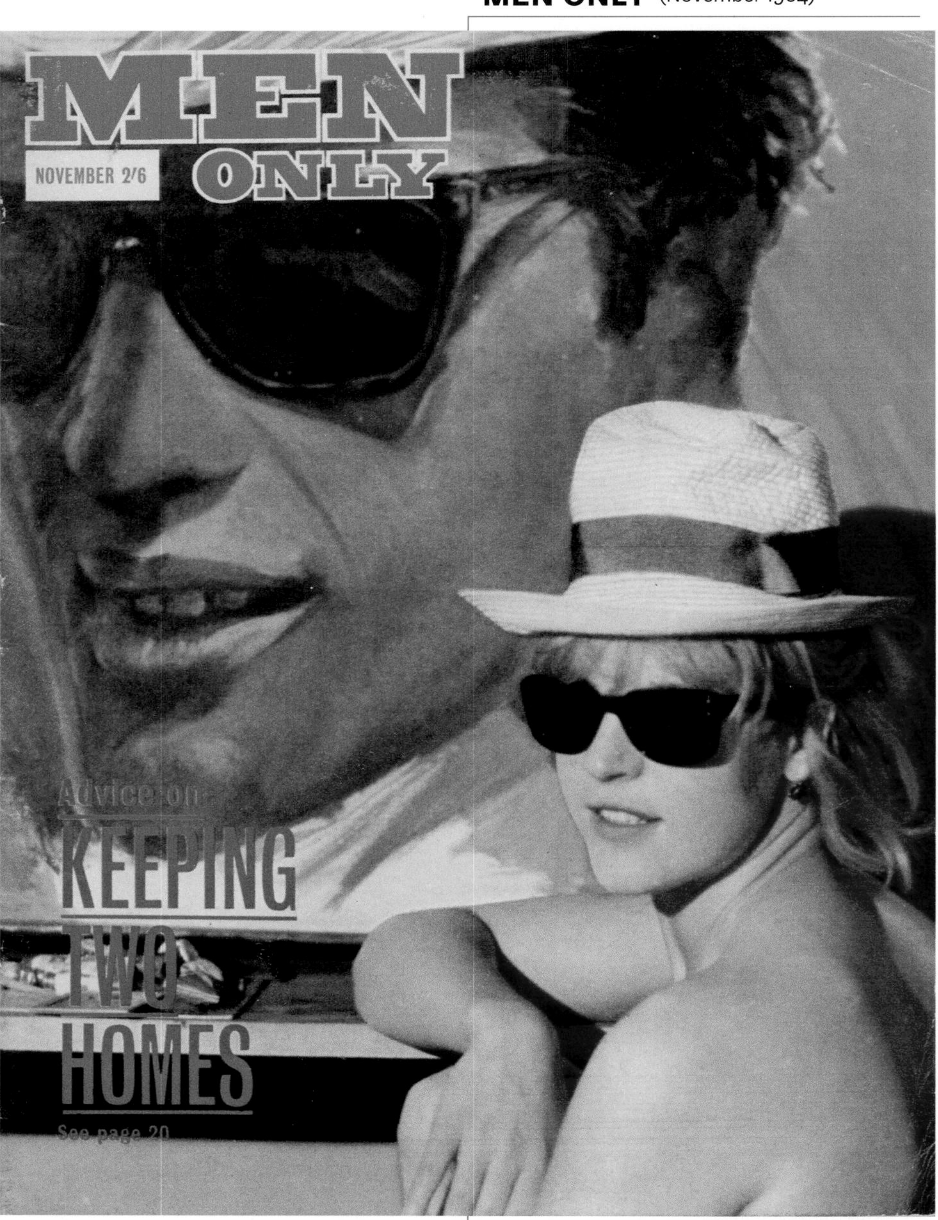

Keeping Two Homes

'A HOME where you work, a home in the sun'. That is the slogan behind the biggest property boom the Mediterranean countries have ever known. In these 1960's every man can own two homes, even when they are a thousand miles apart, and as long as he can afford to pay for both of them.

It is a boom where prices seldom stand still. In London a man built a villa in Spain and sold it three years later for exactly 100 per cent profit. Last June an advertisement in the Evening Standard offered bungalows on Majorca for £2,400 and six weeks later inquirers were told the price had gone up to £2,700. Plots of land have been known to be worth half as much again in under two years.

But as prices soar, the estate agents claim that getting that second home is much cheaper than you think. You can sub-let and have the rents pay most of your mortgage repayments. After eight years the villa can be yours, an extra income as well as a cheap holiday for your family.

Three years ago there were only a handful of estate agents in Britain selling homes in the sun. Today there are nearly a hundred, offering plots of land for as little as £25 down and extolling such exotic names as Torremolinos, Costa Brava, Fuengirola, Campamento, Marbella and Pinar de los Franceses.

by **DAVID ROXAN**

Once they just offered a villa here, the odd flat there. But now they handle enormous estates, complete with shops, cinema, launderette, bowling-alley, golf-course, night-clubs and restaurants. They run special chartered flights for clients to view before they buy and if they clinch the deal, the trip is free. They bang on the big drum and attract attention, knowing how powerful an ally is sunshine that you can rely on for many months of the year.

This is a boom that is as logical as it is inevitable. In Northern Europe men are prosperous but live in grime-

Don't expect to gain an income —though it's possible. A villa in the sun can be a profitable, pleasurable, investment provided normal house buying care is taken

20

there's a holiday in the sunspots

ridden industrial cities where it always seems to be raining. Southern Europe has over 2,000 hours of sunshine a year every year, beautiful scenery, the blue Mediterranean and utter poverty. It cries out for capital investment that will mean jobs and a higher standard of living.

Doubtless the marriage was hastened by hoteliers who are today accused of killing the goose that lay their golden eggs. They have made the cost of a holiday in the sun so expensive for a family with two or three children that it has been forced to consider alternative measures.

And certainly buying a house or flat for holidays as an investment figures high on its list.

Some of the larger estate agents in London are getting as many as 300 enquiries a week, though only from 2 to 5 per cent lead to a sale. One single advertisement can bring in well over 500 serious replies.

But if high prices of hotels has hastened the marriage, in Britain the troth has been plighted by the Bank of England who thought up an ingenious method by which people could buy a home in the sun without loss of sterling to the Treasury.

The Bank introduced a special type of currency, known as 'investment dollars' or 'switch funds.' If you live in Wigan and want to buy a villa on the Costa Brava, you go to a banker. On the money-market he finds another resident in Britain who owns the necessary Spanish currency or assets.

The man from Wigan is permitted to buy 'investment dollars' from him up to the amount he needs, but he has to pay a premium that varies between 11 and 14 per cent of the sum bought.

He has to get the Bank's permission to clinch the deal and he is

villa boom of Europe

firmly told that each family is allowed to buy only one home abroad in order to curb the activities of the speculator.

'Investment dollars' aren't needed if the person intends to emigrate and live permanently in his Villa. He is permitted to take the necessary sterling out of the country.

The Bank also makes two other rules. If you want the money to buy a plot of land, you must undertake to build on it within a year. And you are not permitted to spend a penny of your travelling allowance on buying property. If you do and are caught out, you are in deep trouble.

Even with these reservations, the Bank's main decision to permit people to buy a second home in the sun, as long as they pay extra for the privilege, has been like an official blessing to the property developers. They now pour out expensive brochures by the thousand, printed in three languages — English, French and German — and as likely to offer you "Ein Haus an der Sonne" as "A House In the Sun".

It is on Mediterranean coastline spots such as this that the holiday-maker-cum-landlord is encouraged to buy land.

Today the British are as big a customer as the Germans in the move to entice the prosperous middle-classes southwards to the sun by offering big-scale property development schemes, backed by millions of pounds in capital.

One of the biggest is Rosa Marina on the Italian Adriatic coast, a bare spot that is being transformed into a seaside resort. Covering 350 acres, more than half the 900 building plots have been sold for an average price of £700, made up of £25 down and the rest over four years.

So highly desirable is this land half-way between Bari and Brindisi, say the Rosa Marina people, that its value has gone up by 60 per cent in 18 months. And they believe it will get dearer still.

The first fifty villas will be completed at Rosa Marina by the end of 1964. There are 17 different designs in all shapes and sizes, ranging from £2,175 for a conventional one-bedroom villa to £6,500 for a three-bedroom effort that even the brochure admits to be of "ultra modern design."

Last October 80 people flew from Britain on a chartered flight. They inspected their Rosa Marina plots and every one of them said they still wanted to buy. This October another 80 will be going out on another chartered flight.

What sort of people are they? Firstly, those with a bit of brass. Mostly grammar school products, they have made their own way up →

A winter's dream of a holiday in the sun—and it could be just outside your second home.

21

Pop artist Pauline Boty is on the cover in front of her 1962 tribute to French New Wave cinema, 'With Love to Jean-Paul Belmondo' (the painting appears to have been reversed, left to right). Boty, at one time nicknamed 'the Wimbledon Bardot', was part of the Royal College of Art generation that included Derek Boshier and David Hockney. She was featured with them in *Pop Goes the Easel* by Ken Russell for BBC Television's *Monitor* series, along with Peter Blake and Peter Phillips. Not only did Boty feature on the cover of a men's magazine, but she appears to have based one of her Marilyn Monroe paintings on another, *Town* from November 1962. Boty was working on a set design for Kenneth Tynan's production of *Oh! Calcutta!* when she died of cancer, aged 28, in 1966. Inside the issue, the colour centre spread is used for a topless pin-up; the only other colour page was also used for a pin-up.

As this spread shows, the layouts had the feel of a newspaper and aimed for a punchy look; many of the articles were about crime.

City Magazines
(215 × 275 mm, stapled, 72 pages)

KING (July 1966)

King was more upmarket than *Men Only* and the cover price of 7s 6d (compared with 2s 6d) reflected that. Paul Raymond had backed the first two issues of *King*, but then pulled out of a magazine that saw itself as England's answer to *Playboy*. *King* was kept going by a group of backers that included Peter Sellers, Bryan Forbes, Bob Monkhouse and David Frost, but ended up being taken over by *Mayfair*. Designer Dave Chaston fronts the 'Celebrating the Peacock Male' cover.

Inside, the left-hand page shows jazz pundit Danny Halperin; on the right in front is designer Dave Chaston, illustrations editor Mike Foreman (made a Royal Designer for Industry in 1985) and picture editor Roy Giles. Today, Foreman is known as a book illustrator, but he previously worked as a designer on *Playboy* in the US.

Europress Publishing
(235 × 295 mm, stapled, 108 pages)

MEN ONLY (1971)

This is the first issue produced under Paul Raymond's ownership. A reader commented on the letters page of *Men Only* in the 1930s: 'I only fear it will get vulgar; this kind of paper does in time.' The art editor was Roger Watt and the photographer Michael Dyer. The image, to illustrate a short story, 'The Connoisseurs' by Alfred Mazure, betrays Surrealist influences, such as Dalí's lobster and Meret Oppenheim's *Cannibal Feast* from 1959. The issue includes an interview with *Oz* pioneer and 'hippy spokesman' Richard Neville, who was in the process of launching *Ink*. Top-shelf magazines achieved very high sales and were able to pay top rates, which allowed illustrators and photographers great creative freedom and indulgence. Among the other men's magazines that fell into the hands of top-shelf publishers were the 1950s pocket pin-up *Escort*; *Razzle* from the 1930s; *Parade*, originally the forces magazine *Blighty* from the two world wars; and the Victorian pioneer of mass media, *Tit-Bits*.

Paul Raymond Publications
(235 × 295 mm, stapled, 84 pages)

NEW SCIENTIST (28 January 1965)

NEW SCIENTIST

28 January 1965

Churchill and science
Professor R. V. JONES

The controversy about world health research
NIGEL CALDER

Artificial speech
Dr J. R. PIERCE, *Bell Telephone Laboratories*

A curious collision 800 miles up
DAVID FISHLOCK

Junk in space
J. A. PILKINGTON, *The London Planetarium*

Working with molten salts
Dr DOUGLAS INMAN, *Northampton College of Advanced Technology, London*

VOLUME 25 NUMBER 428 1s. 3d. WEEKLY

Ruari McLean was brought in to redesign the magazine, and a new title and typography were introduced for the first issue of 1961. The production values were little changed – there was still uncoated paper, with the same stock used for the cover and internal pages, but the size increased slightly and there were more photographs. Later in 1965, illustrations and spot colours were introduced on the cover.

Harrison, Raison & Co.
(227 × 304 mm, stapled, 62 pages)

NEW SCIENTIST (21 January 1971)

21 January 1971
Weekly 2s (10p)
new scientist
and SCIENCE JOURNAL
Australia 30 cents / Canada 60 cents / New Zealand 35 cents / South Africa 30 cents / USA (airfreight) 75 cents / BF 20 / FF 2.65 / DM 2 / hfl 1.25 / skr 2.50 /

...the science weekly of the 70's
Lord Kennet: when we run out of England / Irradiated food
Science in North Vietnam / Serendipity and cancer research

At the end of 1970, *New Scientist* took over rival *Science* which led to bigger issues, design changes and a switch to full-colour covers. Although photographs would sometimes be used, most covers were illustrated. Notice the modernist lower-case sans-serif typeface and the different weights of type for the two words of the title – an approach that became common in the next decade.

IPC
(215 × 295 mm, stapled, 164 pages)

NEW SCIENTIST (9 August 1979)

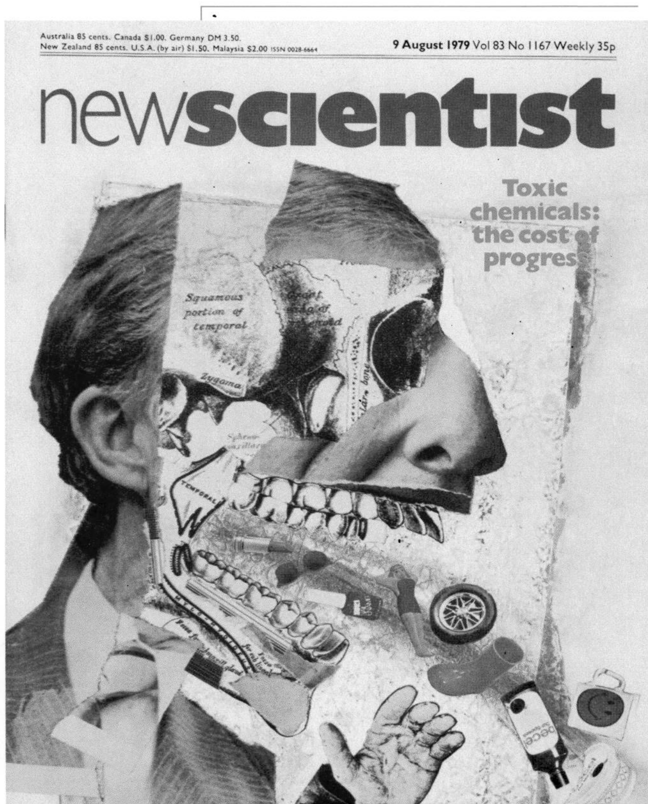

Illustrator and film-maker George Snow produced the collage for this *New Scientist* cover on toxic substances used in everyday products. Snow lists John Heartfield, Stewart Mackinnon, Ian Pollock and Russell Mills among his influences, and was part of a group known as the 'Radical Illustrators'. With Robert Mason, he edited an edition of the Association of Illustrators magazine called *Radical Illustrators* in 1981 (No. 38). Mackinnon, who had illustrated articles for *Nova* and *Oz*, has told Rick Poynor how the offer of a commission from *Playboy* turned him away from illustration: 'I went to the Park Lane Hotel and there was Roger Law, Gerald Scarfe and Ralph Steadman [who had spawned 'Gonzo journalism' with Hunter S. Thompson and covered the Watergate scandals with him for *Rolling Stone*]. There was a woman in a huge room and she said, "My company would like to bring you all to the States to cover different events." I was to cover trials. And what was the magazine? It was *Playboy*! Here's me wanting to do politics and here is this capitalist magazine. I wouldn't go.'[1] Such was his fear of 'selling out' and being dragged into the commercial world that Mackinnon rejected *Playboy*'s offer and turned to film-making. *New Scientist* excelled in commissioning covers to illustrate often highly abstract ideas. The image here led to a legal problem in that one of the companies whose product was seen in the collage objected to being linked to toxic materials. The magazine apologized.

1 Rick Poynor, 'Stewart Mackinnon: Ruptured and Remade', *Varoom*, No. 3, 2007

IPC
(280 × 295 mm, stapled, 76 pages)

HARPERS & QUEEN (early April 1971)

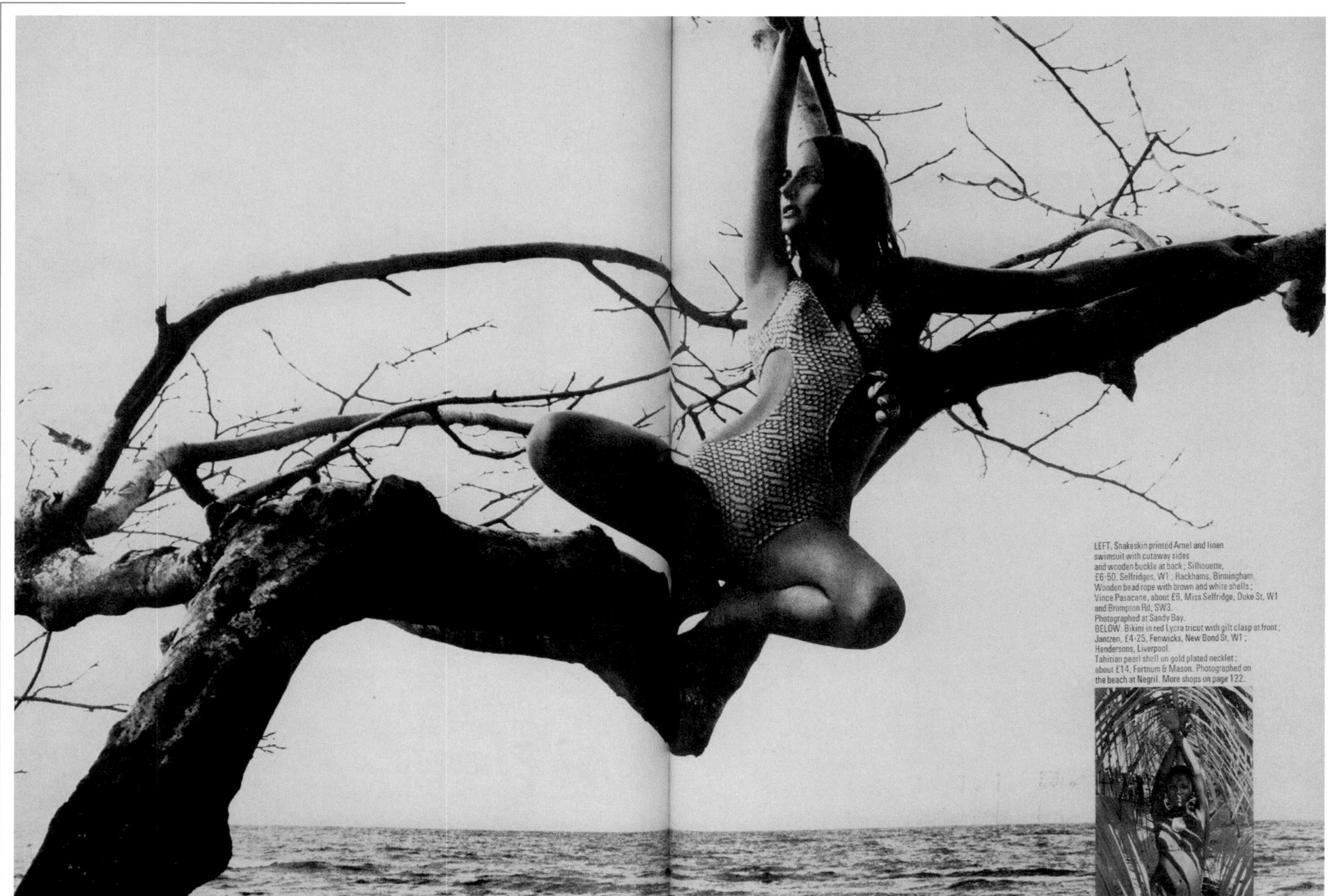

LEFT. Snakeskin printed Arnel and linen
swimsuit with cutaway sides
and wooden buckle at back; Silhouette,
£6·50, Selfridges, W1; Rackhams, Birmingham.
Wooden bead rope with brown and white shells;
Vince Pasacane, about £6, Miss Selfridge, Duke St, W1
and Brompton Rd, SW3.
Photographed at Sandy Bay.
BELOW. Bikini in red Lycra tricot with gilt clasp at front;
Jantzen, £4·25, Fenwicks, New Bond St, W1;
Hendersons, Liverpool.
Tahitian pearl shell on gold plated necklet;
about £14, Fortnum & Mason. Photographed on
the beach at Negril. More shops on page 122.

US-owned *Harper's Bazaar* and *Queen* merged in November 1970. Usually in the case of such a merger the subordinate title quickly disappears from the cover, to be relegated to the masthead inside, eventually going even from that. In this case, the full title was retained until 2006, when the internationalization of the magazine market, particularly for advertising sales, led the company to revert to *Harper's Bazaar*. NatMags has claimed it to be 'the only true successful merger in the women's market'. Advertising had long supported the publishing of 16 issues a year of the big fashion magazines, known as 'double months'. The cover photograph by Helmut Newton is of an uncredited model wearing Biba make-up. Willie Landels was editor, with John Herbert as assistant art director. Future *Vogue* editor Anna Wintour was fashion assistant.

The photographs for a swimsuit fashion spread in Jamaica were by Just Jaeckin, a French photographer who would achieve greater fame with the soft-porn film *Emmanuelle* three years later.

National Magazine Company
(228 × 308 mm, perfect bound, 132 pages)

Harpers
& Queen
JAMAICA:
RUM,
WOMEN
AND STEEL DRUMS,
BANANAS,
SUGAR
AND PALM TREES,
PLAY CLOTHES,
PRINTED COTTONS
AND SWIMSUITS,
SUN,
SUN
AND SUN
ART:
CHRISTO, THE MAN
WHO WRAPS THINGS UP
RUTH DAYAN:
A MOTHER IN ISRAEL

VOGUE

75p

DIAMOND
JUBILEE
1916-1976

VOGUE (October 1976)

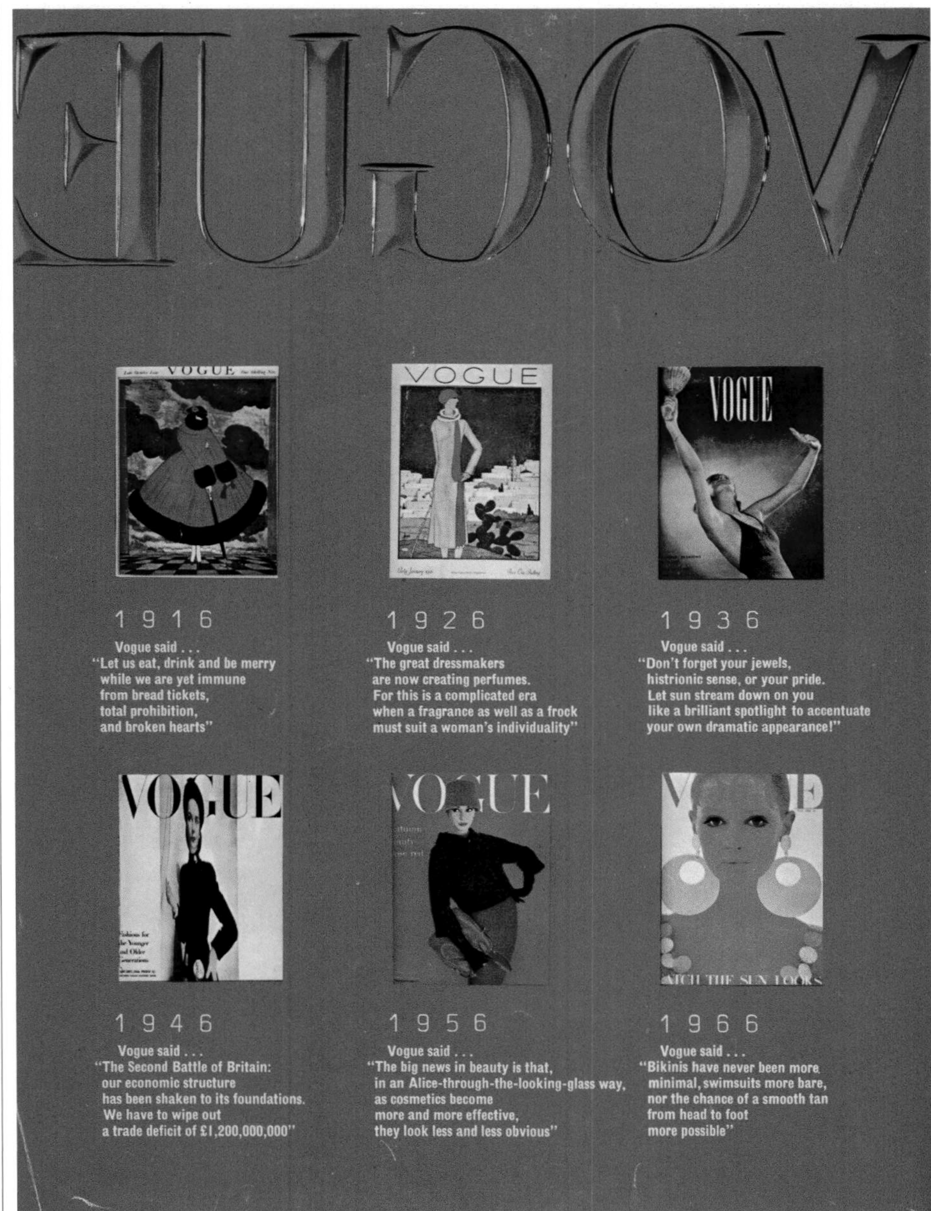

To celebrate 60 years in Britain, *Vogue* commissioned Waterford Crystal to engrave the title in glass; this was then photographed by James Mortimer against a red background. Robin Derrick, who became *Vogue*'s art director in 1993 and later creative director, has identified record covers and this cover as his inspiration: 'David Bowie on the back of Ziggy Stardust and everything about them. Roger Dean books and Hipgnosis [a 1970s design team responsible for the Pink Floyd record covers] led to an interest in graphic design. Then, as a 16-year-old A-level student at Filton Tech in Bristol, I found a Diamond Jubilee copy of *Vogue* with a cut-glass logo, plain red cover and pictures by Guy Bourdin and David Bailey; I put all the pictures on my wall. And in order to meet girls in the fashion department at Central St Martin's College of Art and Design, I designed some clothes for its Alternative Fashion Show, which I photographed. This led me to *i-D* magazine and I met Terry Jones. He'd been the art director of *Vogue* and had done the 1976 cover that I had seen when I was 16. On his desk was the cut-glass *Vogue* logo.'[1]

1 'My Life in Media: Robin Derrick', *Independent*, 17 October 2005, p. 20

Condé Nast
(222 × 304 mm, perfect bound, 256 pages)

SPARE RIB (July 1972)

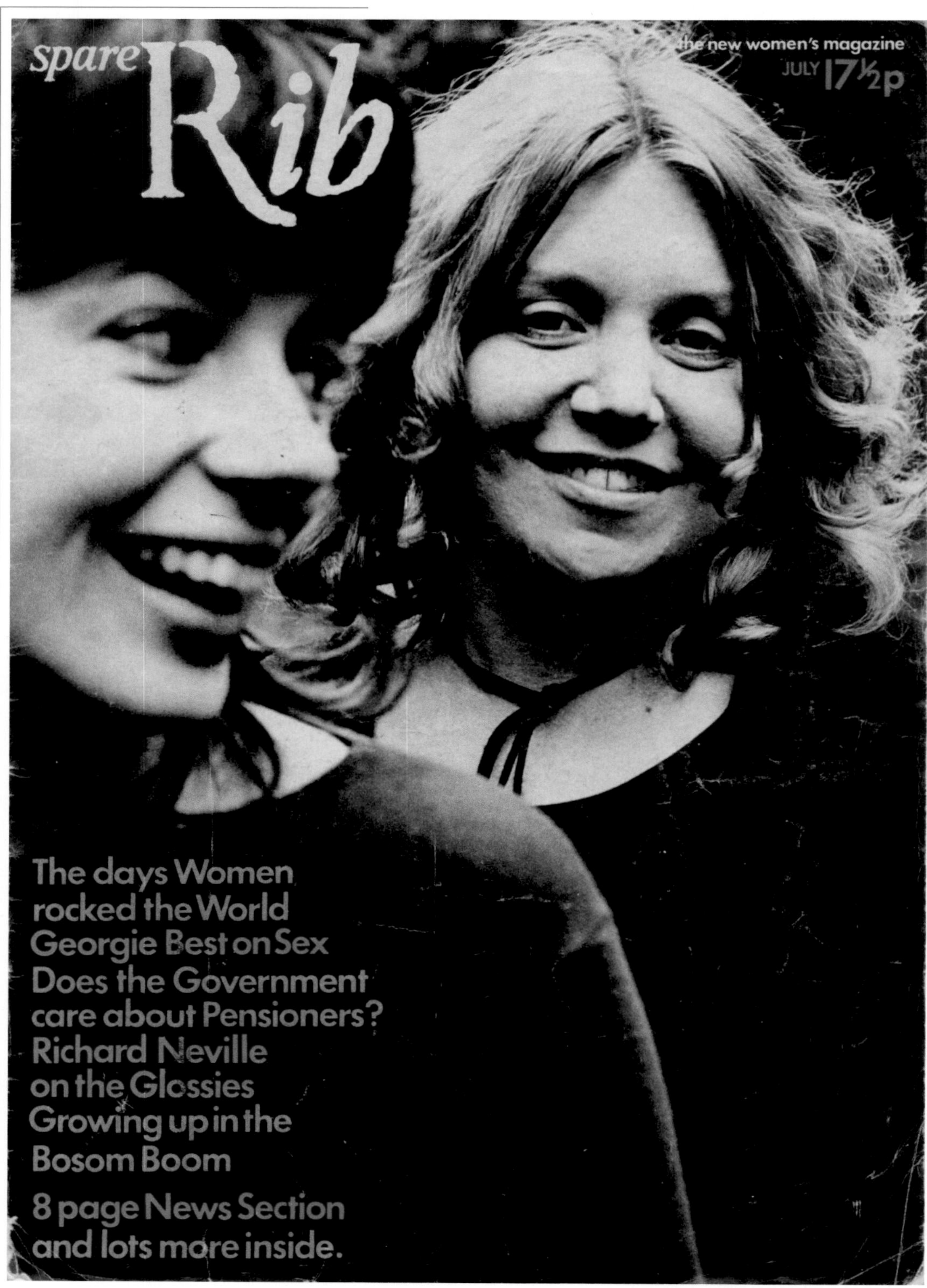

Spare Rib grew out of the underground press to promote the ideas of the women's liberation movement. It included a 'men's page' as a riposte to the women's pages in newspapers. The first issue was designed by Katy Hepburn and Sally Doust. Hepburn also worked with Derek Birdsall (a former art director of *Town*, *Nova* and German magazine *Twen*) on the Monty Python *Big Red Book* and *Papperbok*, both of which included pastiches of magazines, including the *Radio Times* and teenage girls' magazines. One of the *Spare Rib* editors, Rosie Boycott, went on to edit *Esquire*, as well as the *Independent* and *Independent on Sunday* newspapers. The cover photograph was by Angela Phillips and Michael Foreman contributed a cartoon of footballer George Best.

Spare Ribs Ltd
(210 x 280 mm, stapled, 40 pages)

COSMOPOLITAN (March 1972)

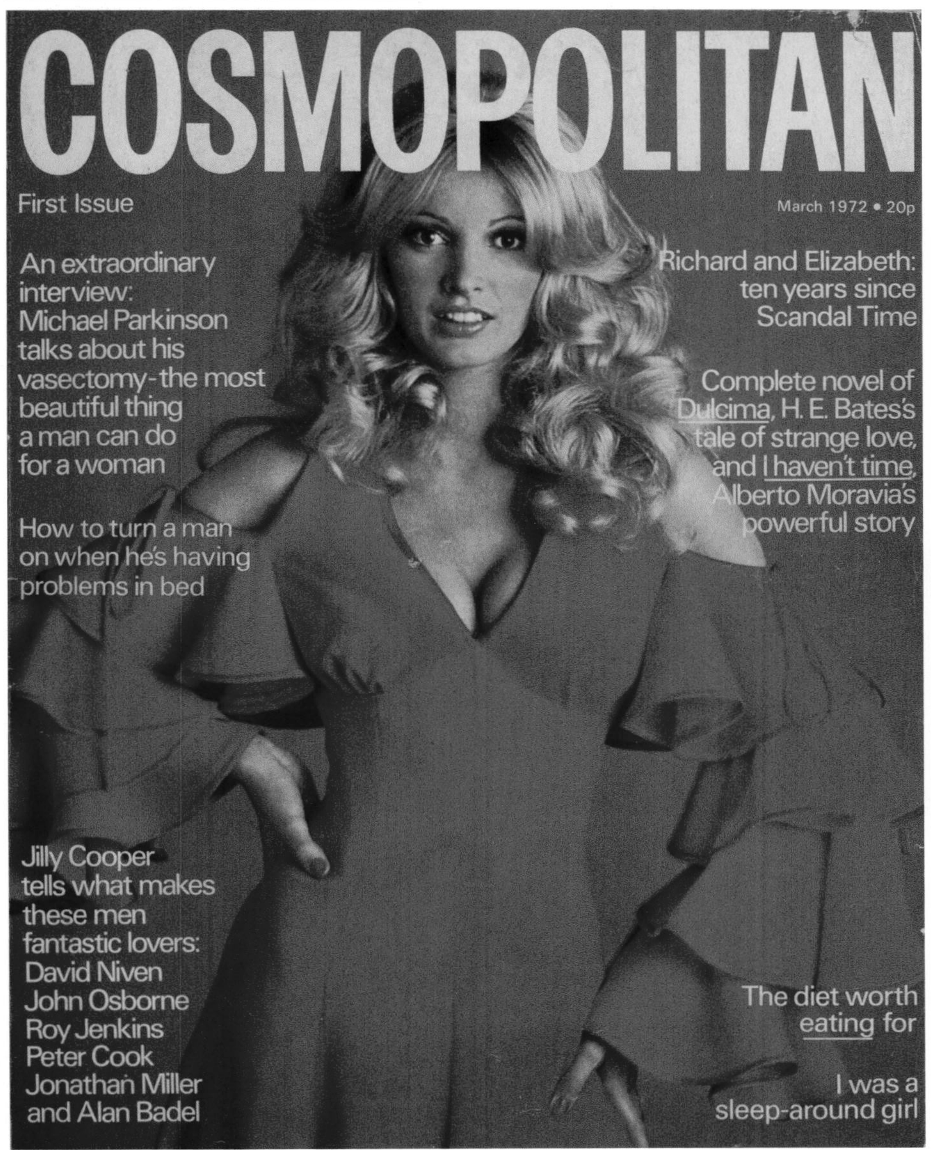

COSMOPOLITAN
First Issue
March 1972 • 20p
An extraordinary interview: Michael Parkinson talks about his vasectomy-the most beautiful thing a man can do for a woman
How to turn a man on when he's having problems in bed
Jilly Cooper tells what makes these men fantastic lovers: David Niven John Osborne Roy Jenkins Peter Cook Jonathan Miller and Alan Badel
Richard and Elizabeth: ten years since Scandal Time
Complete novel of Dulcima, H. E. Bates's tale of strange love, and I haven't time, Alberto Moravia's powerful story
The diet worth eating for
I was a sleep-around girl

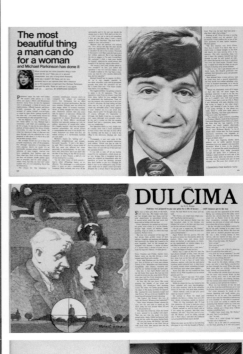

Cosmopolitan chose an aggressive red to dominate the cover with the model Julie Crosthwait surrounded by cover lines. The photograph was by David Magnus; the title set in Franklin Gothic extra condensed. Crosthwait was chosen by editorial director Helen Gurley Brown – the *Sex and the Single Girl* author who had already revamped the US edition – and told the *Daily Mirror* 30 years later: 'I didn't live the *Cosmopolitan* lifestyle at all. I must admit I was a bit shocked when I actually read the magazine.'[1]

Art editor Sue Wade used a sans-serif typeface for most of the features, in this case Helvetica bold for chat-show host Michael Parkinson talking about his vasectomy. Note the very large dateline at the foot of the right-hand page. The face of a cat reversed out of black was used to signify the end of the article.

Despite its editorial innovations, *Cosmo* followed the tested formula of illustration for fiction. Michael Foreman was chosen for the short story 'Dulcima' by H.E. Bates. A Windsor bold typeface was used for the fiction headlines.

1 *Sunday Mirror*, 24 February 2002, p. 30

National Magazine
(214 × 278 mm, perfect bound, 146 pages)

COSMOPOLITAN (November 1992)

Two decades later, the cover approach has evolved but is essentially the same (and is much copied). Notice that the cover model is not allowed to obscure the title, which is now even more condensed. The cover lines are far more aggressive and the bar code and web address have become standard elements. The art director was David Dowding and the cover photograph of Rhea Durham was by Davis Factor.

National Magazine
(216 × 290 mm, perfect bound, 388 pages)

TIME OUT (29 November 1974)

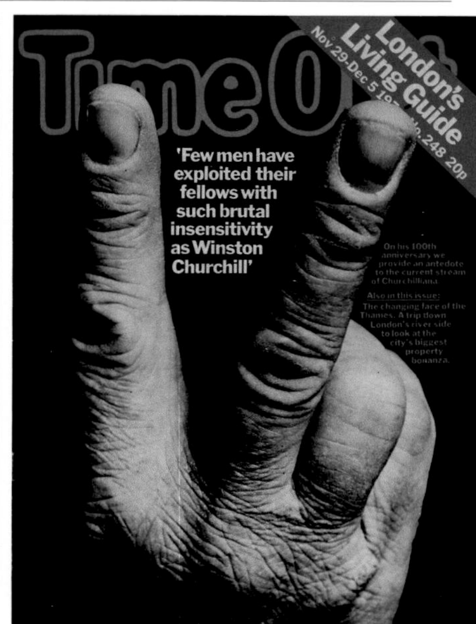

Pearce Marchbank redesigned the magazine for the 14 November 1970 issue, adopting a larger format and developing the neon title treatment. He did the covers himself, often overnight. Emily King has described in *Eye* magazine (No. 44) how Marchbank made the logo: 'The *Time Out* logo is created from two sets of slightly out-of-focus Franklin Gothic characters shot as line, the smaller reversed out of the core of the larger. Marchbank ran the resulting typographic halo through a half-tone filter, lending it the appearance of a gentle glow, suggestive of a radiant neon sign.' He was made a Royal Designer for Industry in 2004.

Time Out Publications
(215 × 290 mm, stapled)

NME (7 October 1978)

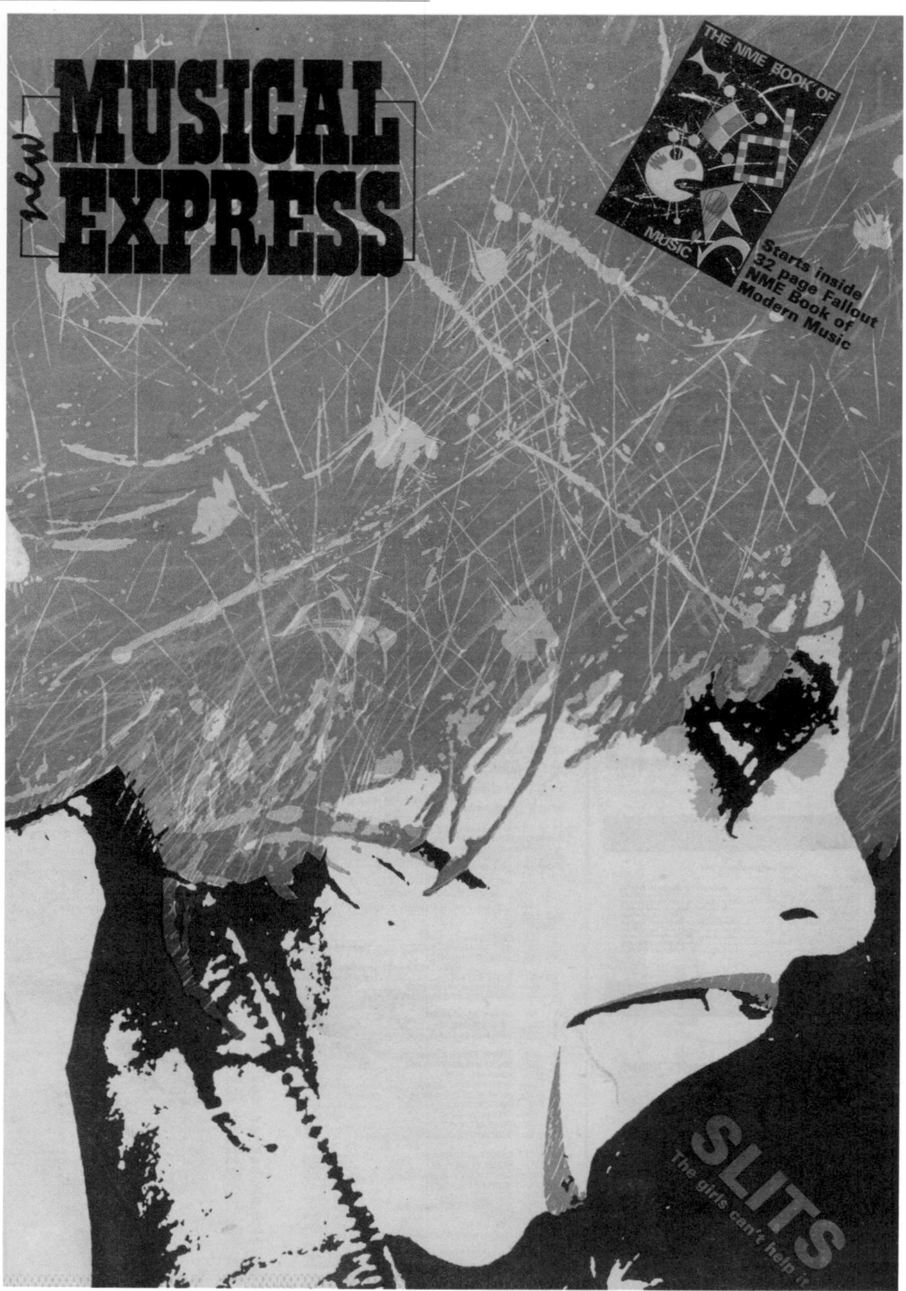

Barney Bubbles (who had changed his name from Colin Fulcher) redesigned *New Musical Express*. He had illustrated articles in the 'inky', as such newspaper-style music weeklies were known, and brought a punk aesthetic to the design. *Never Mind the Bollocks* by the Sex Pistols and the single 'God Save the Queen' had been released the year before.

IPC Magazines
(298 × 422 mm, loose, 60 pages)

NME (7 October 1978)

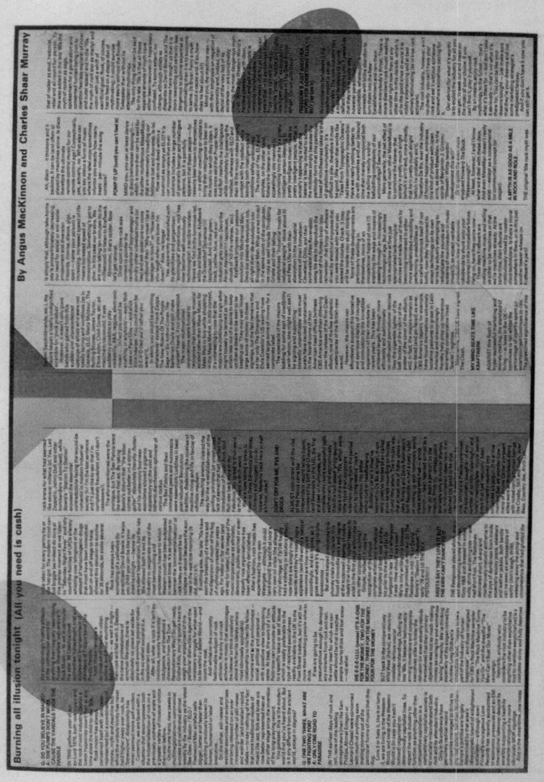

The four centre pages of the issue were designed to be taken out and folded into *NME's Book of Modern Music*, with a colour cover as the start of a series. In the week of 3 July 1977, Stiff Records had run double-page adverts designed by Bubbles in *New Musical Express*, *Sounds* and *Melody Maker*. They combined to make a poster of Elvis Costello to promote his single 'My Aim Is True'.

IPC Magazines
(298 × 422 mm, loose, 60 pages)

NME (2 December 1978)

A new title design by Bubbles, with *New Musical Express* abbreviated to *NME* in block lettering, was not used until the 2 December 1978 issue.

IPC Magazines
(298 × 422 mm, loose, 60 pages)

SMASH HITS (November 1978)

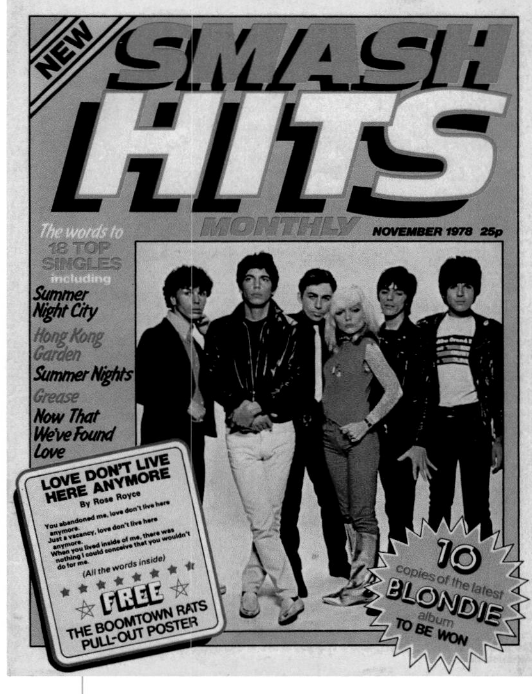

This first issue ran New York punk band Blondie on the cover and, after three monthly issues, *Smash Hits* was published fortnightly. *Smash Hits* was aimed at a younger pop audience, with an A4 format as opposed to the tabloid-newspaper style of *NME*, *Melody Maker*, *Sounds* and *Record Mirror*. All the 'inkies' would later adopt a magazine format.

Emap
(215 × 280 mm, stapled)

Style bibles and computers, lads' mags and celebrities

The 1980s ushered in the widespread use of computers for typesetting and layout and, increasingly, illustration. The decade was also the era of 'style bibles'. It saw the revival of the mainstream men's magazine and, continental influences again made their mark.

First, though, the *Face*. Its founder, Nick Logan, had been editor of *New Musical Express* at IPC and launched pop weekly *Smash Hits* for Emap in 1978. The *Face* had high production values for what, at first, was a music magazine – the third issue described itself as 'the photomagazine that's kind to your hands', a dig at the weekly 'inkies' such as *NME* and *Melody Maker*. The content expanded to cover lifestyle, design, fashion and media, and it became the de facto leader of a trio of style magazines, *Blitz* and *i-D* being the other two. Apart from the masthead with its bold graphic, the first issue gave little clue to the influence it would have on graphic design, but Neville Brody took over as designer and developed his own 'graphic language'. By the late 1980s, the *Face* was a style bible for young adults, selling 88,000 copies a month. Logan went on to launch *Arena* for male readers and again Brody's look helped to define the title. Only *i-D* now remains of the original style trio.

At the London College of Printing (since renamed London College of Communication), Brody was influenced by punk, Dada and Pop art. He designed album covers before moving to the *Face*. Former *Vogue* designer Terry Jones founded *i-D* in 1980. Its defining visual device is the winking cover subject, mimicking the 'emoticon' the title forms when rotated clockwise through 90 degrees. A punk influence on *i-D* is seen in the early issues, with an anarchic, DIY look, often using type and artwork produced on cheap dot-matrix printers.

Alongside the style boom came magazines for computer users. *Personal Computer World* was launched in 1978 with a restrained, classic look – appropriate for business and serious readers. In March 1981, Clive Sinclair's ZX81 brought computing within reach of the general public. In December the same year came Acorn's BBC Micro, competing with US imports from Commodore and Atari. They sold in their millions, spawning a generation of home users who wrote (or copied) their own games, utilities and documents.

Using computers in magazine production, for electronic mail and for illustration was pioneered within computer magazines but spread quickly to other titles. Also, the early home-computer aesthetic – dot-matrix typefaces, pixellated imagery, circuit boards and glowing neon lines – became pervasive. The £400 BBC Micro opened up the world of computers to artists and illustrators. One of those to begin experimenting was an art teacher called Jonathan Inglis. He reviewed software for *Acorn User* (later *BBC Acorn User*) magazine and the images he produced were used to illustrate articles and for covers. His artwork was supplied as hard copy – a colour printout or as four separate printouts, one for each process colour – or on a floppy disk. Inglis, who was killed in a cycling accident in July 1997, explored drawing and colouring programs – which had to run in a maximum of 32kb of RAM on a BBC Micro – to mimic Pointillism and Impressionist techniques, as well as exploiting the 'blocky' look that was a feature of low-resolution imagery.

By 1988, a 'holy trinity' of software was available for the Apple Macintosh: QuarkXPress for typesetting and layout; Adobe Photoshop for image cropping and manipulation; and Adobe Illustrator for creating vector graphics and charts. One immediate effect of DTP layouts was that complex grid structures could be designed into page templates and a great amount of text formatting could be applied quickly and accurately, giving the sort of control over pages that had been impossible to achieve previously. However, it was also the case that DTP resulted in a level of typographical and design experimentation that could be painful to behold.

One of the first companies to exploit the potential of micro-computers was contract magazine publisher Redwood, which set up large networks of BBC Micros in place of typewriters and experimented with sending disks to typesetters. The idea of companies producing magazines to give to customers as publicity vehicles for their products was not new, but the mid-1980s saw the professionalization of a group of publishing companies initially called 'contract publishers' but later 'customer publishing' and 'content marketing' agencies, and the formation of an industry that took its cues from advertising and marketing. At first, such titles were not taken seriously by advertisers and the industry more widely, but by 2005 they accounted for most of the top-circulating magazines (though they were still given away rather than sold).

In mainstream periodicals, marketing became ever more important as publishers saw themselves as controlling brands and wanted to develop editorial strategies that differentiated their products among readers. The strongest magazine brand is *The Economist*, with editorial values that have enabled it to see off competitors even when they have copied its look, as with the *Statist* in the 1960s. The foundation for *The Economist*'s look was laid in the late 1950s under art editor Peter Dunbar; before then it looked like an academic journal. Dunbar replaced the 1937 masthead by Eric Gill with one from Reynolds Stone, who had redesigned the clock logo of *The Times* in 1949 and was responsible for the war memorial in the grand entrance of the Victoria and Albert Museum (V&A: A.39–1952), near Eric Gill's memorial tablet for the First World War (V&A: A.4–1999).

The Economist still sports Stone's white-out-of-red title treatment (though the typeface has been tweaked to work better with different printing techniques). The style of the cover, mixing photography, illustration and typography over different issues, is as successful now as it was in the 1960s, and sales have grown from about 85,000 to exceed a million worldwide. As its design moved into the mainstream, Alistair Burnet, who became editor in 1965, tried to take the editorial tone in the same direction, striving for less formal writing. 'Nobody,' he told *Time* magazine, 'not even treasury officials and financiers, talks the way the quality press has been written for so long. If there is a larger audience to be talked to – and I don't mean talked down to – we must write more nearly the way ordinary educated people write. We must use the vernacular more often.'[1] Even then, half of its sales were outside the UK. As the design helped attract readers and the writing became more inclusive, *The Economist* could use the simplicity of its masthead to create an international brand. In 2007, it launched a new set of adverts by leading illustrators. The themes were juvenile in many ways – dissecting frogs, losing brain cells, swallowing spiders and six-year-olds in the dark – but they served, as always, to flatter current (and potential) readers. *The Economist* has always called itself a newspaper – partly to ensure concessions on postage costs, but also to reflect its commitment to daily journalism combined with analysis.

Another veteran, *Woman's Own*, celebrated its 50th anniversary in 1982 by including a free gift – a plastic shopping bag sporting a reproduction of the first issue's cover on one side and that of the latest issue on the other. 'A golden past – a golden future,' said the magazine, but its prospects were upset five years later with another wave of German influence on British industry. In this case, it was not just a style of editing or design that was exported but a different concept of how to publish women's magazines. Gruner & Jahr's *Prima* was devoid of the white space beloved by graphic designers; instead, material was densely presented on the page. Also, articles were limited to a page or spread in length: every time the reader turned the page, the subject changed. The 'unique selling proposition' for *Prima* was a giant pull-out pattern, offering readers detailed instructions for sewing and knitting clothes for themselves and their children. 'You have to have respect for the national culture, but we are living in a period of international ideas, of global behaviour,' said publisher Alex Ganz.[2] Although the women's magazine sector was regarded as crowded, within six months *Prima* was the best-selling domestic women's monthly.

Other continental titles followed. IPC launched a British version of Hachette's *Marie Claire*, while *Hello!* arrived from Spain, bringing with it a conservative design approach and introducing a system whereby subjects were paid for access and given sight of pictures before publication.

Hello! and its rival *OK!* fed a demand for celebrity news, while television invented an industry for creating an endless supply of minor, mini and micro celebrities through reality shows and talent competitions. The weekly *Heat* switched from an entertainment strategy to focus on celebrities and soon many mainstream magazines had ditched unknown models from their covers in favour of people with names, if not profiles. This trend was seen across magazine publishing, from *Vogue* to *Marie Claire*, from newspaper supplements – some relaunched with names such as *Celebs* and *Fabulous* – to *Woman's Own*.

Loaded – James Brown's launch 'For men who should know better' – plugged into an era of culture propagated and proliferated by *Viz*, stand-up comedians and TV's *Men Behaving Badly* and *A Question of Sport* to define the 'lads' mag'. Sales exceeded 100,000 copies with the ninth issue, surpassing *GQ*. Brown was quoted in *Vanity Fair* (March 1997, p. 141): 'I told the publishers it would be *Arena* magazine edited by Hunter S. Thompson'; Alan McGee, head of Creation Records, described it as 'More like a cross between a fanzine and *Penthouse*'. It was soon followed by Emap's *FHM*, which overtook *Loaded* to rival the sales of *Cosmopolitan* for a time. The laddish look influenced many other magazines in different segments, from the men's fashion monthlies to the BBC's *Top Gear* and women's monthly *Minx*, but ultimately the approach was a design dead end, with lads' mags falling over each other to go downmarket with pin-ups.

CD-ROMs were seen initially as offering a multimedia future to magazines, but physical distribution of digital media never truly made sense. In 1995, IPC launched *Uploaded.com* 'for men who should net better'. That website failed, though *NME.com* was a success, as publishers tried various strategies, with some sites devoted to a specific title and others offering subject 'portals' based on the content of several magazines.

At the end of the 1990s, a worry resurfaced from the 1960s. Simon Esterson, Vince Frost and Ken Garland were among 22 designers who signed a manifesto railing against the overbearing influence of advertising on graphic design. 'We propose a reversal of priorities in favour of more useful, lasting and democratic forms of communication – a mindshift away from product marketing and towards the exploration and production of a new kind of meaning.'[3] The issue – first set out by Garland in 1964 – was taken up internationally as *First Things First 2000* and published in *Eye* and *Blueprint*.

By this time, the dominance of clean, modernist design was starting to break up, with asymmetric, sans-serif typography no longer being seen as the one true path. Decoration and script typefaces made a return, with magazines beginning to go back to the 1950s in so far as the inspiration for a layout was unique to a feature rather than dictated by a uniform look throughout the issue.

1 Alistair Burnet, quoted in 'A Vigorous Moderation', *Time*, 21 July 1967
2 Alex Ganz, quoted in 'A Battle for Britain's Women', Jonathan Miller, *Sunday Times*, 27 September 1987, p. 2
3 'Big Names Unite against the Commercial Nature of Design', *Design Week*, 17 September 1999, p. 12

THE FACE (March 1985)

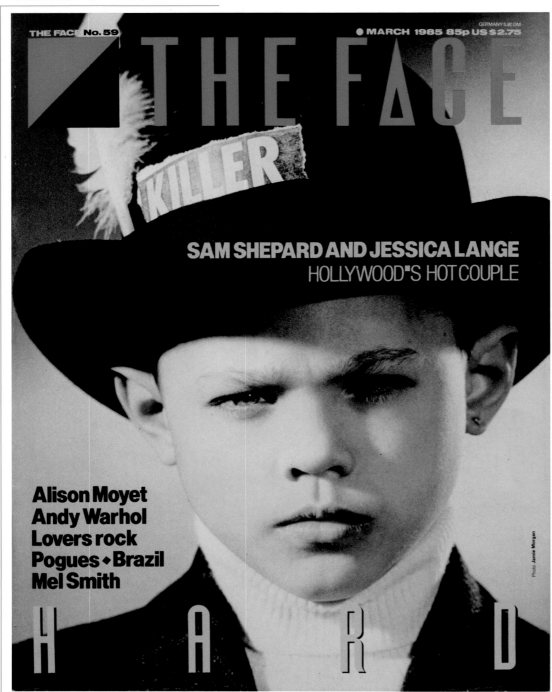

Nick Logan's brainchild set out from the start in May 1980 to be a mainstream magazine with a 75,000 print run. Its high production values for what was initially a music magazine attracted photographers and writers. This 1985 cover of teen model Felix, shot by Jamie Morgan, marked the beginning of stylist Ray Petri's Buffalo movement. Petri, who died in 1989, also worked on *i-D* and *Arena*. The opening spread of the eight-page feature, which used three models besides Felix, read: 'Hard is the graft when money is scarce. Hard are the looks from every corner. Hard is what you will turn out to be. Look out, here comes a buffalo! "The harder they come, the better (Buffalo Bill)".' Felix starred in Madonna's 'Open Your Heart' video a year later.

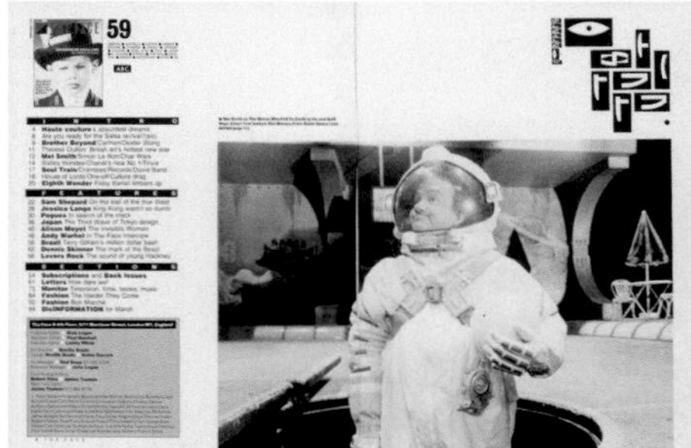

The opening spread shows art director Neville Brody manipulating the word 'contents' into a set of graphic symbols. The V&A held an exhibition of Brody's work in 1988.

An interview with singer Alison Moyet shows Neville Brody using all the elements of the page to turn them into a dynamic graphic shape. The photograph was by Robert Erdman.

Wagadon
(234 × 302 mm, stapled, 96 pages)

i-D (March 1983)

WORLDWIDE MANUAL OF STYLE I-D NO.13
£1
i-D
FLASH
CRASH
SPLASH
N'DASH
WET 'n' WILD

Former *Vogue* art director Terry Jones adopted a punk ethos with Letraset, handwritten and dot-matrix type on *i-D* from August 1980. It was a 'fashion, people, music and ideas' magazine, driven by street style rather than the fashion industry. Thomas Degen, Malcolm Garrett and Steve Johnston did early covers. The winking model was a visual pun on the name *i-D*, which turns into a winking face when turned on its side. The initial print run was 2,000 copies and the format for the first 13 issues was landscape A4 before the magazine 'went commercial', using a portrait A4 size. Nick Knight – then a student at Bournemouth and Poole College of Art and Design (now the Arts University Bournemouth) – did the first 'commercial' cover, featuring the singer Sade; there were other covers by Marc Lebon, David Bailey and Mario Testino by the end of 1984.

People on the street were photographed full-length, with captions added as crude typesetting from a dot-matrix printer to create a fanzine feel. Photos by Steve Johnston.

Levelprint
(302 × 234 mm, stapled, 56 pages)

i-D (May 1990)

i-D ©
i-D MAGAZINE
i-DEAS, FASHION, CLUBS, MUSIC, PEOPLE
Warning!
This magazine is dangerous
fashion fallout
– poisonous looks
USA $4.95
9 770262 357006 05
Water – is it safe to drink? ● Julian Clary, the man behind the make-up ● 'The Krays' and the Kemps – can pop stars act? ● Monie Love and the changing face of rap ● Viking Combat – have martial arts gone mad? ● Hip hop fashion adopts the suit ● The man behind 'The Toxic Avenger' ●

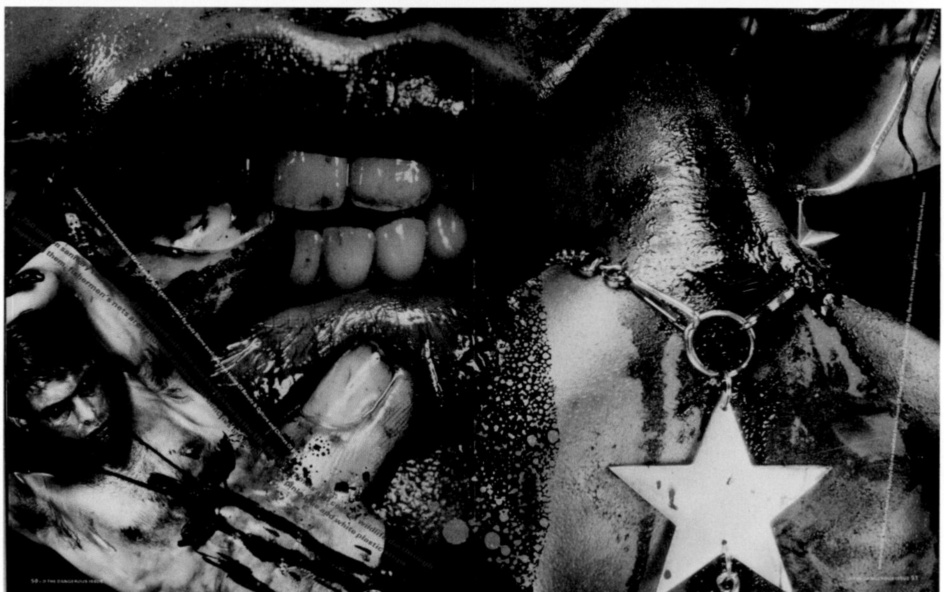

'The dangerous issue', with a 'noxious substances' cover image of Marni at the Viva modelling agency by French fashion photographer and music video director Jean-Baptiste Mondino. Stephen Male was art director and Neil Edwards art editor. The styling was by 'Buffalo Boy' Judy Blame. The cover and centre spread photomontage were part of a 14-page anti-pollution feature entitled 'Dying water'. All told, 23 people are credited for the article, not including the clothes and accessories.

The issue 14 centre spread uses photos by Thomas Degen and Nick Knight.

Levelprint
(230 × 300 mm, stapled, 100 pages)

DAZED & CONFUSED

(September 1998)

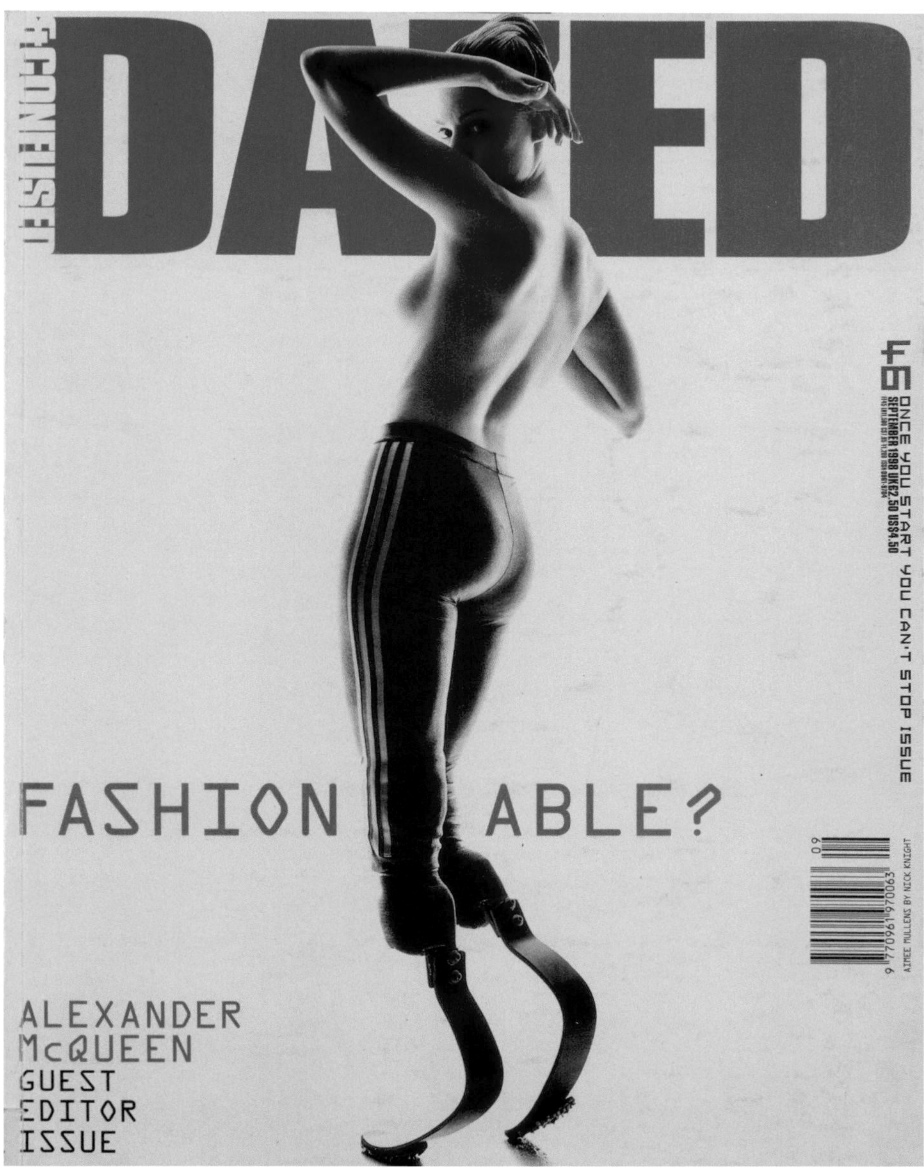

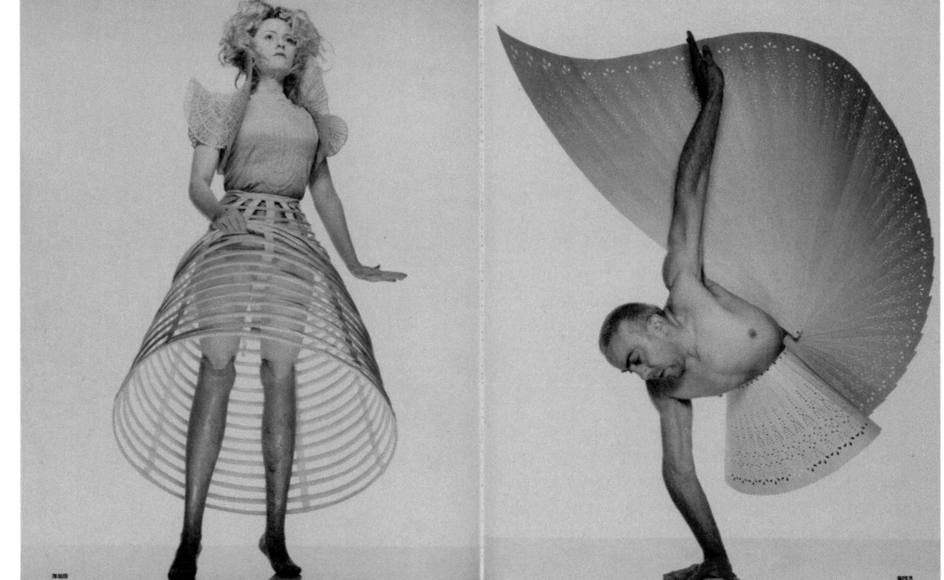

Dazed & Confused built its reputation on collaborative relationships with artists, designers and photographers. The 'Fashion-able?' issue featured fashion designer Alexander McQueen as guest editor. McQueen decided to run an article based around people with physical disabilities. Nick Knight was the photographer, with stylist Katy England (who would soon become the magazine's fashion director and later take on the same role at *AnOther*). McQueen handled the art direction and designers at several fashion houses created looks for the shoot. Jefferson Hack, *Dazed* co-founder, has identified this issue as pivotal: 'That was the point where the magazine grew up. With that issue we were on page two or three of the world's newspapers. We realized that you didn't have to be the best-selling magazine to have an influence on culture. That has been our philosophy ever since.' The other founder of *Dazed* was Rankin, as John Rankin Waddell, the portrait and fashion photographer, is known. The pair met at the London College of Printing and the magazine's name was inspired by the Led Zeppelin track.

The spread shows athlete and model Aimee Mullins[1] with prosthetic legs and David Toole in an Alexander McQueen wooden skirt.

1 V&A: E.633–1998

Waddell
(230 × 298 mm, perfect bound, 148 pages)

INTERIORS (November 1981)

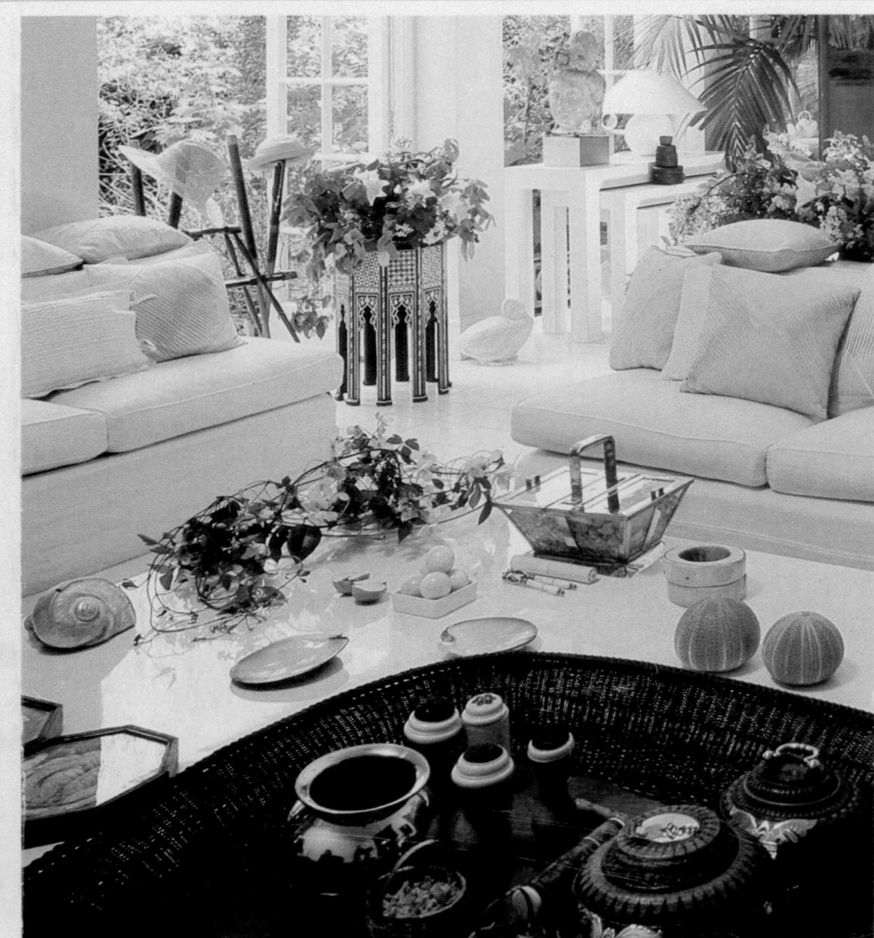

CITY LIMITS (9 October 1981)

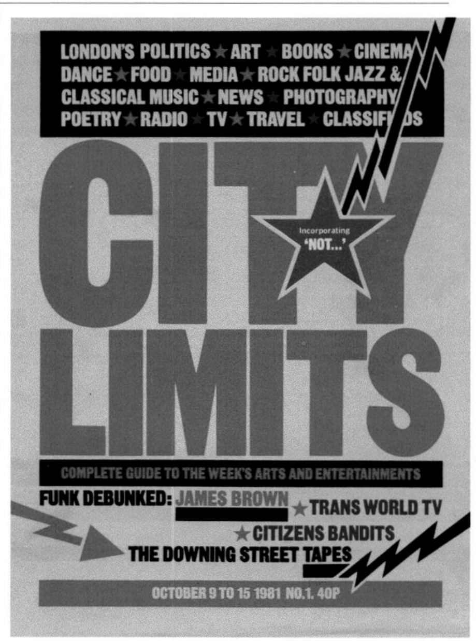

LONDON'S POLITICS ★ ART ★ BOOKS ★ CINEMA
DANCE ★ FOOD ★ MEDIA ★ ROCK FOLK JAZZ &
CLASSICAL MUSIC ★ NEWS ★ PHOTOGRAPHY
POETRY ★ RADIO ★ TV ★ TRAVEL ★ CLASSIFIEDS
CITY
Incorporating 'NOT...'
LIMITS
COMPLETE GUIDE TO THE WEEK'S ARTS AND ENTERTAINMENTS
FUNK DEBUNKED: JAMES BROWN ★ TRANS WORLD TV
★ CITIZENS BANDITS
THE DOWNING STREET TAPES
OCTOBER 9 TO 15 1981 NO.1. 40P

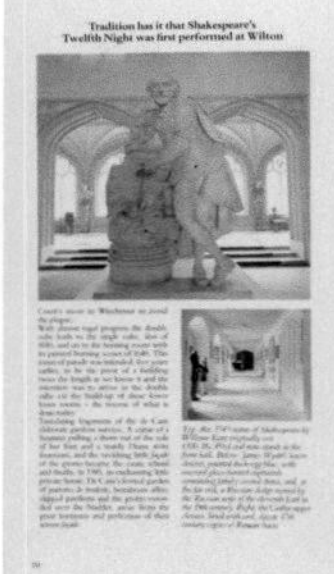

City Limits was set up by former *Time Out* staff after a dispute with owner Tony Elliott over his ending of the system of equal pay for everyone. During the dispute, *Time Out* staff produced a protest news-sheet called *Not...* and this explains the blue star on the front cover of the first *City Limits* that says 'Incorporating "NOT..."'. The cover was by former *Sunday Times Magazine* designer David King, who used a Constructivist style derived from his interest in Bolshevik-era Russia. Inside, art director Carol Warren made use of strong graphic shapes that came across effectively on the newsprint paper the magazine used.

London Voice
(212 × 298 mm, stapled, 92 pages)

Publisher Kevin Kelly set up *Interiors* with Min Hogg as editor-in-chief and Wendy Harrop as art director. It was later bought by Condé Nast, who changed its name to *World of Interiors*. The design is classically understated, with excellent photography used to show off the world's most beautiful homes at a leisurely pace.

Two spreads showing the unrushed style of the magazine, with photographs of sumptuous houses by Nic Barlow and Richard Davies.

Pharos Publications
(215 × 278 mm, perfect bound, 208 pages)

TATLER (September 1982)

TATLER
Sassy September
£1.20
OH, EDIE, EDIE, WHY SO SEEDY?
(The wrecking of an American deb)
FURTHER TOMES FROM MARY SOAMES
(Winston's winning daughter)
STUFF IT UP YOUR EMPIRE
(Jan Morris strikes back)
TERENCE STAMP
JOHN ASPINALL
STING
PIERRE BALMAIN
MARC
MARTIN AMIS
HENRY POST
&
THE FAB FORBES BALLOON

When Mark Boxer's *London Life* variant of *Tatler* closed in 1967, the Thomson organization sold the name to the Illustrated County Magazine Group (publishers of *East Anglia Life*), who revived it as a monthly in 1968 and reverted to the advertising-dominated cover design of 1903. In 1979, it changed hands again and Tina Brown was appointed as editor. Her success led Condé Nast to buy the title, and she later went to the US to salvage *Vanity Fair* and pep up the *New Yorker*. Brown brought a sharper feel to the contents and wit to cover lines. Even months of the year developed attitude, such as this 'Sassy September' issue with 'Last of the Summer Wine' on the spine – where the bowing *Tatler* gent was incorporated. The cover shot here by Norman Parkinson is of Paula Yates, complete with tattoo – which *Cosmopolitan* had avoided showing for a July 1981 cover. The assistant art editor was Lawrence Morton.

Tatler and Bystander Magazine and Publishing
(224 × 304 mm, perfect bound, 156 pages)

BLUEPRINT (November 1983)

Blueprint confirmed the reputation of Simon Esterson, who would later be appointed a Royal Designer for Industry. It published in a large format and focused on strong photographs using heavy Helvetica Condensed headlines in an editorial approach aimed at an international readership, appealing to readers interested in design, architecture and style. This theatrical cover by Phil Sayer from the second issue is of industrial designer Daniel Weil.

Blueprint gave portraits space on its large pages. Another photograph by Phil Sayer, this time of US graphic designer April Greiman, dominates this spread – it has been cropped to exploit the angles of the image. The art editors were Simon Esterson and Stephen Coates.

Wordsearch
(295 × 420 mm, stapled, 28 pages)

ELLE (November 1983)

The cover photograph by Gilles Tapie was of model Yasmin Parveneh, who married Duran Duran singer Simon Le Bon in December 1985. Inside, clean modernist design values are expounded by an international template based around Futura display type – ready for the expansion of the French original into the UK and US. Contrasting weights of Futura were used for the headlines, with Univers for the body copy. Inside, the cover motif of text set at an angle was picked up in the layouts. Fleet Street and *Cosmopolitan* veteran Joyce Hopkirk was editorial director, with Sally Brampton as editor and Malgosia Szemberg as deputy art director.

Elle set out to take a different angle on style, with a gossip column opening the fashion pages, which featured strong shapes that bled off and contrasted with the white backgrounds. Gilles Tapie took the knitting pictures with styling by Debbi Mason.

News International-Hachette
(230 × 300 mm, perfect bound, 228 pages)

PRIMA (October 1986)

Prima brought modern-day German design and editorial values to the UK, and focused on getting good value for money for readers. There was little advertising and a lot of text on each page alongside images that were small compared with those of British competitors. Page margins were narrow and the layouts busy, with tip boxes and other designed elements. The 'white space' and open layouts of British magazines were anathema. The giant pattern sheet – a 'unique selling point' in marketing jargon – folded out to a size about equal to 16 A4 pages; readers of other magazines would have to pay for such patterns. All the elements of a domestic women's magazine were included, apart from fiction. There were pages of cookery cards to cut out and keep, with prices for the ingredients in the four recipes on each page. Iris Burton was editor and Anthony Essam art director, with typesetting by Solecast in London and gravure printing in Germany. A year before, *TV Times* publisher Independent Television Publications also used a German model, *Bild der Frau* published by Axel Springer, to launch *Chat*, a colour tabloid weekly with target sales of a million and a price of 18p, half that of a typical women's weekly. It did not reach the target and was turned into an A4 weekly by IPC.

The three spreads here demonstrate classic women's magazines features: winter wardrobe on a budget (photography by Ursula Steiger); practical crafts (Belinda Banks); practical fashion based on the giant pattern sheet (Nigel Limb).

Gruner & Jahr
(210 × 280 mm, stapled, 140 pages)

GARDENERS' WORLD (April 1991)

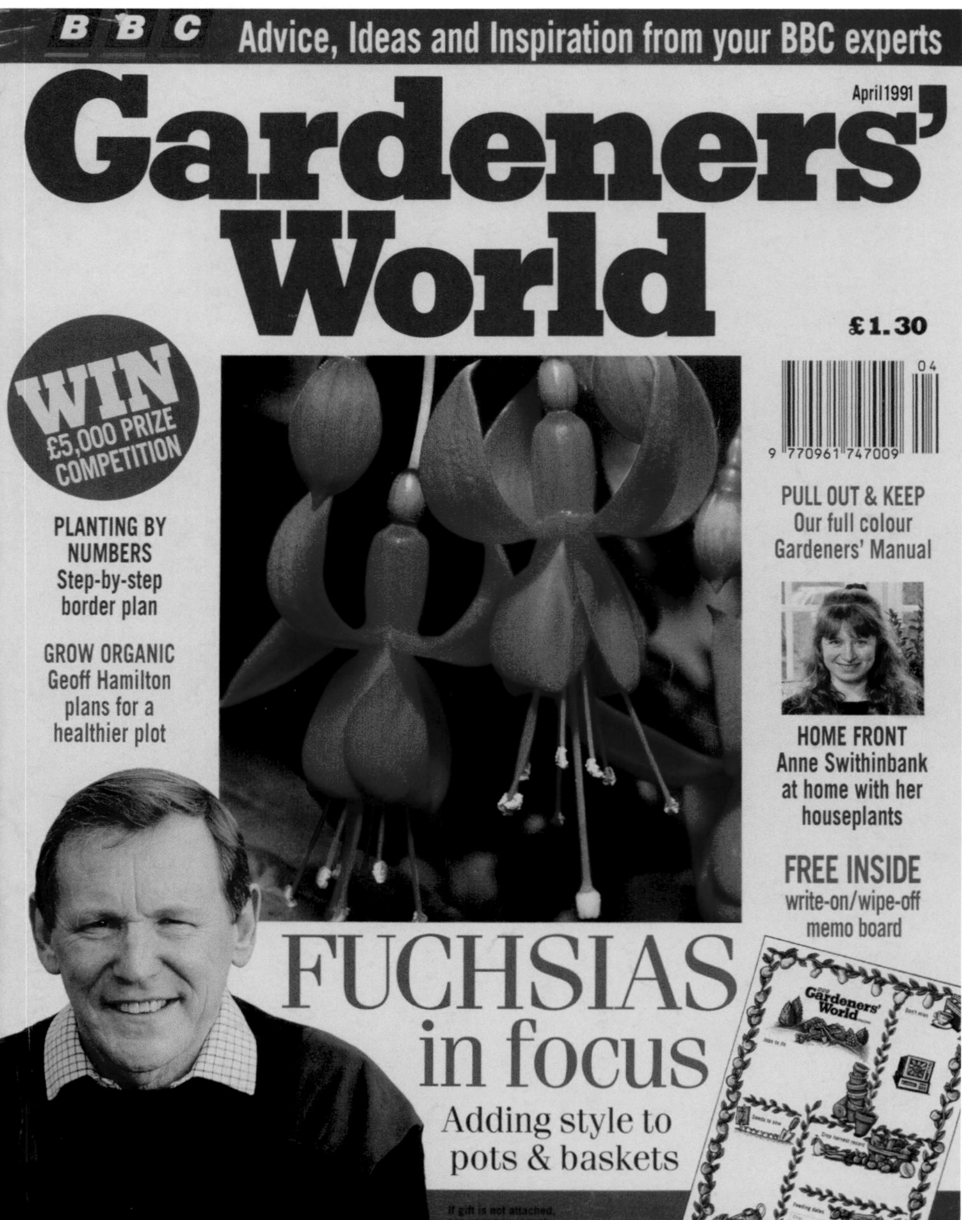

Early BBC launches produced by Redwood featured a coloured strip with the corporation's lozenges above the cover title, and all had the same design 'feel', featuring pictures and cut-outs laid on a white background. Every page was printed in full colour. 'Previous titles went for the niche market; we wanted to appeal to all recent home buyers and gardeners,' said publisher Seamus Geoghegan. He also gave away cover gifts, including gloves, a spade and a trug that was bigger than the magazine, and for subscribers there was a garden gnome reading the magazine. Rivals responded by redesigning their gardening magazines, some with a similar look to the BBC version. The result was that all the titles added sales and the size of the sector almost doubled within a year.

Presenting value for money was a key element in the BBC's strategy and the magazines packed in editorial pages, an approach reminiscent of that of German group Gruner & Jahr when they launched *Prima* in the UK in 1986. Editor Adam Pasco used the inside front cover for the contents spread of *Gardeners' World*. The art editor was Abigail Dodd, with Paul Harpin as creative director.

BBC/Redwood
(225 × 300 mm, stapled, 108 pages)

HELLO! (26 November 1988)

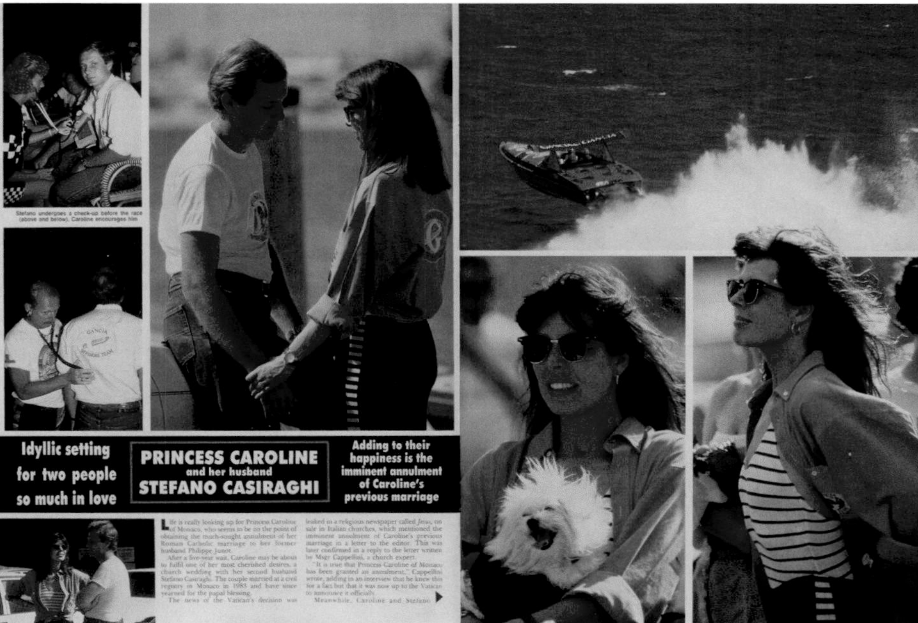

Spain's royalty-driven women's weekly *¡Hola!* was launched in Britain as *Hello!*, complete with the original's idiosyncratic design approach and copy-approval for its subjects. The popularity of Diana, Princess of Wales, encouraged *Hello!* and the development of the celebrity magazines sector more widely. *OK!* followed quickly, first as a monthly and then a direct weekly rival. Other titles, such as *Now*, *Closer* and *Heat* joined the fray, pushing up prices for paparazzi shots and – in tandem with reality TV shows like *Big Brother* – spawning a celebrity-manufacturing industry. The cover is reminiscent of *Illustrated* in the 1950s and points to the contents on page 27. The position of the contents page was dictated by its place at the start of the last section to go to the printers, the 16 monochrome news pages, which were inset between the colour features sections.

The boxy spread with a head-shot cut out and overlaid on an adjoining photograph is typical of *Hello!*

Hello! Ltd
(240 × 330 mm, stapled, 100 pages)

BLAH BLAH BLAH (April 1996)

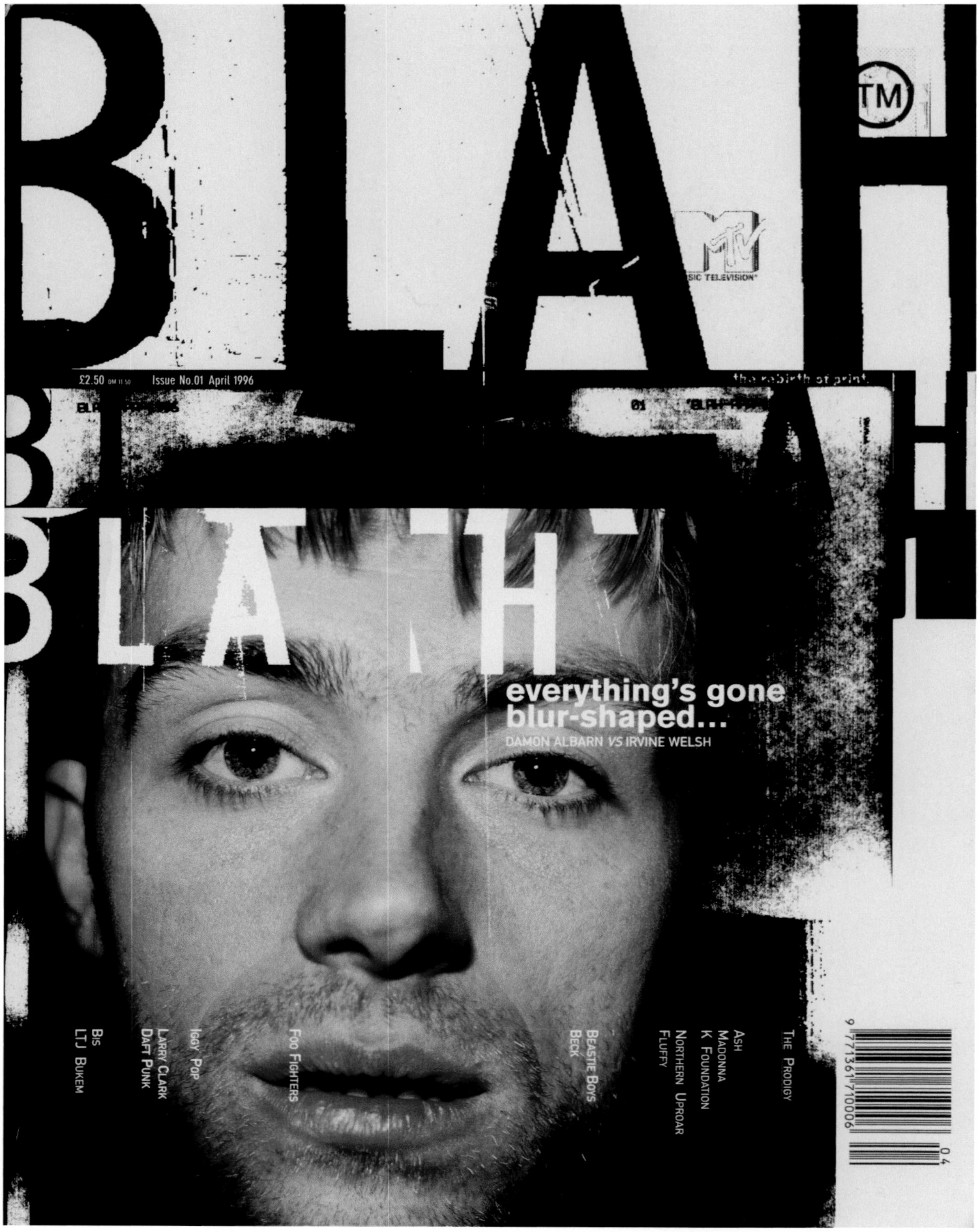

This sponsored magazine for MTV (the company's logo is part of the title) was launched by *Ray Gun* founder Marvin Scott Jarrett. It brought US designer David Carson's look to the UK, interpreted by art directors Chris Ashworth and Neil Fletcher, who were recruited in London. The cover photo was by Phil Poynter; Malcolm Garrett was credited for his instant lettering. Note the barely legible strapline 'The Rebirth of Print', a reference to Carson's book, *The End of Print*. The whole approach is reminiscent of the underground look that established *i-D*.

The headlines are Letraset that's been mulched through photocopiers and fax machines. Typographic rules are ignored and the pages reject any concept of a grid. The content is focused on music, as in this Iggy Pop interview – *Blah-Blah-Blah* was the title of his 1986 album.

Ray Gun Publishing
(230 × 300 mm, stapled, 100 pages)

SCENE (Aug/Sept 1998)

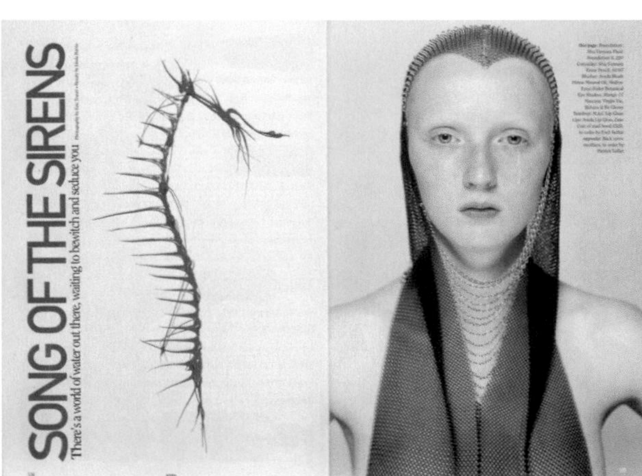

Scene used metallic ink under a heavy laminated gloss varnish for this 'steamy' cover photograph. Cutting-edge fashion photography under editor Deborah Bee became a trademark of the magazine, which started out more as a catalogue. In 1998, *The Times* quoted photographer David Bailey criticizing modern magazine design and praising *Scene* as second only to Italian *Vogue*: 'For photography, *Scene* is the best magazine in England. You know it will use your pictures well, unlike the others, where complicated design has taken over.'[1] In its November issue, *Scene* became one of the first magazines to use 70-year-old model Daphne Selfe for a shoot, sparking media debate about older models. The *Independent on Sunday* commented: 'Both *Scene* and *Vogue* are educating the fashion-literate eye, sated with "Youth Is Beauty", to see the aesthetics of age.'[2] Soon after, Bee left to try to revive *Nova* for IPC and the title closed.

This fashion spread under the auspices of *Scene* beauty editor Linda Burns featured French products portrayed by Parisian photographer Eric Traoré. The left page is of a sculptural necklace by Patrick Veillet. On the right, the model wears a coat of mail hood by Fred Sathal and a teardrop painted on with lip gloss.

1 Imogen O'Rorke, 'Big and Bold', 2 October 1998, p. 46
2 James Sherwood, 'Old is Pure Gold', 1 November 1998, p. 2

Scene Spiro Group
(210 × 297 mm, perfect bound, 132 pages)

BIG K (April 1984)

Computer magazines were the fastest-growing sector of the 1980s and early 1990s. They tended to rely on either photographs of hardware or illustrations to put across the software. Screen resolutions were crude and games or characters could not be portrayed realistically. This cover for the first issue of *Big K* was by Ron Embleton, who had worked on *Eagle*, *Look and Learn* and *TV21* – for which he drew the *Stingray* series; he also did the artwork for the closing credits of a later Gerry Anderson TV series, *Captain Scarlet and the Mysterons*. *Big K* carried a software cassette tape stuck to the cover, which is why there is little detail in the bottom left corner of the cover.

This was the era of computer users typing in programs from magazines. This spread (pp. 70–1) is a BASIC listing to generate *Downfall*, a game for the BBC Micro. The background illustration is by Robin Smith, who drew both Judge Dredd and Strontium Dog for *2000 AD*. Longer programs could go on for many pages and most magazines ran them in this way – with a background illustration, or surrounded by text. In contrast, *Acorn User* printed all the listings to a standard measure and gathered the programs together in a section at the centre of the magazine, an idea adopted from the data presentation in car magazines.

IPC Magazines
(208 × 298 mm, perfect bound, 108 pages)

BIG K (March 1985)

'Shatter' claimed to be the world's first comic strip drawn on an Apple Macintosh. The strip, by Mike Saenz, Peter B. Gillis and Mike Gold, later appeared as the one-off comic *Shatter* in the US (June 1985). This is the opening spread of four pages.

IPC Magazines
(208 × 298 mm, perfect bound, 84 pages)

TIME OUT (22 August 1985)

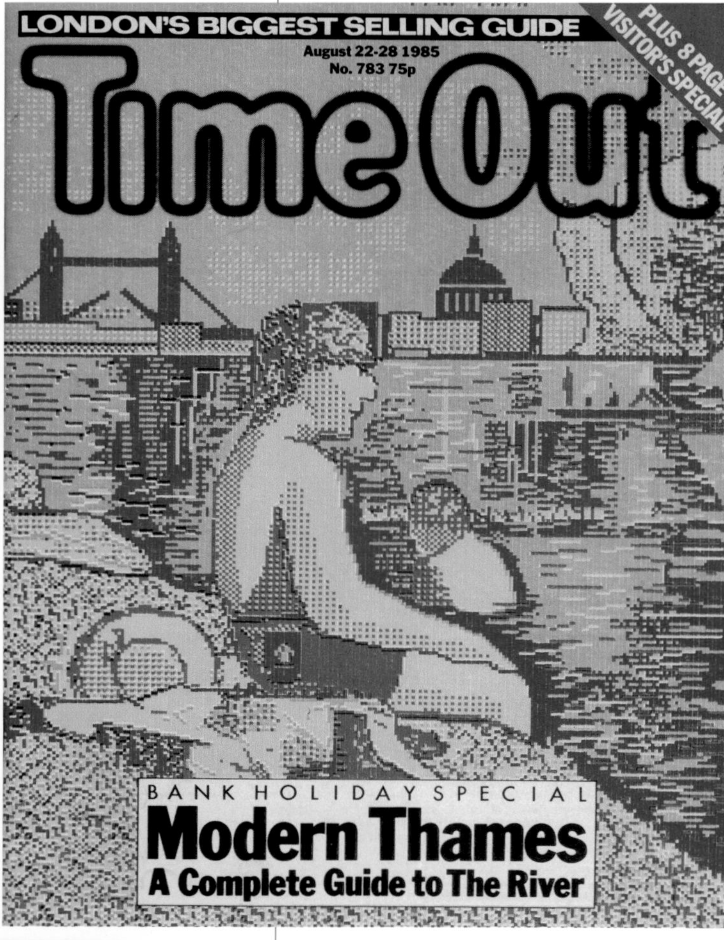

This is one of the first consumer magazine covers to incorporate a computer-generated illustration. It was done by Jonathan Inglis, a former art teacher, who was inspired by the introduction of computers into schools and the BBC's Computer Literacy Project of 1982. Inglis had already used BASIC programs running on a BBC Micro to illustrate articles for *Acorn User*. For the *Time Out* cover, he used a paintbox package written by Rob Fenton that had been published in the February 1985 *Acorn User*. The *Time Out* cover mimicked the Pointillist style of Georges Seurat. Inglis did work for other magazines, including the *Sunday Times Magazine* and the *Spectator*. He told *Creative Review*: 'I have reservations about trying to make computer images look realistic. They look like poor copies of airbrushing or photography. I think you have to express the state-of-the-art and accept it as a medium in its own right.'[1] Inglis used a BBC Micro and later a Commodore Amiga. He printed separate artwork for each of the four printing colours on a black-and-white dot-matrix printer using software filters. *Acorn User* also used a screen photograph of an Inglis design on one cover.

1 Lesley Chisholm, 'Jonathan Inglis', *Creative Review*, 1 July 1987, p. 40

Time Out Publications
(216 × 300 mm, stapled)

APPLE BUSINESS (May 1989)

Apple Business was supported by Apple Computer (the company has now dropped the 'Computer') to demonstrate the potential of desktop publishing (DTP) for magazines. It was 'produced entirely on a network of Macintosh computers' and sent free to 'serious buyers and users of Apple Macintosh computers'. The art editor was Mike Wright. Martin Leeks's photograph illustrated a case study by Alan Pipes about Macintoshes being used to design around-the-world race yachts. Pipes had published his own punk magazine, *Barbed Wire*, in the late 1970s, and edited academic journals and trade magazines about computer-aided design; he later wrote textbooks, such as *Production for Graphic Designers* (1992).

Emap
(228 × 275 mm, perfect bound, 124 pages)

WIRED (April 1995)

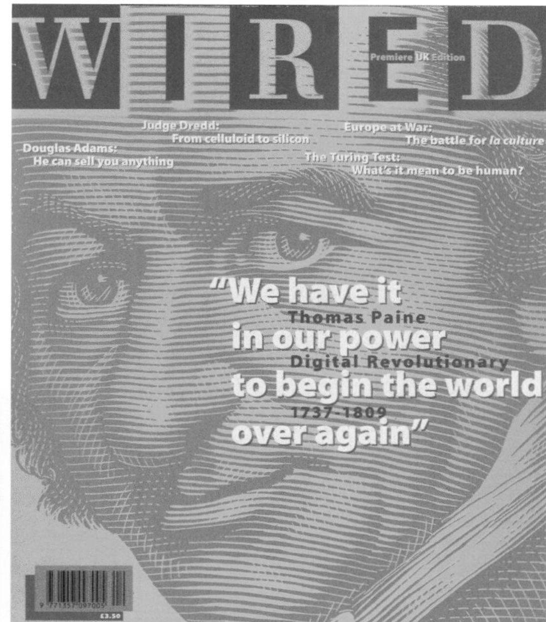

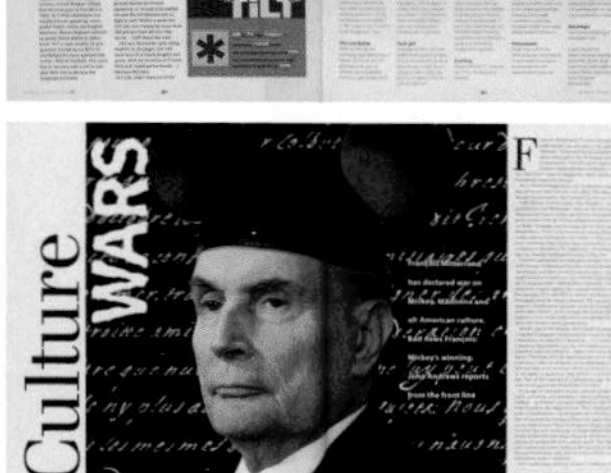

Wired attempted to bring a Silicon Valley approach and design ethic to the UK. The design director was Mark Porter, who had worked on the Benetton customer magazine *Colors* and later led the redesign of the *Guardian* when it switched to a Berliner format in 2005. A large part of the masthead page was devoted to listing the hardware, software and networking technology used, as well as the paper stock and typefaces.

The magazine was full colour throughout and used background tints and special inks extensively, as on this news spread. Readability was a challenge at times, however. Note the news item about *Unzip*, which IPC advertised as 'the UK's first fully interactive magazine on CD-ROM'.

French president François Mitterrand had taken a stand against the incursion of US culture, but is here satirized with Mickey Mouse ears.

Wired Ventures
(227 × 274 mm, perfect bound, 116 pages)

FORTEAN TIMES (August 1998)

More powerful and inexpensive computers put the ability to manipulate images into the hands of designers and art editors. The art director was Etienne Gilfallan.

John Brown Publishing
(210 × 295 mm, stapled, 70 pages)

INTERCITY (November 1985)

THE FISH CONNECTION

Eating fish regularly can be very good for you, reveals Oliver Gillie, The Sunday Times Medical Correspondent

ICE CREAM WARS

INTERCITY (July/August 1985)

Former *Nova* and *Observer Magazine* editor Peter Crookston launched *InterCity* with Jim Brewster as art editor and Mike Lackersteen as art director; Barbara Bellingham did the cover montage. In May 1988, Lackersteen later went into partnership with Simon Esterson (*Architects' Journal*, *Blueprint*, *Eye*) and former Wolff Olins designer Sharon Ellis to form Ellis Esterson Lackersteen, a consultancy advising publishers on magazine launches and relaunches.

Redwood/British Rail
(210 × 288 mm, stapled, 68 pages)

InterCity magazine was designed to attract business travellers and copies were left in wall-mounted racks in first-class carriages. This, however, had two drawbacks: first, the metal rack obscured both the bottom centimetre and a band about 4 cm deep just above the middle of the cover; and second, many travellers walked past the racks, assuming the magazine was a brochure. To get around these problems, editor Tony Quinn relaunched the magazine with a design by creative director Paul Harpin implemented by Adam Hay. The word 'magazine' was added to the title; cover lines were positioned to be visible above or below the band; and cover images were chosen to work despite being partly covered up. In this case, the eyes in Brian Moody's photograph appeared to peek under the band. The magazine's readership nearly doubled within 18 months.

BBC Redwood/British Rail
(210 × 288 mm, perfect bound, 60 pages)

INFORMATION RESOURCES MANAGEMENT (April 1983)

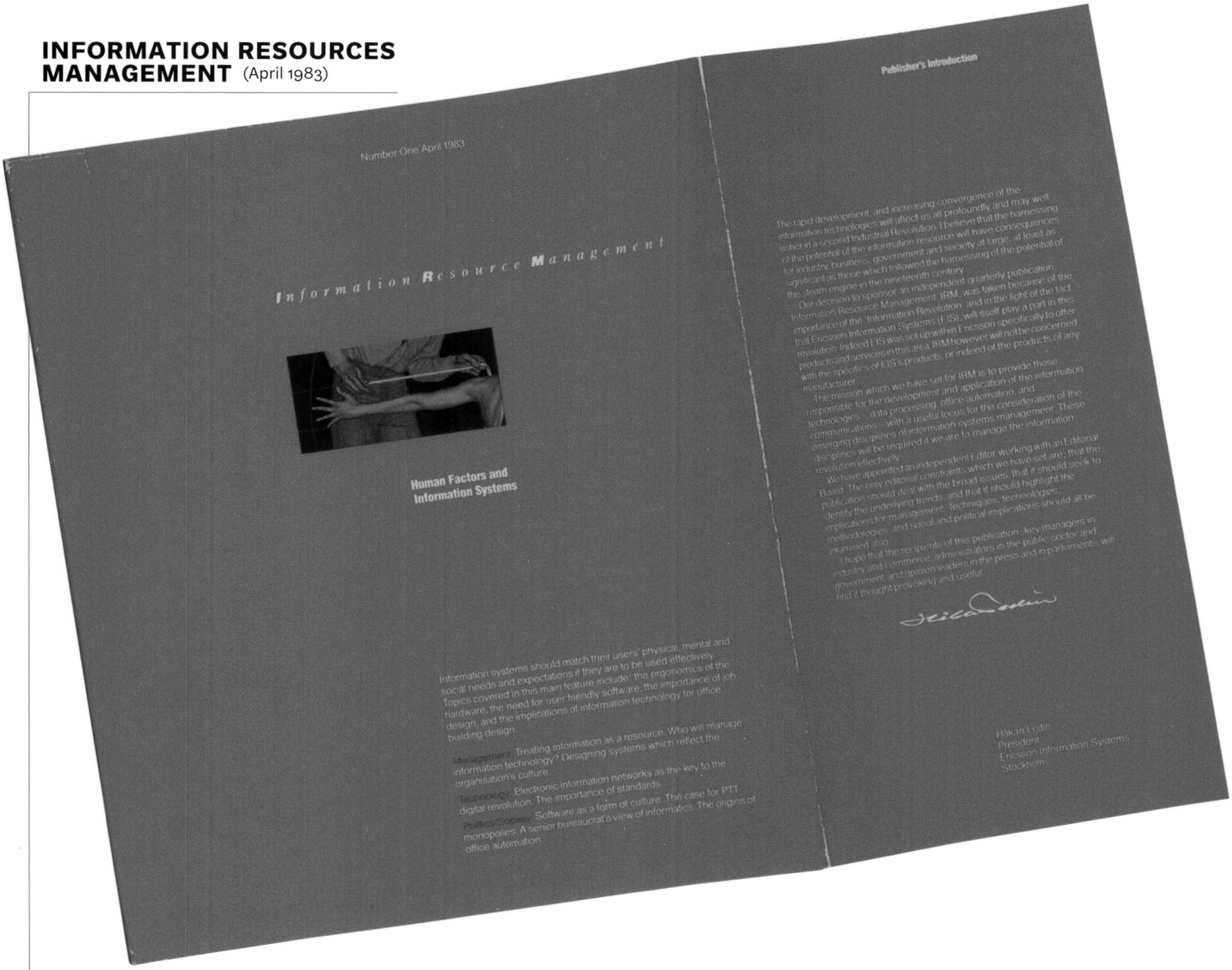

INFORMATION RESOURCES MANAGEMENT (September 1984)

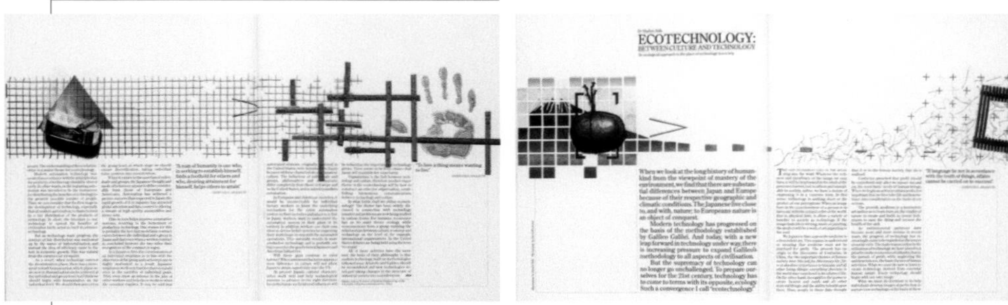

The histories of book and magazine design have been intertwined since periodicals began, but this contract title for the telecoms equipment manufacturer Ericsson presents the magazine entirely as a book, complete with dust jacket. The actual cover was blank; the design was by David Hillman at Pentagram. It set out to attract director-level executives using high production values and, in this case, an academic journal approach with an international editorial board. The editor was Graham Bunting.

Anderson & Lembke/Ericsson (234 × 280 mm, perfect bound, 52 pages plus jacket)

Illustrator Russell Mills used three-dimensional constructions for his work. The photographs were by David Buckland. The layouts show the use of a strict horizontal grid throughout the features, with the images commissioned to fit the design.

Anderson & Lembke/Ericsson (234 × 280 mm, perfect bound, 52 pages plus jacket)

ARENA (Winter 1986/87)

A R E N A

C O N T E N T S

S P R I N G 1 9 8 7

6 **ARENA** DESPATCHES 12 **SPECTATOR** ARCHITECTURE BY DEYAN SUDJIC 14 STEPHEN FRY ON **THE WORLD SERVICE** 16 **BOOKS** BY GORDON BURN 19 **CINEMA** THE VANISHING DIRECTORS 20 **TRAVEL** BY DON MACPHERSON 24 **HARRISON FORD** INTERVIEWED BY TONY PARSONS 32 WET 'N'WILD: **WINTER WINDSURFING** 38 HARRY MACKLOWE AND THE **MANHATTAN SKYLINE** 44 **MANDY SMITH** BY GORDON BURN 52 **FICTION** BY TAMA JANOWITZ 58 **PARIS FASHION** BUSTER KEATON BOUNCES BACK 70 **RAGAMUFFINS** HAND ME DOWN MY WALKING CANE 80 THE BOYS IN THE BAND 88 **FASHION** CHAIN REACTION 96 **VANITY** CREW CUTS, THAI FOOD, DRYCLEANING, MONEY ETC 100 **OLIVER STONE** PROFILED BY JAMES TRUMAN 106 **COWBOYS** DON'T SHOOT STRAIGHT ANY MORE 110 **PRODUCT DESIGN** IN THE AGE OF STEAM 114 **PEOPLE** DAVID BOWIE, JEFF GOLDBLUM, TIM POPE, SIMON STRINGER, CHARLOTTE LEWIS, DANNY LANE ETC 127 **ARENA RECOMMENDS**

ARENA THE OLD LAUNDRY, OSSINGTON BUILDINGS, LONDON W1 **01 935 8232**. © WAGADON LTD

A R E N A **3** S P R I N G

Male readers who grew out of Nick Logan's the *Face* had no lifestyle titles dedicated to them, so Logan thought up *Arena* as a quarterly, niche title, with an editorial mix of fashion, fads and fiction – again designed by Neville Brody. His company, Wagadon, was backed financially by Condé Nast. The first cover shows actor Mickey Rourke. It's not a strong image for a cover and the contents summary on the left is difficult to read against the changing background tones. Copies of the magazine arranged in order spell out the name *Arena* on the spine.

The opening spread for a fashion feature gives prominent credits for 'Buffalo' pairing Ray Petri, stylist, and photographer Mark Lebon.

The contents page moves away from the use of rules that dominated much of the decade.

Opening spread for a rock-climbing fashion feature. The white background, cut-out figure and detailed captioning are reminiscent of book publisher Dorling Kindersley. Such techniques became much cheaper with the advent of desktop publishing.

Wagadon
(230 × 300 mm, perfect bound, 132 pages)

GQ (December/January 1989)

Pit-bull terriers are the Tysons of dog-fighting: mean, ugly, and astoundingly vicious. William Leith investigates the low life world of the pets who live to kill.

DOG EAT DOG

SUITABLE COLOURS

Made in the shades: A classic quartet of tailored suits in four traditional colours, with the added impact of cleverly chosen accessories.

Photographs by Robert Erdmann Still Lifes by Hugh Johnson.

In the UK *GQ* started out under editor Paul Keers with a straight interpretation of the US magazine's original name: *Gentleman's Quarterly*. Keers had worked on *Cosmo Man*, on contract titles at Redwood and as editor of *Sunday Times Style*. His cover model was Conservative politician (and founder of publisher Haymarket) Michael Heseltine. There was a certain irony here, given Heseltine's failed attempt to address the men's market almost 30 years earlier with *Town* (see page 146–7). Keers aimed to steer *GQ* clear of any top-shelf connotations – a sensitive issue for *Town* – and any perception of being a gay magazine. Heseltine was seen as a buccaneer and as such an exemplar for the business-driven 'yuppie' 1980s. He was a power dresser and potential prime minister. Margaret Donegan was art director. Note the bar code on the cover: these were ubiquitous by the end of the year for news-stand titles – another example of computers influencing the look of magazines.

Condé Nast (220 × 300 mm, perfect bound, 272 pages, including rear cover gatefold)

Along with features on boxing and the Cresta Run, dog fighting provided a macho feel for *GQ*.

The 'still lifes' of the accessories for this fashion article were by Hugh Johnson, with photographs by Robert Erdmann.

The main photograph is by Mike McQueen. Other articles addressed gritty issues such as testicular cancer and innocent men being accused of rape. Elsewhere, Daniel Day-Lewis was photographed by Herb Ritts for a profile.

VOGUE (December 1987)

Editor Elizabeth Tilberis ran a Patrick Demarchelier photograph of Naomi Campbell for this cover. In 2007, former *Cosmopolitan* editor Linda Kelsey blamed the conservative nature of the industry for a lack of black models on magazine covers – and the fact that there were so few black celebrities. Speaking on BBC Radio 4's *Woman's Hour* (10 October 2007), she said that when she was *Cosmopolitan* editor, distributors had warned her against using a black model because such covers did not sell. The magazine did use the cover and Kelsey said there was no discernible effect on sales. Campbell had appeared on eight *Vogue* covers by 2012.

Condé Nast
(220 × 284 mm, perfect bound, 284 pages)

VOGUE (January 1990)

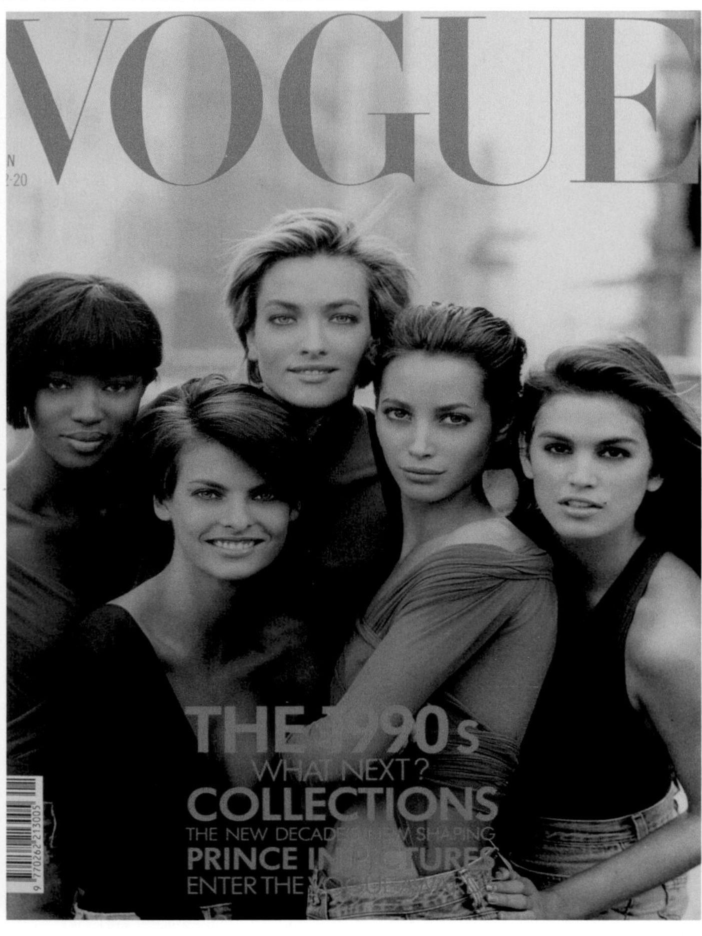

In the 1980s *Vogue* mainly ran covers of uncredited models. For this cover, Peter Lindbergh photographed five models – Naomi Campbell, Cindy Crawford, Christy Turlington, Linda Evangelista and Tatjana Patitz – kicking off the supermodel phenomenon. George Michael cast the same five in his music video for 'Freedom! '90'. Mario Testino's first cover for *Vogue* was of Turlington (January 1993). *Vogue* described Testino as making 'anyone he photographs look the best they ever will', with a style described as 'luxury realism'. Rather than pay high supermodel fees, Testino 'championed a new breed of model', including Kate Moss and Stella Tennant – but all the supermodels were front-page celebrities. Crawford was on the cover of *Vogue* in December 1995, accompanied by an article inside about her, 'Fame and the Single Girl'. The main cover line was: 'Supermodel style: Naomi, Amber and Shalom dress for themselves'. *Vogue*'s April 1999 cover line, 'An icon bares all', alongside a topless Kate Moss by Nick Knight, was for a seven-page profile. The January 2002 cover was a gatefold by Mario Testino of 18 leading British models. However, journalist Tony Parsons called time on the supermodels in *GQ* of March 2011. In an interview with Naomi Campbell, who had recently appeared as a witness in the 'blood diamonds' trial of former African warlord Charles Taylor, he wrote: 'Naomi Campbell, Christy Turlington, Linda Evangelista, Claudia Schiffer, Kate Moss – we will not see their like again ... they have not been replaced by a new generation of supermodels. The axis of celebrity has shifted – it is now singers and actresses who do not get out of bed for less than ten grand.'

Condé Nast
(220 × 284 mm, perfect bound, 164 pages)

THE FACE (July 1990)

Corinne Day's black-and-white cover, styled by Melanie Ward, of Kate Moss, then aged 16, was part of an eight-page photo shoot titled 'The 3rd summer of love'. The first such summer was 1968, the second the summer of 1988 as ecstasy-fuelled raves swept the British Isles. The *Face* christened 1990 the third, and Moss its queen, as underground raves, acid house and smiley badges became mainstream. The waifish Moss went on to become the 'anti-supermodel'. Day, a self-taught photographer, brought a documentary feel to her images.

Wagadon
(234 × 302 mm, stapled, 96 pages)

VOGUE (March 1993)

VOGUE
MAR
£2·50
MOVE INTO SPRING... The colours the layers the freedom that make the difference
Sex, drugs and science: their future together
SHOULD WOMEN DIE FOR THEIR COUNTRY?
LONDON STYLE... LONDON GIRLS
fashion's new spirit

Corinne Day's first *Vogue* cover was also Kate Moss's and was shot in the model's flat. This was the start of the 'heroin chic' controversy, at a time when the drug had become more accessible and therefore cheaper. The look was driven by an advertising campaign from Calvin Klein featuring Moss looking thin and hung-over, and then by films such as *Trainspotting* (1996). *Vogue* discussed Moss checking into an addiction clinic in its April 1999 issue. Day, who died of cancer in 2010, said of her work: 'Photography is getting as close as you can to real life, showing us things we don't normally see. These are people's most intimate moments, and sometimes intimacy is sad.' The June 2012 issue would see Moss's 32nd *Vogue* cover. By contrast, Jean Shrimpton – regarded as a Sixties supermodel – fronted the magazine five times, Twiggy just twice.

Condé Nast
(220 × 284 mm, perfect bound, 260 pages)

LOADED (May 1994)

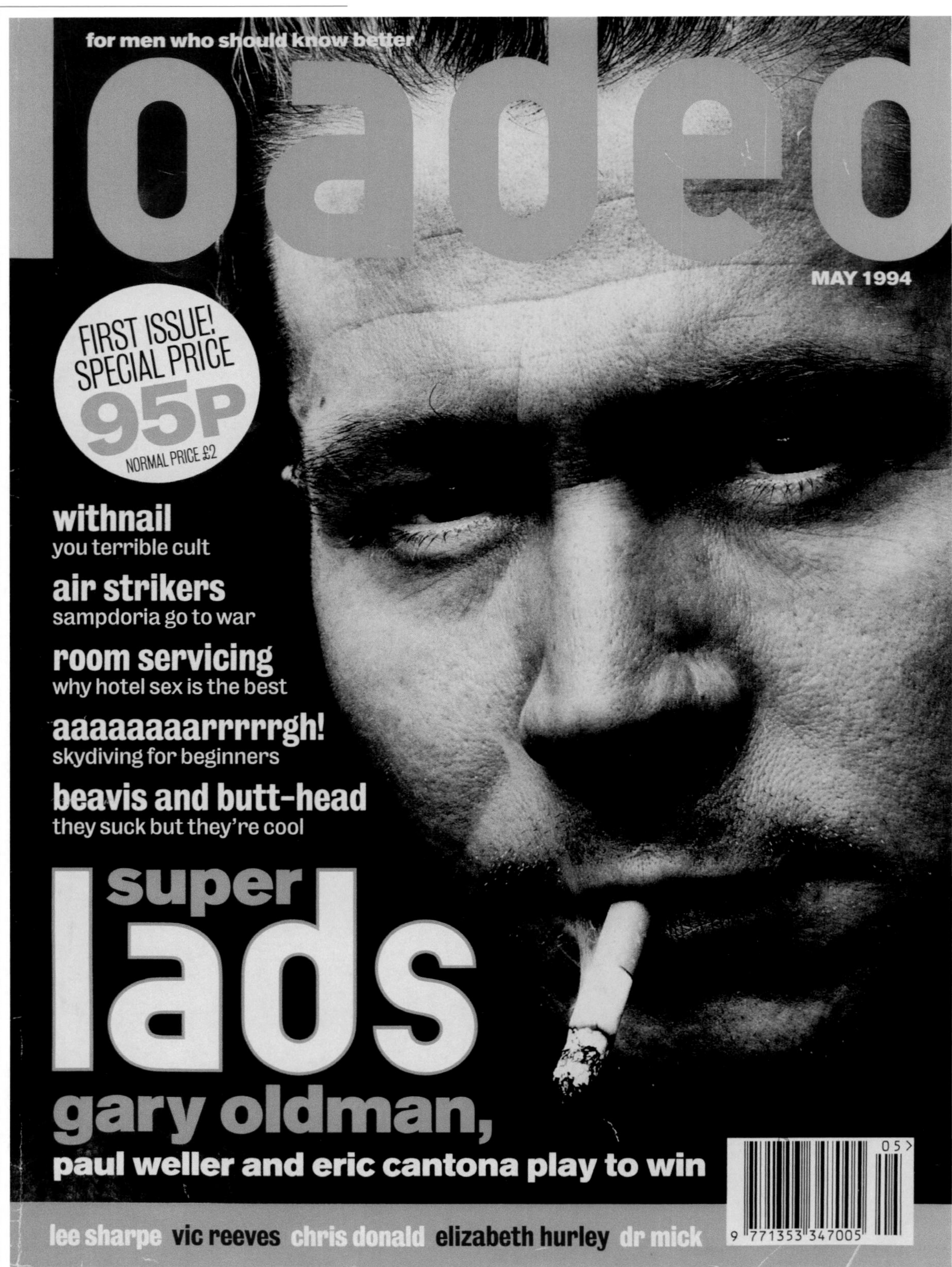

for men who should know better
loaded
MAY 1994
FIRST ISSUE! SPECIAL PRICE
95P
NORMAL PRICE £2
withnail
you terrible cult
air strikers
sampdoria go to war
room servicing
why hotel sex is the best
aaaaaaaarrrrrgh!
skydiving for beginners
beavis and butt-head
they suck but they're cool
super
lads
gary oldman,
paul weller and eric cantona play to win
lee sharpe vic reeves chris donald elizabeth hurley dr mick
05
9 771353 347005

Nigel Parry took the Gary Oldman portrait, with the dangling cigarette suggesting Michael Caine-like attitude. *Loaded* carried on using male celebrities for most of its covers until March 1998, when it adopted the all-women strategy of the previous two years at rival *FHM*. Four-colour black and mono covers with fluorescent type were widely used at the time. The art director was Stephen Read.

IPC Magazines
(220 × 298 mm, perfect bound, 124 pages)

LOADED (May 1995)

berk ETHIC

story by PETE 'THE LOAFER' STANTON
photos by LAWRENCE WATSON

So you think that crazed slapstick comic Lee Evans came out of nowhere? Well, you're wrong. He came out of somewhere. And that somewhere is Southend

THE WOMAN BEHIND THE COUNTER OF THE BARN CHIP SHOP IN HIGHBURY, NORTH LONDON, HAS NEVER HEARD of Lee Evans or **loaded** for that matter. "**loaded**, you say? So, er, what… are you delivering something?" she asks. With only £2.47 between us (£2.10 of which is mine), we split a saveloy and chips and huddle around a lime green table on a couple of rickety chairs. We're even short of fags and resort to sharing Lee's one and only Silk Cut. Her theory that we're just a couple of cheapskate urchins looks pretty hot.

"So you're a comedian, then?" the woman behind the counter says to Lee. She's giving Lee that look up and down. You know, the 'do something funny then' look.

Lee's used to all this, but today he can't think of anything to do. The woman shuffles back behind the counter muttering something like, "Comedian, my arse."

Lee Evans is the nicest bloke you could possibly share saveloy, chips and a fag with. His stage persona might be one of an insane, neurotic wind-up toy, but face to face he's immeasurably shy and incredibly polite. Later he admits to massive bouts of paranoia concerning upsetting people.

"I've had words with a doctor about it," he confides. "It was snapping me brain up inside. The doctor told me to just 'let it go, son, let it go'. So I said to him, 'That's easier said than done.' I worried that I'd upset him that night." Berk. ⇒

50 • loaded

LOADED (May 1994)

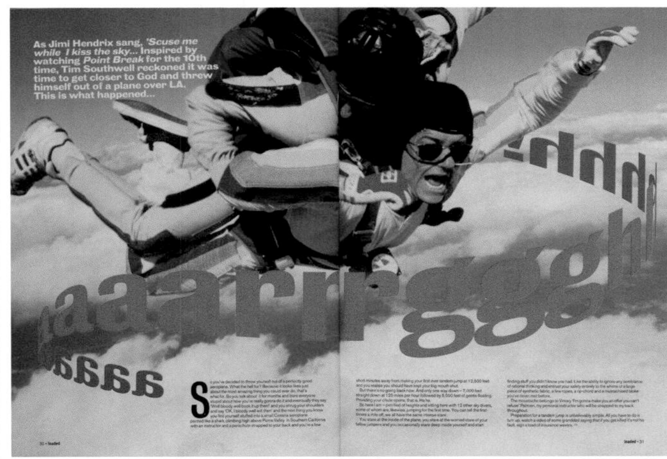

Writers set out on daring tasks that were reflected by increasingly 'in your face' page designs.

IPC Magazines
(220 × 298 mm, perfect bound, 124 pages)

Shouting type was a trademark of *Loaded*, but comics such as Lee Evans were increasingly pushed off the covers in favour of pin-ups, as publishers sought to catch up with the ballooning sales of rival *FHM*, which was more aggressive in its use of women for its covers. The cover for this issue was Kimberley Evans, and there was a double-gatefold poster of her and Kylie Minogue inside.

IPC Magazines
(220 × 298 mm, perfect bound, 148 pages)

MAXIM (October 1995)

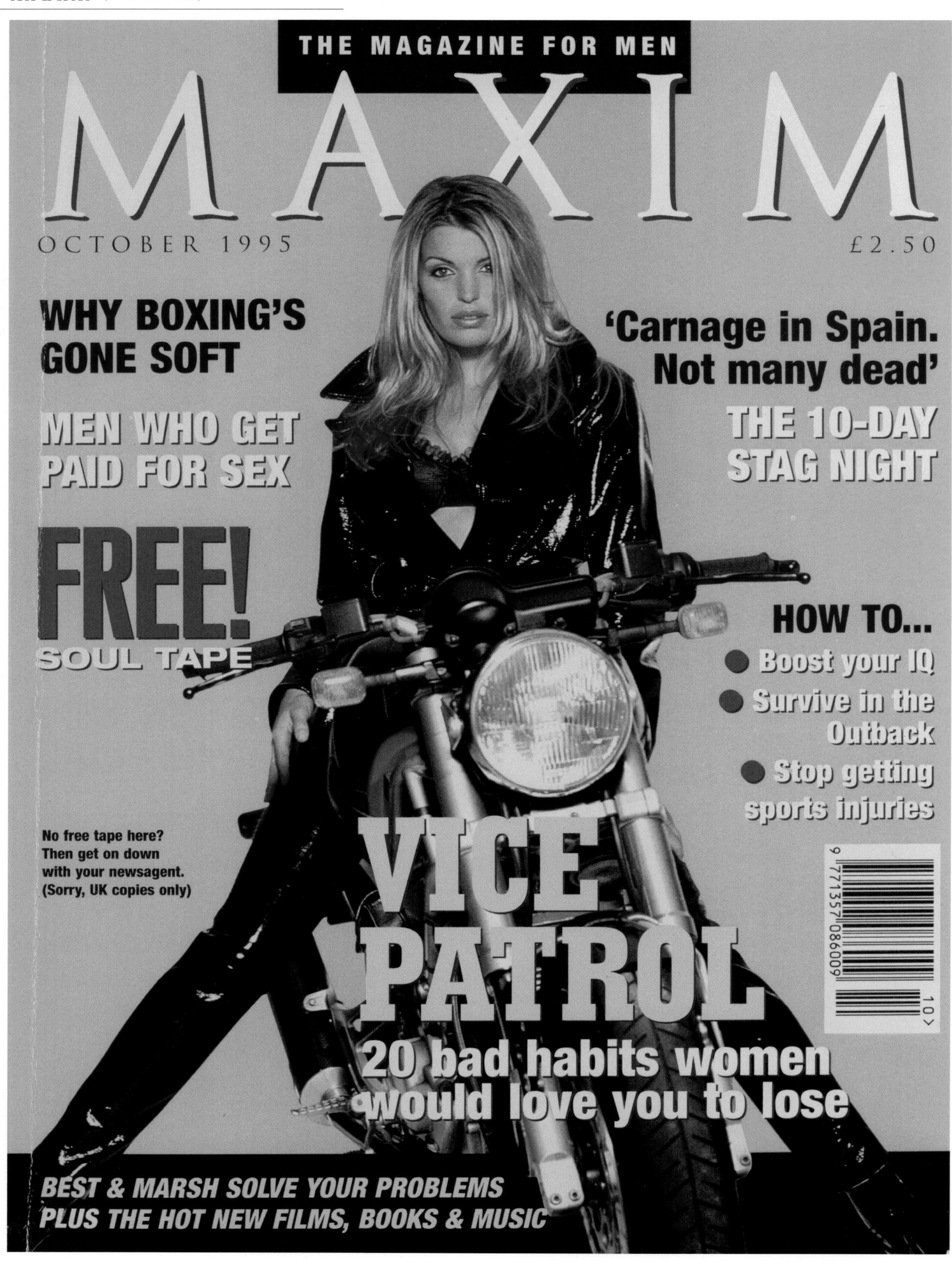

THE MAGAZINE FOR MEN
MAXIM
OCTOBER 1995
£2.50
WHY BOXING'S GONE SOFT
MEN WHO GET PAID FOR SEX
FREE! SOUL TAPE
No free tape here? Then get on down with your newsagent. (Sorry, UK copies only)
'Carnage in Spain. Not many dead'
THE 10-DAY STAG NIGHT
HOW TO...
Boost your IQ
Survive in the Outback
Stop getting sports injuries
VICE PATROL
20 bad habits women would love you to lose
BEST & MARSH SOLVE YOUR PROBLEMS
PLUS THE HOT NEW FILMS, BOOKS & MUSIC

The title was designed by typographic consultant Dave Farey, who based it on lettering from the V&A's 1864 cast of the 1,900-year-old Trajan's Column in Rome, which contains the word MAXIMO (incidentally, Trajan is a favourite font of the film industry). Farey also worked on *The Times*, the *European* and *Design Week*, among others, developing typefaces and titles. This cover promoted a feature on leather jackets by photographer James Martin. Jadene at Elite Premier was the model. The art editor was Peter Green and the editor Gill Hudson.

Dennis Lifestyle
(212 × 286 mm, perfect bound, 140 pages)

TOP GEAR (October 1993)

With three BBC launches behind it, Redwood took a different design approach for the motoring monthly, using a split cover in silver ink wrapped around a gatefold. In keeping with the strategy Seamus Geoghegan established on *Gardeners' World*, *Top Gear* offered more than just a magazine. The issue came with a poster of the full-cover shot and car window stickers; in addition, membership of a Top Gear Club was included in the subscription. The magazine was typical of the laddish 1990s in the way it throbbed with attitude: 'Our Bell Jet Ranger helicopter cleared the trees, and there, lined up on the banking of the legendary Brooklands race track, was just about every new car you can buy. It was perhaps the most awesome automotive spectacle of all time. This was a 15,000 horsepower, £12 million metal orgy. And this is the only car magazine with the clout to stage a shot like this.' The cover was by Frank Herholdt, with reportage photography by Phil Starling.

'They don't like it up 'em', a quote from Corporal Jones in the 1970s BBC TV series *Dad's Army*, is the headline for a test that puts 'England's secret weapon', the TVR Griffith 500, up against continental and US sports cars. The wartime metaphor runs through the copy and the spread shows 'burnt out' tanks and a Maxim machine gun – a regular metaphor in men's magazines. The photograph was by Aart aan de Wiel.

Top Gear started from the outset with a cars database put together by consultant Ivan Berg. This was 'milked' to feed straight into the page layouts with drop-in cartoons by Gray Jolliffe. The opening spread for the section was illustrated by Ian Pollock.

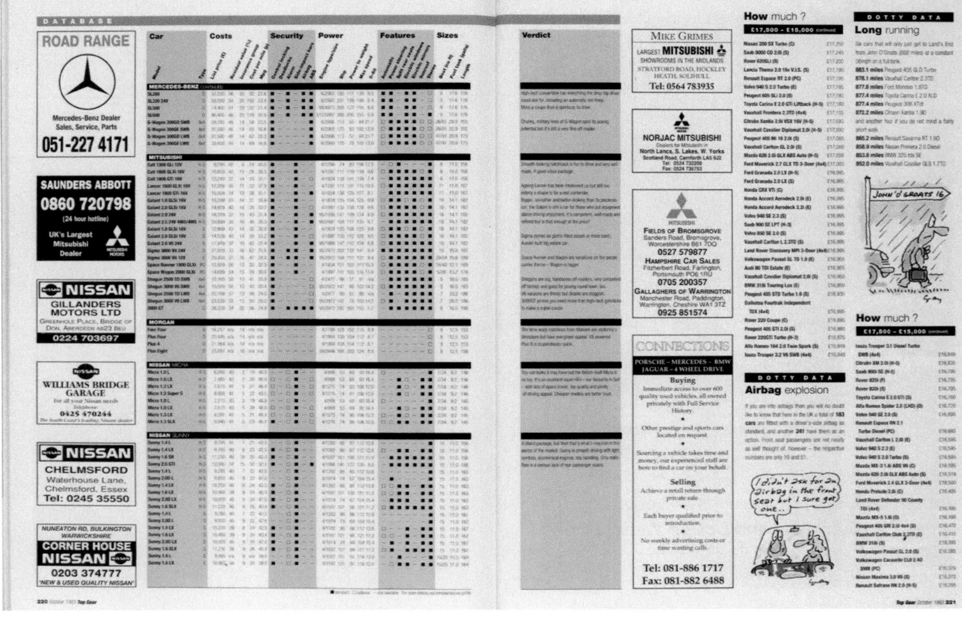
DATABASE

ROAD RANGE
Mercedes-Benz Dealer Sales, Service, Parts
051-227 4171

SAUNDERS ABBOTT
0860 720798
(24 hour hotline)
UK's Largest Mitsubishi Dealer

NISSAN
GILLANDERS MOTORS LTD
0224 703697

WILLIAMS BRIDGE GARAGE
0425 470244

NISSAN
CHELMSFORD
Waterhouse Lane, Chelmsford, Essex
Tel: 0245 35550

CORNER HOUSE NISSAN
0203 374777

Car | Costs | Security | Power | Features | Sizes

Verdict

MIKE GRIMES
LARGEST MITSUBISHI
Tel: 0564 783935

NORJAC MITSUBISHI

0527 579877
0705 200357
0925 851574

CONNECTIONS
Buying
Selling
Tel: 081-886 1717
Fax: 081-882 6488

How much?
£17,500 – £15,000

DOTTY DATA
Long running

DOTTY DATA
Airbag explosion

How much?

BBC/Redwood
(230 × 298 mm, perfect bound, 252 pages)

ELLE (December 1996)

blocking traffic and bending barriers, is a yardstick of how 'hot' the show inside will be. It's rumoured that certain designers will contrive to whip up that last-helicopter-out-of-Saigon atmosphere, for that extra, extra edge of exclusivity.

Everyone's got a ticket, but favoured friends are picked out of the crowd and plucked to safety by men wearing earpieces, talking earnestly into radios. Cashmere-coated arms claw at each other over the barriers, emotions are tested to breaking point. These are desperate scenes. These people have to get inside. It's their job; it's their passion; being on the inside is their *raison d'être*. When you finally make it past that barrier, you have once again proved that you are one of the chosen few – on the inside of the most 'in' business in the world.

'Inside' is probably dark and cavernous, some vast, dank warehouse with chairs grouped in blocks to form a 70-yard runway between them. These are the flat shows – the ones that take place in meat markets, with survival blankets supplied to protect the audience from the cold – as opposed to the staggered terraces of the specially built 'theatres' beneath the Louvre. The hipper the show, the bleaker and more minimalist the venue. But even in these surroundings, the traditional rules apply.

These are desperate scenes; these people must get inside. It's their job, their passion. It's their *raison d'être*

The first of these is that you, the audience, are on show as much as the clothes you've come to see, and your clothes are everyone's business. You score points for a coveted 'piece' (Gucci jacket, Prada Mary Janes), double for something 'directional' (the jersey top everyone will be wearing next spring); points for endurance (hypodermic heels) and a few more for innovative styling (worn by the French stylist Carin Routfeld, a safety-pin holding up a hem could start a new look).

No one in fashion is ever off patrol. In these circles, it isn't rude to look someone up and down, it is diligent. As a matter of course you stroke your neighbour's thigh (is it a wool mix?), check their coat label (No! Really?), or confer as to whose shoes the woman opposite is wearing (as in the designer, rather than whether or not they're borrowed). In any conversation between members of the fashion sorority, the observation 'great skirt' is a request for information, not a compliment.

The second rule is, of course, who sits where. To avoid conflicts of interest, the seats are allocated according to country, company and status – press on one side, buyers on the other. Fashion editors, top stylists and celebrities are front row, rivals are separated, and the allocation of the second and even third and fourth rows is crucial. If you're further back than the 10th, you are not a significant player, and for those with a reputation to think of, it's better not to see the show at all than to be seen anywhere but the front. Among the front-row icons are the massive black figure of *Vanity Fair*'s André Leon Talley, Italian *Vogue*'s Anna Piaggi (who dyes her hair to match her outfits, which are rarely black) and Suzy Menkes, the *International Herald Tribune*'s correspondent, with the Wilma Flintstone hairdo.

At this point there is usually a skirmish, when a ball of photographers – hand-held spotlights and furry microphones brandished on booms – swarm into position opposite someone in the front row. The ball gathers momentum, collecting newspaper editors looking for quotes, fashion editors with Instamatics and anyone who can't stand the suspense. When they are sated, it gradually disperses to reveal Joan Collins or Madonna or Hugh and Liz (or Tamara Beckwith, depending on the calibre of the show). Across the room, blinding white lights indicate TV crews ➤

34 ELLE

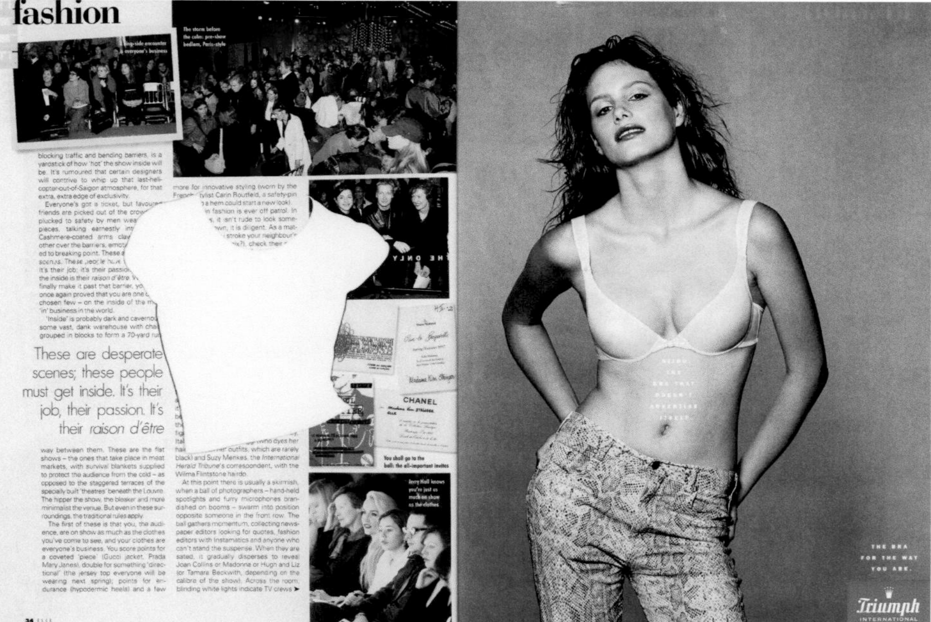

Advertising agency Delaney Fletcher Bozell and 20/20 Media produced a unique advert in *Elle* for the launch of a new bra. When the reader turns the page, an acetate overlay on which the white T-shirt is printed is removed, revealing the bra and the copy: 'Bijou, the bra that doesn't advertise itself.' Other adverts from the time employed special card, embossing and unusual inks; and issues would often open up at inserts loaded with perfume strips or tipped-on sachet samples of lotions. Such techniques would become more popular a decade later, for both editorial and advertising, as magazines sought to make themselves more of a luxury, interactive product.

Emap Elan
(223 × 298 mm, perfect bound, 228 pages)

DAZED & CONFUSED

(August 1997)

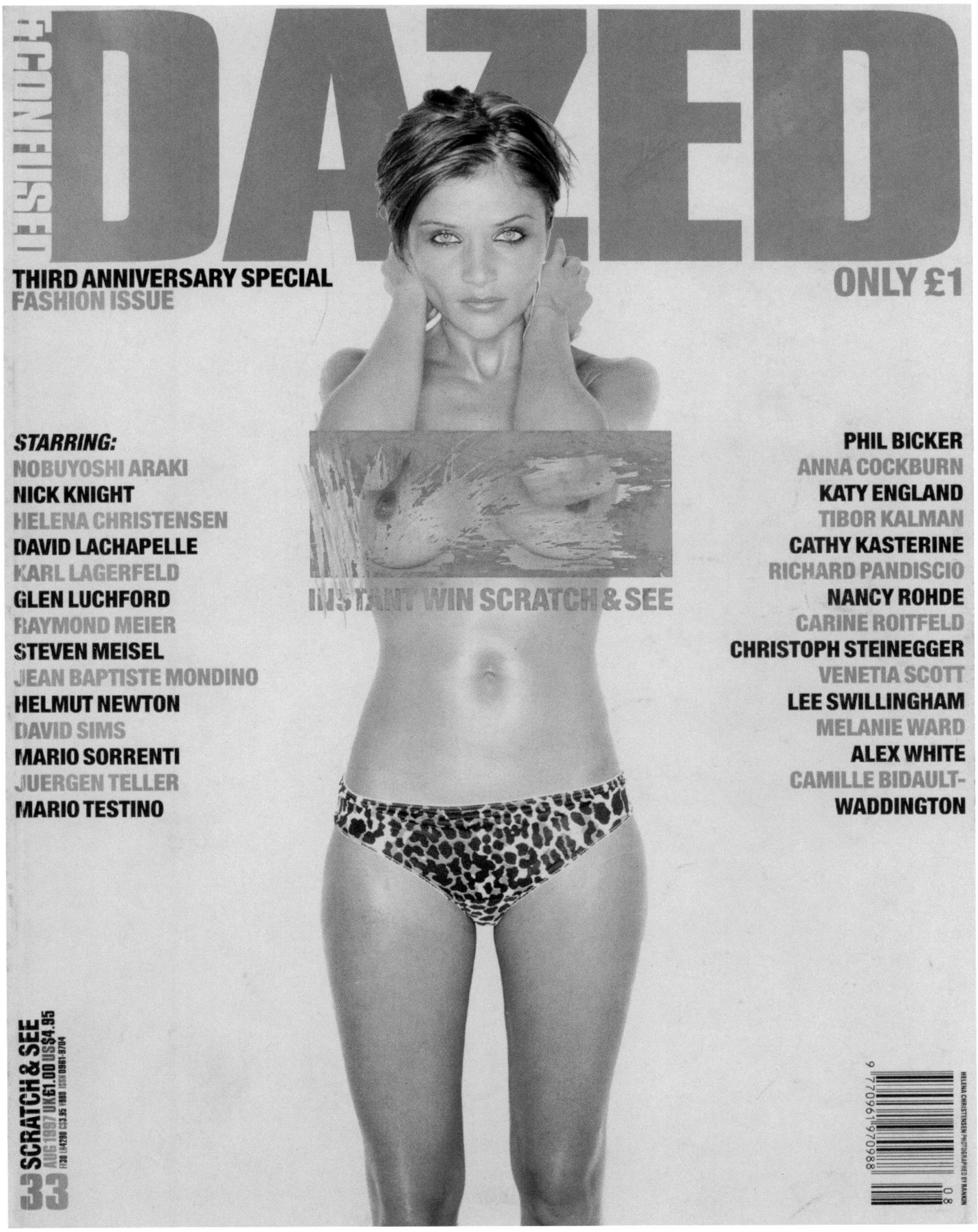

DAZED & CONFUSED

THIRD ANNIVERSARY SPECIAL
FASHION ISSUE

ONLY £1

STARRING:
NOBUYOSHI ARAKI
NICK KNIGHT
HELENA CHRISTENSEN
DAVID LACHAPELLE
KARL LAGERFELD
GLEN LUCHFORD
RAYMOND MEIER
STEVEN MEISEL
JEAN BAPTISTE MONDINO
HELMUT NEWTON
DAVID SIMS
MARIO SORRENTI
JUERGEN TELLER
MARIO TESTINO

PHIL BICKER
ANNA COCKBURN
KATY ENGLAND
TIBOR KALMAN
CATHY KASTERINE
RICHARD PANDISCIO
NANCY ROHDE
CARINE ROITFELD
CHRISTOPH STEINEGGER
VENETIA SCOTT
LEE SWILLINGHAM
MELANIE WARD
ALEX WHITE
CAMILLE BIDAULT-WADDINGTON

INSTANT WIN SCRATCH & SEE

33 SCRATCH & SEE
AUG 1997 UK£1.00 US$4.95

For its third anniversary, *Dazed & Confused* ran a Helena Christensen cover with a 'scratch and see' panel. One of the articles was a question and answer session with photographers Nick Knight, David Sims, Glen Luchford and Juergen Teller.

Waddell
(210 × 276 mm, perfect bound)

EDGE (October 1998)

Art editor Terry Stokes used foil embossing for the title and embossing combined with five-colour printing on the cover to announce a review of the *Turok 2: Seeds of Evil* console and computer game. The issue also included a bookmark taped to the back cover. A panel on the contents page identified the hardware (Power Macintosh G3, PowerBook and Quadra) and software (QuarkXPress, Adobe Photoshop, Macromedia Freehand, Pixar Tapestry and Nisus) used, as well as the typefaces (Adobe Formata, Vectora and Univers) and Pantone special colours (five metallic shades for the cover and inside pages). Colour reproduction was by Colourworks in Bristol and printing by Cradley in Warley, West Midlands.

Future
(210 × 280 mm, perfect bound, 156 pages)

VANITY FAIR (March 1997)

The use of the Union flag on covers has a long history. The art director here was David Harris. The 'London Swings Again!' issue led with zeitgeist couple actress Patsy Kensit and Liam Gallagher from the band Oasis, photographed by Lorenzo Agius.

Alongside 'coolish' politicians such as Tony Blair, pop and film stars, aristocratic beauties and the fashion world, here represented by Alexander McQueen and Isabella Blow in a Philip Treacy hat, were presented as British 'heroes'. The photograph was by David LaChapelle. Other spreads showed London tailors, the Conran family, restaurateurs, the Spice Girls and hedonists – *Loaded*'s Martin Deeson, James Brown, Michael Holden and Tim Southwell with models and actresses Annabelle Rothschild, Sophie Anderton and Sophie Dahl.

Condé Nast
(203 × 275 mm, perfect bound, 206 pages)

MODERN REVIEW (October 1997)

The Modern Review

Number 1 October 1997 £2.95

Bye bye baby
Julie Burchill on
her abortions
Posh Spice
Like f**k she is
New Labour paranoia
They're bonkers!

Swinging London

The myth of a
British renaissance

10>

9 770964 232007

A *Guardian* article about *Modern Review* quoted a Tina Brown spine line from *Tatler*: 'the magazine that bites the hand that feeds it'. It was a relaunch of a 1991 magazine from Julie Burchill, but in a glossy format designed by the Esterson Lackersteen consultancy. It lasted for only a few issues. The cover, by Rankin, attacks the 'Cool Britannia' label that New Labour under Tony Blair was trying to promote.

Modern Media
(218 × 284 mm, perfect bound, 92 pages)

PULP (13 November 1998)

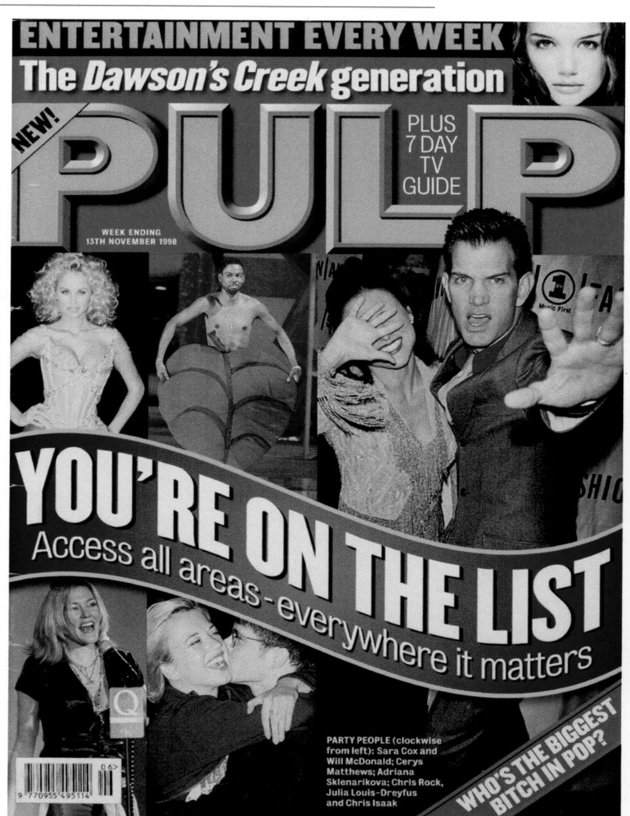

Pulp was a dummy issue for *Heat*, a TV-based entertainment weekly. There were 40 pages of programme listings and previews. The big publishers would spend millions launching a magazine and do several dummy covers – and even full issues – to test the editorial strategy and design among people seen as target buyers.

Emap
(222 × 298 mm, stapled, 106 pages)

HEAT (6 February 1999)

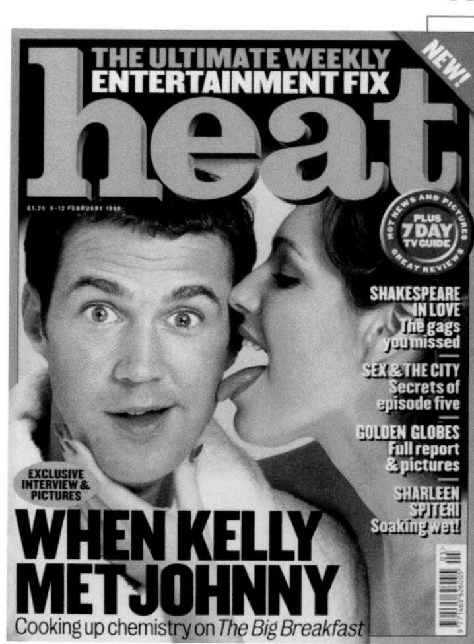

The cover of the first issue shows Johnny Vaughan and Kelly Brook, presenters of Channel 4's *Big Breakfast*; it was taken by Paul Rider. The style of the cover is influenced by *Loaded*'s approach. Hot TV was the name for the 42 pages of TV listings and previews at the back. The art director was Jonathan Sellers.

The photograph of Kate Winslet on this profile spread was by Katz.

Emap
(222 × 298 mm, stapled, 116 pages)

HEAT (3 February 2001)

Heat was not a success initially but sales jumped when it switched from being the 'ultimate weekly entertainment fix' to carrying the 'hottest celebrity news', usually based on reality TV series such as *Big Brother* or *Popstars*. The listings section was reduced to 28 pages, with the contents a single-column strip on page 3. The art director was Lottie Berridge.

The first 18 pages were made up of celebrity photographs.

Emap
(222 × 298 mm, stapled, 100 pages)

ZEMBLA (September 2003)

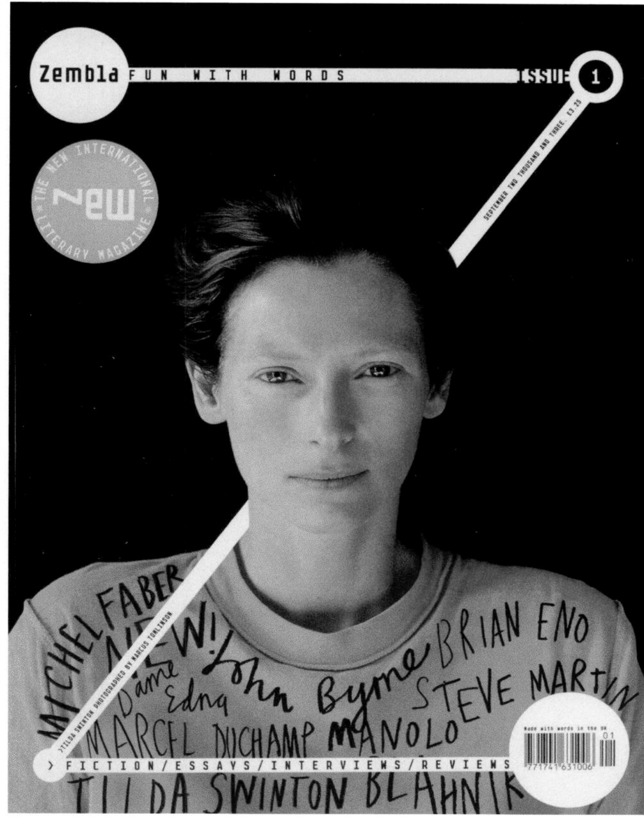

'Fun with words' is the strapline on this international literary bimonthly, which was funded by antiquarian bookseller Simon Finch and drew on celebrities and glossy production values to boost its appeal, though it lasted only nine issues. The design was contracted out to Vince Frost and his agency, Frost Design, with Matthew Willis as designer. In 2005 editor Dan Crowe told the online magazine *3:AM Magazine*: 'I think people don't buy literary magazines because they *are* dull and boring, but because they *look* dull and boring. That's a very big marketing problem. So we have Rachel Weisz and Tilda Swinton or Jimi Hendrix on our covers. We were hoping to have Johnny Depp on this cover but that didn't work out.'[1] The title, he told *Design Week* in August 2003, referred to a fictional land in Vladimir Nabokov's novel *Pale Fire*, one of Crowe's favourites: 'I wanted to find a word that wasn't in use. It's typographically neat too, starting with a Z and ending in an A.' The photograph of actress Tilda Swinton on the cover of the first issue was by Marcus Tomlinson. Her T-shirt acts as a form of cover line: for example, French artist Marcel Duchamp is the subject of a fictional interview by Michel Faber in the first of a series of interviews with dead subjects. Another interview included crime writer Ian Rankin 'interviewing' Sir Arthur Conan Doyle. The 'Z' title was used on all the covers, but the cover lines on later issues were more conventional. Celebrity names associated with the magazine included Swinton, photographer Henri Cartier-Bresson and shoe designer Manolo Blahnik.

1 Richard Marshall, 'Writing for All', *3:AM*, February 2005

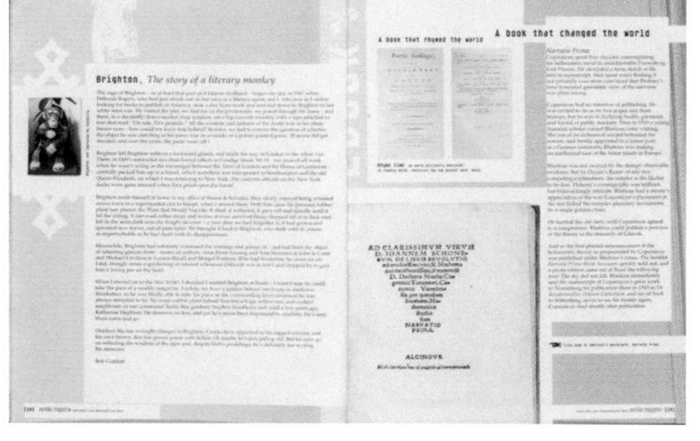

This spread of literary tales has the look of a scrapbook. The typefaces are eclectic, but relatively modern: the 1999 typewriter-like face Arete Mono by American 'grunge' typographer and musician Jim Marcus for the headlines and captions, and Hermann Zapf's 1951 Palatino for the body copy. The pointing hands and decoration feel Victorian.

A visual pun for the letters spread.

Zembla Magazine
(232 × 300 mm, perfect bound, 124 pages)

FT WEEKEND MAGAZINE (28 May 2011)

Even the *Financial Times* embraced the celebrity trend. This cover shows Lady Gaga, who was being interviewed by Stephen Fry. They took tea at the Lanesborough hotel in London. Both were celebrities – the actor and technology enthusiast Fry was one of the world's most popular bloggers and tweeters, chosen as 'blogger in residence' for the reopening of the Savoy hotel in 2010. The cover portrait was by Shamil Tanna. This interview was part of the trend for celebrities interviewing each other, acting as guest editors or launching their own magazines. Examples include artist Tracey Emin as guest editor of the *Guardian*'s *Weekend* magazine (October 2002), comedian Russell Brand editing the *New Statesman* (October 2013), Prince Charles editing *Country Life* (November 2013) and Sir Tom Jones interviewing cover bunny girl Kate Moss for the 60th anniversary issue of *Playboy* (January/February 2014).

The typography reflects the subject, with overblown italic script and handwritten display text on covers and for headlines.

Financial Times weekend supplement
(242 × 298 mm, stapled, 56 pages)

THE ECONOMIST (12 May 2001)

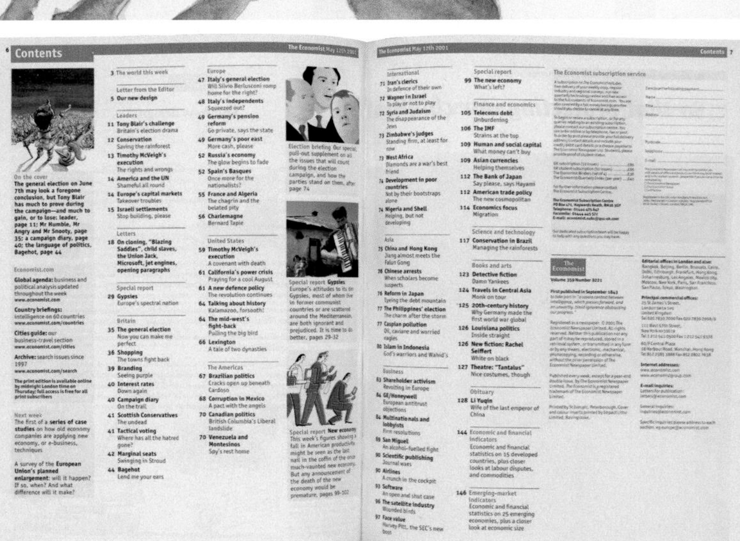

6 Contents

The Economist May 12th 2001

On the cover
The general election on June 7th may look a foregone conclusion, but Tony Blair has much to prove during the campaign—and much to gain, or to lose: leader, page 11; Mr Humble, Mr Angry and Mr Snooty, page 35; a campaign diary, page 40; the language of politics, Bagehot, page 44

Economist.com
Global agenda: business and political analysis updated throughout the week www.economist.com
Country briefings: intelligence on 60 countries www.economist.com/countries
Cities guide: our business-travel section www.economist.com/cities
Archive: search issues since 1997 www.economist.com/search
The print edition is available online by midnight London time on Thursday; full access is free for all print subscribers

Next week
The first of a series of case studies on how old economy companies are applying new economy, or e-business, techniques

A survey of the European Union's planned enlargement: will it happen? If so, when? And what difference will it make?

Election briefing Our special pull-out supplement on all the issues that will count during the election campaign, and how the parties stand on them, after page 74

Special report Gypsies Europe's attitudes to its Gypsies, most of whom live in former communist countries or are scattered around the Mediterranean, are both ignorant and prejudiced. It is time to do better, pages 29-32

Special report New economy This week's figures showing a fall in American productivity might be seen as the last nail in the coffin of the once much-vaunted new economy. But any announcement of the death of the new economy would be premature, pages 99-102

The Economist May 12th 2001 Contents 7

The Economist subscription service

The Economist
Volume 359 Number 8221
First published in September 1843

Editorial offices in London and also:

Principal commercial offices:

Internet addresses:

E-mail inquiries:

Editor Bill Emmott launched the first full redesign of the weekly since 1987 (though it had introduced its own body face, Ecotype, by Gunnlaugur Briem in 1991, replacing Goudy Old Style, under art director Aurobind Patel). Emmott set out the magazine's approach: 'There are few things more boring than long articles by editors about how their redesigns are going to produce a sharper, more modern, publication, brightening readers' lives and furthering world peace ... Good design, like good writing, should blend into the background; it should be the servant of editors and readers alike, not their master.' Colour was introduced on all pages 'in a cool, restrained way' and there was more navigational information, including expanding the contents page to a spread. New typefaces were used: Officina for cover lines and navigation boxes, plus a redrawn Ecotype.

The Economist Newspaper Ltd
(217 × 282 mm, stapled, 148 pages)

SELECT (December 1995)

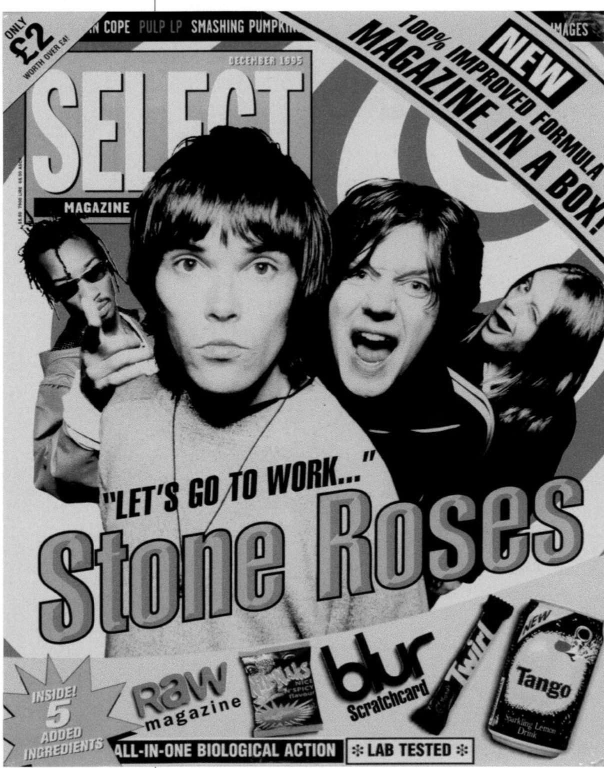

Emap put a copy of the relaunched *Raw* into a box with *Select* and snack samples. The snacks were probably a 'contra deal', with free samples provided in exchange for promotion within the issue. The design mimicked a soap powder packet. The 'mag in a box' strategy was also used by other publishers. The cover photographer was by Simon Fowler and the art editor was Keith Drummond.

Emap Metro
(224 × 296 mm, stapled, 148 pages)

WALLPAPER*

(September/October 1996)

wallpaper*
*The stuff that surrounds you
sept | oct 1996
launch issue
urban Modernists
£3.00 UK
ISSN 1364-4475
interiors * entertaining * travel

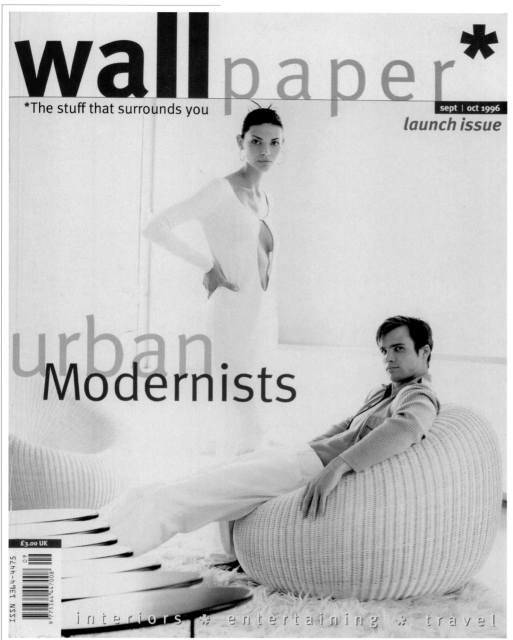

As well as having Herbert Winkler as art director, Martin Jacobs as consultant creative director, contributing editors and contributing photographers, Canada-born founder Tyler Brûlé appointed six contributing illustrators – Geoff Waring, Demetrios Psillos, New York-based Swede Laura Ljungkvist, Canadian Maurice Velekoop, Chris Long and Stuart Patterson – in a statement marking the start of a return to popularity for illustration after decades of decline. The magazine had an international outlook, and typified the slick décor of late 1990s urban living. Along with *Elle Deco* and *Blueprint*, *Wallpaper** nurtured a generation of young, brand-conscious internationalists with retro-modern tastes. The magazine was bought up within a year by Time Life, which stated: 'We were impressed by *Wallpaper**'s freshness. In the US we already have several lifestyle magazines but none with quite such broad appeal ... Time Inc.'s international sales and distribution network will enable *Wallpaper** to become a truly global brand.' Brûlé led two other launches, fashion titles *Line* and *Spruce*, for the company, but both failed.

Wallpaper Media in association with Ahead Media
(230 × 298 mm, perfect bound, 164 pages)

A spread from the 'Intelligence' section, the second section simply being 'Features'. Both began with their own right-hand title page that listed the main contents.

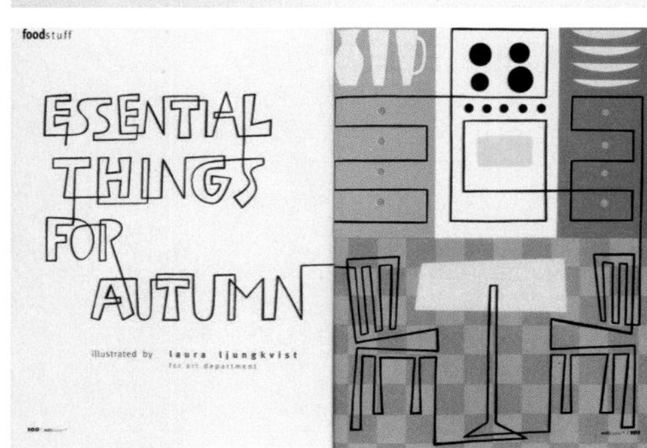

The opening spread of an eight-page list of essential kitchen items illustrated by Laura Ljungkvist, such as Belgian linen kitchen cloths, a pepper mill 'that can double as a lethal weapon', a 'Waring blender for mixing the perfect cocktail' and a grill pan for searing scallops.

VIZ (April/May 1993)

Chris Donald started *Viz* in his bedroom in 1979 and sales grew to exceed a million copies an issue by 1990. Its success spawned copycats and it was blamed, along with *Private Eye*, for driving *Punch* to close in 1992. At this stage it was designed with the production values of the comics that inspired its spoof cartoon strips. *Viz* has been identified as an inspiration for *Loaded* by founder James Brown, who later bought the magazine and relaunched it with colour covers, but sales fell sharply. Although *Beano* and *Dandy* comic characters provided the main inspiration for *Viz*, it also ran *Jackie*-style photo strips, spoof adverts and newspaper pages.

House of Viz/John Brown Publishing
(210 × 296 mm, stapled, 48 pages)

SPECTATOR (14 July 1990)

Nicholas Garland's cover – showing Nicholas Ridley adding a Hitler moustache to a poster of German chancellor Helmut Kohl – was seen as a big factor in the trade minister's resignation. In the interview with editor Dominic Lawson, 'Saying the Unsayable about the Germans', Ridley described the proposed Economic and Monetary Union as 'a German racket designed to take over the whole of Europe' and said that giving up sovereignty to Europe was as bad as giving it up to Adolf Hitler. The *Spectator* lays claim to the record of being the oldest continuously published English-language magazine.

Spectator 1928
(210 × 275 mm, stapled, 72 pages)

THE OLDIE (21 February 1992)

News from Stump Cross Roundabout

Germaine Greer

begins a love-hate relationship

Even as *Punch* was dying, former *Private Eye* editor Richard Ingrams was launching a magazine that 'began as a joke' and a 'protest against the cult of youth'. Backing came from Naim Attallah, a book publisher and backer of the *Literary Review*.

Germaine Greer had been a gardening contributor to *Private Eye* in the 1960s under the pen name Rose Blight. The wood-engraving that accompanied her article here was commissioned from 80-year-old John O'Connor, who had been trained by Eric Ravilious and worked for many magazines since the war. A gargoylish graphic signs off the article.

Oldie Publications
(224 × 298 mm, stapled, 52 pages)

PUNCH (September 1996)

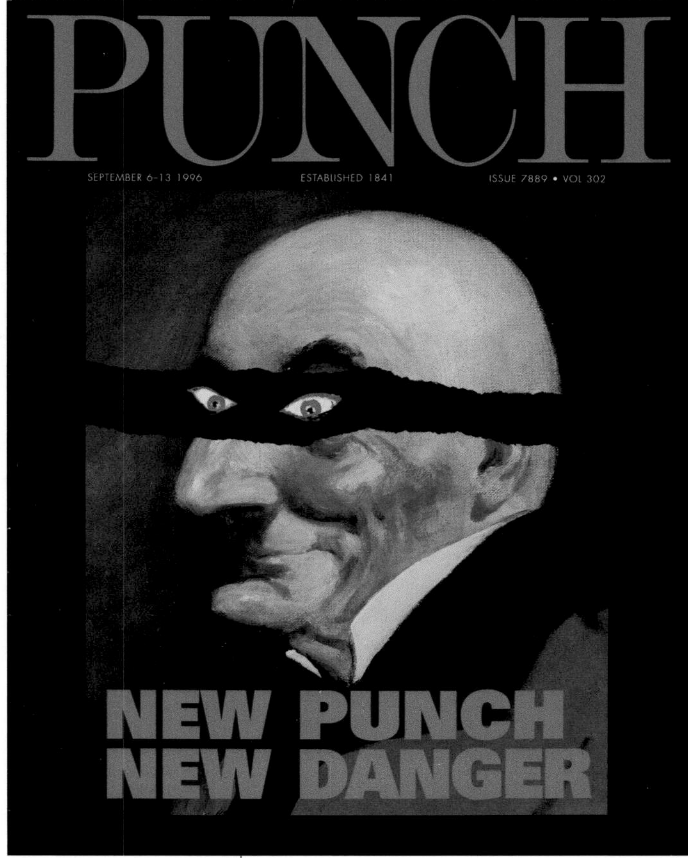

Punch had closed in April 1992, but was resurrected with this cover mimicking a recent Conservative Party poster attacking Tony Blair ('New Labour, New Danger'). Former *Daily Mirror* editor Mike Molloy was involved in buying the *Punch* name on behalf of Harrods owner Mohammed Fayed, and another Fleet Street veteran, Peter McKay, became editor. It was, said McKay, 'at last something special to read at the weekend'. The publishers, Liberty, used better paper and a larger format, with richly illustrated covers and whole-page paintings, by Annie Farrell and Diane Broadley in this issue, as well as cartoons from the grandiloquent John Glashan, Mike Williams and Willie Rushton. Byline portraits were by Michael Grimsdale. However, it failed to thrive, the format was reduced to a standard A4 with fewer pages, and it folded a year later.

Liberty Publishing
(232 × 298 mm, stapled, 100 pages)

Beyond print – and back again

The launch of 'handbag'-format fashion monthly *Glamour* was a big success – knocking *Cosmopolitan* from its long-standing position as the biggest-selling monthly within a year – and it led to a debate among designers about a lack of innovation. Jeremy Leslie, creative director at contract publisher John Brown Citrus, used it as evidence of a problem, telling *Design Week*: 'When it's big news that someone has produced something smaller, it highlights in the broader context how little diversity the market has seen.' For Leslie, design hadn't evolved since the 1970s. 'There's a perceived way glossies should look. All these magazines have the same, clichéd way of presenting themselves. All the front covers are the same. It's formulaic and very repetitive.'[1] The small format – 'travel size' – was adopted by many other titles, including *Elle*, *Marie Claire*, *GQ* and *Cosmopolitan* – alongside their usual size.

Creativity was alive and well elsewhere, however, among independent magazines – a sector today documented and promoted in Leslie's *magCulture* blog. One independent title, *Marmalade*, dated its inspiration to July 2001 when the *Face* carried David Beckham on its cover. 'We knew that the whole idea of "cool" was over right there and then,' co-editor Sasha Teulon told the *Guardian*. 'At that same time *Dazed & Confused* was busy rewriting press releases and nobody was going out there to discover the new creativity that has always been one of Britain's biggest exports.'[2]

Free magazines produced by contract publishers for the customers of companies such as Marks & Spencer and Sky TV were dominating the twice-yearly circulation figures. In 2003, Virgin Atlantic launched an 'upper class suite' in its aircraft and introduced a free luxury quarterly, *Carlos*, for its customers that was designed to break the mould in contract publishing. The idea was that it had been left behind by a rich traveller whose name was Carlos and there was no Virgin branding on the pages. The magazine only lasted a couple of years, but customer titles carried on expanding: by 2010, they would hold a third of the places for the top 100 circulations.

The 2006 film *The Devil Wears Prada* put fashion magazines back in the public mind again, but much of the talk in the industry was of decline in the face of online competition. The same year saw the launch of digital facsimiles with built-in interactive features and searches by Exact Editions and other 'digital news-stands'. The *Spectator* (which dates back to 1828), the *Scientist*, *London Review of Books* and *Literary Review* were the first four. Six years later, there were more than 100 magazines available from Exact Editions alone, including the *Lady*, launched in 1885, and *Dazed & Confused*. During the severe weather of early 2010, Hachette Filipacchi made issues of *Elle* available free as digital editions so subscribers were not inconvenienced by late delivery of their magazines. A digital subscription would typically cost about half that of a UK postal print subscription, and the cost advantage would be far greater to subscribers overseas.

Tablet computers such as Apple's iPad seemed to offer a lifeline to large publishers, which feared a loss of readers and advertising to digital services in the same way that commercial television had affected magazines since 1955. The iPad was seen as providing a way for publishers to develop magazine apps that would deliver the visual richness of print and so earn money from subscriptions, rather than just ploughing investment into free websites that offered little in the way of advertising revenue. The industry displayed a lack of confidence in print not seen since the 1970s, with some titles closing and launches drying up.

Yet, even as many big publishers seemed to lose their faith in print, there was a blossoming of independent magazines as well as fashion and style magazines with a global outlook. *Wallpaper** founder Tyler Brûlé returned to magazines with *Monocle*. He ignored prevailing design approaches and rejected the view that newspapers and magazines were a failing medium, arguing that publishers were not investing in their main product and were being distracted by digital media. They did not appreciate that a highly mobile international audience was willing to pay for quality content. *Monocle* launched its own branded products, from notebooks to luggage and bicycles, and its own shops around the world. And the magazine that had made Brûlé's name continued to develop. For the August 2010 issue, *Wallpaper** produced a 'handmade' issue with seven paper stocks, and 21,000 unique covers designed by readers and printed on digital presses. Furthermore, every object featured was commissioned by the magazine. To top it off, there was a paper house to cut out and build.

But it is among independent magazines that design is blooming. Their praises were sung on blogs and at conferences and high design values could support premium prices – typically twice the price of a monthly. *Marmalade* has been accompanied by a stream of titles, some of which returned to illustration, *Little White Lies* and the delightful *Anorak* quarterly for children being two examples; the *Chap* is a 'satirical magazine for modern gentlemen' espousing pipes, slippers and knitted jumpers alongside steam punk. To Simon Esterson, *Karen* – based around everyday life in Malmesbury – is 'as beautiful as a bubble and as complicated as a snowflake'. *Delayed Gratification* brings the power of data-based illustration – infographics – to a review of the previous quarter's news, while *Pretty Nostalgic* feels more like a book than a magazine. For many of these titles, a move to environmentally friendly paper means they eschew the varnishing and lamination of the glossies.

Such magazines wear their heart on their covers. They bring an enthusiasm – and occasional wackiness – that may have otherwise been lost. The 'blockbuster' approach to launches adopted by the biggest publishers mimicked that of the US film studios, in the same way that they fall over themselves to put film stars on the cover of their magazines. However, for small, independent publishers, the relative cheapness of the production technology and the ability to reach potential readers though social media coupled with online payments really has opened up a whole new world of print.

1 Trish Lorenz, 'Close Ranks', *Design Week*, 7 October 2004, p. 18
2 Will Hodgkinson, 'Content Still King on Quality Street', *Guardian*, 20 November 2006

GLAMOUR (November 2001)

Glamour adopted the 'handbag' size used by the magazine's Italian edition since 1992, in the process rediscovering a format that had been a standard for many of the best-selling Victorian monthlies, such as the *Strand*, right up to the Second World War. Condé Nast found from focus groups that people 'loved its dinkiness, the way it fitted into their handbags', while rival National Magazine accused it of devaluing the sector with a £1.50 cover price – half that of *Cosmopolitan*. Celebrities fronted the covers.

The dimensions chosen and the advent of digital production technology meant that advertisers could scale down their adverts from other magazines without redesigning them, but it was not so simple for creative director Geoff Waring and art editor Anton Jacques. To keep large headline and readable text sizes, the design had to squeeze in more text, by, for example, putting headlines and other display text over images and experimenting with changing sizes within a headline.

Condé Nast
(203 × 275 mm, perfect bound, 276 pages)

CARLOS (Winter 2004)

44. *Two decades ago, the New Romantic heroes of British pop music wowed the USA just as The Beatles had 20 years before. The second British invasion owed its success to style, the emergence of MTV and one killer haircut. Peter York was there to salute...*

HOW THE WEDGE WAS WON

Carlos was designed by Warren Jackson at consultancy Fifty-One for customer publisher John Brown Citrus and creative director Jeremy Leslie. Its unusual look and feel – illustrated, with a brown paper cover and 4,000-word features – was more akin to a fanzine than the usual glossy. The rough paper and lack of full colour and photography (except for a central section of advertising, which was on glossy paper) were intended to feel 'authentic'; the cover was by Jonathan Schofield. However, Virgin closed the title in 2006, favouring screen entertainment systems – the start of a trend for some long-haul airlines as they looked to save weight in the face of rising fuel prices.

The text on this spread was set in Hoefler Text Swash – a swash being an exaggerated serif, as seen on the capitals – and printed in dark blue ink on off-white uncoated paper. The all-capitals headline was set in Mrs Eaves, a Baskerville-like typeface designed by Zuzana Licko in 1996 and named after the woman who became the mistress, assistant and later wife of 18th-century typographer John Baskerville. The illustration for the Peter York article was by Jamie Cullen.

John Brown Citrus/Virgin Atlantic
(170 × 240 mm, stapled, 52 pages)

GRAZIA (21 February 2005)

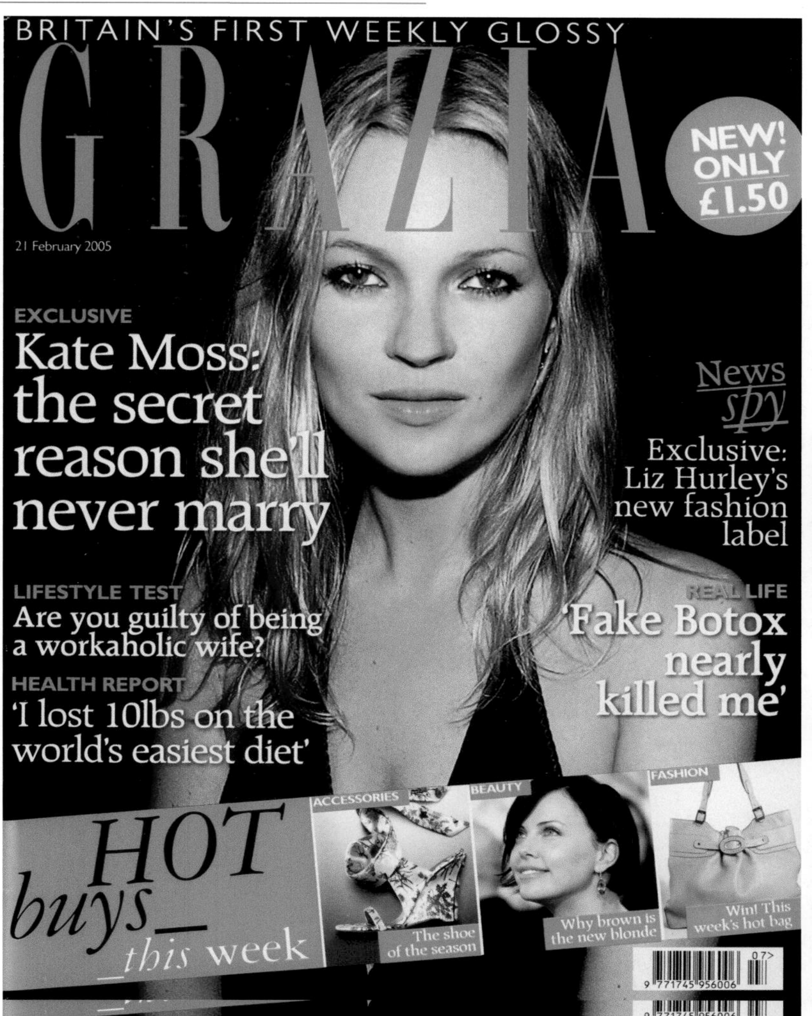

SHORTLIST (5 July 2012)

Catwalk scrapbook: NEW YORK

GRAZIA NEWS

WHAT'S HIP IN NEW YORK

«From wasp waists and curvy hips at Roland Mouret, to Oscar de la Renta's tulle cocktail dresses, next season will be all about the girl»

A topical celebrity was vital to the 'first glossy weekly', a mix of fashion and gossip. 'Kate Moss: the secret reason she'll never marry' is the cover story for the first issue, with a newsy photograph by Dimitrios Kambouris. The art director was Suzanna Sykes. 'I've finally found a magazine I can pore over, drool over and dream over,' wrote one reader in reaction to the previous week's free sample issue.

The paper was a silky matt inside, with lots of fluorescent yellow ink and gravure printing (by Polestar Purnell in Bristol). The magazine was an early adopter of 'soft' proofing – on-screen proofs to check colour reproduction rather than 'hard' colour proofs from film produced by systems such as Cromalin – using Kodak's Matchprint and inkjet proofs.

So much black is rarely used on magazine pages because ink can come off on the facing page (a problem called 'set-off') and it becomes tricky to achieve a balance across other pages on the larger printed sheet. However, production techniques such as 'undercolour removal' – in which some of the yellow, magenta or cyan inks that would combine to create a near black are replaced with black ink during colour separation can save ink, reduce the danger of set-off and cut drying times.

Emap
(234 × 298 mm, stapled, 124 pages)

Shortlist adopted a model pioneered in London by *Sport*, a free newsprint weekly launched in 2005 based on a French model by Sports, Medias & Strategie. They both built on the success of free morning papers such as *Metro* in the capital. Along with *Stylist*, a sister magazine to *Shortlist* for women, the three formed a 'freemium' magazine sector. As free magazines with advertising as the only source of revenue, issues tended to consist of alternating advertising and editorial pages in the first half and editorial spreads only in the latter half of each issue. The titles also sometimes sold an outer cover on glossy paper as a four-page advertorial for an event – a film launch, perhaps, with the magazine's title appearing above the advertiser's image on the front – very reminiscent of motoring titles from 60 years earlier or a trade magazine. This outer cover, which promotes *The Amazing Spider-Man*, used a thick spot UV varnish printed over parts of the character's suit. The main magazine was printed at Polestar Sheffield and the outer cover at Polestar Chantry on heavier paper, with the varnish overprinted using a screen press. As well as UV varnish, the Chantry plant could print special colours and fragrant inks. Note that there is no cover date. The word 'advertising' is printed in the bottom left corner to meet industry guidelines on such promotions.

Shortlist Media
(225 × 296 mm, stapled, 52 pages)

MONOCLE (March 2007)

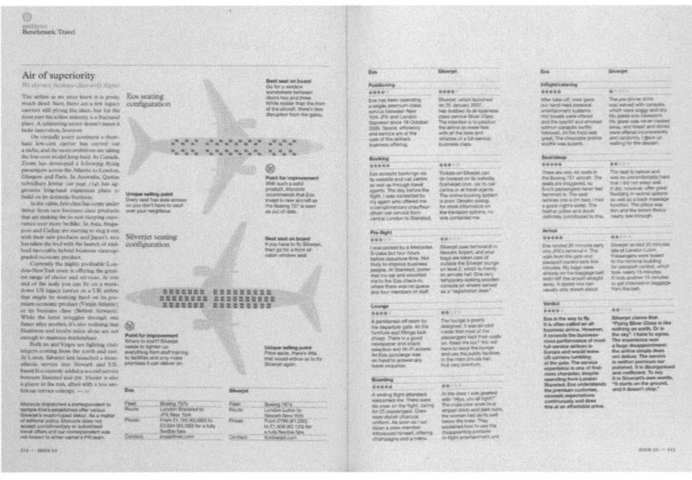

*Wallpaper** founder Tyler Brûlé ignored prevailing design approaches to launch a global magazine brand selling its own goods. The launch also went against the prevailing opinion that print was dying and that readers would inevitably be lost to digital media. Brûlé's theory was that publishers were neglecting their print products (where they had expertise) in favour of digital, where they were unskilled. The art director was Richard Spencer Powell and the title was meant to sound old-fashioned and established. Matt paper was used for most of the issue, with lots of small images.

The travel section is an example of *Monocle*'s obsession with detail: the diagrams show the best place to sit on various aircraft (Brûlé is a very frequent traveller).

This inside spread is from the manga-style comic bound into the back of *Monocle*. As with any Japanese magazine, the comic is read from what Westeners would regard as the back cover. Here, Copenhagen cop Kita Koga, drawn by Takanori Yasaka, defeats the baddies. The comic included two covers printed on glossy paper to take colour advertising for Breitling watches.

Winkontent
(200 × 264 mm, perfect bound, 244 pages)

ANOTHERMAN (Autumn/Winter 2005)

AnOtherMan

ISSUE 1 AUTUMN/WINTER 2005 UK £ 4.95 IT € 13.00 US $ 14.99 CAN $ 15.95

JOAQUIN PHOENIX PHOTOGRAPHED BY CRAIG MCDEAN

HANDLE WITH CARE

JOAQUIN PHOENIX ON JOHNNY CASH

KATE MOSS DRESSES UP IN DIOR HOMME, RICHARD PRINCE AND GLENN O'BRIEN TAKE ON OUTSIDER AMERICA, AND ASIA ARGENTO REVEALS HER SWEET SIDE. EXCLUSIVE ESSAYS TACKLING GLOBAL ECONOMIC MELTDOWN, SEXUAL DEVIANCE, ADULTERY, AND THE NEW ART REVOLUTION. SOVIET MODERNIST ARCHITECTURE, PLUS THE ESSENTIAL FASHION FOR MEN THIS SEASON BY THE PUBLISHERS OF DAZED & CONFUSED AND ANOTHER MAGAZINE

David James was art director, with Nichola Formichetti as senior fashion editor, in this spin-off from the team behind *Dazed & Confused* and *AnOther* magazines. The cover shot of actor Joaquin Phoenix was by Craig McDean, with styling by Beat Bolliger.

The playful type for the main cover line continued inside, as in these pages, where the headline continues over to the next spread.

Another Man Publishing
(234 × 300 mm, perfect bound, 322 pages)

SHINE (June 2001)

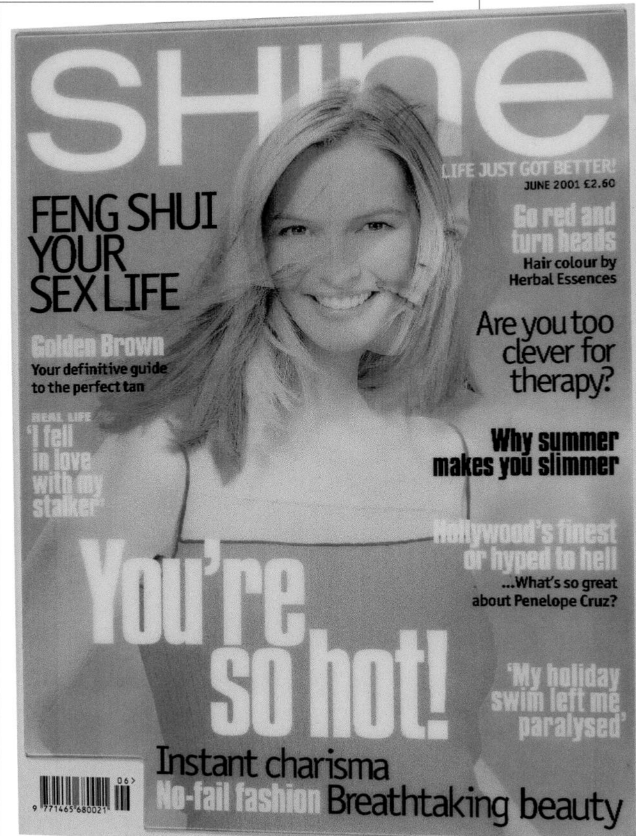

The young women's glossy was one of the early users of a 'lenticular' cover. The technique had been used for promotional purposes for many years, on film posters and postcards as long ago as the 1960s, with two images printed behind plastic 'lenses'; as the sheet is tilted or the viewer moves, one or the other image is seen, creating an animated effect. The lenticular sheets have to be printed separately and then mounted on the cover.

Attic Futura
(225 × 290 mm, perfect bound, 132 pages)

GOOD FOOD (July 2001)

Split covers are not unusual, but *Good Food* went a step further with a split cover that was also a cut-out. This is rarely done, not only because of the extra expense, but also because the edges of the cut-out tend to get bent over on the newsagents' shelves and copies can end up looking dog-eared. Note the white 'halo' around each chef's head.

BBC Magazines
(230 × 300 mm, stapled, 132 pages)

WOMAN'S OWN (7 October 2002)

The star treatment was rolled out to celebrate 30 years of ITV soap *Emmerdale*. *Woman's Own* used a gatefold – unusual on a women's weekly because of the lack of moneyed advertisers to fund the cost. Note the lucky-number competition on the cover, harking back to *John Bull*'s (see page 74) promotional strategy of a century earlier.

IPC Connect
(224 × 284 mm, stapled, 62 pages)

FHM (February 2004)

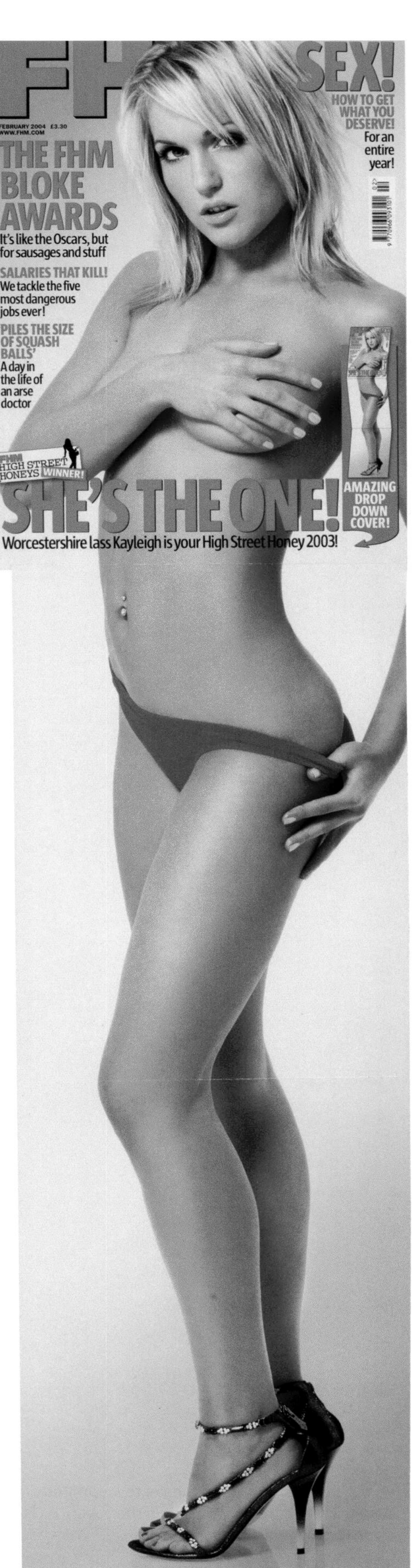

The monthly lads' mag claimed that this was the UK's first 'double drop-down' cover, intended to promote the winner of its 'High Street Honey' competition, Kayleigh Pearson. The cover folded out into a 90cm poster – three times the height of the magazine. The inside of the cover was an advert for a Sony-Ericsson T610 camera phone. The technique is rare because it wastes so much paper, though *Time Out* used the same idea later in the year to mark the London Film Festival. *FHM* was the market-leading men's magazine – selling about 600,000 copies monthly – but had started to lose sales to the weekly *Nuts* (IPC) and *Zoo* (a sister title at Emap). It was redesigned for the September 2004 issue with a title that filled the width of the cover.

Emap
(224 × 300 mm, perfect bound, 124 pages)

SFX (January 2004)

Spot-varnishing is a technique where varnish is printed over parts of a sheet as a fifth 'ink'. For this cover, the black areas of the Spider-Man image are overprinted with a glossy varnish, resulting in both a visual and a tactile effect.

Future
(222 × 300 mm, perfect bound, 124 pages)

TIME OUT (25 September 2008)

For its 40th anniversary, *Time Out* ran a triple-gatefold cover showing people important to the magazine. In pole position was *Queen* actress Helen Mirren.

Time Out Publications
(205 × 272 mm, stapled, 196 pages)

NEW SCIENTIST (7 August 2010)

DIGITAL GENESIS
Artifical life forms evolve basic intelligence
FAT EARTH NEWS
The obesity epidemic is on the wane
INSTANT EXPERT
Cloning: the second in our collectable series
NewScientist
WEEKLY 7 August 2010
INSIDE: WHY THIS COVER TWISTS YOUR MIND p32
END OF SPACETIME
Has the fabric of the universe unravelled?
£3.40 US/CAN$5.95 No2772
News, ideas and innovation www.NewScientist.com The best jobs in science

The scientific weekly turned to 'neuromarketing' techniques to choose the best cover for this issue. Eye-tracking technology and electroencephalographics were used to examine the subconscious responses of a group of test subjects to three covers. Several measures – attention, awareness, memory retention, novelty, purchase intent and emotional engagement – helped determine the winning design. The issue claimed a 12 per cent increase in sales over the previous year, making it the title's second most popular issue of 2010.

Reed
(216 × 282 mm, stapled)

GQ (February 2003)

Kate Winslet was photographed by Jason Bell for this cover. The image was subsequently altered to make her look taller and thinner. Winslet described the 'stretching' as 'excessive', but it resulted in great publicity for the magazine. Editor Dylan Jones said: 'With Kate, we were thrilled. It was a full page in all the tabloids ... And the fourth bong on the *News at Ten*.' For some celebrities, however, digital manipulation is a way to alter their public image. Photographers are also divided about whether images should be altered. Nick Knight defends manipulation: 'Originally, photography was seen as a better recorder of truth than painting – that's why it became popular. It's taken us 100 years to realise that is not the case and neither should we want it to be.'[1] Rival fashion photographer Juergen Teller is against: '[Retouched images are] not what I find beautiful. Beauty advertisers change everything and it doesn't do any good for the psyche of a woman.'[2] Another Condé Nast publication, *Tatler*, saw similar controversy with its April 2008 issue when photographs of Princess Eugenie, then sixth in line to the throne, were touched up both on the cover and inside. Whitening eyes and teeth and removing skin blemishes would be standard on such magazines, but the treatment here included smoothing the jawline and nose, removing puppy fat, whitening the skin and slimming the neck, shoulders, upper arms and torso by a dress size. Articles about the changes were carried in many papers, from the *Daily Mirror* to the *Telegraph*.

1 Susannah Frankel, 'Master of Illusion', *Independent Life*, 4 November 2009, pp. 2–5
2 Camilla Long, 'The Master Manipulator', *Sunday Times*, 18 May 2008, p. 14

Condé Nast
(220 × 285 mm, perfect bound, 188 pages)

DAZED & CONFUSED
(March 2007)

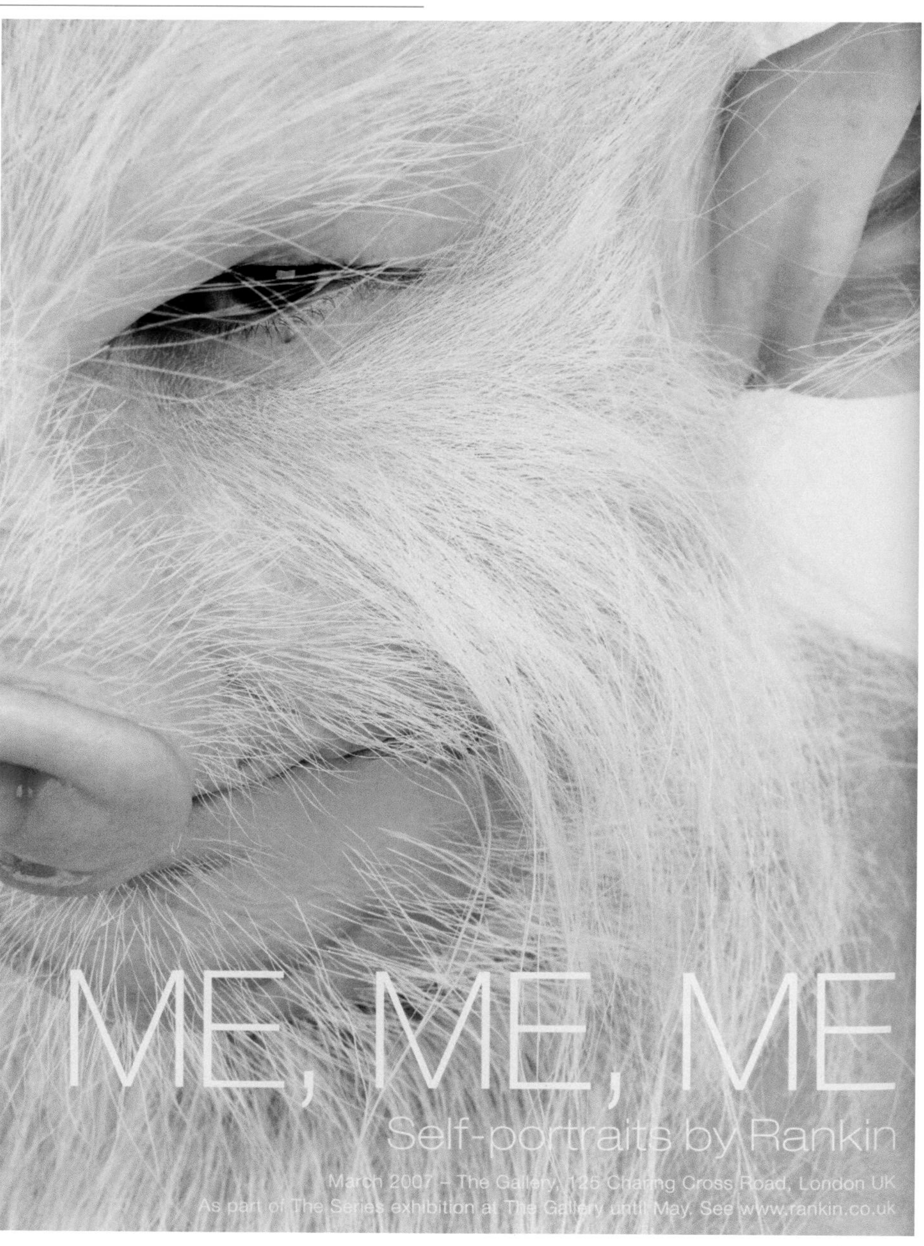

A 'self-portrait' by photographer and joint *Dazed* founder Rankin demonstrates the potential of digital manipulation.

Waddell
(230 × 300 mm, perfect bound, 342 pages)

METAL HAMMER (December 2009)

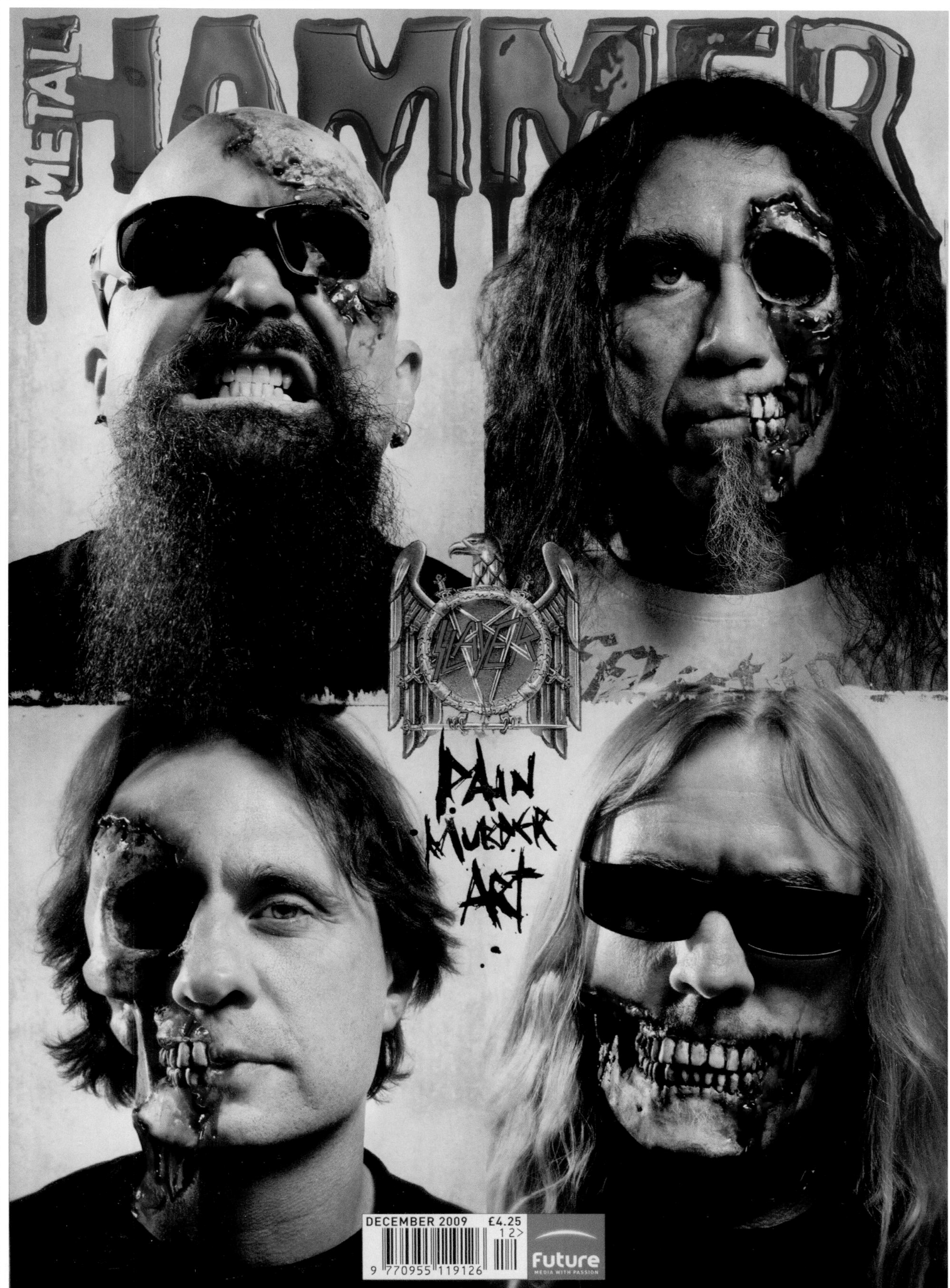

While debate was raging elsewhere about digital manipulation of photographs, the world of heavy metal gloried in the gruesome possibilities and *Metal Hammer* used this cover to shock and celebrate the music.

Future
(208 × 295 mm, perfect bound, 132 pages)

James Isaacs, art editor, commissioned Steve Brown to take portraits of the band members of Slayer. Lucy Darkness, a prosthetic make-up artist who worked on the *Harry Potter* films, created 'wounds' to match the photos of the band and attached them to ceramic skulls. These were then photographed and the images combined with the portraits by Brown using Photoshop. The title appeared to be written in blood.

MONKEY (November 2006)

Dennis Publishing used its experience in computing – it had several computer and technology magazines – to launch *Monkey*, a free weekly online lads' mag: 'The world's first weekly digital men's magazine'. The company followed this up with the fortnightly *iMotor* and *iGizmo*. The art editor for this issue of *Monkey* was Andrew Mook; Mohammed Oli did the digital design. The front and back 'covers' are displayed as single pages. Users can show and use a contents menu tab on the left of the screen to click through to pages or 'turn' pages by clicking on the bottom corners.

Once at a spread, the viewer can zoom in on details, listen to music, watch videos and film trailers or play games. The interactive elements flash to attract attention.

Dennis Publishing
(28-page email weekly, www.monkeymag.co.uk)

STANDPOINT (January 2010)

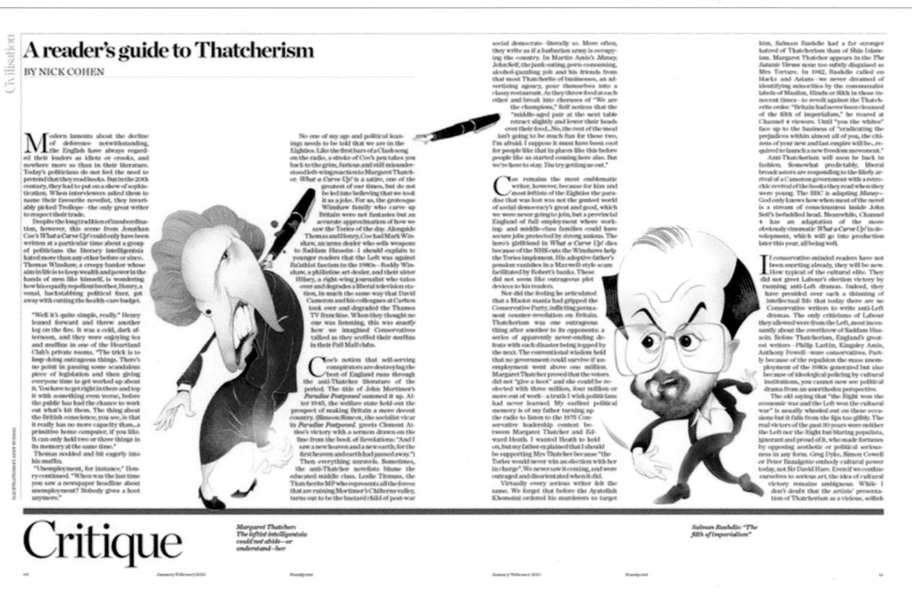

Civilisation

A reader's guide to Thatcherism

BY NICK COHEN

Critique

The screenshot here of a sample issue of *Standpoint*, a political monthly, shows how pages are accessed from a flatplan. The buttons below the subscription bar include a search option, allowing terms to be found within an issue, across a title or from all the magazines on the Exact Editions site.

Here, a spread is blown up in size. The pages, designed by art director James Brewster, are identical to the print edition, but any web or email addresses on the pages would be 'activated' as if they were on a web page.

Exact Editions (digital subscriptions website, www.exacteditions.com)

CAR (September 2006)

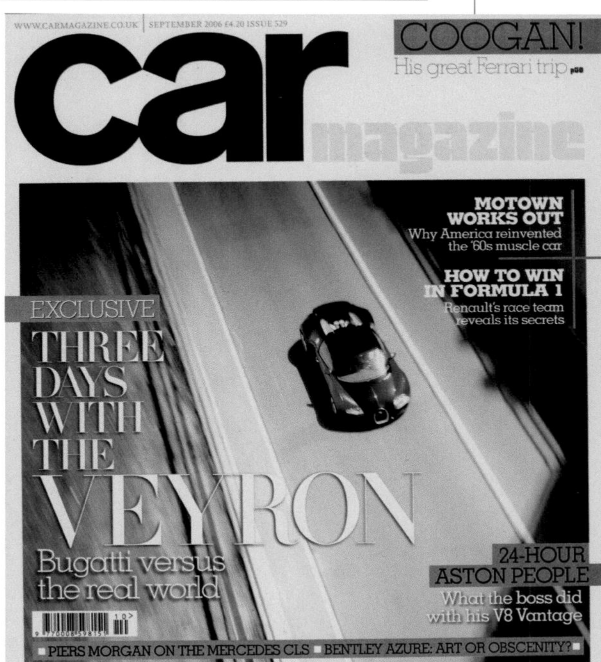

Since its inception in the 1960s, *Car* had been one of the best-designed titles. It was not until it was taken over by Emap in 1991 that it switched from hot metal typesetting straight to DTP, so bypassing photosetting. This relaunch of *Car* by editor Jason Barlow and art director Andrew Thomas was a response to the popularity of the web with the magazine's print sales static or declining. The magazine switched to a squarish format, with a lot of white space and gold ink, and dropped almost 100 pages of price listings and news. Just four issues later, the title returned to a portrait shape. Although the square format is associated in book publishing with modernity, it rarely works in the long run with magazines. The exception that proves the rule is the design monthly *Creative Review*.

A spread was devoted to explaining the changes and two others to promoting the website, which focused on the latest news and data.

Emap
(230 × 264 mm, perfect bound, 180 pages)

GRAZIA (23 March 2010)

This was promoted as a '3-D issue' using 'augmented reality' techniques with 2D tags linking to a website with animation. 'Welcome to walk-in, talking *Grazia*, this week's all-singing, all-dancing issue,' wrote editor-in-chief Jane Bruton. 'With just a few clicks (you'll need an iPhone or webcam) you can make our fabulous cover girl Florence Welch sing, dance and spin around!' There were five other pages where 'Quick Response' graphical bar codes linked to online videos and animations. Magazines had run such interactive advertising since at least the December 2007 issue of music monthly *Kerrang!*, which linked to a mobile internet site for the rock group Pendulum. The 1990s experience with multimedia CD-ROM technology suggests that customers can come to see such ideas as gimmicks.

Note the graphic in the bottom left of the page: the technology was developed for stock-keeping in the motor industry.

Bauer London Lifestyle
(235 × 300 mm, stapled, 148 pages)

STUFF (May 2012)

The iPad has encouraged many magazine publishers to launch their own apps. Magazines as varied as *Reader's Digest*, *Wired UK*, *Vogue*, *The Economist* and *Good Food* all created digital versions within a year of the iPad's appearance. This issue of technology monthly *Stuff* focused on the second version of Apple's tablet.

Haymarket
(220 × 295 mm, perfect bound, 164 pages)

LITTLE WHITE LIES
(November/December 2009)

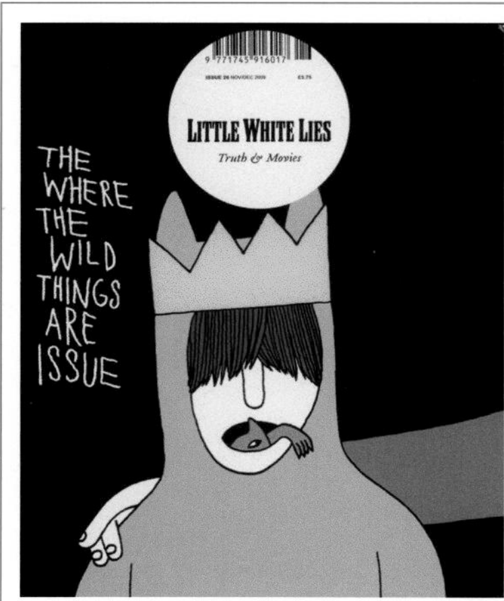

HUCK
(December 2009/January 2010)

These two magazines have no immediate content link – one is about film, the other surfing, skating and snowboarding lifestyle – but they each ran parts of a single illustration by Geoff McFetridge. Having a link between the final covers of the year has become a tradition at publisher the Church of London, a creative agency run by Rob Longworth, Danny Miller and Paul Willoughby.

Little White Lies focuses on illustration, and this issue was devoted to the Spike Jonze film of Maurice Sendak's *Where the Wild Things Are*, with Max, the book's main character, on the cover. *Huck* carried director Jonze being overrun by 'wild things' on the cover and an interview with him inside. Jonze, director of influential skate videos in the 1990s, provides the visual link between the covers.

Church of London
(200 × 245 mm, perfect bound, 110 pages)

BUCK (December 2008)

Buck was a monthly for the 'modern dandy', focusing on fashion, furniture and food. Steve Doyle launched the magazine at the age of 26 after working for *Wonderland*, *Dazed & Confused* and *Vogue*. This was a 'seat of the pants' launch, aimed at 20-somethings and 'Broadway Market man' (a trendy Saturday market in Hackney, east London). The covers all featured men with moustaches and bearded models were common inside. His inspiration was *Men's Non-no*, a Japanese men's magazine that was selling 300,000 copies a month. Doyle set out the angst of producing a cover in a blog entry: 'A cover has to do so many different things. It must entice and excite, but also acknowledge the regular readers, not just those who may not have tried the magazine before. A first cover is therefore even more difficult. You're selling not just one magazine issue but the whole concept of that magazine ... in one image. It is near impossible to get it right.' *Buck* lasted for three issues.

Buck Publishing
(230 × 300 mm, perfect bound, 164 pages)

ROTTEN APPLES (August 2010)

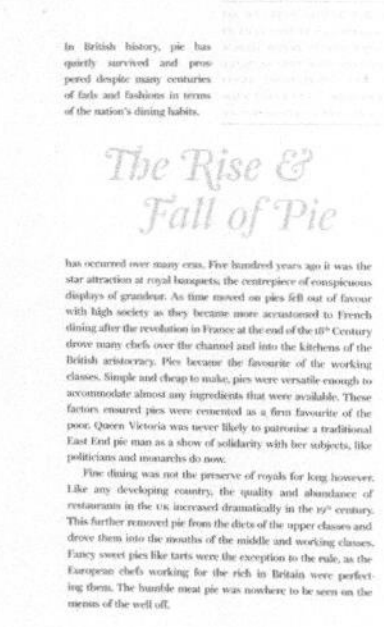
The Rise & Fall of Pie

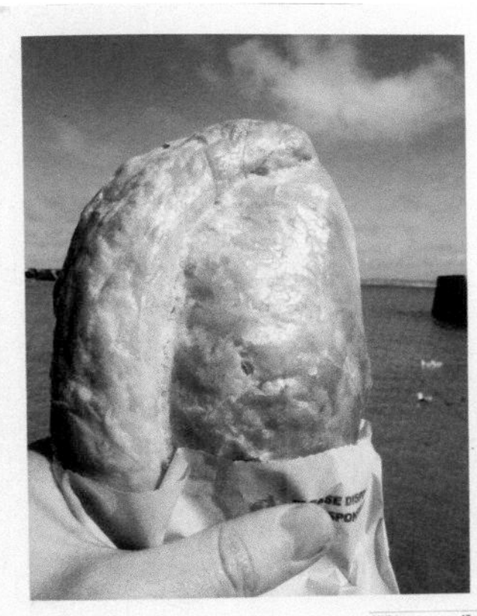

This short-lived magazine was about 'the extremes of food culture', with articles relating food to art, design, film, history, death and sex. The cover photograph was by William Hundley as part of a project about cheeseburgers; the designer was Jono Lewarne. Of the cover, editor Ed Vaughan said: 'We are not suggesting that the funny little pup is in any way a delicacy or should be eaten à la cheeseburger.' Questions asked include: 'Does Sophie Dahl really represent what we truly think about food?'

Vaughan sought out 'enthusiastic food writers who write in a left-field style and whose work never gets the chance to see the light of day in the mainstream food magazines. I am very keen to give these writers a chance to get published.' The not-so-humble pie was the topic of this spread by Jono Lewarne (author of *The Encyclopiedia*); dining on death row was the subject for another feature.

Rotten Apples Magazine
(perfect bound)

DELAYED GRATIFICATION
(January 2011)

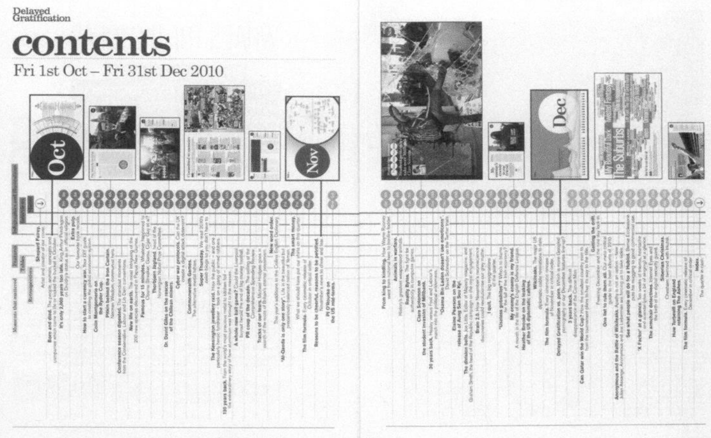

Delayed Gratification took its inspiration from the slow food movement, applying the idea to come up with the concept of 'slow journalism' as an antidote to throwaway media. Each issue applies hindsight to consider the big news stories of the previous three months with the aim of producing 'a beautifully designed and printed publication'. The cover was by US graffiti artist Shepard Fairey.

A graphic approach to the contents page shows lengthy analysis pieces sitting alongside infographics.

A spread of more complex infographics, providing a different way to present facts and data.

Slow Journalism Company
(194 × 240 mm, perfect bound, 112 pages)

AUTHOR'S ACKNOWLEDGEMENTS

My Mum and Dad, for funding my early comic and magazine habit; it was the *Beano*, *TV21* and *Look & Learn* that helped make me, as well as the Jesuits.

Ice lollies for running limerick and drawing competitions to win subscriptions to comics (and the week's top 10 singles). Alan 'Fred' Pipes, who showed me the publishing ropes in my first job in journalism at IPC and is still showing people how to do it with his books.

Magazine sellers on eBay who put up lots of photos and information.

Among the many people who have helped me along the way are: Cathy van Abbe; David Abbott; Ian Bott; Alison Chapman Andrews; Caroline Archer; Gordon Cruickshank; Dave Farey; Pepita de Foote; Seamus Geoghegan; Peter Greenhill; James Isaacs; Paul Keers; Lawrence Mackintosh; Liz Miller; Graham Parrish; Bob Richardson; Rupert Sanders; Jane Smedley; George Snow; Larry Viner; and Dr Lesley Whitworth.

Finally, none of this would have happened without the help of the Victoria and Albert Museum and the National Art Library, particularly Marc Ward and John Meriton.

My thanks to you all.